Classical Latin
An Introductory Course

Classical Latin
An Introductory Course

JC McKeown

Hackett Publishing Company, Inc.
Indianapolis/Cambridge

14 13 12 11 10   1 2 3 4 5 6 7

For further information, please address
  Hackett Publishing Company, Inc.
  P.O. Box 44937
  Indianapolis, Indiana 46244-0937

  www.hackettpublishing.com

Cover and interior designs by Elizabeth L. Wilson
Composition by Agnew's, Inc.
Printed at Sheridan Books, Inc.

Library of Congress Cataloging-in-Publication Data
McKeown, JC
    Classical Latin : an introductory course / by JC McKeown.
    p.   cm.
    Includes index.
    ISBN 978-0-87220-851-3 (pbk.)—ISBN 978-0-87220-852-0 (cloth)
    1. Latin language—Grammar—Problems, exercises, etc. I. Title.
    PA2087.5.M38 2010
    478.82′421—dc22   2009040619

The paper used in this publication meets the minimum requirements of American National Standard for Information Sciences—Permanence of Paper for Printed Library Materials, ANSI Z39.48–1984.

∞

For Jo, Maeve, and Tanz
tribus Grātiīs meīs

Contents

Contents

Preface

Latin is one of the world's most important languages. Some of the greatest poetry and prose literature ever written is in Latin, the language spread by the conquering Romans across so much of Europe and the Mediterranean region, and it continues to exert an incalculable influence on the way we speak and think nowadays. The purpose of this course is to enable students to learn the basic elements of the Latin language quickly, efficiently, and enjoyably. With this knowledge, it is possible to read not only what the Romans themselves wrote in antiquity, but any text written in Latin at any later time.

Classical Latin has developed over many years. Successive annually revised versions of it have been used at the University of Wisconsin–Madison and in other universities. As will, I hope, be evident as you work through it, writing the course has been great fun, but I could not have produced it on my own; at every stage I have benefited from the perceptions, knowledge, enthusiastic support, and practical common sense of so many colleagues, friends, and students. It is a great pleasure to acknowledge at least some of the greatest debts I have accumulated throughout the long process. I have received much useful advice and criticism on many topics from, among many others, Peter Anderson, William Batstone, Jeff Beneker, Stephen Brunet, David Califf, Jane Crawford, Aileen Das, Sally Davis, Andrea De Giorgi, Laurel Fulkerson, Brian Harvey, Doug Horsham, Thomas Hubbard, Helen Kaufmann, Mackenzie Lewis, Matthew McGowan, Arthur McKeown, James Morwood, Blaise Nagy, Mike Nerdahl, Jennifer Nilson, Alex Pappas, Roy Pinkerton, Joy Reeber, Colleen Rice, Crescentia Stegner-Freitag, Bryan Sullivan, Holly Sypniewski, William Short, Matt Vieron, Jo Wallace-Hadrill, Tara Welch, and Cynthia White. As well as compiling the index, Josh Smith read through the whole work with extraordinary acumen. Katherine Lydon meticulously edited the text for clarity, correctness and content, and suggested many changes to the presentation of the material, which have greatly enhanced its effectiveness in the classroom. I have no doubt that, without her good-humored but determined cajoling, the introductions to many chapters would have been dull, pedantic, and obscure. Needless to say, I alone am responsible for any errors that remain. I am also very grateful to Brian Rak and Liz Wilson at Hackett Publishing Company for their limitless patience and wise advice in the preparation of the course for publication.

I would not have come to enjoy Latin, much less write this course, had I not had the great good luck to have such wonderful teachers when I first started to learn Latin nearly fifty years ago. My earliest appreciation of such immortal writers as Virgil and Ovid, Cicero and Tacitus I owe to Charlie Fay and John Rothwell, and the latter's habit of drawing attention to errors in homework by ornamenting them with cartoon pigs is a treasured and abiding memory.

Finally, I owe a particular debt to my wife, Jo. She has listened tolerantly to so many ramblings about arcane aspects of Latin grammar, and stoically formulated so many versions of *Classical Latin,* that the dedication of this work to her can hardly be sufficient recompense. I know she will not mind sharing the dedication with Maeve and Tanz, our Missouri Fox Trotters. After all, the mad emperor Caligula was rumored to have wanted to appoint Incitatus, a horse in the Green Stable, as consul of Rome.

JC McKeown
Madison
Kalendis Novembribus MMIX

Abbreviations

abl.	ablative		intrans.	intransitive
abl. abs.	ablative absolute		irreg.	irregular
acc.	accusative		Ital.	Italian
act.	active		lit.	literally
AD	*annō dominī* (in the year of our Lord)		masc.	masculine
adj.	adjective		n.	note
adv.	adverb		neut.	neuter
BC	before Christ		nn.	notes
c.	*circā* (approximately)		nom.	nominative
cent.	century		obj.	object
compar.	comparative		p.	page
conj.	conjunction		pass.	passive
conjug.	conjugation		perf.	perfect
cf.	*confer* (compare)		pers.	person
dat.	dative		pl.	plural
decl.	declension		pluperf.	pluperfect
dep.	deponent		Port.	Portuguese
e.g.	*exemplī grātiā* (for example)		pp.	pages
Eng.	English		prep.	preposition
etc.	*et cētera* (and the other things)		pres.	present
fem.	feminine		pron.	pronoun
ff./f.	following		pronom.	pronominal
Fr.	French		ps.-	Pseudo-
fut.	future		r.	ruled
gen.	genitive		reflex.	reflexive
Gk.	Greek		rel.	relative
i.e.	*id est* (that is)		s. v.	*sub verbō* (see under)
imp.	imperative		sing.	singular
imperf.	imperfect		Span.	Spanish
impers.	impersonal		subj.	subjunctive
ind.	indicative		superl.	superlative
indecl.	indeclinable		trans.	transitive
inf.	infinitive		voc.	vocative
interrog.	interrogative			

How to Use *Classical Latin*

Classical Latin, a textbook for use in a year-long college course or a single intensive semester, makes learning Latin practical and interesting for today's student. In each chapter, you will

- Master new grammar using a set of vocabulary words that you already know (poets, pirates, and, above all, pigs). Since these words recur in every chapter, they allow you to focus on the unfamiliar grammar until you have understood how the new structures work.

- Go on to practice the structures you have just learned using new words, constantly enlarging your vocabulary and preparing to read real Latin. This section is called *Prōlūsiōnēs*, after the practice fights with which gladiators warmed up for their battles in the arena.

- Read passages by ancient Roman prose authors that use words and grammar you know, and answer simple comprehension questions about them. This will allow you to read Latin for the content and the author's ideas without worrying about a precise translation. You can start getting a feel for what the Romans said, as well as how they said it. This section is called *Lege, Intellege*, "Read and Understand."

- Read passages of Roman poetry that use the grammar and vocabulary you have learned in the chapter and be able to explain how the structures work. Even when Virgil and Ovid use it, the grammar works the same way. This section is called *Ars Poētica*, "The Poetic Art."

- See the chapter's grammar and vocabulary used by great Roman authors in "Golden Sayings" or *Aurea Dicta*.

- Explore how Latin has contributed to English (*Thēsaurus Verbōrum*, "A Treasure Store of Words") and how the Romans thought about their own language (*Etymologiae Antīquae*).

- Learn something about the people who spoke the language you are learning. This section, *Vīta Rōmānōrum* ("The Life of the Romans"), gives you a passage translated from a Classical Latin text, illustrating some aspect of Roman history, social life, culture, or religious beliefs.

The grammar explanations and paradigms and the activities using readings (*Lectiōnēs Latīnae*) are the core of each chapter. The *Thēsaurus Verbōrum* and *Etymologiae Antīquae* sections (starting in Chapter 11), as well as the *Vīta Rōmānōrum* passages, are optional extra material, or as the Romans would have said, *Lūsūs* ("Games").

In addition, the "Vocabulary Notes" give you further information about how to use the words in each vocabulary list, while occasional sections entitled *Notā Bene*, or "notice well," draw your attention to unusual or easy-to-miss aspects of the material.

Introduction

What Is Classical Latin?

The term "Latin" refers to the language used in Latium, the western central region of Italy, which was dominated by the Romans from the early years of the first millennium BC. Through centuries of warfare, followed by military occupation and integration with native populations, the Romans spread the Latin language over a vast empire that embraced the whole Mediterranean basin and stretched north to southern Scotland and east almost as far as the Caspian Sea.

Classical Latin is the written language of the period roughly 80 BC to 120 AD, two centuries that saw the collapse of the Roman Republic and the establishment of the imperial system of government and also produced most of Rome's greatest literary achievements.

Given that the Roman empire was so vast and endured so long, one might expect that Latin would vary from one region of the empire to another and change over time (as American English differs from British English, and Elizabethan English from modern English). Here we have to distinguish between spoken Latin and written Latin. Such variations and developments were, in fact, always a feature of the spoken language: regional versions of spoken Latin would later evolve into the Romance languages—Italian, Spanish, Portuguese, French, and so on in the west, Romanian in the east. This evolution took place very gradually, as Latin replaced other languages in various parts of the empire. In strong contrast to spoken Latin, however, the written language was never much influenced by the different dialects and was very resistant to change for several reasons.

Roman rule was firmly centralized in Rome itself, which was also the cultural heart of the empire. Not surprisingly, therefore, standards for the correct use of Latin were set by Rome. Even though the majority of the great Roman writers came originally from distant parts of Italy and from the provinces, they conformed to these standards, so that their writing hardly ever included localized idioms and vocabulary that they might have used in speaking.

A further reason why written Latin is so standardized is that the great age of Roman literature was very brief, and it is this period that produced the texts that constitute and define Classical Latin. For more than half a millennium after its founding, Rome was essentially a military state, struggling for survival and expansion. Such a society was not congenial to literary and cultural creativity. Then the second century BC brought Rome greater security through the subjugation of Carthage, the only rival power in the western Mediterranean. It also brought wider intellectual horizons through contact with Greece. The way was therefore open for the flowering of Roman culture over the next two centuries.

Throughout Europe until recent times, the education system was extremely conservative. A very few great prose writers and poets, Cicero and Virgil above all, were adopted as models of Latinity, and the language was codified, restricted, and then transmitted century after century in accordance with these models. Depending on one's point of view, this conservatism either ensured the purity of Classical Latin or prevented the written language from evolving. As spoken Latin gradually dropped out of use or was transformed into the Romance languages, those who continued to write in Latin still wanted to imitate the great authors of the classical period. This means that once you know Classical Latin you will have the basis for reading texts written at any time from pagan antiquity through to the Renaissance and more modern periods.

The Cultural Context

The influence of the Romans on the modern world is hard to overstate. Without them, our language, our literature, the way we think would have been very different. That said, however, it is important to realize that Roman society was quite alien to ours. Women had almost no role in public life and were generally under the legal control of their fathers, husbands, or brothers. The economy depended on slavery: at the end of the first century BC, perhaps as much as one-third of the population of Italy were slaves. All classes of society enjoyed the bloody spectacle of gladiatorial contests, which were first introduced in the third century BC as a form of human sacrifice in honor of the dead: in AD 107, at the games celebrating his subjugation of the lower Danube, the emperor Trajan had five thousand pairs of gladiators fight each other. Accounts of the empire's expansion, since they were written by the Romans themselves, naturally tended to glorify their military exploits: Julius Caesar's conquest of Gaul is an extraordinary achievement, but it was based on what we would probably call genocide, with perhaps more than a million people being exterminated in less than a decade.

For these reasons we may not always sympathize with the Romans, but it would be difficult not to respect their accomplishments. In order to provide some insight into Roman culture, this book uses, as much as possible, Latin texts written by Roman authors themselves.

You Already Know More Latin Than You Think: Using English to Master Latin Vocabulary

English belongs to the Germanic branch of the vast Indo-European family of languages, whereas Latin belongs to the quite separate Italic branch. These two branches lost contact with each other several millennia ago in the great migration westward from the Indo-European homeland. English derives its basic grammatical structure and almost all of its most commonly used words from its Germanic background. Nevertheless, Latin came to have a dominant influence on English, vastly increasing its vocabulary, after the Normans conquered the British Isles in 1066. Latin was the language of both the church and the legal system, and French, a Romance language derived directly from Latin, was the Normans' mother tongue. It is estimated that well over 60 percent of nontechnical modern English vocabulary is Latinate.

To appreciate the extent of the influence of Latin on English vocabulary, study the following paragraph of German for a few minutes. How many of the words are familiar enough for you to guess their meaning?

Nilpferde sind grosse, dicke Tiere, die in Afrika im Nil leben. Zahlreiche afrikanische Tiere sind furchterregend und sehr wild, nämlich Krokodile, Löwen, Leoparden, Nashörner, Hyänen, Skorpione, Aasgeier, Schlangen (z.B. Riesenschlangen, Nattern und Vipern). Ängstlich jedoch sind Nilpferde nicht. Sie haben grosse Körper, grosse Zähne und grosse Füsse, aber ihre Ohren sind klein und ihr Schwanz kurz. Afrika ist ein heisses Land, darum liegen Nilpferde stundenlang im Wasser und dösen. Erst wenn nachts der Mond am Himmel scheint, steigen sie aus dem Fluss und grasen ausgiebig.

Now look at exactly the same paragraph, this time translated into Latin. How many of these words can you guess at?

Hippopotamī sunt animālia magna et obēsa, quae in Africā habitant, in flūmine Nīlō. bestiae numerōsae Africānae sunt terribilēs et ferōcissimae—crocodīlī, leōnēs, pardī, rhīnocerōtēs, hyaenae, scorpiōnēs, vulturēs, serpentēs (exemplī grātiā, pythōnēs, aspidēs, vīperae). sed hippopotamī nōn sunt timidī. corpora magna habent, dentēs magnōs, pedēs magnōs, sed aurēs minūtōs et caudam nōn longam. Africa est terra torrida. ergō hippopotamī hōrās multās in aquā remanent et dormitant. sed, cum nocte lūna in caelō splendet, ē flūmine ēmergunt et herbās abundantēs dēvorant.

Despite the fact that English is a Germanic language, you probably found it much easier to guess at the meaning of the Latin version. In the same way, throughout this book, you will be able to use your knowledge of English to identify the meaning of many Latin words. This Latinate aspect of English will also make it easier for you to remember the Latin vocabulary once you have studied it.

Inflection

Most Latin words change their form according to the particular function they perform in a sentence. This change, which usually involves a modification in the word's ending, while the basic stem remains the same, is known as inflection. Latin uses inflection much more than English does, and this is by far the most significant difference between the two languages. Latin nouns, pronouns, and adjectives all have many different endings, depending on their function in a sentence, while even adverbs can have three different endings. As an example, compare the English adverb "dearly" to its Latin equivalent:

cārē "dearly," *cārius* "more dearly," *cārissimē* "most dearly."

The basic form in English stays exactly the same, using a helping word to define the precise meaning, but in Latin the endings change dramatically, and it is this change that tells you how to translate the form. In general, English nouns, pronouns, adjectives, and adverbs change hardly at all, and almost all English verbs keep exactly the same form with only minimal changes. As you will see in the very first chapter of this book, you need to know the various endings in order to understand what a Latin word is doing in its sentence.

Not surprisingly, the concept of inflection takes some getting used to for speakers of English. In particular, English depends heavily on very strict conventions of word order to convey meaning;

for example, the subject of an English sentence will almost always come first. In Latin, by contrast, word order tells you nothing about a word's function; this information comes from the word's ending. At first the order of words in Latin sentences will seem arbitrary. Be patient. By the time you have worked through the first few chapters of this book, you will be used to the structure of Latin sentences.

Adjusting to the different structure of a Latin sentence will be much easier if you learn the paradigms (the examples of how to form the various parts of speech) by heart right away, and don't go on to the next chapter until you can use them confidently and accurately. You can use the exercises in each chapter (and online at www.hackettpublishing.com/classicallatin) to help you gain this confidence and accuracy. Here are some suggested strategies to help you learn the paradigms by heart more easily:

- All the paradigms have been recorded online. Listen to them several times and repeat them to be sure you are familiar with the way they are pronounced. This will make it easier to learn them quickly and correctly, because you will be using three of your language-learning skills: reading, listening, and speaking.

- You will notice many similar patterns in the various systems for verbs, nouns, and so on. This book emphasizes these similarities by putting similar systems together. Again, you can use these patterns to make your learning and memorization much easier.

- Write the paradigms out from memory, and then check that you have written each form correctly. Don't rely solely on repeating them to yourself, since the difference between one ending and another can be quite small, and it's easy to confuse them if you don't write them down. Again, using more than one of your language-learning skills makes it more likely that you will remember what you're studying.

- Don't try to master large amounts of material at any one time.

- Constantly review the material you have already learned.

Almost immediately, you will be able to go from memorizing paradigms to real translation, including translating sentences from actual Latin writers. Enjoy the sense of achievement when you can turn theory into practice. If it sometimes seems that you'll never reach the end of the tables of adjectives, nouns, pronouns, and verbs, you can take comfort in knowing that, after working through this book, there will be practically no more to learn. You will have mastered the essentials needed for reading Latin texts of any period.

The Pronunciation of Latin

There is no universally accepted pronunciation of Latin nowadays. In some countries, particularly those influenced by the Catholic Church, Latin is pronounced in a manner broadly similar to Italian. Toward the end of the nineteenth century, English-speaking countries adopted reforms in an attempt to return more closely to the classical pronunciation. This is the system that will be followed in the rules for pronunciation below, as well as in almost all of the audio files online (at www.hackettpublishing.com/classicallatin). You should realize, however, that any system of pronunciation is, to some extent, a modern convention: there are some features of ancient pronunciation about which we are largely or entirely ignorant, and others that almost no one nowadays attempts to reproduce, even though we know they existed.

Listening to the paradigms and texts recorded online will make these general rules about pronunciation easier to understand.

- Latin is easy to read, since spelling is phonetic, and every letter and syllable is pronounced in a largely consistent manner. There are no silent letters. As an example, "facile" is a two-syllable word in English meaning "easy" or "excessively easy"; the final letter *e* is not pronounced. In Latin, however, *facile*, also meaning "easy," has three separate syllables.

- The sounds you will use in pronouncing Latin are much the same as those used in English. There are very few unfamiliar combinations of letters. For example, the Latin for "pig" is *porcus*; by contrast, in German it is *Schwein*, in Hungarian it is *disznó*, in Swahili it is *nguruwe*.

- Every vowel is long or short, a very important distinction in Latin. In many cases, you will simply have to learn this for each individual word. But you will start to see some patterns; that is, you will often be able to predict the length of a particular vowel in a new word based on your knowledge of other words. To help you master this variation in vowel length, in this book long vowels are marked with a macron (-) written above them; you can assume that any vowel without a macron is short. To show you how important vowel length can be, two grammatical forms of the same word may be spelled in exactly the same way but differ in the length of one vowel. This difference will affect the word's meaning. For example, *puella*, with a short *a*, has a different grammatical function from *puellā*, with a long *a*; *legit* means "he reads" (present tense) but *lēgit* means "he read" (past tense).

- The following combinations of vowels, known as diphthongs, are usually run together and pronounced as one sound: *ae* (pronounced to rhyme with "sty"), *au* (pronounced to rhyme with "cow"), *eu* (pronounced like "ewe"), *oe* (pronounced like *oi* in "oink").

- The letters *c* and *g* are always hard, as in English "cat" and "goat," never soft, as in "cider" and "gin."

- The letter *h* is always pronounced when it occurs at the beginning of a word, so it is like the *h* in "hot," not the *h* in "honor." The combinations *ph* and *th*, used in Greek words adopted by the Romans (such as φιλοσοφία [*philosophia*], θέατρον [*theatrum*]), are pronounced as in English, while *ch* (a fairly rare combination) is pronounced like *c*.

- The only letter which needs special attention is *i*. It is usually a vowel, as in English, but sometimes it's a consonant, pronounced like English *y*; this "consonantal *i*" evolved into our *j*. To illustrate the difference, *Iūlius* (or *Jūlius*) and *iambus* both have three syllables. When you see a word in a vocabulary list in this book presented with *j* as an alternative to *i*, for example, *iam* (*jam*), *iubeō* (*jubeō*), you will know that the *i* is a consonantal *i*.

- The letter *v* is pronounced like English *w*.

- The letter *w* was not used by the Romans. The letters *j*, *k*, and *z* are very rare. Otherwise, the alphabet in Classical Latin is exactly like the English alphabet.

The accent always falls on the first syllable of two-syllable words, such as *Róma*. It always falls on the second-to-last or penultimate syllable in words of three or more syllables if that syllable is long, as in *Románus*, but otherwise it falls on the preceding syllable, as in *Itália*.

Punctuation

Since there were few rules for the punctuation of Latin in antiquity, and since in any case we know Classical Latin texts mostly from manuscripts written many centuries later, when new systems of punctuation had evolved, we simply apply modern practices. Nouns and adjectives denoting proper names are capitalized, as in English. Otherwise, capitalization is optional, even at the beginning of sentences. This is a matter of individual choice—just be consistent.

CHAPTER 1

The Present Active Indicative, Imperative, and Infinitive of Verbs

A verb expresses an action or a state; for example, "I *run*," "she *sees* the river" are *actions*, "you *are* clever," "they *exist*" are *states*. Nearly all sentences contain verbs, so they are an especially important part of speech.

Verbs in most Western languages have three **PERSONS (1st, 2nd, and 3rd)**, and two **NUMBERS (Singular and Plural)**. Each PERSON exists in both NUMBERS, yielding six separate forms. Compare how English and Latin handle these six forms of the verb "to love."

1st person singular	I love	am**ō**
2nd person singular	You love	am**ās**
3rd person singular	He/She/It loves	am**at**
1st person plural	We love	am**āmus**
2nd person plural	You love	am**ātis**
3rd person plural	They love	am**ant**

The biggest difference is that Latin does not normally use pronouns such as "I," "you," "he," "she," "we," or "they." Instead, an ending is added to the basic stem, and this ending signals both the PERSON and the NUMBER. So the form of the verb in Latin changes a great deal, whereas in English the form "love" hardly changes at all.

When we give commands ("Run!" "Stop!" "Listen!"), we use the **IMPERATIVE**. Imperatives are in the second person singular or plural, depending on the number of addressees, and the singular and plural have different endings. "Love!" would be either *amā* (singular) or *amāte* (plural).

One important form of the verb has neither person nor number, because it does not refer to a specific action or event. This is the **INFINITIVE** form, which in English is "to run," "to see," "to be," "to exist." Here, too, Latin forms the present infinitive by adding a specific ending: "to love" is *amāre*.

Almost all Latin verbs belong to one of five groups, known as **CONJUGATIONS**. A conjugation is a group of verbs that form their tenses in the same way. You can see one basic pattern in the way in which all the conjugations form their tenses. All conjugations use the same personal endings, *-ō, -s, -t, -mus, -tis, -nt*, and the same infinitive ending, *-re*.

It is the stem vowel that tells you which conjugation a verb belongs to. For example, *a* is the stem vowel of the first conjugation, so you know that *amāre* belongs to the first conjugation (in early Latin, *amō* was *amaō*, but the stem vowel dropped out). The stem vowels for the second and fourth conjugations are *e* and *i*.

The third conjugation is unusual: the stem vowel was originally *e,* but several persons of the present tense and the plural imperative use *i* instead. A small number of third conjugation verbs have this *i*-stem in all the persons of the present tense, so they are considered a separate conjugation, called "third conjugation *i*-stems."

Paradigm Verbs

In this book the paradigm verbs for the five conjugations will be **amāre** (1st) "to love," **monēre** (2nd) "to warn," **mittere** (3rd) "to send," **audīre** (4th) "to hear, listen to," and **capere** (3rd *i*-stem) "to take, capture." The third person singular of the present tense (for example) of the five conjugations shows you that they are all variations on one basic pattern:

am	+	a	+	t	=		amat
mon	+	e	+	t	=		monet
mitt	+	i	+	t	=		mittit
aud	+	i	+	t	=		audit
cap	+	i	+	t	=		capit

You have already seen *amāre* fully conjugated in the present tense. Here are all the present-tense forms for the other four model verbs.

Second Conjugation

1st sing.	mon**eō**	I warn
2nd sing.	mon**ēs**	You warn (sing.)
3rd sing.	mon**et**	He/She/It warns
1st pl.	mon**ēmus**	We warn
2nd pl.	mon**ētis**	You warn (pl.)
3rd pl.	mon**ent**	They warn
Imperative	mon**ē**	Warn! (sing.)
	mon**ēte**	Warn! (pl.)
Infinitive	mon**ēre**	To warn

Third Conjugation

1st sing.	mitt**ō**	I send
2nd sing.	mitt**is**	You send (sing.)
3rd sing.	mitt**it**	He/She/It sends
1st pl.	mitt**imus**	We send
2nd pl.	mitt**itis**	You send (pl.)
3rd pl.	mitt**unt**	They send
Imperative	mitt**e**	Send! (sing.)
	mitt**ite**	Send! (pl.)
Infinitive	mitt**ere**	To send

Fourth Conjugation

1st sing.	aud**iō**	I hear, listen to
2nd sing.	aud**īs**	You hear, listen to (sing.)
3rd sing.	aud**it**	He/She/It hears, listens to
1st pl.	aud**īmus**	We hear, listen to
2nd pl.	aud**ītis**	You hear, listen to (pl.)
3rd pl.	aud**iunt**	They hear, listen to
Imperative	aud**ī**	Listen! (sing.)
	aud**īte**	Listen! (pl.)
Infinitive	aud**īre**	To hear, listen to

Third Conjugation *i*-stem

1st sing.	cap**iō**	I take
2nd sing.	cap**is**	You take (sing.)
3rd sing.	cap**it**	He/She/It takes
1st pl.	cap**imus**	We take
2nd pl.	cap**itis**	You take (pl.)
3rd pl.	cap**iunt**	They take
Imperative	cap**e**	Take! (sing.)
	cap**ite**	Take! (pl.)
Infinitive	cap**ere**	To take

Using the imperative is simple:

audī!	"Listen!" (to one person)
audīte!	"Listen!" (to more than one person)
cape!	"Take!" (to one person)
capite!	"Take!" (to more than one person)

To give a *negative* command (to order someone *not* to do something), Latin uses *nōlī* or *nōlīte*, the imperative forms of the irregular verb *nōlō, nolle, nōluī* "be unwilling" (you will learn its other forms in Chapter 10) with the appropriate infinitive.

nōlī audīre!	Don't listen! (to one person)
nōlīte audīre!	Don't listen! (to more than one person)
nōlī capere!	Don't take! (to one person)
nōlīte capere!	Don't take! (to more than one person)

Mood, Voice, and Tense

You should learn some technical terms now, since they are convenient ways to describe the form and function of verbs.

Latin verbs have four **moods**:

- indicative
- subjunctive
- imperative
- infinitive

You already know how the imperative works for giving commands. The infinitive is almost always used with another, conjugated verb; it rarely stands alone. The indicative and the subjunctive complement each other. Basically, the indicative is used for events or situations that actually happen, whereas the subjunctive is used when an event or situation is somehow doubtful or unreal. We will go into this in detail in Chapter 22.

Latin verbs have two **voices**:

- active
- passive

An active verb tells us what the subject does, but a passive verb tells us what is done to or for the subject by someone or something else.

Active: "I love my pig."   Passive: "My pig is loved by me."

Latin verbs have six **tenses**:

- present
- future
- imperfect
- perfect
- future perfect
- pluperfect

How to Translate the Latin Present Active Indicative

So far, we have been translating *amō* simply as "I love," *moneō* as "I warn," and so on, but of course in English we have three forms to express three different aspects of an action in the present: "I love," "I am loving," and "I do love." Latin has only one form to express all three of these ideas.

When you are translating, therefore, you will need to rely on context to help you choose which of the three English forms to use. Consider, for example, the following dialogue:

"My friends never <u>listen</u> to me."
"They <u>do listen</u> to you."
"They <u>are</u> not <u>listening</u> to me now."

In all three sentences, the Latin verb would be simply *audiunt.*

Verbs are also divided into **transitive** and **intransitive** verbs. Transitive verbs always have a direct object, which is a noun or pronoun referring to the person or thing that the verb affects directly. The meaning of intransitive verbs is complete without a direct object.

Transitive: "My pig <u>likes</u> turnips."   Intransitive: "My pig <u>dances</u>."

Principal Parts

In order to be able to conjugate a verb correctly, you must know the conjugation to which it belongs. If you know both the first person singular of the present indicative active (*amō*) and the present infinitive active (*amāre*), then you can tell which conjugation the verb belongs to. For example, these 3rd person present forms look exactly alike, even though they belong to three different conjugations:

mittit "he/she/it sends"   *audit* "he/she/it hears"   *capit* "he/she/it takes"

But if you know the forms *capiō* and *capere*, you have a lot more information. *Capiō* can't be a 3rd conjugation 1st person singular present, and *capere* can't be a 4th conjugation infinitive. So you know that *capit* is the 3rd person singular of the present tense of a 3rd conjugation *i*-stem verb.

amō and *amāre*, *capiō* and *capere* are the first two **principal parts** of those particular verbs. Most Latin verbs have four principal parts:

amō	**amāre**	**amāvī**	**amātum**
"I love"	"to love"	"I have loved"	"having been loved"

capiō	**capere**	**cēpī**	**captum**
"I take"	"to take"	"I have taken"	"having been taken"

These principal parts give you the basis for constructing all the tenses of all regular verbs (and almost all Latin verbs are regular in this way). You will learn how to use the 3rd and 4th principal parts in later chapters, but you will save yourself time and trouble by learning them now. The principal parts of the model verbs for the other conjugations are **moneō, monēre, monuī, monitum** (2), **mittō, mittere, mīsī, missum** (3), **audiō, audīre, audīvī, audītum** (4).

Vocabulary

First Conjugation Verbs

amō, amāre, amāvī, amātum	love
dō, dare, dedī, datum	give
spectō, -āre, spectāvī, spectātum	watch
vocō, -āre, vocāvī, vocātum	call

Second Conjugation Verbs

dēbeō, -ēre, dēbuī, dēbitum	owe, ought to, must, should
habeō, -ēre, habuī, habitum	have
moneō, -ēre, monuī, monitum	warn
sedeō, -ēre, sēdī, sessum	sit
terreō, terrēre, terruī, territum	frighten
timeō, timēre, timuī	fear
videō, -ēre, vīdī, vīsum	see

Third Conjugation Verbs

bibō, bibere, bibī	drink
dīcō, -ere, dixī, dictum	say
dūcō, -ere, duxī, ductum	lead
legō, -ere, lēgī, lectum	read
lūdō, -ere, lūsī, lūsum	play
metuō, metuere, metuī	fear
mittō, -ere, mīsī, missum	send
petō, petere, petiī (or -īvī), petītum	seek
vincō, vincere, vīcī, victum	conquer
vīvō, -ere, vixī, victum	live

Fourth Conjugation Verbs

audiō, -īre, audīvī, audītum	hear, listen to
reperiō, -īre, repperī, repertum	find

Third Conjugation *i*-stem Verbs

capiō, -ere, cēpī, captum	take, capture
rapiō, -ere, rapuī, raptum	seize
nōlī, nōlīte irregular imperative verb	don't

Vocabulary Notes

dō, dare, dedī, datum 1: Unlike all other 1st conjugation verbs, *dare* has a short *a* in the present infinitive, and in the 1st and 2nd person plural, *damus* and *datis*.

dēbeō, -ēre, dēbuī, dēbitum 2: *audīre dēbeō* means "I ought to listen" or "I must listen" or "I should listen." Like all of the English equivalents ("ought," "must," and "should"), *dēbeō* is combined with another verb, which is in the infinitive: "to listen." Don't be confused by the fact that the "to" is left out in some of the English translations; this is still the infinitive.

habeō, -ēre, habuī, habitum 2: "I have to listen" is *audīre dēbeō*. Latin does NOT use *habēre* to express need or obligation. "Audīre habeō" is not correct Latin.

For largely unknown reasons, some verbs (e.g., **timeō, timēre, timuī** 2, **bibō, bibere, bibī** 3, **metuō, metuere, metuī** 3) do not have a fourth principal part.

timeō, timēre, timuī 2 and **metuō, metuere, metuī** 3 mean the same thing and can be used interchangeably.

Prōlūsiōnēs

Use English Words Derived from Latin to Memorize Latin Vocabulary

One of the ways to remember Latin vocabulary is to think of English words derived from a given word in Latin. Every one of the verbs in this chapter's vocabulary list survives in English. For each of the English words listed below, find the Latin verb from which it originates. If you know what the English word means, you can guess—and easily remember—what the Latin word means. In five instances, a prefix has been added to the basic Latin verb. In only two instances has the word's original meaning evolved beyond easy recognition in English: *meticulous* work is motivated by *fear* of error, and a *repertoire* is a list in which things can be *found*.

amiable	"easy to like or love"	**amō, amāre, amāvī, amātum** 1
admonish	"warn not to do something"	*Mōneō monēre monuī monitum 2*
audition		*Audiō Audīre audivī audītum 4*
imbibe	"drink in"	*bibō, bibere, bibī 3*

capture		Capio, capere, cepi, captum 3I
data	"information given"	do, dare, dedi, datum 1
debt		debeo, debere, debui, debitum 2
diction		dico, dicere, dixi, dictum 3
evoke	"call to mind"	voco, vocare, vocavi, vocatum 1
have		habeo, habere, habui, habitum 2
legible	"which can be read"	lego, legere, legi, lectum 3
ludicrous	"silly"	ludo, ludere, lusi, lusum 3
meticulous		metuo, metuere, metui 3
omit		mitto, mittere, misi, missum 3
petition		peto, petere, petii, petitum 3
rapture	"experience that seizes you"	rapio, rapere, rapui, raptum 3I
reduce		duco, ducere, duxi, ductum 3
repertoire		reperio, reperire, repperi, repertum 4
sedentary	"not active, sitting a lot"	sedeo, sedere, sedi, sessum 2
spectator	"one who watches"	specto, spectare, spectavi, spectatum 1
terrify		terreo, terrere, terrui, territum 2
timid		timeo, timere, timui 2
victory		vinco, vincere, vici, victum 3
vision		video, videre, vidi, visum 2
vivid		vivo, vivere, vixi, victum 3

Your knowledge of English words derived from Latin will make learning Latin vocabulary easier. For example, you can tell right away that *video* has something to do with seeing and *audio* has something to do with hearing. You are free to concentrate on new facts: that *videre* belongs to the second conjugation, and *audire* belongs to the fourth. You will also find the online electronic flashcards useful for learning vocabulary.

ostmustis (handwritten, top left)

Parsing

Parsing a word means describing it grammatically, by stating its part of speech, its grammatical form, and its relation to the rest of the sentence. So far, you have only encountered verbs, and only in one tense, so parsing is relatively simple. As you learn other parts of speech in subsequent chapters, parsing will become more challenging and more interesting. For now, simply parse verbs as follows:

amō: 1st person singular present active indicative of the verb *amō, amāre, amāvī, amātum* 1 "love"

mittitis: 2nd person plural present active indicative of the verb *mittō, mittere, mīsī, missum* 3 "send"

audiunt: 3rd pers. pl. pres. act. ind. of the verb *audiō, audīre, audīvī, audītum* 4 "hear"

capere: pres. act. inf. of the verb *capiō, capere, cēpī, captum* 3 *i*-stem "take"

Parsing a word is a convenient and precise way of describing its form. As soon as more parts of speech are introduced (in the next chapter), you will see how parsing also explains grammatical function.

Complete the following.

1. The 1st pers. pl. pres. act. ind. of the verb *audiō, audīre, audīvī, audītum* 4 "hear" is ___Audimus___.

2. The 2nd pers. sing. pres. act. ind. of the verb *amō, amāre, amāvī, amātum* 1 "love" is ___Amas___.

3. The 3rd pers. pl. pres. act. ind. of the verb *mittō, mittere, mīsī, missum* 3 "send" is ___Mittunt___.

4. The 2nd pers. pl. pres. act. ind. of the verb *moneō, monēre, monuī, monitum* 2 "warn" is ___Monetis___.

5. The 3rd pers. sing. pres. act. ind. of the verb *capiō, capere, cēpī, captum* 3 *i*-stem "take" is ___Capit___.

Parse the following.

1. monēmus.
2. mitte.
3. capit.
4. amant.
5. audītis.

(handwritten answers)

1: 1st per Pl prs act ind of moneo, monere, monvi, monitum [2 warn]
2: IMP of mitto, mittere, misi, missum [3 send]
3: 3rd per sing prs act ind of capio, capere, cepi, captum [3i Take]
4: 3rd per Pl pres act ind of amo, amare, amavi, amatum [1 Love]
5: 2nd per Pl pres act ind of audio, audire, audvi, auditum [4 hear]

Supply the correct verb ending.

1. am_atis_;   you (pl.) love.
2. aud_ire_;   to hear.
3. cap_iunt_;   they are taking.
4. mon_es_;   you (sing.) warn.
5. mitt_it_;   she sends.

6. mitt_ere_;   to send.
7. mon_ete_;   warn (pl.)!
8. cap_imus_;   we take.
9. aud_io_;   I hear.
10. mitt_ent_;   they send.

Change from singular to plural or vice versa, and then translate.
e.g., *amat – amant* "They love"; *mittimus – mittō* "I send"

1. audit. – audiunt
2. capitis. – capis
3. amāmus. – amo
4. monent. – monet
5. mittis. – mittitis

6. audīte. – audi
7. amātis. – amas
8. capit. – capiunt
9. moneō. – monemus
10. mittit. – mittunt

Translate.

1. vocant. He calls
2. dūcitis. You all lead
3. sedēmus. we sit
4. reperiō. I find
5. legite! Read!
6. metuis. You fear
7. nōlite rapere! Don't seize!
8. habētis. You all have
9. legere dēbēs. You must lead
10. vīvimus. we live
11. dīcitis. You all sey
12. habēre. To have
13. pete! Seek!
14. vincite! conquer!
15. vidēmus. we see
16. terrēs. You frighten
17. timent. They fear
18. petit. He seeks
19. bibunt. They drink
20. lūdis. You play

21. He reads. Legit
22. You (pl.) have. habetis
23. You (sing.) are leading. duces
24. To sit. Sedere
25. I am drinking. bibo
26. They watch. Spectunt
27. She does hear. audit
28. We fear. termemus
29. It is watching. Spectat
30. Do not (sing.) take! Noli capere
31. I am calling. Voco
32. They seize. rapiunt
33. She sees. vidit
34. You (sing.) must lead. ducere debes
35. To say. dicere
36. We are reading. Legemus
37. He fears. temit
38. You (pl.) must conquer. vincere debetis
39. They seek. petevunt
40. We frighten. terremus

Lectiōnēs Latīnae

Lege, Intellege

Nothing is known about Lucius Ampelius. His *Liber Memoriālis* (Memory Book), full of briefly stated information on history, religion, geography, cosmography, and marvels, is dedicated to a boy named Macrinus, identified by some scholars with the soldier-emperor who reigned AD 217–18.

Rēgēs Rōmānōrum

Rōmulus quī urbem condidit.
Numa Pompilius quī sacra constituit.
Tullus Hostilius quī Albam dīruit.
Ancus Marcius quī lēgēs plūrimās tulit et Ostiam colōniam constituit.
Priscus Tarquinius quī insignibus magistrātūs adornāvit.
Servius Tullius quī prīmum censum ēgit.
Tarquinius Superbus quī ob nimiam superbiam regnō pulsus est.

—Ampelius, *Liber Memoriālis* 17

1. Which king established Rome's religious practices? *Numa Pompilius*
2. Which king conducted the first census? *Servius Tullius*
3. Which king established most laws and founded the colony at Ostia? *Ancus Marcius*
4. Which king founded the city? *Romulus*
5. Which king destroyed Alba Longa, Rome's mother city? *Tullus Hostilius*
6. Which king gave the magistrates insignia? *Priscus Tarquinius*
7. Which king was expelled from his kingdom on account of his excessive arrogance? *Tarquinius Superbus*

English obviously owes a lot of vocabulary to Latin. Here are some familiar expressions that English took from Latin unchanged or in abbreviated form:

AD	*annō dominī*	in the year of our Lord
a.m./p.m.	*ante/post mērīdiem*	before/after midday
CV	*curriculum vītae*	course of life
DTs	*dēlīrium tremens*	shaking madness
e.g.	*exemplī grātiā*	for the sake of an example
etc.	*et cētera*	and the other things
i.e.	*id est*	that is
n.b.	*notā bene*	note well
p.s.	*post scriptum*	written afterward
RIP	*requiescat in pāce*	(may he/she) rest in peace

aurōra boreālis	dawn of the north wind
data	things that have been given
homō sapiens	intelligent person
rigor mortis	stiffness of death
viā	by way (of)

Ars Poētica

Publilius Syrus was brought to Rome as a slave in the mid-first century BC and became an extremely successful writer of mimes, a not very sophisticated but extremely popular type of dramatic performance. Unlike modern mime, it involved speech. None of the scripts of his mimes has survived. From the first century AD, however, collections of Syrus' maxims were excerpted from the mimes for use in schools, as texts to be copied and memorized. The younger Seneca, St. Augustine, and Shakespeare were among the countless generations of schoolboys who studied him.

How many verbs can you find in the following quotations from Publilius Syrus?

1. *contrā fēlīcem vix deus vīrēs habet.*
   Against a happy person, god scarcely has power.

2. *crūdēlem medicum intemperans aeger facit.*
   An intemperate patient makes his doctor cruel.

3. *īrācundiam quī vincit, hostem superat maximum.*
   A person who conquers his anger defeats his greatest enemy.

4. *effugere cupiditātem regnum est vincere.*
   To escape desire is to conquer a kingdom.

5. *lex videt īrātum, īrātus lēgem nōn videt.*
   The law sees an angry man, but an angry man does not see the law.

6. *mortuō quī mittit mūnus, nīl dat illī, sibi adimit.*
   A person who sends a gift to a dead man gives him nothing and deprives himself.

Lūsūs

Thēsaurus Verbōrum

Many English verbs are formed from the present stem of Latin verbs, without the linking vowel or the inflecting suffix; for example, "absorb" is derived from *absorbeō, -ēre* 2, "ascend" from *ascendō, -ere* 3. To emphasize that the English verb and the present stem of the Latin original are the same, only the first two principal parts of the Latin verbs are given in the following list of further examples:

commendō, -āre 1	dēfendō, -ere 3	ponderō, -āre 1
condemnō, -āre 1	disturbō, -āre 1	reflectō, -ere 3
consentiō, -īre 4	errō, -āre 1	reformō, -āre 1
consīderō, -āre 1	expandō, -ere 3	respondeō, -ēre 2
consistō, -ere 3	insultō, -āre 1	reportō, -āre 1
damnō, -āre 1	infestō, -āre 1	vīsitō, -āre 1

Vīta Rōmānōrum

Roman Superstitions

The Romans believed that the universe is controlled by a vast range of deities: not just the Olympian family (Jupiter, Juno, etc.), whom they shared with the Greeks, but also more primitive spirits such as Imporcitor, Subruncinator, and Stercutus, agricultural deities responsible for plowing, weeding, and manure-spreading. Such representatives of Roman public religion are quite alien to us, but the following glimpse into Roman private beliefs, from the *Natural History* of Pliny the Elder, does not sound terribly different from modern superstitions:

On New Year's Day, why do we wish one another happiness and prosperity? At public sacrifices, why do we pick people with lucky names to lead the victims? Why do we use special prayers to avert the evil eye, with some people calling on the Greek Nemesis, who has a statue for that purpose on the Capitol at Rome, even though we have no name for the goddess in Latin? . . . Why do we believe that uneven numbers are always more powerful? . . . Why do we wish good health to people when they sneeze? . . . (It is sometimes thought more effective if we add the name of the person.) There is a common belief that people can sense by a ringing in their ears that they are being talked about somewhere else. It is said that if one says "two" on seeing a scorpion it is prevented from striking. . . . In praying, we raise our right hand to our lips and turn our whole body to the right, but the Gauls think it more effective to turn to the left. Every nation agrees that lightning is propitiated by clicking the tongue.... Many people are convinced that cutting one's nails in silence, beginning with the index finger, is the proper thing to do on market days at Rome, while a haircut on the 17th or 29th day of the month ensures against baldness and headaches.... Marcus Servilius Nonianus, one of our leading citizens [he was consul in AD 35], was afraid of contracting inflammation of the eyes, and would not mention that disease till he had tied round his neck a piece of paper inscribed with the Greek letters *rho* and *alpha* [their significance is unknown], while Gaius Licinius Mucianus, who was consul three times, did the same sort of thing with a living fly in a little white linen bag.

—Pliny the Elder, *Historia Nātūrālis* 28.22–29

CHAPTER 2
First Declension Nouns, Prepositions

Nouns

A noun is a word denoting a person, place, or thing, for example, "man," "goddess," "pig," "Italy," "beauty." Compare the way in which English and Latin deal with the noun "Brutus" in the following sentences (and don't worry about the other words, which you will be learning soon):

Brutus kills Caesar.	**Brūtus** Caesarem interficit.
Caesar is **Brutus'** friend.	Caesar **Brūtī** amīcus est.
Caesar gives a book to **Brutus**.	Caesar librum **Brūtō** dat.
Caesar loves **Brutus**.	Caesar **Brūtum** amat.
Caesar was killed by **Brutus**.	Caesar ā **Brūtō** interfectus est.
Brutus, kill Caesar!	**Brūte**, Caesarem interfice!

In each of these sentences, the noun "Brutus" performs a different grammatical function. As you can see, however, in English the form of "Brutus" never changes. Instead, function is indicated either by word order (if you wrote "Caesar kills Brutus" you would change the meaning) or by the addition of extra words ("to," "by") or, in the last sentence, by punctuation. In Latin, by contrast, the form of the noun itself, not word order, indicates the function, usually without the addition of extra words. So you see five different forms of "Brutus" in these six sentences, depending on the noun's function in the sentence.

You already know that almost all Latin verbs belong to one of five conjugations. Similarly, almost all Latin nouns belong to one of five **DECLENSIONS**. A declension is a group of nouns that change their forms in the same way when their function in the sentence changes. You saw in Chapter 1 that the five conjugations of verbs don't look all that different from each other. Much greater differences exist between the five declensions, however, and each declension needs to be studied separately. This chapter will introduce only the **FIRST DECLENSION**.

Just as you need to know the **PERSON** and **NUMBER** of a verb in order to understand its function in the sentence (for example, *amāmus* is 1st pers. pl.), you need to know a noun's **NUMBER**, **GENDER**, and **CASE**.

NUMBER: just as a verb will be either SINGULAR (*amō* "I love") or PLURAL (*amāmus* "we love"), so also a noun will be either SINGULAR ("girl") or PLURAL ("girls"). Just as the ending -*āmus* tells you that *amāmus* is a plural form, you can tell whether a noun is singular or plural from the ending attached to the stem.

GENDER: all Latin nouns belong to one of three genders, MASCULINE, FEMININE, or NEUTER. You need to know a noun's gender because that will affect the form of any adjective or pronoun used with that noun. The meaning of some nouns determines their gender. The words for "boy," "man," "god" are masculine, whereas the words for "girl," "woman," "goddess" are feminine. In general, however, there are no clear guidelines for gender. There is no natural reason why, for example, the words for "family," "rose," and "house" should be feminine, whereas those for "field," "flower," and "garden" should be masculine, and those for "finger," "hand," and "arm" should be, respectively, masculine, feminine, and neuter. As you learn each noun, you need to learn its gender also.

CASE: A noun (for example, "Brutus") will have different forms—that is, different endings—depending on its function in a sentence. The ending tells you which case the noun is in, and therefore what the noun is doing in this particular sentence, and you will soon learn to recognize the endings for each case. The following are explanations of the basic meanings of each case, which apply to all nouns whatever their declension.

The **NOMINATIVE** case of a noun (or pronoun) is used for the subject of a verb, indicating the person or thing doing the action. In our sentence, "Brutus kills Caesar," Brutus is the subject, so in Latin it is in the nominative.

The **GENITIVE** case is used to give more information about another noun. Most frequently it indicates possession, so it is used where English would use either "of" or else an apostrophe. Our sentence "Caesar is Brutus' friend" could also be phrased as "Caesar is the friend of Brutus." Whatever the phrasing in English, in Latin Brutus is in the genitive.

The **DATIVE** case is used for the indirect object, the person or thing indirectly affected by the action of the verb. The dative is often used where English would use "to" or "for," or simply word order. For example, our sentence "Caesar gives a book to Brutus" could also be phrased in English as "Caesar gives Brutus a book." Whatever the phrasing in English, in Latin Brutus will be in the dative. If the sentence were "Caesar bought a book for Brutus," Brutus would also be in the dative.

The **ACCUSATIVE** case has two main functions. It is used for the direct object, the person or thing directly affected by the action. In our sentence "Caesar loves Brutus," Brutus is the direct object, so in Latin Brutus is in the accusative. It is also the case required by most prepositions; *contrā* "against," *post* "behind," *trans* "across" are some examples of prepositions that, to use a common technical term, GOVERN nouns and pronouns in the accusative case.

The **ABLATIVE** case has a wider range of functions than any of the other cases. Historically, this is because it combines what were, in the pre-classical period, three distinct cases: the true ablative, usually meaning "from" or "because of"; the instrumental case, expressing how something is done (usually equivalent to "with"); and the locative case, indicating the place in which something is done. In the Latin translation of "Caesar was killed by Brutus," Brutus is in the ablative because some prepositions, such as *ā* "from" (in our sentence "by"), *cum* "with," and *sine* "without," govern nouns and pronouns in the ablative case. You will learn the different uses of the ablative as you encounter them in future chapters.

Finally, Latin has the **VOCATIVE** case, used in addressing people or things. Our sentence "Brutus, kill Caesar!" is spoken by someone telling Brutus to kill Caesar, so Latin uses the vocative form of Brutus. When you see a noun fully declined, like *puella* below, the vocative will often be omitted because it is usually the same as the nominative.

First Declension Paradigm Noun: *puella*

Nouns in the first declension are nearly all feminine, a small minority are masculine, and none are neuter. Once you have memorized how *puella* is declined, you will know how to decline almost any first declension noun. (The only exceptions are names borrowed from Greek, which you will meet when you read Roman literature.)

	SINGULAR	PLURAL
NOMINATIVE	puell**a**	puell**ae**
GENITIVE	puell**ae**	puell**ārum**
DATIVE	puell**ae**	puell**īs**
ACCUSATIVE	puell**am**	puell**ās**
ABLATIVE	puell**ā**	puell**īs**

Here is a sentence using *puella* and *nauta*, another first declension noun, which means "sailor":

nauta puellam videt   means   "The sailor sees the girl."

Since Latin uses inflection, and not word order, to signal a noun's function in a sentence, the following five sentences also mean "The sailor sees the girl":

nauta videt puellam

puellam nauta videt

puellam videt nauta

videt nauta puellam

videt puellam nauta

BUT, if the cases change, the meaning changes. Thus,

acc. sing	nom. sing.	
nautam	*puella*	*videt*

means "The girl sees the sailor."

Now look at a longer sentence, with two more nouns, *fīlia* "daughter" and *agricola* "farmer":

nom. sing.	acc. sing.	gen. sing.	
nauta	*fīliam*	*agricolae*	*videt*

means "The sailor sees the farmer's daughter."

That same meaning can be expressed, however, by the same four words in almost any other order:

nauta agricolae fīliam videt   videt fīliam agricolae nauta

nauta videt agricolae fīliam   fīliam agricolae nauta videt

nauta videt fīliam agricolae   fīliam agricolae videt nauta

videt nauta fīliam agricolae   agricolae fīliam nauta videt

videt nauta agricolae fīliam   agricolae fīliam videt nauta

videt agricolae fīliam nauta

In English, of course, the subject is very often the first word in a sentence. This is not true in Latin; the most you can say is that Latin has a distinct preference for the order Subject, Object, Verb, as in *nauta puellam videt*. The longer the sentence, the more likely it is that the subject will not come first.

Notā Bene

You can see that in the translation "**The** sailor sees **the** girl," the definite article "the" has been added. Latin does not have either the definite article or the indefinite article ("a/an"). To make your translation sound like correct English, you often need to supply these. Similarly, although Latin has a full range of words meaning "my," "your," "his," and so on (and you will learn them in later chapters), they are not used as much as in English.

How to Break Down a Latin Sentence

When you are trying to determine what a Latin sentence means, it is best to start by looking for the verb, not the subject (which is what speakers of English intuitively look for), since the verb, which you can usually identify quite easily, will give you the clearest guidance in understanding the functions of the other words.

Latin verbs do not always have a specific subject. For example, *videt puellam* could mean simply "he (or she or it) sees the girl." When you do have a specific subject expressed, it will have to be in the **NOMINATIVE**, the subject case, and its **NUMBER** must also match the number of the verb: singular with a singular verb, plural with a plural verb. Take, for example, the sentence

nauta agricolae fīliam videt.

Our verb, *videt*, is singular, so we're looking for a NOMINATIVE SINGULAR noun for our subject. We have two candidates, *agricolae* and *nauta*. *agricolae* could only be a PLURAL nominative, so it can't be the subject of *videt*. Therefore, *nauta* must be the subject of *videt*.

Subject
nauta   agricolae fīliam videt.

By beginning our translation with the verb, we also know to look for a noun in the accusative case, since *videt* is a **transitive verb**, that is, a verb that takes a **direct object**. Here there is just one possibility: only the accusative *fīliam* can be the direct object of *videt*.

	direct object	
nauta agricolae	*fīliam*	*videt.*

As you can see from the declension of *puella*, some noun forms can represent more than one case. *puellae*, for example, is the form used not only for the genitive and dative singular but also for the nominative and vocative plural. It can therefore serve four different functions in a sentence. In practice, however, context will usually tell you which case and number to choose. Consider, for example, the following story:

> *nauta fīliam agricolae amat. ergō rosās puellae dat.*
> The sailor loves the farmer's daughter. Therefore roses <u>puellae</u> he gives.

What are the case and number of *puellae*? It cannot be nominative plural, that is, the subject of the sentence, because the verb, *dat*, is singular. In theory, *puellae* could be genitive singular, "Therefore he gives the roses of the girl," or vocative plural, "Therefore, girls, he gives roses," but neither of these possibilities makes very good sense. You can see that the dative singular is the most appropriate case in the context, especially since the verb, *dat*, typically takes an indirect object: "The sailor loves the farmer's daughter. Therefore he gives roses *to the girl*."

You can often use context to determine the meaning. Here is a different story:

> *nautae fīliās agricolae amant. ergō rosās puellīs dant.*

The meaning may be

> The <u>sailors</u> love the <u>farmer's</u> daughters. Therefore they give roses to the girls.

It is, however, equally possible that the meaning is

> The <u>farmers</u> love the <u>sailor's</u> daughters. Therefore they give roses to the girls.

Without further information, we have no way to tell whether *nautae* is nominative plural and *agricolae* genitive singular or vice versa. Usually the complete context will provide this information, perhaps describing the sailors' lonely life at sea, or the farmers' cultivation of flowers. If the context does not help, word order may give you a hint. For example, a noun in the genitive tends in Latin to come immediately before or after the noun to which it refers. If our sentences were

> *fīliās agricolae amant nautae. ergō rosās puellīs dant*

word order indicates that the writer meant to say "The sailors love the farmer's daughters."

Alternatively, a subordinate clause (here using the conjunction *quod* "because") can make the relationship between the nouns clear:

> *nautae, quod fīliās agricolae amant, rosās puellīs dant.*

This would mean "The sailors, because they love the farmer's daughters, give roses to the girls."

Apposition

As a general rule, the various nouns in a clause or sentence will be in different cases, each having a different function. Often, however, as in English, a noun may appear next to another noun, with both referring to the same person, place, or thing, so as to give further information. The second noun is said to be in apposition. **A noun in apposition always agrees in case, and usually also in gender and number, with the noun to which it is in apposition.** In Latin, as in English, nouns in apposition are usually marked off by commas. For example:

dat. sing. fem.	dat. sing. fem. (in apposition to *puellae*)	
puellae,	*fīliae*	*agricolae, rosās dat nauta.*

This means "The sailor gives roses to the girl, the daughter of the farmer."

acc. pl. fem.	acc. pl. fem. (in apposition to *puellās*)	
puellās,	*fīliās*	*agricolae, nautae amant.*

This means "The sailors love the girls, the daughters of the farmer."

Prepositions

As in English, prepositions are used in Latin to define the relationship between words—frequently between a verb and a noun or pronoun. "Against," "behind," "with," and "without" are prepositions, and their Latin equivalents are *contrā, post, cum,* and *sine*. Unlike verbs, nouns, and some other parts of speech, **prepositions do not decline**, so they have only one form. Nearly all Latin prepositions govern nouns (or pronouns) in either the **accusative** or the **ablative** case; *contrā* and *post* govern the accusative case, *cum* and *sine* the ablative. Here are some examples:

contrā puellam	against the girl
cum puellā	with the girl
post puellās	behind the girls
sine puellīs	without the girls

Nearly all prepositions govern only one case, either the accusative or the ablative, but two prepositions are exceptional because they govern two cases and must be translated differently with each case. The prepositions *in* and *sub* govern the accusative when the situation involves motion toward someone or something. If no motion is involved, they govern the ablative. For example:

acc.

in casam pīrātam dūcō means "I lead the pirate INTO the house," but

abl.

in casā pīrātam videō means "I see the pirate IN the house"

Similarly,

acc.

sub statuam deae agricola fīliam mittit means
"The farmer sends his daughter under the statue of the goddess," but

abl.

sub statuā deae sedet agricolae fīlia means
"The farmer's daughter is sitting under the statue of the goddess"

Vocabulary

This list presents nouns in the format that will be used for nouns in all the vocabulary lists in this book. You will notice that the nominative and genitive singular of each noun are given. Knowing both these forms will become essential later on, so get into the habit of learning both of them now.

First Declension Nouns
Feminine

audācia, audāciae 1	boldness	**ōra, ōrae** 1	shore
avāritia, avāritiae 1	greed	**pecūnia, pecūniae** 1	money
casa, casae 1	house	**porta, portae** 1	gate
dea, deae 1	goddess	**potentia, potentiae** 1	power
familia, familiae 1	family	**praeda, praedae** 1	booty
fīlia, fīliae 1	daughter	**puella, puellae** 1	girl
flamma, flammae 1	flame	**Rōma, Rōmae** 1	Rome
iānua (= *jānua*), **iānuae** 1	door	**rosa, rosae** 1	rose
insula, insulae 1	island	**statua, statuae** 1	statue
Ītalia, Ītaliae 1	Italy	**taberna, tabernae** 1	tavern
lacrima, lacrimae 1	tear(-drop)	**unda, undae** 1	wave

Masculine

agricola, agricolae 1	farmer	**pīrāta, pīrātae** 1	pirate
nauta, nautae 1	sailor	**poēta, poētae** 1	poet

Prepositions

ā/ab + abl.	from	**ad** + acc.	to
cum + abl.	with	**contrā** + acc.	against
ē/ex + abl.	out of	**post** + acc.	behind, after
sine + abl.	without	**trans** + acc.	across
in + abl.	in, on	**sub** + abl.	under
in + acc.	into, on to	**sub** + acc.	(to) under

Conjunctions/Adverbs

ac conj.	and	**sed** conj.	but
atque conj.	and	**nōn** adv.	not
et conj.	and	**sī** conj.	if
at conj.	but		

Vocabulary Notes

ā and **ē** are found primarily before a consonant, **ab** and **ex** before a vowel or *h* (which the Romans did not regard as a consonant); for example, *ā tabernā* and *ē tabernā*, but *ab Ītaliā* and *ex Ītaliā*. The variation makes pronunciation easier, just as *an* is used in English instead of *a* before a word beginning with a vowel or, in some cases, *h*; there is no difference in meaning.

You must translate the English word "to" with **ad** when it involves motion, but with the **dative and no preposition** when motion is not implied.

pecūniam ad nautam mittō	"I send the money to the sailor"
pecūniam nautae dō	"I give the money to the sailor"

In other words, "pecūniam ad nautam dō" is not correct Latin. Similarly, you use the dative without a preposition in translating sentences such as "I say many things to the sailor," "I read the book to the sailor," and "I show the pig to the sailor."

Of the words given here for "and" (**ac, atque, et**) and "but" (**at, sed**), *et* and *sed* are the commonest.

nōn is usually positioned directly before the word that it negates.

Prōlūsiōnēs

Parsing

You already know that verbs are parsed in a certain format, as in these examples:

amō:	1st person singular present active indicative of the verb *amō, amāre, amāvī, amātum* 1 "love"
mittitis:	2nd person plural present active indicative of the verb *mittō, mittere, mīsī, missum* 3 "send"
audiunt:	3rd pers. pl. pres. act. ind. of the verb *audiō, audīre, audīvī, audītum* 4 "hear"
capere:	pres. act. inf. of the verb *capiō, capere, cēpī, captum* 3 *i*-stem "take"

Nouns are also parsed in a prescribed format, as follows:

puellam: accusative singular of the noun *puella, puellae* feminine 1 "girl"

nautārum: genitive plural of the noun *nauta, nautae* masculine 1 "sailor"

agricolās: acc. pl. of the noun *agricola, agricolae* masc. 1 "farmer"

familiā: abl. sing. of the noun *familia, familiae* fem. 1 "family"

Since you have now encountered nouns and prepositions as well as verbs, you can construct more complex sentences. When you are parsing, you will need to explain not only a word's part of speech and grammatical form but also its relation to the rest of the sentence. For example, in the sentence

pecūniam pīrātīs agricola dat

pecūniam is accusative singular of the noun *pecūnia, pecūniae* fem. 1 "money," the direct object of the verb *dat*; *pīrātīs* is dat. pl. of the noun *pīrāta, pīrātae* masc. 1 "pirate," the indirect object of the verb *dat*; *agricola* is nom. sing. of the noun *agricola, agricolae* masc. 1 "farmer," the subject of the verb *dat*.

In the sentence

fīlia poētae nautās ē tabernā vocat

fīlia is nom. sing. of the noun *fīlia, fīliae* fem. 1 "daughter," subject of the verb *vocat*; *poētae* is gen. sing. of the noun *poēta, poētae* masc. 1 "poet," indicating to whose daughter *fīlia* refers; *nautās* is acc. pl. of the noun *nauta, nautae* masc. 1 "sailor," the direct object of the verb *vocat*; *tabernā* is abl. sing. of the noun *taberna, tabernae* fem. 1 "tavern," governed by the preposition *ē*.

Parse the words in bold.

1. in **tabernā** sedet **nauta**.
2. agricola **pīrātam** cum **filiā** videt.
3. pecūniam, **nauta**, **habēmus**.
4. **poētae rosās** dat agricola.
5. puella ad **casam agricolae** statuam mittit.

Change from singular to plural, or vice versa, and then translate.

For example:

filiās agricolārum videō – filiam agricolae vidēmus – We see the farmer's daughter.

1. agricola familiam nautae amat.
2. pīrātae in tabernā cum nautīs bibunt.
3. pīrātae rosam dō.
4. ad ōram insulae undam mittit dea.
5. poētae rosam sub statuā deae reperiunt.

Translate.

1. nauta cum filiā agricolae in ōrā insulae lūdit.
2. rosās ac pecūniam nautae ad pīrātam mittit filia agricolae.
3. pecūniam agricola habet, nōn pīrātae.
4. pīrāta pecūniam nautae atque agricolae capit.
5. trans insulam agricolās dūcunt pīrātae.
6. sine audāciā agricolae pīrātās nōn vincunt.
7. flammae portās Rōmae rapiunt, sed dea Rōmae potentiam dat.
8. in Ītaliā nōn poētās vidēs, sed agricolās.
9. ad Ītaliam filiās mittunt nautae.
10. familia pīrātae Rōmam videt.
11. in tabernā cum agricolae filiā sedēre dēbeō.
12. pīrātae praedam post iānuam casae reperītis.
13. nōlī pīrātae lacrimās spectāre, poēta!
14. statuās deārum sine lacrimīs nōn vidēmus.
15. avāritia pīrātārum agricolās terret, et contrā pīrātās dēbēmus mittere nautās.

16. rosās post casam, sed nōn sub statuā deae, reperiunt puellae.
17. nautae fīliās agricolārum amant, sed agricolārum fīliae nautās nōn amant.
18. sī puellās amātis, nautae, rosās ad agricolārum casās mittite.
19. agricolārum fīliae amant pīrātam, at pīrāta rosās puellārum nōn amat.
20. agricola, sine pecūniā familiam ex Ītaliā nōlī mittere.

21. I give roses to the sailor's daughter.
22. The poet is drinking behind the door of the tavern.
23. We must send the poet out of Italy.
24. The farmers fear the pirates' greed and boldness.
25. They see and hear the farmer's daughters in the house.
26. They are sending the statue of the goddess to the shore of the island.
27. Sailor, listen to the farmers' daughters.
28. Farmers, you do not see the girl's roses.
29. Sailors, do not give the girls roses!
30. The girls must warn the farmers and the sailor.
31. The pirates are seizing the statues of the goddesses.
32. The poets do not have money in the tavern.
33. Sailor, do not give roses to the pirates!
34. If the farmers see the pirates, they lead the sailors to the house.
35. I love the pirate's daughter, but I live with the farmer's family.

Lectiōnēs Latīnae

Lege, Intellege

Florus wrote a brief history of Rome, known as the *Epitomē Bellōrum Omnium Annōrum DCC* (Digest of All Wars for 700 Years). It is largely based on Livy's *Ab Urbe Conditā* (From the Foundation of the City).

Rōmulus et Remus

prīmus ille et urbis et imperiī conditor Rōmulus fuit, Marte genitus et Rheā Silviā. Amūliī rēgis imperiō abiectus in fluvium cum Remō frātre nōn potuit exstinguī; relictīs catulīs lupa ūbera admōvit īnfantibus mātremque sē gessit. sīc repertōs sub arbore Faustulus rēgiī gregis pastor tulit in casam atque ēducāvit . . . ut ōmen regnandī peterent, Remus montem Aventīnum, Rōmulus Pālātīnum occupat. prior ille sex vulturēs, hīc posteā, sed duodecim vīdit.

—Florus, *Epitomē* 1

imperiī can mean both "rule" and "command" as well as "empire"

abiectus "thrown"

nōn potuit "he could not"

relictīs catulīs "leaving her cubs"

mātremque sē gessit "and she behaved as a mother"

ut ōmen regnandī peterent "to seek an omen about ruling"

1. What was the name of the shepherd who discovered the twins?
2. Who was the founder of both Rome and the empire?
3. Who stood on the Palatine hill to watch for signs from the gods about ruling Rome?
4. Who were the parents of Romulus and Remus?
5. Remus saw six vultures. How many did Romulus see?

Many familiar expressions are prepositional phrases drawn directly from Latin. For example:

ad hōc	to this thing (= for this specific purpose)
ad infīnītum	to infinity
ad nauseam	to sickness
dē factō	from the fact
ē plūribus ūnum	one from several
ex officiō	by virtue of one's office
in locō parentis	in the place of a parent
in memoriam	to the memory (of . . .)
per annum/diem	by year/day
per capita	by heads
per sē	in (through) itself
post mortem	after death
post partum	after giving birth
prō patriā	on behalf of one's country
quid prō quō	exchange (what for what)
sub poenā	under penalty
summā cum laude	with highest praise

Ars Poētica

Publilius Syrus II
Identify and explain the case of the nouns in bold.

1. *bona **fāma** in tenebrīs proprium splendōrem obtinet.*
   A good reputation maintains its own splendor in darkness.

2. *damnum appellandum est cum malā **fāmā** lucrum.*
   Profit with bad reputation should be called loss.

3. *comes fācundus in **viā** prō vehiculō est.*
   An eloquent companion on a journey is as good as a vehicle.

4. *cuius mortem amīcī exspectant, **vītam** cīvēs ōdērunt.*
   His fellow citizens hate the life of any man whose death his friends are watching for.

5. ***iniūriam** aurēs quam oculī facilius ferunt.*
   Our ears bear an injury more easily than our eyes.

6. ***iniūriārum** remedium est oblīviō.*
   Forgetting them is the cure for injuries.

7. ***mora** omnis odiō est, sed facit **sapientiam**.*
   All delay is odious, but it creates wisdom.

Lūsūs

Thēsaurus Verbōrum

Many English verbs add a silent *-e* to the present stem of Latin verbs; for example, "cede" comes from *cēdō, -ere* 3, "continue" comes from *continuō, -āre* 1.

dēclārō, -āre 1	explōrō, -āre 1	persuādeō, -ēre 2
dēfīniō, -īre 4	exspīrō, -āre 1	purgō, -āre 1
dēscrībō, -ere 3	inclūdō, -ere 3	revolvō, -ere 3
dīvidō, -ere 3	inquīrō, -ere 3	salūtō, -āre 1
ēmergō, -ere 3	interveniō, -īre 4	sēparō, -āre 1
excitō, -āre 1	invādō, -ere 3	solvō, -ere 3
excūsō, -āre 1	moveō, -ēre 2	surgō, -ere 3
explōdō, -ere 3	observō, -āre 1	urgeō, -ēre 2

Vīta Rōmānōrum

Witches

Pliny the Elder, who catalogued the superstitions listed in Chapter 1, was himself a serious scientist. A rather different attitude to superstition appears in this anecdote from the *Satyricōn*, a comic novel by Pliny's contemporary Petronius. Trimalchio, the main character, tells the story after one of the guests at his banquet has told a tale about a werewolf:

> When I still had all my hair . . . our master's favorite slave died—my god, he was a real treasure, a perfect young fellow! Anyway, when his wretched mother was wailing and we were all mourning with her, suddenly witches began to screech; you'd have thought there was a dog chasing a hare. At that time we had a Cappadocian slave, a tall chap, very reckless and strong enough to lift an angry bull. He boldly drew a sword and rushed out the door with his left hand carefully wrapped [for lack of a shield] and ran a woman through the middle—just about here (may the gods preserve the part I'm touching!). We heard a groan, and—well, of course, I'll tell you no lies—we didn't actually see the witches themselves, but the big fellow came back and threw himself on the bed with bruises all over his body, for he'd been touched by an evil hand. We closed the door and returned to our mourning, but when the mother went to embrace her son's body, she touched it and saw that it was just a little handful of straw. It had no heart, no insides, nothing: the witches had stolen the boy, of course, and substituted a straw dummy. I'm telling you, you'd better believe that there are wise women who go about at night and can turn everything upside down. That big strong chap was never the same again; in fact, a few days later he died in a fit of delirium.

> —Petronius, *Satyricōn* 63

CHAPTER 3
The Future and Imperfect Active Indicative of Verbs

In Chapter 1 we saw that the five verb conjugations form the present active tense in a similar way. The similarities are almost as close in the formation of the future and imperfect active.

To form the FUTURE active of the **first and second conjugations**, simply add the endings *-bō, -bis, -bit, -bimus, -bitis, -bunt* to the present stem, with the appropriate stem vowel (long *a* or long *e*) between stem and ending:

	1st	**2nd**
1st sing.	am**ābō**	mon**ēbō**
2nd sing.	am**ābis**	mon**ēbis**
3rd sing.	am**ābit**	mon**ēbit**
1st pl.	am**ābimus**	mon**ēbimus**
2nd pl.	am**ābitis**	mon**ēbitis**
3rd pl.	am**ābunt**	mon**ēbunt**

To form the FUTURE active of the **third, fourth, and third *i*-stem conjugations,** you use the present stem but with a completely different set of endings: *-am, -ēs, -et, -ēmus, -ētis, -ent.* There is no linking vowel for the third conjugation, but the fourth and the third *i*-stem conjugations both use a short *i*:

	3rd	**4th**	**3rd *i*-stem**
1st sing.	mitt**am**	aud**iam**	cap**iam**
2nd sing.	mitt**ēs**	aud**iēs**	cap**iēs**
3rd sing.	mitt**et**	aud**iet**	cap**iet**
1st pl.	mitt**ēmus**	aud**iēmus**	cap**iēmus**
2nd pl.	mitt**ētis**	aud**iētis**	cap**iētis**
3rd pl.	mitt**ent**	aud**ient**	cap**ient**

To form the IMPERFECT active of all five conjugations, you add the endings *-bam, -bās, -bat, -bāmus, -bātis, -bant* to the present stem. The linking vowel for the first conjugation is a long *a*, for the second and third a long *e*, and for the fourth and the third *i*-stem conjugations, a combination of short *i* and long *e*:

	1st	**2nd**
1st sing.	am**ābam**	mon**ēbam**
2nd sing.	am**ābās**	mon**ēbās**
3rd sing.	am**ābat**	mon**ēbat**
1st pl.	am**ābāmus**	mon**ēbāmus**
2nd pl.	am**ābātis**	mon**ēbātis**
3rd pl.	am**ābant**	mon**ēbant**

	3rd	**4th**	**3rd *i*-stem**
1st sing.	mittēbam	audiēbam	capiēbam
2nd sing.	mittēbās	audiēbās	capiēbās
3rd sing.	mittēbat	audiēbat	capiēbat
1st pl.	mittēbāmus	audiēbāmus	capiēbāmus
2nd pl.	mittēbātis	audiēbātis	capiēbātis
3rd pl.	mittēbant	audiēbant	capiēbant

The **future** tense in Latin covers both meanings of the future tense in English, whether simple (I will love, you will love, etc.) or continuous (I will be loving, you will be loving, etc.).

amābō	I will love, I will be loving, etc.
amābis	You (sing.) will love
amābit	He/She/It will love
amābimus	We will love
amābitis	You (pl.) will love
amābunt	They will love

The **imperfect** tense describes a past action that was

- **in progress when something else happened**
- **repeated over time**
- **begun**
- **attempted**

For example, the biographer Suetonius tells us that the emperor Domitian used to spend a lot of his time alone, catching flies and killing them with a sharp *stilus*, or pen. Here are descriptions of Domitian's behavior that would all require the **imperfect** tense in Latin.

1. When the senators came to the palace, Domitian **was killing** flies. (In progress)
2. Every afternoon, Domitian **used to kill** flies. (Repeated)
3. Since he was bored, Domitian **began killing** flies. (Begun)
4. Domitian **tried to kill** the fly. (Attempted)

If you were translating any of these sentences into Latin, you would use the imperfect tense. The first two instances (an action in progress and a repeated action) correspond to the way we use the imperfect in English. But the last two (an action begun and an action attempted) seem surprising to English speakers. As you translate more Latin sentences into English, however, you will get used to considering all four possibilities.

When translating from English into Latin, you will sometimes have more than one Latin past tense to choose from, depending on the context. **For the moment, you should use the imperfect for any past action.** In Chapter 7 you will learn other past tenses, how they differ from the imperfect, and how to use all of them accurately.

Vocabulary

Verbs

iuvō (= *juvō*), **iuvāre, iūvī, iūtum** 1	help
pugnō, pugnāre, pugnāvī, pugnātum 1	fight
oppugnō, oppugnāre, oppugnāvī, oppugnātum 1	besiege
stō, stāre, stetī, statum 1	stand
tolerō, tolerāre, tolerāvī, tolerātum 1	tolerate
rīdeō, rīdēre, rīsī, rīsum 2	laugh
teneō, tenēre, tenuī, tentum 2	hold
frangō, frangere, frēgī, fractum 3	break
fundō, fundere, fūdī, fūsum 3	pour
surgō, surgere, surrexī, surrectum 3	rise
tangō, tangere, tetigī, tactum 3	touch
dormiō, dormīre, dormīvī, dormītum 4	sleep

First Declension Nouns

aqua, aquae fem. 1	water
āra, ārae fem. 1	altar
cōpia, cōpiae fem. 1 sing.	amount, supply
pl.	military forces
cūria, cūriae fem. 1	Senate(-house)
fortūna, fortūnae fem. 1	fortune
īra, īrae fem. 1	anger
lūna, lūnae fem. 1	moon
spēlunca, spēluncae fem. 1	cave
stella, stellae fem. 1	star
turba, turbae fem. 1	throng, mob
via, viae fem. 1	road
victōria, victōriae fem. 1	victory
villa, villae fem. 1	country house
vīta, vītae fem. 1	life

Adverbs

adhūc	still	**māne**	in the morning
cottīdiē	every day	**paene**	almost
fortasse	perhaps	**praesertim**	especially
frustrā	in vain	**tandem**	at last

Prepositions

ante + acc.	before, in front of
dē + abl.	down from, about
prō + abl.	on behalf of

Conjunctions

aut	or	**ergō**	therefore
aut . . . aut	either . . . or	**igitur**	therefore
vel	or	**itaque**	therefore
vel . . . vel	either . . . or	**quia**	because
cum	when	**quod**	because
dum	while	**quoniam**	because

Vocabulary Notes

cōpia, cōpiae is one of a number of nouns that have different meanings in the singular and the plural. You will find more such nouns in Chapter 10.

There is a difference in the way **aut** and **vel** are used:

aut: Only two alternatives exist.

aut cum praedā aut sine praedā in tabernā sedent pīrātae

"Either with their plunder or without their plunder, pirates sit in a tavern"

vel: We're discussing two alternatives selected from a larger range of possibilities.

vel aquam vel vīnum bibēmus

"We will drink either water or wine [not milk, beer, or anything else]"

Don't confuse the preposition **cum** (which governs nouns and pronouns) with the conjunction **cum**, which introduces clauses containing verbs.

ergō, igitur, itaque: These three words for "therefore" are all very common and interchangeable. Some authors prefer to put *igitur* or *itaque* as the second, not the first, word in its clause.

quia, quod, quoniam: These three words for "because" are also all very common and, when used with indicative verbs, generally interchangeable. With subjunctive verbs, which you will find starting in Chapter 22, *quod* is the most frequent word for "because."

Prōlūsiōnēs

Parse the following words.

1. frangēbant.
2. pugnābitis.
3. surgitis.
4. dormiēs.
5. tenēs.

6. tangēmus.
7. habēmus.
8. tolerābam.
9. legam.
10. puellam.

Supply the future and imperfect forms for the following verbs, in the same person and number.

For example, if you are given *amō*, write *amābō − amābam*.

1. pugnātis.
2. dormiō.
3. tenēs.
4. capis.
5. stō.

6. iuvāmus.
7. rīdent.
8. tangimus.
9. funditis.
10. frangunt.

Translate.

1. tenēbās.
2. fundent.
3. rīdēbunt.
4. surgētis.
5. pugnābāmus.
6. iuvābitis.
7. capiēbat.
8. stābunt.
9. dormiēs.
10. habēs.

11. You (sing.) used to stand.
12. We began to send.
13. He used to fight.
14. They will tolerate.
15. We used to stand.
16. They began to pour.
17. They will be hearing.
18. You (sing.) will take.
19. She was trying to sleep.
20. You (pl.) were taking.

Translate.

1. praesertim sī rīdet fortūna, pecūniam habent agricolae.
2. in tabernā māne sedēbant poētae, nōn nautae.
3. sine cōpiā aquae vītam nōn tolerābimus.
4. statuam deae tangere nōn dēbētis, pīrātae.
5. statuam deae post victōriam dabimus.
6. dum surgunt undae, pīrātae fīlia dormit.
7. fortūna vītam sine victōriā nautīs nōn dabit.
8. contrā insulam undās fortasse mittēbat dea.
9. sine īrā vīvere dēbēmus, sed cottīdiē surgit īra.
10. vel pecūniam vel praedam pīrātārum nauta deae dabit.
11. agricola nōn rīdēbit, et lacrimās ante deae āram frustrā fundet.
12. agricolārum turbam tenet īra, et māne in tabernā sedēbunt.
13. rosās praesertim amābāmus, sed sine pecūniā rosās nōn habēbimus.
14. fortūna tandem rīdēbat; itaque pecūniam habēbant agricolae.
15. in casā surgēbant flammae, sed agricolae familia adhūc dormiēbat.

16. While the moon is rising, we see the stars at last.
17. You were holding roses, sailors, not money.
18. We will send either the pirates or the farmers out of the cave.
19. We had to sleep under the moon and stars.
20. The poets will have to give either money or roses to the sailors.
21. He tried to watch the stars when the moon was rising.
22. A crowd of sailors used to sleep every day either in front of the cave or behind the tavern.
23. The poet was trying to read in the country house, but he was not listening to his daughter.
24. In the morning, the farmers will be sitting in front of the house with the pirates.
25. When the goddess rises out of the waves, we ought not to call the pirate and the sailor's daughters to the shore.

Lectiōnēs Latīnae

Lege, Intellege

Probably early in the third century AD, Gaius Julius Solinus published his *Collectānea Rērum Memorābilium* (Collections of Memorable Things), which he mostly plagiarized from the *Natural History* of Pliny the Elder and the *Geography* of Pomponius Mela. He is, however, the earliest source to mention that there are no snakes in Ireland—but he also claims that there are no bees there, either.

More About the Roman Kings

Rōmulus mūrōrum fundāmenta iēcit duodēvīgintī nātus annōs, XI Kalendās Maiās, hōrā post secundam ante tertiam, sīcut Lūcius Tarruntius prōdidit mathēmaticōrum nōbilissimus, Iove in Piscibus, Saturnō Venere Marte Mercuriō in Scorpiōne, Sōle in Taurō, Lūnā in Librā constitūtīs. . . . Tatius in arce habitāvit, ubi nunc aedēs est Iūnōnis Monētae. Numa in colle Quirīnālī, propter aedem Vestae. Tullus Hostilius in Veliā, ubi posteā deōrum Penātium aedēs facta est. Ancus Marcius in summā Sacrā Viā, ubi aedēs Larum est. Tarquinius Priscus ad Mūgiōniam portam suprā summam Novam Viam. Servius Tullius suprā clīvum Orbium. Tarquinius Superbus ad Fāgūtālem lacum.

—Solinus, *Collectānea* 1

prīmum . . . deinde "at first . . . then"

1. At what time on April 21 did Romulus lay the foundations of Rome?
2. The temple of which goddess later stood on the citadel where Tatius once lived?
3. The Sun was in which zodiacal sign when Romulus founded Rome?
4. Where did Ancus Marcius live?
5. Which planets were in Scorpio when Romulus founded Rome?

The following verb forms are used as nouns in English:

affidāvit	he/she has sworn	*interest*	it concerns
caveat	let him/her beware	*mementō*	remember!
exit	he/she goes out	*nōn sequitur*	it does not follow
fac simile	make a similar thing	*placēbō*	I will please
habitat	he/she lives	*vetō*	I forbid

Ars Poētica

Ovid's Love Poetry I

Ovid (Publius Ovidius Naso; 43 BC–AD 17?) was the author of several collections of love poetry (*Amōrēs*, *Hērōides*, *Ars Amātōria*, *Remedia Amōris*), a versified calendar of the Roman year from January to June (*Fastī*), and a fifteen-book collection of myths called the *Metamorphōsēs*. After the emperor Augustus exiled him to the Black Sea in AD 8 for some unknown offense, he produced two melancholy collections of poetic letters to persuade the emperor to let him come back (*Tristia*, *Epistulae ex Pontō*), and a long curse-poem against a disloyal friend (*Ībis*).

Give the person, number, mood, and tense of the verbs in bold in the following quotations from Ovid's love poetry.

1. ***dīcēbam*** *"medicāre tuōs* **dēsiste** *capillōs!"*
   I kept saying, "Stop dyeing your hair!"

2. *vix mihi* **crēdētis**, *sed* **crēdite**.
   You will scarcely believe me, but believe me.

3. ***errābat*** *nūdō per loca sōla pede.*
   She was wandering with naked foot through lonely places.

4. *Īlia,* **pōne** *metūs! tibi rēgia nostra* **patēbit**.
       tēque **colent** *amnēs. Īlia, pōne metūs!*
   Ilia, lay aside your fears! My palace will be open for you, and rivers
   will revere you. Ilia, lay aside your fears! [A river god is trying to seduce Ilia, the future mother of Romulus and Remus.]

5. ***vīvet*** *Maeonidēs, Tenedos dum* **stābit** *et Īdē,*
       dum rapidās Simoīs in mare **volvet** *aquās;*
   vīvet et Ascraeus, dum mustīs ūva **tumēbit**,
       dum **cadet** *incurvā falce resecta Cerēs.*
   Homer ["the man from Maeonia"] will live, as long as Tenedos and Ida [places mentioned in the *Iliad*] stand, as long as the [river] Simois rolls its rushing waters into the sea; Hesiod [archaic Greek poet c. 700 BC] also will live, as long as the grape swells with juice, as long as Ceres [the goddess of harvest, here representing grain] falls, cut by the curved sickle.

6. *prīmus ego* **aspiciam** *nōtam dē lītore puppim,*
       et **dīcam** *"nostrōs advehit illa deōs!"*
   I will be the first to catch sight of your familiar ship from the shore, and I will say, "That ship is carrying my gods." [Ovid is imagining his mistress' return.]

Lūsūs

Thēsaurus Verbōrum

English has adopted many words from Latin with little or no change. As a result, when you see a first conjugation verb, you often just need to add the suffix -*ate* to the stem to find its meaning: for example, "celebrate" is derived from *celebrō, -āre, -āvī, -ātum* and "congregate" from *congregō, -āre, -āvī, -ātum*. Here are some more examples:

cremō	germinō	narrō	sēparō
creō	hībernō	nāvigō	simulō
decorō	implicō	palpitō	stimulō
dēmonstrō	irrigō	penetrō	subiugō (= *subjugō*)
dēvastō	locō	plācō	terminō
dictō	migrō	prōcrastinō	tolerō
exaggerō	mīlitō	satiō	vibrō
excruciō	mītigō	saturō	violō
generō	mūtō	sēgregō	vōciferō

Mors Rōmānōrum

Fear of Death

The Romans did not make anything like as great a contribution to philosophy as the Greeks did. Nevertheless, Lucretius' *On the Nature of Things*, which draws on the teachings of the Greek Epicurus of Samos (341–270 BC), is arguably the greatest philosophical poem ever written. His calm explanation of why no one should fear death contrasts starkly with the Roman superstitions recounted in Chapters 1 and 2.

> "Your home and your excellent wife will never again welcome you happily, and your sweet children will not run to snatch kisses and fill your heart with silent joy. You will not be able to protect your prosperity and your family. A single hateful day has deprived you, unhappy wretch, of all the many rewards of life." What people do not add when they say this is that desire for those things no longer troubles you, either. If they could see this clearly in their minds and speak accordingly, they would free themselves from great anxiety and fear. "You have fallen asleep in death, and will be spared every distressing sorrow for all time to come, but we have wept inconsolably for you, standing by when you were turned to ashes on the dreadful pyre, and time will never take our everlasting sorrow from our hearts." Then we should ask: if [in death] things return to

sleep and rest, what can be bitter enough to cause anyone to waste away with eternal grief? This is just what people often do at banquets, when they are holding their wine cups and shading their faces with garlands. They say with sincerity: "Petty humans have only a short life to enjoy; soon it will be over and we will never be able to call it back again." As if in death this should be their greatest trouble, that a parching thirst should be burning them up or that the desire for anything else should be weighing upon them.

—Lucretius, *Dē Rērum Nātūrā* 3.894–918

CHAPTER 4

Direct Questions, Irregular Verbs, Compound Verbs

Direct Questions

When English speakers want to ask a question, they often change the word order and use a compound verb tense: "Does the farmer listen to the sailor?" "Is the farmer listening to the sailor?" But Latin has only one form of each tense (remember that *audit* means "he listens to," "he is listening to," and "he does listen to") and word order does not have the same significance as in English. So this method won't work in Latin. Instead, as in English, you can change a statement into a question by simply adding a question mark. You can also signal a question by adding *-ne* to the end of the first word in the sentence:

> *agricola nautam audit?* and *agricolane nautam audit?* both mean "Does the farmer listen to the sailor?"

In English we can show that we expect a certain answer to a question by using various kinds of emphasis. The questions

> "<u>Surely</u> the farmer listens to the sailor?"
>
> "<u>Doesn't</u> the farmer listen to the sailor?"
>
> "The farmer listens to the sailor, <u>doesn't he</u>?"

all assume that the answer will be "Yes, he does."

On the other hand,

> "<u>Surely</u> the farmer <u>doesn't</u> listen to the sailor?"
>
> "The farmer doesn't listen to the sailor, <u>does he</u>?"

both assume that the answer will be "No, he doesn't."

In Latin, if the question is introduced with *nonne*, it is assuming an affirmative answer; a negative answer is assumed if the question is introduced by *num*.

Question	Expected Answer
nonne *agricola nautam videt?*	*videt*
num *agricola nautam videt?*	*nōn videt*

Notā Bene

Latin has no simple word for "yes" or "no."

Some questions are really two questions in one, for example:

"Do you see the sailor or the farmer?"

The second part of this "double" question must be introduced using *an* or *anne*. For the first part, you have several possibilities. You can treat it like an ordinary question, using *-ne* or just a question mark. Or you can introduce it with *utrum*.

Question	**Some Possible Answers**
nautam an(ne) agricolam vidēs?	*nautam videō*
nautamne an(ne) agricolam vidēs?	*agricolam videō*
utrum nautam an(ne) agricolam vidēs?	*nautam et agricolam videō*

A question such as "Do you see the sailor or not?" where the answer may be "Yes" or "No" uses the particle *annōn*:

Question	**Possible Answers**
nautam(ne) vidēs annōn?	*videō*
	nōn videō

The interrogative adverbs WHY, WHEN, HOW, and WHERE have Latin equivalents that come at the beginning of their clause, as in English.

WHY will the pirate see the girl?	*CŪR pīrāta puellam vidēbit?*
WHEN will the pirate see the girl?	*QUANDŌ pīrāta puellam vidēbit?*
HOW will the pirate see the girl?	*QUŌMODO pīrāta puellam vidēbit?*
WHERE will the pirate see the girl?	*UBI pīrāta puellam vidēbit?*

Since words such as *cūr*, *quandō*, *quōmodo*, and *ubi* are already interrogative, you do not need to add *-ne*; "cūrne," "quandōne," and so on are not correct Latin.

Irregular Verbs

The present, future, and imperfect tenses of the verb **sum** "I am" are as follows:

	Present	**Future**	**Imperfect**
1st sing.	sum	erō	eram
2nd sing.	es	eris	erās
3rd sing.	est	erit	erat
1st pl.	sumus	erimus	erāmus
2nd pl.	estis	eritis	erātis
3rd pl.	sunt	erunt	erant

The present infinitive is *esse*, and the imperative forms (relatively rare) are *es* or *estō* and *este* or *estōte*. The principal parts are *sum, esse, fuī*; there is no fourth principal part.

Notā Bene

sum is not a transitive verb; that is to say, it does not take a direct object. Instead, it takes a predicate. In the sentence "The poet will be a pirate," "pirate" is the predicate, referring to the poet. Both nouns will be in the nominative case: *poēta pīrāta erit*. "poēta pīrātam erit" is not correct Latin.

Context often tells you to translate third person forms of *esse* as "There is/are," "There will be," "There was/were." For example, *pīrātae in Ītaliā erant* can mean either "The pirates were in Italy" or "There were pirates in Italy," depending on the context.

The verb **possum** "I am able," "I can" is a compound of the adjective *potis* "able" and *sum*. The present, future, and imperfect tenses are as follows:

	Present	**Future**	**Imperfect**
1st sing.	possum	poterō	poteram
2nd sing.	potes	poteris	poterās
3rd sing.	potest	poterit	poterat
1st pl.	possumus	poterimus	poterāmus
2nd pl.	potestis	poteritis	poterātis
3rd pl.	possunt	poterunt	poterant

The present infinitive is *posse*; *possum* has no imperatives. Its principal parts are *possum, posse, potuī*; there is no fourth principal part.

Like *dēbeo*, *possum* usually takes an infinitive. If you remember that "I can see the farmer" is the same as "I am able TO see the farmer," it's easy to remember that both should be translated as *agricolam vidēre possum*.

The present, future, and imperfect tenses of the verb **eō** "I go" are as follows:

	Present	**Future**	**Imperfect**
1st sing.	eō	ībō	ībam
2nd sing.	īs	ībis	ībās
3rd sing.	it	ībit	ībat
1st pl.	īmus	ībimus	ībāmus
2nd pl.	ītis	ībitis	ībātis
3rd pl.	eunt	ībunt	ībant

The present infinitive is *īre*, and the imperatives are *ī* and *īte*. The principal parts are *eō, īre, iī* (or *īvī*), *itum*.

The present active indicative of the verb *ferō* "I carry" is irregular:

1st sing.	ferō
2nd sing.	fers
3rd sing.	fert
1st pl.	ferimus
2nd pl.	fertis
3rd pl.	ferunt

The future, *feram*, and the imperfect, *ferēbam*, are formed regularly, as if *ferō* were a third conjugation verb. (These tenses of *ferō* are given in full in Appendix 2.) The present infinitive is *ferre*, and the imperatives are *fer* and *ferte*. The principal parts are *ferō, ferre, tulī, lātum*.

Compound Verbs

Latin has a rather small base vocabulary. The limited range of verbs is increased by adding to the basic form prepositions such as *ā/ab, ad, cum, dē, ē/ex, in, ob, per, sub*, and the dependent prefixes *di[s]* and *re*. Some examples: **ab***dūcō* "I lead away," **per***dūcō* "I lead through," **ex***eō* "I go out," **in***eō* "I go into," **dē***ferō* "I bring down," **re***ferō* "I bring back," **ab***sum* "I am absent," **ad***sum* "I am present."

Many of these prefixes change slightly when used in compound forms: *ā/ab* becomes *au-* in *auferō* but *abs-* in *abstineō* ("hold back"), *cum* becomes *con-* in *conferō* ("bring together") but *com-* in *committō* ("send together"). This process is called assimilation, and its purpose is usually to make pronunciation easier; *subferō*, for example, is harder to say than *sufferō*. There are no universal rules for assimilation, but the variations are not difficult. The most practical approach is to learn each form as you meet it.

Even if the vocabulary list gives only the basic form of a verb, compound forms will appear in the exercises. Since the meaning of the compound usually equals the meaning of the simple verb plus the meaning of the prefix, you should have no trouble guessing it. Sometimes, however, a compound has a special meaning; for example, *pereō* "perish," *inveniō* (from *in* and *veniō* = "come [up]on") "find," *āmittō* (from *ab* and *mittō* = "send away") "lose." **When the compound has a meaning that can't easily be guessed, it will be included in a vocabulary list.**

A preposition can be part of a compound verb and ALSO appear elsewhere in the clause. For example:

puella ad tabernam adit.	The girl goes to the tavern.
agricola agnōs ē silvā ēdūcit.	The farmer leads his lambs out of the wood.

Alternatively, the simple verb and a prepositional phrase can express the same idea as the compound verb:

> *puella <u>ad</u> tabernam it.*
> *agricola agnōs <u>ē</u> silvā dūcit.*

Finally, the noun (here *tabernam* or *silvā*) may appear on its own, in the case that it would be in if it were governed by the preposition separately from the verb:

> *puella tabernam <u>ad</u>it.*
> *agricola agnōs silvā <u>ē</u>dūcit.*

Vocabulary

Verbs

arō, arāre, arāvī, arātum 1	plow
labōrō, labōrāre, labōrāvī, labōrātum 1	work
līberō, līberāre, līberāvī, līberātum 1	free
portō, portāre, portāvī, portātum 1	carry
vītō, vītāre, vītāvī, vītātum 1	avoid
agō, agere, ēgī, actum 3	drive, do, spend (of time)
āmittō, āmittere, āmīsī, āmissum 3	lose
carpō, carpere, carpsī, carptum 3	pluck
laedō, laedere, laesī, laesum 3	harm
ostendō, ostendere, ostendī, ostentum 3	show
pascō, pascere, pāvī, pastum 3	feed
pellō, pellere, pepulī, pulsum 3	drive away, repel
pōnō, pōnere, posuī, positum 3	place
veniō, venīre, vēnī, ventum 4	come
inveniō, invenīre, invēnī, inventum 4	come upon, find
faciō, facere, fēcī, factum 3 *i*-stem	do, make
sum, esse, fuī irreg.	be
possum, posse, potuī irreg.	be able
eō, īre, iī (or **īvī**), **itum** irreg.	go
pereō, perīre, periī (or **perīvī**)	go through, perish
ferō, ferre, tulī, lātum irreg.	carry

Nouns

capella, capellae fem. 1	she-goat
fera, ferae fem. 1	wild animal
porca, porcae fem. 1	pig, sow
silva, silvae fem. 1	wood, forest
terra, terrae fem. 1	earth, land
ūva, ūvae fem. 1	grape
vacca, vaccae fem. 1	cow

Particles

annōn	or not
-ne	[introduces a question]
nonne	surely
num	surely not
-que	and, both
utrum	[introduces the first part of a double question]

Adverbs

cūr	why	**nec . . . nec . . .**	neither . . . nor . . .
quandō	when	**numquam**	never
quōmodo	how	**nunc**	now
ubi	where	**semper**	always
nec adv., conj.	and not, nor	**tum, tunc**	then

Vocabulary Notes

As noted above, the singular imperative of *ferre* is **fer**. Three other verbs, the otherwise regular *dīcere*, *dūcere*, and *facere*, have similarly unusual singular imperatives: **dīc, dūc, fac**.

The particle signifying a question, **-ne**, is added to the first word in its clause. Particles like this, and other words that do not come first in their clause, are called **enclitics**.

Another important enclitic is the conjunction **-que**, which may be added to the first word in its clause to join that clause with the preceding one.

> *puella post āram sedet porcāsque vocat.*   The girl sits behind the altar and calls the pigs.

It may also be used to join two words that have the same grammatical function; in this case, it will be added to the second word.

> *puella porcās vaccāsque vocat.*   The girl calls the pigs and the cows.

When *-que* is added to both words, it has the special meaning "both . . . and. . . ."

> *puella porcāsque vaccāsque vocat.*   The girl calls both the pigs and the cows.

et may be used in the same way or *et* can be substituted for the second *-que*.

> *puella et porcās et vaccās vocat.*   *puella porcāsque et vaccās vocat.*

Latin repeats **nec** in a similar way to express "neither . . . nor."

> *puella nec porcās nec vaccās vocat.*   The girl calls neither the pigs nor the cows.

You can extend a sequence like this as long as necessary. To say "The girl sits behind the altar and calls the pigs and feeds the goats," you can use either

> *puella post āram sedet porcāsque vocat capellāsque pascit.*
> or
> *puella post āram sedet porcāsque vocat et capellās pascit.*

To say "The girl calls both the pigs and the cows and the goats," you can use any of the following:

> *puella porcāsque vaccāsque capellāsque vocat.*
> *puella porcāsque vaccāsque et capellās vocat.*
> *puella et porcās et vaccās et capellās vocat.*

nec has an alternative form **neque**; they are used interchangeably.

quandō and **cum** both mean "when," but they are quite distinct, since *quandō* introduces questions but *cum* does not. Contrast

> *quandō porcam in silvā vidēs?*   When do you see a pig in the wood?
> with
> *cum in silvā es, porcam vidēs.*   When you are in the wood, you see a pig.

tum is used mostly before words beginning with a consonant, **tunc** mostly before words beginning with a vowel or with *h*.

Prōlūsiōnēs

Parse the words in bold.

1. sī **potes**, puella, porcās ē casā **fer**!
2. **vaccae** nōn sunt **ferae**.
3. in silvā **ūvās** carpere **poterimus**?
4. in silvam sine **capellīs īte**, vaccae.
5. num **cum** porcīs terram arāre **possumus**?

Change from singular to plural, or vice versa, and then translate.

For example:

num porcās tum pascēbat poēta? – num porcam tum pascēbant poētae? – Surely the poets weren't feeding the pig then?

1. ūvam nec capellae nec porcae dabātis.
2. utrum feram anne vaccam in silvīs inveniēmus?
3. semper laborābātis, agricolae, sed fīliae porcās poētīs numquam ostendent.
4. flammaene capellās porcāsque tangēbant?
5. agricola tunc eram, et nauta nunc sum, sed pīrāta numquam erō.

Translate.

1. quandō ad casam vaccās cum porcīs agētis, agricolae?
2. in silvam cum agricolā venī, poēta, ferāsque porcīs ostende!
3. cum ferae ē silvā veniunt, pereunt et porcae et capellae.
4. quōmodo porcās iuvāre poterimus, sī in ōrā insulae sunt?
5. poētaene porcās pascere poterātis, puellae?
6. quōmodo pīrātās poterunt vītāre poētae?
7. tandem ad ōram insulae venient undae, sed statuam deae nōn laedent.
8. cum fīliā agricolae laborā, poēta! in tabernā cum nautīs nōn dēbēs esse.
9. quoniam ferae in villā sunt, porcāsque et vaccās in silvam pellite, nautae!
10. ubi lūdunt capellae cottīdiē cum porcārum turbā?
11. porcās agricola nec līberābit nec pīrātīs dabit.
12. porcae vaccaeque, cūr in casam agricolae venīre nōn potestis?
13. agricolae porcās nautīs ostendere nōlī.
14. utrum porcīs an capellīs ūvās dat agricola?
15. porcās et capellās et vaccās semper habet agricola, sed pecūniam numquam habēbit.
16. sī agricola tunc erās, cūr nautārum vītam nunc amās praedamque in spēluncam fers?
17. ante deārum ārās terram arās dum vaccae in spēluncā sunt?
18. porcīs ūvās semper dabat agricola annōn?
19. quōmodo porcās sine pecūniā pascēs, sī cum agricolīs nunc in tabernā lūdis?
20. ferae ē silvā venient, sed fīlia agricolae nec capellam nec porcās in villam feret.

21. The pirate will lose his life in Italy.
22. Were the farmers not driving the cows from the house?
23. Farmer, carry the goats to the country house now, because the pirates are coming!

24. Why does the farmer's daughter love neither the poet nor the sailor?

25. Where will I be feeding the farmers' pigs?

26. Were the goats able to avoid the farmer's anger?

27. Will I carry the wild animal into the cave?

28. Farmers, always give grapes to pigs, not to wild animals!

29. You weren't driving the farmers' pigs into the wood, were you, pirates?

30. Pluck both roses and grapes in the wood, poets!

31. Surely the farmers will always love their pigs?

32. Will the sailors find the pirate's plunder under the goddess' statue?

33. Are there grapes in the wood or not?

34. How can pigs plow the farmer's land?

35. When will the sailors drive the pirates out of Italy?

Lectiōnēs Latīnae

Lege, Intellege

Marcus Gavius Apicius was a celebrated gourmet in the reign of Tiberius, early in the first century AD; he once sailed across the Mediterranean when informed of a breeding ground in Africa for a particularly fine type of shrimp, but, on finding that it was nothing special, he returned home without even disembarking. The *Dē Rē Coquināriā* (*On Cookery*) that is often attributed to him was actually written in the fourth century AD by an unknown author.

What is the tense of the verbs in bold?

Roman Sauces

> *iūs frīgidum in porcellum ēlixum ita **faciēs**: terēs piper, careum, anēthum, orīganum modicē, nucleōs pīneōs, **suffundēs** acētum, liquāmen, caryōtam, mel, sināpi factum, **superstillābis** oleum, piper aspergēs et īnferēs.*

A recipe for a cold sauce for boiled suckling pig: crush pepper, caraway, dill, a little oregano, pine kernels; pour in vinegar, fish sauce, dates, honey, prepared mustard; drizzle with olive oil, sprinkle with pepper, and serve.

> *iūs in perdīcēs: terēs in mortāriō piper, apium, mentam et rūtam, **suffundis** acētum, **addis** caryōtam, mel, acētum, liquāmen, oleum. simul coquēs et **īnferēs**.*

Gravy for partridge: crush pepper, parsley, mint, and rue in a mortar; pour in vinegar; add dates, honey, vinegar, fish sauce, and olive oil. Cook all together and serve.

—[Apicius], *Dē Rē Coquināriā* 8.7.15, Appendix 31

More Latin words and phrases commonly used in English:

alma māter	nourishing mother
alter ego	the other I
alumnus/a	nursling
bonā fidē	in good faith
compos mentis	in possession of one's mind
ēmeritus	having done one's duty
honōris causā	for the sake of honor
innuendō	by (merely) nodding
meā culpā	by my fault
memorābilia	things worth remembering
modus operandī	way of operating
passim	everywhere
persōna nōn grāta	unwelcome person
prīmā faciē	on first appearance
status quō	the condition in which (i.e., the prevailing circumstances)
terra firma	solid ground
terra incognita	unknown land
verbātim	word for word

Ars Poētica

Publilius Syrus III

Parse the words in bold.

1. *avārus ipse **miseriae causa** est suae.*
   A greedy person is himself the cause of his own misery.

2. *bona mors est hominī, **vītae** quae extinguit mala.*
   It is a good death for a person, that extinguishes the evils of life.

3. *caecī **sunt** oculī, cum animus aliās rēs agit.*
   The eyes are blind when the mind is dealing with other things.

4. *dēlīberandō saepe **perit** occāsiō.*
   In deliberating an opportunity is often lost.

5. *in venere semper dulcis est **dēmentia**.*
   There is always a sweet madness in love.

6. ***invidiam ferre** aut fortis aut fēlix **potest**.*
   Either a brave man or a lucky one is able to endure envy.

Lūsūs

Thēsaurus Verbōrum

Many English nouns are exactly the same as the first declension nouns from which they are derived, except that the ending has been dropped; for example, "catapult" is derived from *catapulta, -ae* fem. and "cavern" from *caverna, -ae* fem.

cisterna, -ae fem. 1	persōna, -ae fem. 1
columna, -ae fem. 1	planta, -ae fem. 1
forma, -ae fem. 1	poēta, -ae masc. 1
herba, -ae fem. 1	ruīna, -ae fem. 1
massa, -ae fem. 1	tunica, -ae fem. 1
mātrōna, -ae fem. 1	urna, -ae fem. 1

Vīta Rōmānōrum

The Circus Maximus

Chariot-racing was the most popular spectator sport in ancient Rome. The Circus Maximus, as its name implies, was the largest but not the only venue in Rome for the races. In the Augustan Age it held possibly 150,000 spectators, but later almost a quarter of a million people could attend. (The Colosseum, where gladiatorial shows were held, accommodated about 50,000. The world's largest modern soccer venue, the Maracana Stadium in Rio de Janeiro, has a capacity of approximately 200,000.)

> I've spent all this recent time very pleasantly and restfully with my notes and my books. "How," you ask, "could you do that in the city?" The Circus games were taking place, but I'm not the least bit interested in that sort of spectacle. There's nothing new about them, nothing different, nothing that it's not sufficient to have seen just once. So I'm all the more amazed that so many thousands of grown men should time after time have a childish desire to see horses running and people driving chariots. There would be some reason to it, if they were attracted either by the speed of the horses or by the skill of the drivers. In fact, it's a piece of cloth [the team colors] that they favor, a piece of cloth they love. If these colors were to be transferred from one team to another, their enthusiasm and their support would change sides, and immediately they would abandon those charioteers and those horses that they can recognize even at a distance and whose names they call out. Such is the influence and the power wielded by a single

cheap tunic—and I don't just mean over the mob, who are cheaper than the tunic, but over certain important people: when I think of their insatiable passion for such a vacuous, dull, and vulgar pursuit, I feel a certain pleasure in not being attracted by this pleasure myself. During these days that other people have been wasting in the idlest of pursuits I've been very pleased to devote my leisure to my books.

—Pliny the Younger, *Epistulae* 9.6

CHAPTER 5
Second Declension Nouns

In the second declension, most nouns are **masculine** and some are **neuter**; only a few are feminine.

Second declension **masculine nouns** almost all decline like *dominus, -ī*, "master," "owner." You will notice that, whereas almost all other nouns are identical in the nominative and vocative singular, **the vocative singular of these second declension masculine nouns has its own ending**. A good way to remember this is to think of Julius Caesar's dying words (in Shakespeare's play, anyway), when he saw his friend Brutus among his assassins: *et tū, Brūte?* "You also, Brutus?"

	SINGULAR	PLURAL
NOMINATIVE	domin**us**	domin**ī**
GENITIVE	domin**ī**	domin**ōrum**
DATIVE	domin**ō**	domin**īs**
ACCUSATIVE	domin**um**	domin**ōs**
ABLATIVE	domin**ō**	domin**īs**
VOCATIVE	domin**e**	domin**ī**

Second declension **neuter nouns** almost all decline like *saxum, -ī*, "rock."

	SINGULAR	PLURAL
NOMINATIVE	sax**um**	sax**a**
GENITIVE	sax**ī**	sax**ōrum**
DATIVE	sax**ō**	sax**īs**
ACCUSATIVE	sax**um**	sax**a**
ABLATIVE	sax**ō**	sax**īs**
VOCATIVE	sax**um**	sax**a**

As you can see, masculine and neuter nouns of the second declension have identical endings except in the **nominative** and **vocative singular** and in the **nominative, accusative**, and **vocative plural**. In addition, the **nominative, accusative**, and **vocative plural** of ALL NEUTER NOUNS, whatever their declension, have the same ending: short *a*, as in *saxa* in our paradigm. Of course, this can make these nouns look like the nominative and vocative singular of first declension nouns, but you can use context and the grammatical structure of the clause to tell the difference.

Now look at a very small group of masculine nouns in the second declension whose nominative and vocative singular do not end in *-us* and *-e*, as with *dominus, domine*. These nouns have a stem ending in *-er* or *-r*. Our examples are *puer, puerī* "boy" and *magister, magistrī* "teacher."[1] **Apart**

---

1. *magistra, -ae* fem. 1 is the feminine equivalent, but women were rarely employed as schoolteachers.

from the nominative and vocative singular, all the other endings remain the same as for *dominus*.

	SINGULAR	PLURAL
NOMINATIVE	puer	puerī
GENITIVE	puerī	puer**ōrum**
DATIVE	puer**ō**	puer**īs**
ACCUSATIVE	puer**um**	puer**ōs**
ABLATIVE	puer**ō**	puer**īs**
VOCATIVE	puer	puerī

	SINGULAR	PLURAL
NOMINATIVE	magister	magistrī
GENITIVE	magistrī	magistr**ōrum**
DATIVE	magistr**ō**	magistr**īs**
ACCUSATIVE	magistr**um**	magistr**ōs**
ABLATIVE	magistr**ō**	magistr**īs**
VOCATIVE	magister	magistrī

You will notice that *magister* drops the *e* of its *-er* ending. This shows how important it is to learn the full form when you are learning a new noun: *puer, puerī,* masc. 2 "boy," *magister, magistrī,* masc. 2 "teacher." The **genitive** is what tells you whether this is a noun that drops the *e* or not. This fact will also be helpful when you are learning other nouns and adjectives, so make sure to get into the habit now, if you haven't already, of learning the full form, not just the nominative singular.

One other important second declension noun has an unusual form: *vir, virī,* masc. 2 "man." The **nominative** and **vocative** singular is *vir*, but the word otherwise declines like any other second declension masculine noun.

humus, humī "ground" (which you will learn in Chapter 15) and a few place names are the only second declension feminine nouns used in this book, and they decline just like *dominus*.

Vocabulary

In the following list, to emphasize that some nouns have first or second declension forms, according to their gender, some first declension feminine nouns (not highlighted in bold) are repeated from earlier chapters and others are introduced for the first time.

Nouns

agna, agnae fem. 1	ewe-lamb
agnus, agnī masc. 2	ram-lamb
amīca, amīcae fem. 1	female friend
amīcus, amīcī masc. 2	male friend

dea, deae fem. 1	goddess
deus, deī masc. 2	god
discipula, discipulae fem. 1	female student
discipulus, discipulī masc. 2	male student
domina, dominae fem. 1	mistress, owner
dominus, dominī masc. 2	master, owner
equa, equae fem. 1	mare
equus, equī masc. 2	stallion
filia, filiae fem. 1	daughter
filius, filiī masc. 2	son
lupa, lupae fem. 1	she-wolf
lupus, lupī masc. 2	male wolf
porca, porcae fem. 1	pig, sow
porcus, porcī masc. 2	pig, boar
serva, servae fem. 1	female slave
servus, servī masc. 2	male slave
vacca, vaccae fem. 1	cow
taurus, taurī masc. 2	bull
puella, puellae fem. 1	girl
puer, puerī masc. 2	boy
fēmina, fēminae fem. 1	woman
vir, virī masc. 2	man
campus, campī masc. 2	plain
hortus, hortī masc. 2	garden
lūdus, lūdī masc. 2	game, school
mūrus, mūrī masc. 2	wall
ager, agrī masc. 2	field
aper, aprī masc. 2	wild boar
capella, capellae fem. 1	she-goat
caper, caprī masc. 2	he-goat
liber, librī masc. 2	book
magister, magistrī masc. 2	teacher
argentum, argentī neut. 2	silver
astrum, astrī neut. 2	star
aurum, aurī neut. 2	gold
caelum, caelī neut. 2	sky, heaven

dōnum, dōnī neut. 2	gift
ferrum, ferrī neut. 2	iron
saxum, saxī neut. 2	rock
templum, templī neut. 2	temple
vīnum, vīnī neut. 2	wine

Non-Declining Parts of Speech

circā and **circum** adv., prep. + acc.	around
per prep. + acc.	through, along
prope prep. + acc.	near
crās adv.	tomorrow
diū adv.	for a long time
herī adv.	yesterday
hodiē adv.	today
saepe adv.	often
enim particle	for
nam particle	for
namque conjunction	for

Vocabulary Notes

Apparently for reasons of pronunciation, second declension masculine nouns in -*ius* have a vocative singular in -*ī*, not -*ie*, for example, *fīlius* (nom.), *fīlī* (voc.), *Antōnius* (nom.), *Antōnī* (voc.) Similarly, the Romans avoided using the vocative singular of *deus*, which would be *dee*. Gods were addressed in prayers either by name or with the related word *dīvus*, vocative *dīve*. (*Dea*, however, is commonly found as a vocative in addresses to goddesses.) For the same reason, *mī*, not *mee*, was used as the masc. voc. sing. of the adjective *meus* (see Chapter 6); a Roman would say *mī fīlī* "my son."

nam and **namque** come first in the clause they introduce. **enim**, however, is postpositive or enclitic, that is, it cannot stand first in its clause. Unlike "for" in English, *nam*, *namque*, and *enim* often introduce independent main clauses. Hence, "The wolves are not in the school, for they are wild beasts" may be translated either as *lupī in lūdō nōn sunt; nam(que) ferae sunt* or as *lupī in lūdō nōn sunt; ferae enim sunt.*

Prōlūsiōnēs

Parse the words in bold.

1. **vaccās**ne prope **templa** deōrum audīre potestis?
2. quandō per **agrōs** agricolae **filiī** venient?
3. puerōrum **magistrō** equum nōlī **dare**.
4. agnōs in **campō**, **porce**, vidēre potes?
5. **sunt** in caelō **astra**.

Change from singular to plural or vice versa, and then translate.

1. aprōsne porcus timet?
2. astra, capella, vidēre poterās?
3. agnum vaccamque in agrum fertis, servī?
4. domina servam nōn semper amābat.
5. taurum ad templī portam dūcent agricolārum fīliī.
6. quandō ē spēluncīs venient magistrī?
7. sine servō per silvam venīre nōn poterō.
8. lupum in campō saepe audīs?
9. porcōs servīs pīrātārum dare dēbēbitis.
10. sub mūrō templī ūvam carpēbat capella.

Translate.

1. porcusne librōs legere potest?
2. pīrāta est amīcus servī.
3. num pīrātam, servī amīcum, amābātis, puerī?
4. agricola porcōs et vaccās in agrum diū vocābat.
5. dominī servīs vīnum dabant.
6. dominīs servī vīnum dabunt.
7. rosās in templō deae pōne, puer, sed vīnum in āram nōlī fundere!
8. deī deaeque dē caelō ad terram saepe veniunt.

9. saxa in hortum ferte, puerī, namque aprōs in agrīs herī audiēbat agricola.

10. agricolae servī prope hortum magistrī sedēbant.

11. lupī, nōn agnī, in agricolārum agrīs māne erant.

12. nōlīte, magistrī, lupum in lūdum dūcere!

13. virōs fēmināsque in deae templō vidēre potestis?

14. fēminae in templum deae venīre possunt, nōn virī.

15. porcus per agrōs ad mūrōs villae venīre nōn dēbet; agricola enim prope templum labōrat.

16. porcī et vaccae, in hortōs venīte! nam circā deī templum et lupōs et aprōs audīre possumus.

17. dominus servōs in silvam crās mittet, quoniam lupum prope villae portam capere hodiē nōn poterant.

18. sub terrā aurumque argentumque et ferrum invenīre poterāmus, sed astra in caelō vidēre potestis, amīcī?

19. sub caelō diū sedēbat dominus servōrum cum discipulōrum magistrō, quod vīnum in hortō saepe bibēbant.

20. filiōs filiāsque ad templum mitte, agricola, tum porcōs agnāsque in agrōs age!

21. The gods and goddesses are in the sky.

22. Boys, give wine to your owner, the teacher's friend!

23. There is gold, the pirate's gift, on the god's altar.

24. When was the wild boar near the teacher's garden?

25. Were you able to see the cows in the fields yesterday, poet?

26. We will be able to catch the wolves in the wood tomorrow.

27. Will you place the money in the temple, girls?

28. Surely the poet will not be able to give silver to the slaves' owners?

29. Why did the students not love their teachers?

30. Slaves, drive the cows across the plain to the temple of the goddess!

31. Tomorrow we will not work, for the teacher's sons will free the slaves.

32. When wolves are on the plain in the morning, the bulls, lambs, and pigs sleep in the temple.

33. While the pigs are going into the wood, the slave pours wine onto the altar of the god.

34. Pig, don't listen to the she-wolf, for you must not go into the cave!

35. The pirates were able to live on the island, because there was an abundance of water under the rocks.

Lectiōnēs Latīnae

Lege, Intellege

The Roman View of the World

mundus est ūnīversitās rērum, in quō omnia sunt et extrā quem nihil; quī Graecē dīcitur cosmos. elementa mundī quattuor: ignis ex quō est caelum, aqua ex quā mare Ōceanum, āēr ex quō ventī et tempestātēs, terra quam propter formam eius orbem terrārum appellāmus. caelī regiōnēs sunt quattuor: oriens occidens merīdiēs septentriō. caelum dīviditur in circulōs quinque: arcticum et antarcticum, quī ob nimiam vim frīgoris inhabitābilēs sunt; aequinoctiālem, quī ob nimiam vim ardōris nōn incolitur; brūmālem et solstitiālem sub quibus habitātur (sunt enim temperātissimī); per quōs oblīquus circulus vādit cum duodecim signīs, in quibus sōl annuum conficit cursum.

—Ampelius, *Liber Memoriālis* 1

1. What is the universe called in Greek?
2. Which two of the five regions are uninhabitable because of their excessive cold?
3. The universe is composed of what four elements?
4. Why is the equinoctial region uninhabitable?
5. What exists outside the universe?

Ars Poëtica

Publilius Syrus IV

Identify and explain the case of the nouns in bold.

1. *amor, ut lacrima, ab **oculō** oritur, in pectus cadit.*
   Love, like a tear, rises from the eye, (and) falls into the bosom.

2. ***beneficia** plūra recipit, quī scit reddere.*
   The person who knows how to return them receives more favors.

3. *cum **vitia** prōsunt, peccat quī rectē facit.*
   When vices bring advantage, a person who acts correctly is doing wrong.

4. *dolor **animī** multō gravior est quam corporis.*
   Pain of the mind is much heavier than that of the body.

5. *habet suum **venēnum** blanda ōrātiō.*
   A flattering speech has its own poison.

6. *improbē **Neptūnum** accūsat, quī iterum **naufragium** facit.*
   A person who is shipwrecked for a second time wrongly blames Neptune.

7. ***lucrum*** *sine **damnō** alterius fierī nōn potest.*
   Profit cannot be made without someone else's loss.

8. *nēmō timendō ad summum pervenit **locum**.*
   No one attains the highest place by being afraid.

Aurea Dicta

1. *animum aliquandō dēbēmus relaxāre.* (Seneca the Younger)

2. *est animī medicīna philosophia.* (Cicero)

3. *facere docet philosophia, nōn dīcere.* (Seneca the Younger)

4. *in oculīs animus habitat.* (Pliny the Elder)

5. *odium est īra inveterāta.* (Cicero)

6. *nōn vīvere sed valēre vīta est.* (Martial)

7. *servā mē, servābō tē.* (Petronius)

8. *vītam regit fortūna, nōn sapientia.* (Cicero)

aliquandō adv. sometimes

valeō, -ēre, valuī 2 be strong

Lūsūs

Thēsaurus Verbōrum

English changes the final *-ia* of many first declension feminine nouns to a *-y*; for example, "colony" is derived from *colōnia, -ae,* "controversy" from *contrōversia, -ae.*

custōdia	glōria	memoria
fallācia	infāmia	miseria
familia	iniūria (= *injūria*)	modestia
furia	luxuria	victōria

Vīta Rōmānōrum

The Birth of Virgil, Rome's Greatest Poet

Publius Vergilius Maro was from Mantua. His parents were of humble status, especially his father. By some accounts, his father was a potter, but it is more generally believed that he started out as a hired laborer for a man called Magus, a civil servant, subsequently becoming Magus' son-in-law thanks to his hard work. It is also said that he bettered himself financially by buying up woodlands and keeping bees. Virgil was born on the Ides [15th] of October in the first consulship of Gnaeus Pompeius Magnus and Marcus Licinius Crassus [70 BC], in a village called Andes, not far from Mantua. When his mother was pregnant with him, she dreamed that she had given birth to a laurel branch, which took root as soon as it touched the earth and immediately grew to the size of a mature tree covered in fruits and flowers of different kinds. On the following day, as she was going to a neighboring district with her husband, she stopped and gave birth in a nearby ditch. They say that the child did not cry when he was born and had such a gentle expression that even then you could see that he was destined to be unusually successful. There was another omen as well: a poplar twig, planted in the spot where he was born, as was the custom in that region, grew strong in such a short time that it was soon as tall as other poplars planted much earlier. It was therefore called "Virgil's tree" and was worshipped with great reverence by pregnant women and new mothers, who made vows and left offerings there.

—Donatus, *Vīta Vergiliī* 1

CHAPTER **6**
First and Second Declension Adjectives and Adverbs

An adjective is a word that describes a noun: "good," "intelligent," "omnivorous," and "your" are all adjectives. Almost all Latin adjectives are formed in one of two ways: like nouns of the first and second declensions or like nouns of the third declension. In this chapter you will be learning how to use the first group, first and second declension adjectives; third declension adjectives are introduced in Chapter 9.

The adjective *cārus* "dear" is our paradigm for first and second declension adjectives. **The endings these adjectives use are the endings you already know from first and second declension nouns.** When one of these adjectives modifies any feminine noun, it will use the endings of, for example, **puella**. When it modifies any masculine noun, it will use the endings of **dominus** (including the exceptional vocative singular ending, as in *et tū, Brūte*). When it modifies any neuter noun, it will use the endings of **saxum**.

	MASCULINE	**FEMININE**	**NEUTER**
Singular			
NOMINATIVE	cār**us**	cār**a**	cār**um**
GENITIVE	cār**ī**	cār**ae**	cār**ī**
DATIVE	cār**ō**	cār**ae**	cār**ō**
ACCUSATIVE	cār**um**	cār**am**	cār**um**
ABLATIVE	cār**ō**	cār**ā**	cār**ō**
VOCATIVE	cār**e**	cār**a**	cār**um**
Plural			
NOMINATIVE	cār**ī**	cār**ae**	cār**a**
GENITIVE	cār**ōrum**	cār**ārum**	cār**ōrum**
DATIVE	cār**īs**	cār**īs**	cār**īs**
ACCUSATIVE	cār**ōs**	cār**ās**	cār**a**
ABLATIVE	cār**īs**	cār**īs**	cār**īs**
VOCATIVE	cār**ī**	cār**ae**	cār**a**

All but a small minority of first/second declension adjectives decline like *cārus*. They will appear in vocabulary lists in the form *cārus, -a, -um*, giving the nom. sing. form of all three genders.

One group of first/second declension adjectives ends in *-er* in the nominative and vocative masculine singular: **miser** "unhappy" and **pulcher** "beautiful" are examples. Just like the second declension nouns *puer* and *magister*, some of these adjectives change their stem by dropping the *e* from the nominative ending (like *magister, magistrī*), but some do not (like *puer, puerī*). To know whether or not one of these adjectives drops the *e* when it modifies a noun in any case other than the nominative or vocative masculine singular, you need to learn the full form of the adjective as presented in the vocabulary lists: for example, *miser, misera, miserum* "wretched," *pulcher, pulchra, pulchrum* "handsome," "beautiful."

Adjectives agree in **GENDER**, **NUMBER**, and **CASE** with the noun that they modify. For example:

fem. sing. nom.	fem. sing. nom.	masc. sing. acc.	masc. sing. acc.	
puella	*Rōmāna*	*taurum*	*pulchrum*	*videt.*

The Roman girl sees the handsome bull.

masc. pl. nom.	masc. pl. nom.	masc. sing. dat.	masc. sing. dat.	masc. pl. acc.	masc. pl. acc.	
puerī	*miserī*	*magistrō*	*cārō*	*porcōs*	*pigrōs*	*dant.*

The wretched boys are giving the lazy pigs to their dear teacher.

These examples may give you the impression that adjectives will always have the same endings as the nouns they modify. This is because so far we are using nouns of only the first and second declensions. Nouns of the third, fourth, and fifth declensions will have completely different endings from any first/second declension adjectives. **Even in the first two declensions, adjectives will not always have the same endings as the nouns they modify.** For example:

agricola Rōmānus pīrātās miserōs videt.   The Roman farmer sees the wretched pirates.

servus pulcher nautam magnum audit.   The handsome slave is listening to the big sailor.

As you can see, *Rōmānus* agrees with *agricola*, *miserōs* with *pīrātās*, *pulcher* with *servus*, *magnum* with *nautam*: none of the adjectives has the same ending as the noun it modifies. Notice also that *agricola*, *pīrātās*, and *nautam* are all **masculine** nouns in the **first** declension, so adjectives modifying them must use a **masculine, second** declension ending. You will never see "agricola Rōmāna," "pīrātās miserās," "nautam magnam." Adjectives only use first declension endings when they are modifying **feminine** nouns.

Notā Bene

There is no Latin term for a female farmer, pirate, sailor, and so on. There are, however, some nouns that are not specific to one gender; what tells you the gender is the adjective. These nouns are nearly all in the third declension. *Sacerdōs*, for example, means both "priest" and "priestess" and therefore may be modified by, for example, either *cārus* or *cāra*.

You learned in Chapter 4 how to connect a string of nouns using *et* or *-que*. In the same way, when a noun is modified by two adjectives, they are almost always linked by *et* or *-que*:

porcum magnum pulchrumque habeō.   I have a lovely big pig.

When three or more adjectives are used together, they may all be linked by *et* or *-que*: for example, *porcōs parvōs et pigrōs et stultōs lupus videt* ("The wolf sees the small, lazy, and stupid pigs"). Sometimes the connecting words are simply omitted: *porcōs parvōs, pigrōs, stultōs lupus videt.*

Generally *et* and *-que* are not used to connect ordinary adjectives with pronominal adjectives, such as *meus, -a, -um* "my," *tuus, -a, -um* "your" (sing.), *noster, nostra, nostrum* "our" and *vester, vestra, vestrum* "your" (pl.):

porcum magnum et pigrum videō	means	I see the big, lazy pig.
porcum meum pigrum videō	means	I see my lazy pig.
porcum meum magnum pigrumque videō	means	I see my big, lazy pig.

Notā Bene

The third person pronominal adjectives "his," "her," "its," "their" have only limited equivalents in Latin and are not given in this chapter along with words for "my," "our," "your." In any case, when the context makes possession clear, pronominal adjectives are usually omitted.

As you begin translating nouns and their adjectives into Latin, try translating the noun first and then the adjective(s). Adjectives agree with their nouns, so you need to determine the gender, number, and case of the noun in order to determine the correct form of the adjective.

Predicate Adjectives

In Chapter 4 you saw how the verb *esse* "to be" takes a **predicate**, not an object: for example, in the sentence *nauta pīrāta est*, "the sailor is a pirate," *pīrāta* is the predicate of *nauta*, and both nouns are in the same case, the nominative. Adjectives are also used as predicates. For example:

fem. sing. nom.   fem. sing. nom.
puella   est   *pulchra.*
The girl is beautiful.

  masc. pl. nom.   masc. pl. nom.
servī   sunt   *miserī.*
The slaves are wretched.

You can just as easily say *puella pulchra est* and *servī miserī sunt*, but when an adjective is separated from its noun, the reason is often that it is a predicate adjective.

Adjectives Used as Nouns

English often uses adjectives as nouns, for example, "Fortune favors the brave," with the noun "people" implied, or "The best is yet to come," with the noun "thing" implied. Latin does the same:

piger vīnum miserae dat.	The lazy (man) gives wine to the wretched (woman).
fessa dōnum aegrī nōn amat.	The tired (woman) does not like the sick (man's) gift.

This is called using an adjective substantivally. *vir* and *fēmina* are usually, as in these examples, the nouns implied when an adjective is used substantivally in its masculine or feminine form. Neuter adjectives are also very often used substantivally, especially in the plural, but without any specific neuter noun being implied. In translating these neuter adjectives, the English noun "thing" is often useful:

stultus stulta facit.   A stupid man does stupid things.

Complex Agreement

In the simple sentences *taurus magnus est* "The bull is big" and *porcus magnus est* "The pig is big," the adjective *magnus* is in the nominative, masculine singular because it is agreeing with nouns in the nominative, masculine singular.

taurus et porcus magnī sunt means "The bull and the pig are big." *magnī* has to be in the nominative, because it refers to the bull and the pig, which are in the nominative; it has to be masculine because both *taurus* and *porcus* are masculine nouns; it has to be in the plural because *taurus* and *porcus* together are equivalent to a plural.

But what if an adjective modifies two or more nouns that are of different genders? How, for example, do you say in Latin, "The boy and the girl are good"? *Puer* is masculine, and *puella* is feminine. Which gender of the nominative plural of the adjective should be used? By convention, it is the masculine that stands for both: *puer et puella bonī sunt.* This holds true even if the boy is heavily outnumbered. In the sentence "The boy and his twelve sisters are good," *bonī* is still the usual form.

When there are two or more inanimate subjects (not people, gods, or animals) of different genders, the modifying adjective is often neuter plural; for example, *terra* is feminine and *caelum* is neuter, but "The earth and the sky are great" will be *terra caelumque magna sunt.* We can interpret *magna* as a neuter adjective here, or as a neuter adjective used substantivally: "great things."

Adverbs

Adverbs modify verbs, adjectives, or other adverbs: for example, "She ran <u>fast</u>," "The plan was <u>beautifully</u> simple," "He spoke <u>extremely</u> well." We have already met some adverbs, such as *adhūc* "still," *fortasse* "perhaps," *frustrā* "in vain," *nunc* "now," *tandem* "at last." As these examples show, adverbs can take many forms and often have to be learned individually. As in English, however, the majority of Latin adverbs are derived from adjectives.

Regular adverbs of the first/second declension type add the ending *-ē* to the adjectival base. Adjectives decline in the same way as nouns, but adverbs have only one form:

Adjective		Adverb	
cārus, -a, -um	dear	*cārē*	dearly
pulcher, pulchra, pulchrum	beautiful	*pulchrē*	beautifully
miser, misera, miserum	wretched	*miserē*	wretchedly

Here are some examples of sentences containing adverbs formed from the adjectives in this chapter's vocabulary:

pīrātae pecūniam agricolae avārē rapiunt.	The pirates greedily seize the farmer's money.
cūr stultē rīdēs, stulte puer?	Stupid boy, why are you laughing stupidly?
porcus pigrē dormiēbat.	The pig was sleeping lazily.
in āram vīnum lentē fundit poēta.	The poet pours wine slowly on to the altar.

Vocabulary

Adjectives

altus, -a, -um	high, deep	**paucī, -ae, -a**	few
āridus, -a, -um	dry	**pūrus, -a, -um**	pure
avārus, -a, -um	greedy	**Rōmānus, -a, -um**	Roman
barbarus, -a, -um	barbarian	**saevus, -a, -um**	savage
bonus, -a, -um	good	**stultus, -a, -um**	stupid
calidus, -a, -um	warm	**asper, aspera, asperum**	rough
cārus, -a, -um (+ dat.)	dear (to)	**līber, lībera, līberum**	free
dīvīnus, -a, -um	divine	**miser, misera, miserum**	wretched
fessus, -a, -um	tired	**aeger, aegra, aegrum**	sick
frīgidus, -a, -um	cold	**niger, nigra, nigrum**	black, dark
lātus, -a, -um	broad	**pulcher, pulchra, pulchrum**	beautiful
lentus, -a, -um	slow	**piger, pigra, pigrum**	lazy
longus, -a, -um	long	**sacer, sacra, sacrum (+ dat.)**	sacred (to)
magnus, -a, -um	big	**meus, -a, -um**	my
malus, -a, -um	bad	**noster, nostra, nostrum**	our
multus, -a, -um	much, pl. many	**tuus, -a, -um**	your (sing.)
novus, -a, -um	new	**vester, vestra, vestrum**	your (pl.)
parvus, -a, -um	small		

Adverbs

iterum	again	**nūper**	recently
rursus	again	**statim**	immediately
mox	soon		

Vocabulary Notes

cārus very often takes a noun or pronoun in the dative case; for example, *porcus agricolae cārus est* means "The pig is dear to the farmer." *sacer* is similarly used with the dative in sentences like *templum deō sacrum est* "The temple is sacred to the god."

paucī is used only in the plural, because of its meaning: *paucī agricolae, paucae fēminae, pauca saxa.*

līber, **lībera**, **līberum** when used substantivally in the masculine plural means "children," more specifically, the freeborn children of a household, as opposed to the slaves.

iterum and **rursus** can be used interchangeably.

Prōlūsiōnēs

Parse the words in bold.

1. porcō **pigrō** agricola **stultus** aquam calidam dat.
2. caper **nūper aeger** erat.
3. lūnamque et astra **multa** in caelō altō vidēs, **puer**?
4. ad **novam** casam nautae **miserī** dūcit via longa.
5. spēluncā in **nigrā** lupus est magnusque **malus**que.

Change from singular to plural or vice versa, and then translate.

1. porcī pigrī sunt.
2. templum deō sacrum erat.
3. num miserī estis, servī?
4. quōmodo aprōs saevōs in spēluncīs altīs capiet agricola bonus?
5. nautīs, virīs miserīs, librōs magnōs dabunt servī pigrī.
6. agricolae stultī porcum nigrum in campō āridō vidēbam.
7. dominus tuus prope mūrum altum parvī templī sedēbat.
8. aeger fessusque est taurus meus.
9. nautae barbarō malōque parvum dōnum dat magister miser.
10. servus tuus pulcher nōn est, sed agricolae porcō cārus est.

Translate.

1. est in spēluncā magnā lupa frīgida et aegra.
2. via longa lātaque per saxa aspera ad āram deō sacram dūcit.
3. servus, quod piger est, porcīs paucīs cārus est.
4. serve miser, quandō dominō frīgidum vīnum iterum dabis?
5. fīliī fīliaeque agricolārum avārōrum nōn sunt stultī.
6. magister cāre, puerum aegrum ad templum statim mitte!
7. Rōmānī vaccam magnam ad templa alta deārum lentē dūcēbant.
8. nōlīte stultī esse, porcī! in spēluncā est lupus magnus nigerque.
9. cōpiam magnam aurī argentīque ē templīs sacrīs stultē capient pīrātae malī.
10. magistrī stultī, cūr librōs novōs discipulīs vestrīs numquam dabitis?
11. magnam aurī dīvīnī cōpiam ad spēluncās nigrās mox portābunt pīrātae avārī.
12. magister bonus aurum discipulōrum novōrum capere nōn dēbet.
13. nonne magnam pecūniae cōpiam discipulīs bonīs līberē dabis, magister miser?
14. in hortō parvō sunt magna saxa, sed agricola piger nōn est; ergō diū labōrābit.
15. stulte puer, nonne lupum saevum in agrīs dominī tuī vidēre poterās?
16. serva parva in hortō prope asperum villae mūrum diū miserē labōrābat; fīlia enim fīliusque iterum aegrī erant.
17. ūvās carpere nōn poterāmus, quia lupōs paucōs sed magnōs in silvīs saepe audiēbāmus.
18. magnās villās Rōmānōrum mox vidēre poteris; namque crās ad ōram Ītaliae veniēmus.
19. agricolārum fīliī librōs habent, nōn servī; servī enim nōn sunt līberī.
20. dum in campō asperō lūdunt porcī, capellae dominō meō cārae ūvās nigrās rursus carpunt.

21. Master, give cold wine to your lovely pig.
22. Warn our teacher, girls; he ought not to give wine stupidly to his new students.
23. Because the Roman forces are large, they will defeat the barbarians tomorrow.
24. A few students are sitting wretchedly in the lazy teacher's school.
25. Where are the horses sacred to our goddess?
26. Will the big wolves see your tired pigs under the little rocks again?
27. The farmer is not sick, for he has a warm and dry house.
28. The savage wolf will soon harm the wretched farmers' lambs and cows, for they are now coming lazily across the broad plain.

29. How can the goats be dear to their owner if they are greedily seizing the little grapes?

30. Listen to your students, you wicked teacher; don't give wine freely to the barbarian pirate.

Lectiōnēs Latīnae

Lege, Intellege

Famous Peoples and Places

orbis terrārum in trēs partēs dīviditur, totidemque nōmina: Asia, quae est inter Tanain et Nīlum; Libya, quae est inter Nīlum et Gaditānum sinum; Eurōpa, quae est inter Gaditānum sinum et Tanain.

in Asiā clārissimae gentēs: Indī, Sērēs, Persae, Mēdī, Parthī, Arabēs, Bithynī, Phrygēs, Cappadōcēs, Cilicēs, Syrī, Lydī.

in Eurōpā clārissimae gentēs: Scythae, Sarmatae, Germānī, Dācī, Moesī, Thrācēs, Macedonēs, Dalmatae, Pannonī, Illyricī, Graecī, Italī, Gallī, Hispānī.

in Libyā gentēs clārissimae: Aethiopēs, Maurī, Numidae, Poenī, Gaetulī, Garamantēs, Nasamōnēs, Aegyptiī.

clārissimae insulae: in marī nostrō duodecim: Sicilia, Sardinia, Crētē, Cypros, Euboea, Lesbos, Rhodos, duae Baleārēs, Ebusus, Corsica, Gādēs; in Ōceanō: ad orientem Taprobanē, ad occidentem Britannia, ad septentrionem Thūlē, ad merīdiem Insulae Fortūnātae.

—Ampelius, *Liber Memoriālis* 6

1. Into how many parts is the world divided?
2. On which continent do the following peoples live: the Thracians; the Ethiopians; the Phrygians?
3. Which continent lies between the Nile and the Bay of Cadiz?
4. How many very famous islands are there in the Mediterranean ("Our Sea")?
5. Which islands lie in the southern Ocean?

Ars Poētica

Publilius Syrus V
Identify and explain the case of the adjectives in bold.

1. *absentem laedit, cum* **ebriō** *quī lītigat.*
   A person who quarrels with a drunk harms someone who is not there.

2. *animō virum **pudīcae**, nōn oculō, ēligunt.*
   Respectable women choose a husband with their mind, not with their eye.

3. ***avārus**, nisi cum moritur, nīl rectē facit.*
   A miser does nothing right, except when he dies.

4. *cito ignōminia fit **superbī** glōria.*
   The glory of an arrogant person quickly becomes disgrace.

5. *heu vīta **miserō** longa, fēlīcī brevis!*
   Alas! Life (is) long for the wretched, short for the happy!

6. ***multa** ante temptēs, quam virum inveniās **bonum**.*
   You would make many attempts before you find a good man.

Aurea Dicta

1. *animus aeger semper errat.* (Cicero)
2. *antīquōrum vitiōrum remanent vestīgia.* (Seneca the Elder)
3. *certa āmittimus dum incerta petimus.* (Plautus)
4. *immodica īra creat insāniam.* (Seneca the Younger)
5. *magna deī cūrant, parva neglegunt.* (Cicero)
6. *sacra populī lingua est.* (Seneca the Elder)
7. *saepe virī fallunt, tenerae nōn saepe puellae.* (Ovid)
8. *vērae amīcitiae sempiternae sunt.* (Cicero)

tener, tenera, tenerum tender, gentle

Hōrologia Latīna

The following maxims, from medieval and later times but written in Classical Latin, are found on sundials in many parts of Europe. They exemplify the extreme brevity of most Latin inscriptions.

1. *hōram dum petis, ultimam parā.*
   While you seek the hour, prepare for your final one.

2. *hōrās nōn numerō nisi serēnās.*
   I count only the sunny hours.

3. *sōl tibi signa dabit.*
   The sun will give you signs.

4. *ultima latet hōra.*
   Our final hour lies hidden.

5. *umbra sumus.*
   We are a shadow.

Lūsūs

Thēsaurus Verbōrum

English changes the final *-tia* of many first declension feminine nouns to *-ce*; for example, "absence" is derived from *absentia, -ae*, "abundance" from *abundantia, -ae*.

adulescentia	grātia	petulantia
arrogantia	ignōrantia	potentia
avāritia	indulgentia	prōvidentia
benevolentia	innocentia	prūdentia
confidentia	insolentia	repugnantia
constantia	iustitia (= *justitia*)	reticentia
convenientia	licentia	reverentia
differentia	magnificentia	scientia
dīligentia	malitia	sententia
distantia	nōtitia	substantia
ēlegantia	observantia	temperantia
ēloquentia	opulentia	tolerantia
excellentia	patientia	vehementia
experientia	pestilentia	violentia

Vīta Rōmānōrum

Foreseeing the Future

The Romans believed that foretelling the future could protect individuals or the whole state from disaster. There were many methods. You could observe the alignment of the stars and planets, the behavior of birds and other animals, and the condition of the liver of sacrificial victims. You could also interpret unusual events: strange objects in the sky; showers of stones, milk, or blood; lambs born with the hooves of a horse or the head of a monkey. The Romans also believed, however, that some things were inevitably fated to happen.

Here, Cicero meditates on the undesirability of knowing too much about the future, taking as examples the recent violent deaths of Marcus Crassus, Pompey, and Caesar, the members of the First Triumvirate, who illegally controlled Roman politics in the 50s BC.

> Personally, I do not think that it is beneficial for us to know about future events. What sort of life would Priam [the king of Troy] have had if he had known from his boyhood

what he was going to suffer as an old man? But let's leave old stories aside and look at things closer to home. In my treatise on *Consolation*, I have catalogued instances of very distinguished Romans who have died violently. Passing over those in earlier times, do you think it would have been useful to Marcus Crassus, when he was at the height of his power and prosperity, to know that he was going to perish in shame and disgrace on the other side of the Euphrates, after the death of his son Publius and the annihilation of his army? Or do you think Gnaeus Pompey would have been likely to rejoice in his three consulships, his three triumphs, and the glory of his outstanding achievements if he had known that he was going to lose his army and be cut down in the Egyptian desert, and suffer after death things which I cannot mention without weeping? What about Caesar? In what mental agony would he have lived, had he been able to foretell that he was going to lie butchered by our noblest citizens (some of whom owed their position to him) in the Senate (most of whose members he had appointed personally), in Pompey's Senate-house, in front of the statue of Pompey himself, with so many of his own centurions looking on, but with none of his friends, nor even a slave, willing to come near his corpse?

—Cicero, *Dē Dīvīnātiōne* 2.22–23

CHAPTER 7
The Perfect Active Indicative System of Verbs

Latin has six verb tenses. In Chapters 1 and 3, you learned the active indicative forms of the present, future, and imperfect, the three tenses of the indicative that are based on the **present** stem. This chapter introduces the active indicative forms of the other three tenses, the **perfect**, the **future perfect**, and the **pluperfect**, which are all based on the **perfect** stem.

In these three tenses, the endings for all verbs, regardless of conjugation, are the same:

Perfect	Future Perfect	Pluperfect
-ī	*-erō*	*-eram*
-istī	*-eris*	*-erās*
-it	*-erit*	*-erat*
-imus	*-erimus*	*-erāmus*
-istis	*-eritis*	*-erātis*
-ērunt	*-erint*	*-erant*

The ending for the **perfect infinitive** is *-isse*.

You already know the **first person singular of the perfect active** tense, because that is the **third principal part**. In order to form all three tenses in the perfect system, simply add the appropriate ending to the perfect stem, which you get from the **third principal part**:

amāv	+	**ī**	=	**amāvī** "I loved" or "I have loved"
monu	+	**imus**	=	**monuimus** "we warned" or "we have warned"
mīs	+	**erat**	=	**mīserat** "he had sent"
audīv	+	**erātis**	=	**audīverātis** "you had heard"
cēp	+	**erint**	=	**cēperint** "they will have taken"

Look for patterns in the forms of the third principal parts: for instance, almost all verbs in the first conjugation consist of the present stem, plus *-āv*, plus the personal ending: **amāvī**, **spectāvī**, **vocāvī**, and so on. As you work with the perfect system, you will see other patterns in the perfect active stems of verbs in the other conjugations.

The third principal parts of our model verbs are *amāvī*, *monuī*, *mīsī*, *audīvī*, and *cēpī*. Since the perfect system of all verbs is regular, and since the full paradigm of each conjugation is given in Appendix 2, only the first conjugation paradigm is given here.

	Perfect loved/have loved	**Future Perfect** will have loved	**Pluperfect** had loved
1st Sing.	amāvī	amāverō	amāveram
2nd Sing.	amāvistī	amāveris	amāverās
3rd Sing.	amāvit	amāverit	amāverat
1st Pl.	amāvimus	amāverimus	amāverāmus
2nd Pl.	amāvistis	amāveritis	amāverātis
3rd Pl.	amāvērunt	amāverint	amāverant

Perfect Infinitive (To have loved) amāvisse

Here is a list of most of the verbs you have seen so far. Be sure to review especially the third principal part of each:

First Conjugation

amō, amāre, **amāvī**, amātum	love
arō, arāre, **arāvī**, arātum	plow
dō, dare, **dedī**, datum	give
iuvō, iuvāre, **iūvī**, iūtum	help
labōrō, labōrāre, **labōrāvī**, labōrātum	work
līberō, līberāre, **līberāvī**, līberātum	free
portō, portāre, **portāvī**, portātum	carry
pugnō, pugnāre, **pugnāvī**, pugnātum	fight
spectō, spectāre, **spectāvī**, spectātum	watch
stō, stāre, **stetī**, statum	stand
tolerō, tolerāre, **tolerāvī**, tolerātum	tolerate
vītō, vītāre, **vītāvī**, vītātum	avoid
vocō, vocāre, **vocāvī**, vocātum	call

Second Conjugation

dēbeō, dēbēre, **dēbuī**, dēbitum	owe, ought to, must, should
habeō, habēre, **habuī**, habitum	have
moneō, monēre, **monuī**, monitum	warn
rīdeō, rīdēre, **rīsī**, rīsum	laugh
sedeō, sedēre, **sēdī**, sessum	sit
teneō, tenēre, **tenuī**, tentum	hold
terreō, terrēre, **terruī**, territum	frighten
timeō, timēre, **timuī**	fear
videō, vidēre, **vīdī**, vīsum	see

Third Conjugation

agō, agere, **ēgī**, actum	drive, do, spend (of time)
bibō, bibere, **bibī**	drink
carpō, carpere, **carpsī**, carptum	pluck, harvest
dīcō, dīcere, **dixī**, dictum	say
dūcō, dūcere, **duxī**, ductum	lead
frangō, frangere, **frēgī**, fractum	break
fundō, fundere, **fūdī**, fūsum	pour
laedo, laedere, **laesī**, laesum	harm
legō, legere, **lēgī**, lectum	read
lūdō, lūdere, **lūsī**, lūsum	play
metuō, metuere, **metuī**	fear
mittō, mittere, **mīsī**, missum	send
ostendō, ostendere, **ostendī**, ostentum	show
pascō, pascere, **pāvī**, pastum	feed
pellō, pellere, **pepulī**, pulsum	drive, repel
petō, petere, **petiī** (*or* **petīvī**), petītum	seek
pōnō, pōnere, **posuī**, positum	place
surgō, surgere, **surrexī**, surrectum	rise
tangō, tangere, **tetigī**, tactum	touch
vincō, vincere, **vīcī**, victum	conquer
vīvō, vīvere, **vixī**, victum	live

Fourth Conjugation

audiō, audīre, **audīvī**, audītum	hear
dormiō, dormīre, **dormīvī**, dormītum	sleep
reperiō, reperīre, **repperī**, repertum	find
veniō, venīre, **vēnī**, ventum	come

Third Conjugation *i*-stem

capiō, capere, **cēpī**, captum	take
faciō, facere, **fēcī**, factum	do, make
rapiō, rapere, **rapuī**, raptum	seize

Irregular Verbs

sum, esse, **fuī**	be
possum, posse, **potuī**	be able
eō, īre, **iī** (*or* **īvī**), itum	go
ferō, ferre, **tulī**, lātum	carry, bring

How to Use and Translate the Perfect System Tenses

The Perfect

English has two tenses for the past, the simple past and the present perfect, and the Latin perfect is used to translate both of them. In English the simple past tense is used for past actions to which **a particular time, period, or date can be assigned**: "I went [at 5 o'clock]," "I understood [right away]." By contrast, to express an action to which **you can't assign a particular time or date or when the past activity is connected to the present or is still continuing**, you use the present perfect: "I have gone," "I have understood." It's true that English speakers do not always apply this rule strictly, but thinking about it will help you in Latin.

Simple Past in English
Brutus **killed** Caesar on the Ides of March.

Hannibal **defeated** the Romans at the Battle of Cannae.

Present Perfect in English
Brutus **has killed** Caesar and the senators are frightened.

Hannibal **has defeated** us too often in recent times.

All the verbs in bold in these sentences would be in the perfect in Latin. It is important to remember this fact when you are translating from Latin to English and have to decide whether to say "I went" or "I have gone." It is also important in the translation of various types of subordinate clauses that you will be studying later. **For now, when you are translating the Latin perfect, you can use either English tense: the simple past or the present perfect.**

What about the distinction between the **imperfect** tense, which you learned in Chapter 3, and the **perfect**? If you are translating the sentence "I gave food to my pigs" into Latin, which tense of the verb *dare* should you use? There is no way to tell without further information, which the context often gives you:

Specific time in the past
I gave food to my pigs [yesterday].
cibum porcīs **dedī**.   PERFECT

Repeated action in the past
I gave food to my pigs [whenever they were hungry].
cibum porcīs **dabam**.   IMPERFECT

So, depending on the context, you can translate the English simple past tense with either the Latin perfect or the imperfect.

The Pluperfect

The pluperfect expresses an action or event **even further back in the past** than a given past action or event. For example,

In the past: PERFECT
A she-wolf **saved** Romulus and Remus after
The Romans **worshipped** the she-wolf
Before the Romans **realized** the danger,

Further back in the past: PLUPERFECT
the evil king **had thrown** them into the river.
because she **had saved** the two brothers.
Hannibal **had** already **crossed** the Alps.

The Future Perfect

The future perfect is less common than the other tenses of Latin verbs; it expresses **an action or event that will be completely finished at some point in the future**. It is even less common in English, but here are some examples that resemble Latin sentences you will see:

Future action/event	Action/event that will be finished at that point
When you finish Virgil's *Aeneid*,	you **will have read** the greatest of all Latin poems.
The pigs will be safe tonight because	by sunset the shepherds **will have killed** the wolves.

The Latin future perfect is used mostly in various types of subordinate clauses that will be introduced in the last chapters of this book. **Even though you will not need to use it yet, the easiest way to learn its forms is to do so now along with the other tenses in the perfect system.**

Vocabulary

Verbs

aedificō 1	build
ambulō 1	walk
clāmō 1	shout
laudō 1	praise
monstrō 1	show
nāvigō 1	sail
doceō, docēre, docuī, doctum 2	teach
fleō, flēre, flēvī, flētum 2	weep
maneō, manēre, mansī 2	remain
moveō, movēre, mōvī, mōtum 2	move
addō, addere, addidī, additum 3	add
cadō, cadere, cecidī 3	fall
caedō, caedere, cecīdī, caesum 3	cause to fall, kill
claudō, claudere, clausī, clausum 3	shut
cōgō, cōgere, coēgī, coactum 3	gather, force
discō, discere, didicī 3	learn
perdō, perdere, perdidī, perditum 3	lose, destroy
relinquō, relinquere, relīquī, relictum 3	leave behind
scrībō, scrībere, scripsī, scriptum 3	write
aperiō, aperīre, aperuī, apertum 4	open

accipiō, accipere, accēpī, acceptum 3 *i*-stem   accept, receive

cupiō, cupere, cupīvī, cupitum 3 *i*-stem   wish

incipiō, incipere, incēpī, inceptum 3 *i*-stem   begin

ait defective, found mostly in this form   he/she/it says or said

inquit defective, found mostly in this form   he/she/it says or said

Nouns

anima, animae fem. 1	soul		**forum, forī** neut. 2	forum
epistula, epistulae fem. 1	letter		**iugum** (= *jugum*), **iugī** neut. 2	yoke
poena, poenae fem. 1	punishment		**negōtium, negōtiī** neut. 2	business
rēgīna, rēgīnae fem. 1	queen		**officium, officiī** neut. 2	duty
animus, animī masc. 2	mind		**oppidum, oppidī** neut. 2	town
cibus, cibī masc. 2	food		**ōtium, ōtiī** neut. 2	leisure
numerus, numerī masc. 2	number		**proelium, proeliī** neut. 2	battle
oculus, oculī masc. 2	eye		**silentium, silentiī** neut. 2	silence
populus, populī masc. 2	people, race		**somnium, somniī** neut. 2	dream
somnus, somnī masc. 2	sleep		**tēlum, tēlī** neut. 2	spear, missile
ventus, ventī masc. 2	wind		**tergum, tergī** neut. 2	back
bellum, bellī neut. 2	war		**venēnum, venēnī** neut. 2	poison
collum, collī neut. 2	neck		**verbum, verbī** neut. 2	word
fātum, fātī neut. 2	fate			

Conjunctions

antequam	before
postquam	after
quamquam	although

Adverbs

ferē	almost
iam (= *jam*)	now, already
procul	far away
subitō	suddenly
tamen	but, however, nevertheless

Vocabulary Notes

The third person singular and first person plural forms of some verbs are identical in the present and perfect tenses; for example, *bibit* and *bibimus* could be either present or perfect forms. Other examples are *metuit* and *metuimus*, *ostendit* and *ostendimus*. With some other verbs, the only difference between the present and perfect forms is vowel length; contrast *legit* and *legimus* with *lēgit* and *lēgimus*, or *venit* and *venimus* with *vēnit* and *vēnimus*.

The verb forms **ait** and **inquit** are unusual because they can mean either "he (she, it) says" or "he (she, it) said." The other forms of these verbs are rare. They are used particularly for reporting speech directly; *dīcere*, the most frequent word meaning "say," is hardly ever used in this way. They are usually placed within or after the reported speech. For example:

> *agricola "porcus meus" ait "magnus est"*
> and
> *agricola "porcus meus magnus est" inquit*

both mean "The farmer says/said 'My pig is big.'"

tamen does not usually come first in its clause, unless it follows a clause beginning with a word for "although," and then it means "nevertheless." For example:

fessus eram; diū tamen labōrāvī.	I was tired, but I worked for a long time.
quamquam fessus eram, tamen diū labōrāvī.	Although I was tired, nevertheless I worked for a long time.

Prōlūsiōnēs

Parse the following words.

1. fuerant.
2. mōvit.
3. potuerās.
4. vēnistis.
5. venītis.
6. ierātis.
7. dederit.
8. tulisse.
9. carpserint.
10. sēdimus.

Chapter 7

Translate (for review), then give the perfect, future perfect, and pluperfect forms of the following verbs, in the same person and number.

For example: *dās*. You (sing.) give. *dedistī. dederis. dederās.*

1. cadēs.
2. caeditis.
3. movētis.
4. dormit.
5. cōgō.
6. flēs.
7. tangent.
8. relinquit.
9. īs.
10. arābitis.
11. portāmus.
12. fers.
13. perdent.
14. erō.
15. venīs.
16. discētis.
17. docēmus.
18. erat.
19. poteram.
20. ībō.

Translate.

1. agricola "cūr venēnum, nōn aquam," pīrātae clāmāvit "taurīs meīs barbarē dedistī?"
2. discipulī bonī in lūdum nōn vēnērunt, quod oculōs saevōs magistrī asperī timēbant.
3. sine taurīs nigrīs herī labōrāre nōn potuit agricola, quamquam nec aeger nec piger erat.
4. porcōs magister ē lūdō lentē ēgerat; vaccās tamen prope mūrum lūdī altum nōn invēnit.
5. nauta miser ferās nōn paucās ē spēluncā mōverat quia lupumque aprumque timēbat.
6. librōs multōs discipulīs monstrāvit magister, et multa dē caelō astrīsque didicērunt.
7. quamquam lupōs in silvā saepe audīverat, numquam flēvit fīlius agricolae.
8. servus iānuam lūdī subitō aperuit; magister enim epistulam iam scrīpserat inque lūdō aderat.
9. ad lūdum magister iam adierat; serva igitur aquamque cibumque porcīs dedit.
10. agricola Rōmam numquam vīderat, sed herī cum familiā per Viam Sacram ad forum ambulāvit.
11. prope forum Rōmānum multōrum templa deōrum fīliae monstrāvit.
12. templa nostra flammīs stultē dedērunt barbarī, sed nova mox aedificāvimus.
13. "stultī fuērunt barbarī," exclāmāvit puella parva; "cūr deōs nostrōs nōn laudāvērunt?"
14. nauta piger, postquam epistulam accēpit, verba aspera dominī vestrī miserē lēgit et ab ōrā insulae rursus nāvigāvit.
15. taurōs, porcōs, agnōs ad nova templa deōrum dūximus et dōna magna magnīs deīs dedimus.

16. cum fīliae bonae agricolae servīs aquam pūram frīgidamque līberē dedērunt, dormīre cupiēbant.

17. quamquam fīliae bonī agricolae servus aquam pūram frīgidamque dederat, flēbat adhūc puella.

18. sub mūrō longō oppidī parvī pigrē sedēbat servus fessus; nōn labōrābat, quia dominus ā villā abierat.

19. puella servō "sub mūrō nōlī sedēre!" inquit; "cibum enim equō, taurō, capellīs dare dēbēs, quod dominus tuus vir saevus est."

20. quamquam magnam pecūniae cōpiam herī stultē perdidī, tamen negōtia mea fortūna crās pulchrē iuvābit.

21. I came, I saw, I conquered.

22. Before they saw the big wild beast near their new house, they could hear the wolf's wicked words: "Come into our cave, little pigs."

23. Because they often fought against savage peoples far away, the Romans always made broad roads.

24. Before they began the battle, the Romans had received a letter from the barbarians.

25. Although my bull was carrying a yoke on its broad neck, I could not plow the big field yesterday.

26. The moon and stars remained in the sky for a long time, but the wretched pigs had not been able to see the wolves in the dark wood.

27. Although he almost never drinks wine, yesterday the teacher stupidly sat with a small number of friends in a tavern behind the Forum.

28. Tomorrow he will be wretched because he will wish to sleep, but duty forces a teacher to go to school.

29. Tears suddenly fell from the girl's eyes, for her friend had sailed from the shore of the savage island and she feared the wild animals.

30. Sleep and silence brought the wretched woman bad dreams again—battles, poisons, savage barbarians, slow punishments.

Lectiōnēs Latīnae

Lege, Intellege

The Acquisition of the Empire

populus Rōmānus per Flāminīnum consulem Macedonās vīcit; per Paulum consulem Macedonās sub rēge Perse rebellantēs; per Scīpiōnēs Africānōs Carthāginiensēs; per Scīpiōnem Asiāticum in Syriā vīcit rēgem Antiochum; per Scīpiōnem Aemiliānum Celtibērōs et Numantiam; per eundem Scīpiōnem Lūsitāniam et ducem Viriātum;

per Mummium Achāicum Corinthum et Achaeōs; per Fulvium Nōbiliōrem Aetōlōs et Ambraciam; per Marium Numidās et Iugurtham; per eundem Marium Cimbrōs et Teutonēs; per Sullam Ponticōs et Mithridātem; per Lucullum item Ponticōs et Mithridātem; per Pompeium Cilicās pīrātās et Armeniōs cum rēge Tigrāne et plūrimās Asiāticās gentēs; per Gaium Caesarem Galliam Germāniam Britanniam; sub hōc duce nōn tantum vīdit sed etiam nāvigāvit Ōceanum; per Caesarem Augustum Dalmatās Pannōniōs Illyricōs Aegyptiōs Germānōs Cantabrōs tōtumque orbem perpācāvit exceptīs Indīs Parthīs Sarmatīs Scythīs Dācīs quod eōs fortūna Trāiānī principis triumphīs reservāvit.

—Ampelius, *Liber Memoriālis* 47

eundem Scīpiōnem "the same Scipio"

item adv. likewise

1. The Roman people conquered the Macedonians through which two consuls?
2. Which consul conquered Corinth?
3. Which countries did Gaius (Julius) Caesar conquer?
4. Who brought peace to almost the whole world?
5. Which other two peoples besides the Sarmatians, Scyths, and Dacians did Fortune reserve for the triumphs of the emperor Trajan?

Ars Poētica

Ovid's Love Poetry II

Parse the verbs in bold in the following quotations from Ovid.

1. *annua **vēnērunt** Cereālis tempora sacrī.*
   The annual times of Ceres' festival have come.

2. *quae vōbīs **dīcunt**, **dīxērunt** mille puellīs.*
   What they say to you, they have said to a thousand girls.

3. *contrā tē sollers, hominum nātūra, **fuistī**.*
   Human nature, you have been clever against yourself.

4. *saepe petens Hērō iuvenis **transnāverat** undās.*
   The young man [Leander] had often swum across the waves seeking Hero.

5. *causa **fuit** multīs noster amōris amor.*
   Our love has been the cause of love for many.

6. *ingenium quondam **fuerat** pretiōsius aurō.*
   Talent had once been more precious than gold.

7. *quī modo Nāsōnis **fuerāmus** quīnque libellī,*
    *trēs **sumus**; hōc illī **praetulit** auctor opus.*
   We who had recently been Ovid's five little books are three; the author preferred this work to that one.

8. *sīc fera Thrēiciī **cecidērunt** agmina Rhēsī,*
    et dominum captī dēseruistis equī.
   Thus the wild ranks of Thracian Rhesus fell, and you, horses, deserted your owner when you were captured.

Aurea Dicta

1. *adversus miserōs inhūmānus est iocus.* (Quintilian)
2. *aliēna vitia in oculīs habēmus, ā tergō nostra sunt.* (Seneca the Younger)
3. *gaudia nōn remanent, sed fugitīva volant.* (Martial)
4. *magna prōmīsistī, exigua videō.* (Seneca the Younger)
5. *nihil praeter cibum nātūra dēsīderat.* (Seneca the Younger)
6. *nōn ego sum stultus, ut ante fuī.* (Ovid)
7. *rāram fēcit mixtūram cum sapientiā forma.* (Petronius)
8. *ut ager sine cultūrā frūctuōsus esse nōn potest, sīc sine doctrīnā animus.* (Cicero)

aliēnus, -a, -um of other people

exiguus, -a, -um tiny

praeter prep. (+ acc.) beyond

Hōrologia Latīna

1. *aurōra hōra aurea.*
   Dawn is a golden hour.

2. *meam vidē umbram, tuam vidēbis vītam.*
   Look at my shadow, you will see your life.

3. *transit umbra, lux permanet.*
   The shadow passes, the light remains.

4. *umbra mea vīta.*
   Life is my shadow.

5. *vidēs hōram, nescīs tuam.*
   You see the hour, but you don't know your own.

Lūsūs

Thēsaurus Verbōrum

When you are learning principal parts, it may help to notice that a large number of English nouns ending in *-ion* are based on the stem of the fourth principal part of a Latin verb. Here are some from the verbs in this chapter:

action	elaboration	petition
audition	election	position
caption	expectation	premonition
conclusion	faction	prevention
confusion	fraction	proclamation
conviction	incision	projection
deletion	induction	relation
delusion	invasion	resurrection
demonstration	lesion	session
dereliction	liberation	station
derision	mission	toleration
description	motion	transition
donation	navigation	transportation
edification	perdition	vocation

Mors Rōmānōrum

Perfidia Pūnica

The Battle of Cannae in 216 BC was the last in a rapid series of encounters in which the Carthaginians from North Africa (Punic means Carthaginian) defeated the Romans. It was perhaps the worst massacre ever suffered by a Western army. The Romans outnumbered the Carthaginians by about two to one, but they lost more than sixty thousand men due to Hannibal's military genius. The Romans, however, ultimately defeated Carthage, and history is written by the victors.

What should I say about Hannibal? Did he not bring the Roman army to such a lamentable disaster at Cannae by enmeshing it in many crafty nooses before coming out to fight? To start with, he saw to it that the Romans had to face into the sun and the dust that the wind so often stirs up there. Then he ordered part of his troops to pretend to flee during the actual battle; when a Roman legion detached itself from the rest of our army in pursuit of them, he had that legion butchered by troops which he had placed in ambush. Finally, he instructed four hundred horsemen to seek out the Roman commander, pretending to be deserters; when our general ordered them to lay down their arms and retire to the edge of the fighting (as is the usual way of dealing with deserters), they drew swords which they had hidden between their tunics and their breastplates and cut the tendons in the knees of the Roman fighters. This was Punic bravery, fitted out with tricks, treachery, and deceit! That is most definitely the reason why our bravery was foiled: we were cheated rather than defeated.

—Valerius Maximus, *Facta et Dicta Memorābilia* 7.4 *ext.* 2

Third Declension Nouns

The third declension is the biggest, covering a very large proportion of all nouns of all genders. Third declension masculine and feminine nouns decline in exactly the same way. Neuter nouns in the third declension have the same special characteristics as in the second declension; in both singular and plural, the nominative, vocative, and accusative forms are identical, and in the plural these cases all end in *-a*.

Most masculine and feminine third declension nouns follow the same paradigm as *flōs, flōris* masc. "flower":

	SINGULAR	**PLURAL**
NOMINATIVE	flōs	flōr**ēs**
GENITIVE	flōr**is**	flōr**um**
DATIVE	flōr**ī**	flōr**ibus**
ACCUSATIVE	flōr**em**	flōr**ēs**
ABLATIVE	flōr**e**	flōr**ibus**
VOCATIVE	flōs	flōr**ēs**

Most neuter third declension nouns follow the same paradigm as *carmen*, *carminis*, meaning "song" or "poem":

NOMINATIVE	carmen	carmin**a**
GENITIVE	carmin**is**	carmin**um**
DATIVE	carmin**ī**	carmin**ibus**
ACCUSATIVE	carmen	carmin**a**
ABLATIVE	carmin**e**	carmin**ibus**
VOCATIVE	carmen	carmin**a**

These forms show you how important it is to learn the nominative **and** genitive singular when you learn a noun for the first time. As you can see, the stem for these nouns (*flōr-*, *carmin-*) is found first in the genitive singular. With masculine and feminine nouns, the nominative/vocative singular usually do not show the stem; with neuter nouns, the nominative, vocative, and accusative singular almost never do.

Because the third declension covers so many nouns of all three genders, it is particularly important to memorize the gender along with the forms of each noun. With the first declension, you could assume that almost all nouns were feminine; with the second, you could assume that they were masculine or neuter. Here you need to learn the gender of each noun.

Vocabulary

Third Declension Nouns

Masculine

amor, amōris	love	**homō, hominis** masc./fem.	human being
canis, canis masc./fem.	dog	**labor, labōris**	work
dolor, dolōris	pain	**mīles, mīlitis**	soldier
dux, ducis	leader	**pastor, pastōris**	shepherd
flōs, flōris	flower	**pater, patris**	father
frāter, frātris	brother	**rex, rēgis**	king
grex, gregis	flock, herd	**sacerdōs, sacerdōtis** masc./fem.	priest(ess)

Feminine

arbor, arboris	tree	**pecus, pecudis**	flock, herd
lex, lēgis	law	**soror, sorōris**	sister
lux, lūcis	light	**uxor, uxōris**	wife
māter, mātris	mother	**virtūs, virtūtis**	courage, virtue
mulier, mulieris	woman	**vox, vōcis**	voice
pax, pācis	peace		

Neuter

caput, capitis	head	**lūmen, lūminis**	light
carmen, carminis	song, poem	**mūnus, mūneris**	gift
corpus, corporis	body	**nūmen, nūminis**	divinity
flūmen, flūminis	river	**opus, operis**	work
iūs (= *jūs*)**, iūris**	law	**tempus, temporis**	time

A small number of common third declension nouns, both masculine and feminine, have *-ium*, not *-um*, in the genitive plural. For this reason, they are sometimes referred to as "*i*-stem" third declension nouns. Here are the most frequently used of these nouns, which you need to learn separately:

Masculine			*Feminine*		
cīvis, cīvis	citizen		**ars, artis**	art	
collis, collis	hill		**arx, arcis**	citadel	
dens, dentis	tooth		**classis, classis**	fleet	
fīnis, fīnis	end, pl. territory		**mens, mentis**	mind	
fons, fontis	fountain		**mors, mortis**	death	
hostis, hostis	enemy		**nāvis, nāvis**	ship	
ignis, ignis	fire		**nox, noctis**	night	
mons, montis	mountain		**pars, partis**	part	
piscis, piscis	fish		**turris, turris**	tower	
pons, pontis	bridge		**urbs, urbis**	city	

Similarly, a very few important neuter nouns, such as **mare, maris** "sea" and **animal, animālis** "animal," use different endings from our model neuter noun, *carmen*:

	SINGULAR	PLURAL
NOMINATIVE	mar**e**	mar**ia**
GENITIVE	mar**is**	mar**ium**
DATIVE	mar**ī**	mar**ibus**
ACCUSATIVE	mar**e**	mar**ia**
ABLATIVE	mar**ī**	mar**ibus**
VOCATIVE	mar**e**	mar**ia**

Notā Bene

-**ī** in the ablative singular: mar**ī**

-**ium** in the genitive plural: **marium**

-**ia** in the nominative, vocative, and accusative neuter plural: **maria**

Vocabulary Notes

grex, gregis masc. and **pecus, pecudis** fem. are synonyms, as are **labor, labōris** masc. and **opus, operis** neut., **lux, lūcis** fem. and **lūmen, lūminis** neut.

iūs, iūris neut. is a more general concept ("the law"), whereas specific laws were called **lēgēs**.

Like "enemy" in English, **hostis** is frequently used as a **collective singular**, even though more than one person is being referred to. For example, *hostis urbem cēpit* means "The enemy (= the whole enemy army) took the city." Even when Latin uses the plural, as in *hostēs urbem cēpērunt*, English idiom often prefers the singular: "The enemies took the city" will often seem a clumsy translation. Note also that Latin generally distinguishes foreign enemies from personal enemies, the former being *hostēs*, the latter *inimīcī*, (i.e., not *amīcī*); the Carthaginians were the Romans' *hostēs*, whereas Cicero was put on a death-list by his *inimīcus*, Mark Antony.

Prōlūsiōnēs

Give the genitive singular, gender, and meaning of the following nouns.

1. amor.
2. animal.
3. arbor.
4. astrum.
5. canis.
6. caper.
7. caput.
8. cīvis.
9. classis.
10. corpus.
11. dolor.
12. flūmen.
13. fons.
14. frāter.
15. grex.
16. homō.
17. hostis.
18. ignis.
19. iūs.
20. labor.

21. lūmen.
22. lux.
23. mare.
24. mons.
25. mors.
26. mulier.
27. nūmen.
28. nox.
29. opus.
30. pars.
31. pastor.
32. pax.
33. pecus.
34. rex.
35. sacerdōs.
36. soror.
37. turris.
38. urbs.
39. uxor.
40. virtūs.

Chapter 8

Parse the following words.

1. capitī.
2. ignium.
3. mīlite.
4. ducis.
5. dūcis.

6. iūre.
7. dolōrum.
8. mūrōrum.
9. corporum.
10. sorōrī.

Change from singular to plural, or vice versa, and then translate.

1. nox nūminī malō cāra est.
2. nonne hostis vōcem audīre potes?
3. sacerdōtis soror ad montem altum abiit.
4. mulieribus pulchrīs flōrēs vestrōs pastōrēs parvī dederant.
5. pater mīlitis urbis magnae rex erat.
6. canem saevum, mūnus parvum, pastōrī bonō dedī.
7. flūmen in mare fundit aquam.
8. piscium carmen audīvistī?
9. aqua flūminis dē colle magnō cadēbat.
10. num deī sunt Amōrēs, sī dolōrēs saevōs hominibus dant?

Translate.

1. pater māterque sorōrī meae cārī sunt; frāter tamen saepe malus est.
2. sacerdōtī Rōmānō, cīvēs, taurum piscēsque iam dedistis?
3. lūmen magnum in altō monte subitō vīdimus, quamquam nox iam alta erat.
4. pastor miser, in agrō manēre nōn poteris; pecudem trans pontem ad mare cum cane lentē age!
5. ad mātrem epistulam mittere nōn potuī, sed ab altīs montibus hostēs spectābāmus.
6. caput ducis Rōmānī in flūmen lentum cecidit.
7. dux Rōmānus multās turrēs altās prope pontem cecīdit.
8. multōs flōrēs pulchrōs prope fontem frīgidum rursus petēmus.
9. in arce urbis mīlitēs post bellī fīnem vidēre poterātis?
10. corpus animālis pūrum nōn erat; dōnum igitur patrum nostrōrum nōn accēpērunt deī.
11. sub arbore magnā diū sēderat cum grege dominī canis meus.
12. canem pigrum monuī: "Rex, ōtium nōn habēmus; porcī enim dentēs lupōrum, animālium saevōrum, timent."

13. dolōrēs pastōris erant saevī, et mortem timēbat, sed lux dē caelō subitō vēnit et nūminis magnī verba audīvimus: "vir bonus es; nōlī mortem saevōsque dolōrēs hodiē timēre."

14. pīrātae sunt barbarī, quoniam nec virtūtēs nec artēs Rōmānōrum didicērunt.

15. Rōmānārum nāvium magnam classem ab arce urbis iterum vīdērunt hostēs; metuēbant igitur, namque urbem capere dux noster avārē cupiēbat.

16. Peace was always dear to the Romans, but they did not often have peace.

17. The end of the war will be a good time both for the soldiers and for the citizens.

18. "The deep seas have many animals," shouted the sailor again; "there are many fish in the deep sea."

19. I love my wife, the beautiful queen, for she is part of my soul.

20. In part of the high citadel, our dogs had already heard the barbarian voices of the enemy.

21. Although death is the end of life, and our bodies perish, perhaps our souls will be able to live forever.

22. In your city the laws are savage and barbaric, because the stupid citizens have never praised the gods.

23. The king was already leading the bull, a large animal, to the altar, when the high tower fell slowly into the river.

24. Although the gods love humans, the minds of humans are often stupid; therefore we cannot always hear the divine voices of the gods.

25. Silence holds the long night, while the tired shepherds listen lazily to the priests' songs.

Lectiōnēs Latīnae

Lege, Intellege

Only two works by Caesar (Gaius Julius Caesar, 100–44 BC) have survived. Both are accounts of his military actions, the *Commentāriī Dē Bellō Gallicō* (seven books) and the *Commentāriī Dē Bellō Cīvīlī* (three books), with further books added to both works by other writers. From what we know, Caesar's style was normally subtle and polished, but both of these works, and particularly the *Dē Bellō Gallicō*, are written in a consciously simple style intended to persuade his readers of his sincerity and uncomplicated character.

Ancient France

Gallia est omnis dīvīsa in partēs trēs, quārum ūnam incolunt Belgae, aliam Aquītānī, tertiam quī ipsōrum linguā Celtae, nostrā Gallī appellantur. hī omnēs linguā, institūtīs, lēgibus inter sē differunt. Gallōs ab Aquītānīs Garumna flūmen, ā Belgīs Matrōna et

Sēquana dīvidit. hōrum omnium fortissimī sunt Belgae quod ā cultū atque hūmānitāte prōvinciae longissimē absunt, minimēque ad eōs mercātōrēs saepe eunt atque ea quae ad effēminandōs animōs pertinent important, proximīque sunt Germānīs, quī trans Rhēnum incolunt, quibuscum continenter bellum gerunt. quā dē causā Helvētiī quoque reliquōs Gallōs virtūte praecēdunt, quod ferē cottīdiānīs proeliīs cum Germānīs contendunt, cum aut suīs fīnibus eōs prohibent aut ipsī in eōrum fīnibus bellum gerunt.

—Caesar, *Dē Bellō Gallicō* 1.1

ipsī, ipsōrum masc. pron., pronom. adj. they themselves

quibuscum "with whom"

1. Name the three peoples who inhabit Gaul.
2. Do these peoples share a common language, customs, and laws?
3. Which Gallic people has the least contact with the decadent influences of Roman culture and trade?
4. Why are the Helvetii the bravest of the Gallic tribes?
5. What are the Gauls called in their own language?

Ars Poētica

Publilius Syrus VI
Identify and explain the case of the nouns in bold.

1. *amōrī fīnem **tempus**, nōn animus, facit.*
   Time, not the mind, makes an end to love.

2. *amōris **vulnus** īdem, quī sānat, facit.*
   The same person causes the wound of love who cures it.

3. *beneficium accipere **lībertātem** est vendere.*
   To accept a favor is to sell one's freedom.

4. *fulmen est, ubi cum **potestāte** habitat īrācundia.*
   There is lightning, when anger lives with power.

5. *in **venere** semper certant dolor et gaudium.*
   In love grief and joy always contend.

6. *nulla **hominī** maior poena est quam **infēlīcitās**.*
   There is no greater punishment for a person than unhappiness.

7. *dolor quam miser est, quī in tormentō **vōcem** nōn habet!*
   How wretched is grief which in its torture does not have a voice!

8. *omnī **dolōrī** remedium est patientia.*
   Endurance is the remedy for every grief.

Aurea Dicta

1. *crūdēlitātis māter avāritia est, pater furor.* (Rutilius Rufus)
2. *dīvīna nātūra dedit agrōs, ars hūmāna aedificāvit urbēs.* (Varro)
3. *effugere nōn potes necessitātēs, potes vincere.* (Seneca the Younger)
4. *fāta regunt hominēs.* (Juvenal)
5. *hominēs sumus, nōn deī.* (Petronius)
6. *in flammam flammās, in mare fundis aquās.* (Ovid)
7. *in fugā foeda mors est, in victōriā glōriōsa.* (Cicero)
8. *īra odium generat, concordia nūtrit amōrem.* (Ps.-Cato)

Hōrologia Latīna

1. *bulla est vīta hominum.*
   The life of mankind is a bubble.
2. *lux mea lex.*
   The light is my law.
3. *sine sōle nihil.*
   Without the sun, nothing.
4. *sine lūmine pereō.*
   Without the light I perish.
5. *sōl rex rēgum.*
   The sun is the king of kings.

Lūsūs

Thēsaurus Verbōrum

When you are learning principal parts, it may help to notice that a large number of English nouns ending in *-ure* are based on the stem of the fourth principal part of a Latin verb. Here are some from the verbs found in Chapter 7:

adventure	conjecture	rapture
aperture	fracture	scripture
capture	lecture	stature
closure	pasture	

Vīta Rōmānōrum

Roman Scruples

After the Battle of Cannae, Hannibal sent ten captives to Rome to negotiate an exchange of prisoners, with the side receiving more prisoners paying one and a half pounds of silver for each additional man. He made the captives swear to return to the Carthaginian camp if the Romans declined to make the exchange. The captives swore the oath and duly went to Rome where they delivered Hannibal's message, but the Senate rejected the exchange. The captives' parents and families embraced them, declaring that they had been legally restored to their fatherland as free men, and begged them not to return to the enemy. Eight of the captives replied that they were not legally free, since they had sworn an oath, and these eight immediately left to return to Hannibal. The other two stayed in Rome, claiming to be absolved from any obligation because, just after leaving the enemy camp, they returned to it on a pretext so that they could say they had fulfilled their oath. This devious ruse was regarded as so dishonorable that the people in general despised and criticized them, and later the censors punished them with all sorts of fines and reproaches, for not having done what they had sworn to do.

—Aulus Gellius, *Noctēs Atticae* 6.18

CHAPTER 9
Third Declension Adjectives and Adverbs

Adjectives

You already know the forms of first/second declension adjectives, such as *cārus, -a, -um*; *miser, misera, miserum*; and *pulcher, pulchra, pulchrum*. Almost all other adjectives in Latin belong to the third declension.

For almost all third declension adjectives, there is no difference between the masculine and feminine endings, and the neuter endings are the same as those of the third declension neuter noun *mare*.

Here is the adjective *dulcis, dulce* "sweet," "pleasant":

	MASC./FEM.	NEUTER
Singular		
NOMINATIVE	dulc**is**	dulc**e**
GENITIVE	dulc**is**	dulc**is**
DATIVE	dulc**ī**	dulc**ī**
ACCUSATIVE	dulc**em**	dulc**e**
ABLATIVE	dulc**ī**	dulc**ī**
VOCATIVE	dulc**is**	dulc**e**
Plural		
NOMINATIVE	dulc**ēs**	dulc**ia**
GENITIVE	dulc**ium**	dulc**ium**
DATIVE	dulc**ibus**	dulc**ibus**
ACCUSATIVE	dulc**ēs**	dulc**ia**
ABLATIVE	dulc**ibus**	dulc**ibus**
VOCATIVE	dulc**ēs**	dulc**ia**

Notā Bene

-**ī** in the ablative singular: **dulcī**

-**ium** in the genitive plural: **dulcium**

-**ia** in the nominative, vocative, and accusative neuter plural: **dulcia**

Most adjectives of the third declension are like *dulcis, dulce*. The vocabulary lists will give the form for the **nominative singular, both masculine and feminine** (*brevis*), and then the form for the **nominative singular neuter** (*breve*). You do not need to learn a genitive form here, because the stem will not change for any of these adjectives.

Vocabulary

brevis, breve	short
caelestis, caeleste	heavenly
crūdēlis, crūdēle	cruel
dēformis, dēforme	ugly
difficilis, difficile	difficult
dissimilis, dissimile + gen. or dat.	unlike
dulcis, dulce	sweet
facilis, facile	easy
fortis, forte	strong, brave
gravis, grave	heavy, serious
humilis, humile	humble
immortālis, immortāle	immortal
inānis, ināne	empty
incolumis, incolume	safe
levis, leve	light
mollis, molle	soft
mortālis, mortāle	mortal
omnis, omne	all, every
pinguis, pingue	fat
similis, simile + gen. or dat.	like, similar to
tristis, triste	sad
turpis, turpe	shameful

Vocabulary Notes

similis and **dissimilis** can take either the genitive or the dative; the meaning is the same.

"A wild boar is like a pig" can be translated either *aper porcī similis est* OR *aper porcō similis est*.

"A pig is not like a horse" can be translated either *porcus equī dissimilis est* OR *porcus equō dissimilis est*.

In Chapter 6 we saw that possesive adjectives (*meus* "my," *tuus* "your," and so on) are not linked with other adjectives by a word meaning "and." *omnis* is used in the same way.

porcī meī pinguēs in agrō sunt.	My fat pigs are in the field.
omnēs porcī pinguēs in agrō sunt.	All the fat pigs are in the field.

Another group of third declension adjectives DOES change its stem, but the nominative and vocative singular for ALL THREE GENDERS is the same.

	MASC./FEM.	NEUTER
Singular		
NOMINATIVE	fēlix	fēlix
GENITIVE	fēlīc**is**	fēlīc**is**
DATIVE	fēlīc**ī**	fēlīc**ī**
ACCUSATIVE	fēlīc**em**	fēlix
ABLATIVE	fēlīc**ī**	fēlīc**ī**
VOCATIVE	fēlix	fēlix
Plural		
NOMINATIVE	fēlīc**ēs**	fēlīc**ia**
GENITIVE	fēlīc**ium**	fēlīc**ium**
DATIVE	fēlīc**ibus**	fēlīc**ibus**
ACCUSATIVE	fēlīc**ēs**	fēlīc**ia**
ABLATIVE	fēlīc**ibus**	fēlīc**ibus**
VOCATIVE	fēlīc**ēs**	fēlīc**ia**

To help you learn the difference in the stem for these adjectives, the entry in the vocabulary lists will give you the **nominative and genitive singular** (*fēlix, fēlīcis*), forms that are the same for all genders.

audax, audācis	bold, daring	**infēlix, infēlīcis**	unhappy
fēlix, fēlīcis	happy	**ingens, ingentis**	huge
ferox, ferōcis	fierce	**potens, potentis**	powerful

dīves, dīvitis "rich," *pauper, pauperis* "poor," and *vetus, veteris* "old" are irregular and need to be learned separately.

	Singular		Plural	
	Masc./Fem.	*Neuter*	*Masc./Fem.*	*Neuter*
NOMINATIVE	dīves	dīves	dīvitēs	**dītia**
GENITIVE	dīvitis	dīvitis	**dīvitum**	**dīvitum**
DATIVE	dīvitī	dīvitī	dīvitibus	dīvitibus
ACCUSATIVE	dīvitem	dīves	dīvitēs	**dītia**
ABLATIVE	**dīvite**	**dīvite**	dīvitibus	dīvitibus
VOCATIVE	dīves	dīves	dīvitēs	**dītia**

	Singular		**Plural**	
	Masc./Fem.	*Neuter*	*Masc./Fem.*	*Neuter*
NOMINATIVE	pauper	pauper	pauperēs	pauperia
GENITIVE	pauperis	pauperis	**pauperum**	**pauperum**
DATIVE	pauperī	pauperī	pauperibus	pauperibus
ACCUSATIVE	pauperem	pauper	pauperēs	pauperia
ABLATIVE	**paupere**	**paupere**	pauperibus	pauperibus
VOCATIVE	pauper	pauper	pauperēs	pauperia

	Singular		**Plural**	
	Masc./Fem.	*Neuter*	*Masc./Fem.*	*Neuter*
NOMINATIVE	vetus	vetus	veterēs	**vetera**
GENITIVE	veteris	veteris	**veterum**	**veterum**
DATIVE	veterī	veterī	veteribus	veteribus
ACCUSATIVE	veterem	vetus	veterēs	**vetera**
ABLATIVE	**vetere**	**vetere**	veteribus	veteribus
VOCATIVE	vetus	vetus	veterēs	**vetera**

A few adjectives have a special masculine form with the ending -*er* in the nominative and vocative singular. The vocabulary list gives you **all three nominative singular forms, masculine, feminine, and neuter.** Otherwise, these adjectives decline like *dulcis, dulce*. That means that the feminine (and neuter) nominative singular gives you the stem for all cases in all genders. Only the nominative and vocative masculine singular form is exceptional.

ācer, ācris, ācre	sharp, fierce	**salūber, salūbris, salūbre**	healthy
celeber, celebris, celebre	famous	**volucer, volucris, volucre**	flying
celer, celeris, celere	swift		

Adverbs

In Chapter 6 we saw that regular adverbs formed from first/second declension adjectives add the ending -*ē* to the adjectival base; for example, *cārē* "dearly," *pulchrē* "beautifully," *miserē* "wretchedly." Similarly, regular adverbs of the third declension add the ending -*iter* to the adjectival base; for example, *graviter* "heavily," *fēlīciter* "happily," *celeriter* "swiftly."

Latin often uses adjectives where English uses adverbs. This tendency is particularly noticeable in the expression of emotions. For example, "The pig went sadly toward the cave" is *porcus ad spēluncam trist**is*** (rather than "tristiter") *adiit*. Note also that the adverb "incolumiter" does not occur in Classical Latin. "The pig returned safely from the cave" is *porcus ē spēluncā incolum**is** rediit*.

Prōlūsiōnēs

Parse the words in bold.

> **pinguēs** pascēbat porcōs in montibus altīs
> agricola infēlix. pūrō sub **lūmine** lūnae
> crūdēlēsque aprōs et **corpora** magna lupōrum
> **terruerat fortis.** "flōrēs iam carpite" **pigrae**
> clāmāvit pecudī, "dulcēs iam carpite flōrēs."
> sed pīrāta **gregem subitō** malus **abstulit omnem.**

Translate and then change to the plural.

1. rex fortis cecidit.
2. rēgem fortem cecīdit.
3. equus frātris meī dēformis erat, sed celer.
4. flūmen ingens lentumque cum grege pinguī transīre nōn potuerās.
5. vacca animal pigrum et grave est, nōn fera volucris.
6. lupī audācis vōcem magnam nōn timēbit puella pauper.
7. lupe ferox, vox tua nōn dulcis est!
8. num uxōrī tristis agricolae flōrem pulchrum dedistī?
9. quandō cīvis turpis urbis parvae periit?
10. in flūmine magnō nāvis celeris dominum infēlīcem iam vīdistī?

Translate.

1. aqua flūminis frīgidī nūminī magnō sacra erat.
2. porcus pinguis aprō crūdēlī similis est, sed lupus celer vaccae gravī dissimilis est.
3. soror mea semper infēlix erit, quamquam et dīves et rēgīna est.
4. in templō deī immortālis nautae omnēs incolumēs mansērunt.
5. saxa levia sunt, et puerī pauperēs sine labōre multō mūrum ingentem celeriter aedificāre potuerant.
6. agricolae humilis inānis casa est, nam porcōs agnōsque mollēs in hortum remōverāmus.

7. num servī fēlīcis capellās parvās humilēsque prope fontem calidum vidēre potes?

8. nōn stultī sunt porcī, quamquam nec librī verba legunt nec scrībere carmina possunt.

9. poētae pauperis mentem celerem populus Rōmānus laudat, nam carmina difficilia sed dulcia scrībit.

10. cīvium dīvitum vīta semper tristis est; audāciam enim pīrātārum dēformium metuunt.

11. quandō contrā mūrōs fortēs urbium nostrārum audācem mīlitum veterum turbam rex hostium ācriter dūcet?

12. sī via nec difficilis nec aspera per silvam tristem nigramque dūcit, mortem vītābunt puerī omnēs, incolumēsque ad fontem deō sacrum revenient.

13. cum lupō ferōcī, ferā audācī, in templō dīvite deae immortālis īnfēlīciter stābat porcus meus miser.

14. sī fīlius ingens fēminae pauperis pinguēs mīlitēs per flūmen celere nunc dūcit, urbem nostram ferōciter oppugnāre mox incipient.

15. Rōmānī ferē omnēs, et dīvitēs et pauperēs, deīs caelestibus mūnera cottīdiē dant.

16. All good dogs help their sad owners.

17. Although our king is shameful and stupid, he has a beautiful wife.

18. The immortal gods have given good laws to all mortals.

19. The lazy general suddenly saw the swift forces of our cruel enemies on all the hills.

20. Our mother is sad, because the ugly poet's songs are always sad.

21. The rich women, our brave queen's daughters, were already sailing again across the deep and cruel seas.

22. Although the wolves are fierce, don't be afraid of the big animals' long teeth, wretched citizens!

23. If they fear the cold night on the huge mountain, why are you leading the fat pigs slowly across the deep river, soldiers?

24. The shepherd is neither unhappy nor tired, for his goats are big and the old wolves' cave is still empty.

25. We must live happily without much work, because life is short and death is swift.

Lectiōnēs Latīnae

Lege, Intellege

Very little is known about Eutropius. His *Breviārium Ab Urbe Conditā* (*Digest of Roman History from the Foundation of the City*) was written in the mid-fourth century AD, but its style is mostly classical, probably in imitation of the historian Livy who died in AD 17.

Fighting the Carthaginians

annō quartō postquam ad Italiam Hannibal vēnit, Marcus Claudius Marcellus consul apud Nōlam, cīvitātem Campāniae, contrā Hannibalem bene pugnāvit. Hannibal multās cīvitātēs Rōmānōrum per Āpūliam, Calabriam, Brittiōs occupāvit. quō tempore etiam rex Macedoniae Philippus ad eum legātōs mīsit, prōmittens auxilia contrā Rōmānōs. Rōmānī in Macedoniam Marcum Valerium Laevīnum īre iussērunt, in Sardiniam Titum Manlium Torquātum prōconsulem. ita ūnō tempore quattuor locīs pugnābant: in Italiā contrā Hannibalem, in Hispāniā contrā frātrem eius Hasdrubalem, in Macedoniā contrā Philippum, in Sardiniā contrā Sardōs et alterum Hasdrubalem Carthāginiensem.

—Eutropius, *Breviārium* 3.12

1. Which king of Macedon sent ambassadors to Hannibal?
2. Who fought the Romans in Spain?
3. Which Roman proconsul was ordered to invade Sardinia?
4. In how many places were the Romans fighting simultaneously?
5. Near which Campanian city did Claudius Marcellus fight Hannibal successfully?

Ars Poētica

Ovid's Love Poetry III
Identify the case of the adjectives in bold.

1. *parva **levēs** capiunt animōs.*
   Small things captivate light minds.

2. *aspice cognātī **fēlīcia** Caesaris arma.*
   Look at the successful weapons of Caesar, your relative. [To Cupid.]

3. *nōn ego **nōbilium** sedeō studiōsus equōrum.*
   I am not sitting here because I am keen on thoroughbred horses.

4. *tū poterās **fragilēs** pinnīs hebetāre zmaragdōs.*
   You could dim fragile emeralds with your wings. [To his mistress' dead parrot.]

5. ***pauperibus** vātēs ego sum, quia pauper amāvī.*
   I am the poet for poor people, since I loved as a poor man.

6. *cerne cicātrīcēs, **veteris** vestīgia pugnae.*
   Look at his scars, the traces of an old fight.

7. *prōdigiōsa loquor **veterum** mendācia vātum.*
   I speak the prodigious lies of the old poets.

8. ***imbellēs** elegī, **geniālis** Mūsa, valēte.*
   Farewell, unwarlike elegies, my witty Muse, farewell!

Aurea Dicta

1. *dolōris medicīnam ā philosophiā petō.* (Cicero)
2. *hominum generī ūniversō cultūra agrōrum est salūtāris.* (Cicero)
3. *ignis aurum probat, miseria fortēs virōs.* (Seneca the Younger)
4. *impia sub dulcī melle venēna latent.* (Ovid)
5. *iustitia omnium est domina et rēgīna virtūtum.* (Cicero)
6. *nātūram mūtāre difficile est.* (Seneca the Younger)
7. *necessitūdō etiam timidōs fortēs facit.* (Sallust)
8. *omnēs hominēs aut līberī sunt aut servī.* (Justinian's *Dīgesta*)

Hōrologia Latīna

1. *brevis aetās, vīta fugax.*
   Time is short, life is fleeting.

2. *dōna praesentis cape laetus hōrae.*
   Take gladly the gifts of the present hour.

3. *dubia omnibus, ultima multīs.*
   The hour is uncertain for all, the last for many.

4. *dum quaeris, hōra fugit.*
   While you seek it, the hour flees.

5. *tempus edax rērum.*
   Time eats away everything.

Lūsūs

Thēsaurus Verbōrum

Many English nouns are exactly the same as the second declension neuter nouns from which they are derived, except that the ending has been dropped; for example, "argument" is derived from *argūmentum, -ī* and "fragment" from *fragmentum, -ī*.

impedīmentum	ornāmentum
incrēmentum	pigmentum
instrumentum	rudīmentum
līneamentum	sacrāmentum
medicāmentum	segmentum
mōmentum	testāmentum
monumentum	tormentum

Vīta Rōmānōrum

Selling Slaves

The magistrates forbid those who have been slaves for a long time to be sold as if they were newly enslaved. This is a measure to counter the trickery of vendors, for the magistrates protect buyers from vendors' deceit. Most dealers try to pass off slaves of long standing as if they were new slaves, so as to sell them at a higher price, the assumption being that inexperienced slaves are more naive, more adaptable to their duties, easier to teach, and ready for any task, whereas it is difficult to retrain experienced longtime slaves and adapt them to one's own ways. So, since the salesmen know that people are ready to rush to buy new slaves, they mix in longtime slaves and sell them as if they were new. The magistrates ordain that this is not to happen, and a slave passed off on an unsuspecting buyer will be returned.

—Justinian, *Dīgesta* 21.1.37

CHAPTER 10

Volō, Nōlō, Mālō, Numbers, Nouns of Limited Form and Variable Meaning

The Irregular Verbs *volō, nōlō, mālō*

Here is the irregular present indicative active of the verbs **volō** "I wish," **nōlō** "I do not wish," and **mālō** "I prefer":

1st sing.	volō	nōlō	mālō
2nd sing.	vīs	nōn vīs	māvīs
3rd sing.	vult	nōn vult	māvult
1st pl.	volumus	nōlumus	mālumus
2nd pl.	vultis	nōn vultis	māvultis
3rd pl.	volunt	nōlunt	mālunt
Infinitive	velle	nolle	malle
Imperatives	——	nōlī, nōlīte	——

velle, *nolle*, and *malle* conjugate regularly (as third conjugation verbs) in the other tenses: *volam*, *nōlam*, *mālam* (future), *volēbam*, *nōlēbam*, *mālēbam* (imperfect), *voluī*, *nōluī*, *māluī* (perfect). None of these verbs has a fourth principal part.

nōlō is actually *volō* with the negative prefix *ne*, and *mālō* was originally the comparative adverb *magis*, which means "rather," added to *volō*: "I wish rather." You have already met the imperatives *nōlī* and *nōlīte*, when you learned negative commands in Chapter 1; *nōlī ūvās meās carpere*, for example, literally means "Be unwilling to pluck my grapes."

Numbers

Most cardinal numbers do not decline, but *ūnus* "one," *duo* "two," and *trēs* "three" decline as follows:

	MASCULINE	FEMININE	NEUTER
NOMINATIVE	ūn**us**	ūn**a**	ūn**um**
GENITIVE	ūn**īus**	ūn**īus**	ūn**īus**
DATIVE	ūn**ī**	ūn**ī**	ūn**ī**
ACCUSATIVE	ūn**um**	ūn**am**	ūn**um**
ABLATIVE	ūn**ō**	ūn**ā**	ūn**ō**

	MASCULINE	FEMININE	NEUTER
NOMINATIVE	du**o**	du**ae**	du**o**
GENITIVE	du**ōrum**	du**ārum**	du**ōrum**
DATIVE	du**ōbus**	du**ābus**	du**ōbus**
ACCUSATIVE	du**ōs**	du**ās**	du**o**
ABLATIVE	du**ōbus**	du**ābus**	du**ōbus**

	MASC. /FEM.	NEUTER
NOMINATIVE	tr**ēs**	tr**ia**
GENITIVE	tr**ium**	tr**ium**
DATIVE	tr**ibus**	tr**ibus**
ACCUSATIVE	tr**ēs**	tr**ia**
ABLATIVE	tr**ibus**	tr**ibus**

The cardinal numbers four to one hundred are **indeclinable adjectives**. When numbers above twenty are combined with *ūnus, duo,* or *trēs,* such as *vigintī ūnus* (21), *trīgintā duo* (32), *quadrāgintā trēs* (43), then *ūnus, duo,* and *trēs* will decline as usual, but the other component will remain unchanged.

The words for numbers such as two hundred, three hundred, and so on (*ducentī, -ae, -a; trecentī, -ae, -a,* etc.) are also adjectives and they do decline, like the plural forms of *cārus, -a, -um*.

Like most other cardinal numbers, *mille,* "thousand," is an indeclinable adjective, but *mīlia,* "thousands," declines as a third declension neuter plural noun:

NOMINATIVE	mīl**ia**
GENITIVE	mīl**ium**
DATIVE	mīl**ibus**
ACCUSATIVE	mīl**ia**
ABLATIVE	mīl**ibus**

mīlia usually has another noun in the genitive dependent on it, and one of the cardinal numbers as an adjective. If this cardinal number is *ūnus, duo,* or *trēs,* it will decline.

mille	**mīlia**
mille porcī in agrō sunt.	**duo mīlia porcōrum** in agrō sunt.
vōcēs **mille porcōrum** audīmus.	vōcēs **trium mīlium porcōrum** audīmus.
mille porcīs cibum dō.	**quattuor mīlibus porcōrum** cibum dō.
mille porcōs habēmus.	**quinque mīlia porcōrum** habēmus.
ā mille porcīs fugit lupus.	**ā sex mīlibus porcōrum** fugit lupus.

From the following list, you can construct all whole **cardinal** ("one," "two," "three," etc.) and **ordinal** ("first," "second," "third," etc.) numbers. The vast majority of these you will encounter only rarely.

You need to memorize the first ten cardinal and the first ten ordinal numbers, but just understand the rules for forming the rest so that you can recognize them when you meet them in your reading. Here they are divided into groups according to how they are formed.

Cardinal	Ordinal	Roman Numeral
1 ūnus, -a, -um	prīmus, -a, -um	I
2 duo, -ae, -o	secundus, -a, -um/alter, -a, -um	II
3 trēs, tria	tertius, -a, -um	III
4 quattuor	quartus, -a, -um	IV
5 quinque	quintus, -a, -um	V
6 sex	sextus, -a, -um	VI
7 septem	septimus, -a, -um	VII
8 octō	octāvus, -a, -um	VIII
9 novem	nōnus, -a, -um	IX
10 decem	decimus, -a, -um	X
11 undecim	undecimus, -a, -um	XI
12 duodecim	duodecimus, -a, -um	XII
13 tredecim	tertius, -a, -um decimus, -a, -um	XIII
14 quattuordecim	quartus, -a, -um decimus, -a, -um	XIV
15 quindecim	quintus, -a, -um decimus, -a, -um	XV
18 duodēvīgintī	duodēvīcēsimus, -a, -um	XVIII
19 undēvīgintī	undēvīcēsimus, -a, -um	XIX
20 vīgintī	vīcēsimus, -a, -um	XX
21 vīgintī ūnus, -a, -um	vīcēsimus, -a, -um prīmus, -a, -um	XXI
28 duodētrīgintā	duodētrīcēsimus, -a, -um	XXVIII
29 undētrīgintā	undētrīcēsimus, -a, -um	XXIX
30 trīgintā	trīcēsimus, -a, -um	XXX
40 quadrāgintā	quadrāgēsimus, -a, -um	XL
50 quinquāgintā	quinquāgēsimus, -a, -um	L
60 sexāgintā	sexāgēsimus, -a, -um	LX
70 septuāgintā	septuāgēsimus, -a, -um	LXX
80 octōgintā	octōgēsimus, -a, -um	LXXX
90 nōnāgintā	nōnāgēsimus, -a, -um	XC
100 centum	centēsimus, -a, -um	C
101 centum ūnus, -a, -um	centēsimus, -a, -um prīmus, -a, -um	CI

200 ducentī, -ae, -a	**ducentēsimus, -a, -um**	**CC**
300 trecentī, -ae, -a	**trecentēsimus, -a, -um**	**CCC**
400 quadringentī, -ae, -a	**quadrāgentēsimus, -a, -um**	**CD**
500 quingentī, -ae, -a	**quingentēsimus, -a, -um**	**D**
600 sescentī, -ae, -a	**sescentēsimus, -a, -um**	**DC**
700 septingentī, -ae, -a	**septingentēsimus, -a, -um**	**DCC**
800 octingentī, -ae, -a	**octingentēsimus, -a, -um**	**DCCC**
900 nōngentī, -ae, -a	**nōngentēsimus, -a, -um**	**CM**
1,000 mille	**millēsimus, -a, -um**	**M**
2,000 duo mīlia	**bis millēsimus, -a, -um**	**MM**

Notice that the numbers for hundreds from 200 to 900 are plural adjectives declined like *cārus*.

Distributive numbers express the idea of "one, two, three **each**." For example, *agricola fīliīs septēnōs porcōs dedit* means "The farmer gave his sons seven pigs each." **They are also used with nouns that have different meanings in the plural and singular,** which are presented in the next section. For example, *duo castra* means "two forts" but *bīna castra* means "two camps." Here are the most frequently used distributive numbers:

singulī, -ae, -a	one each	**octōnī, -ae, -a**	eight each
bīnī, -ae, -a	two each	**novēnī, -ae, -a**	nine each
ternī, -ae, -a	three each	**dēnī, -ae, -a**	ten each
quaternī, -ae, -a	four each	**vīcēnī, -ae, -a**	twenty each
quīnī, -ae, -a	five each	**centēnī, -ae, -a**	one hundred each
sēnī, -ae, -a	six each	**millēnī, -ae, -a**	one thousand each
septēnī, -ae, -a	seven each		

Indeclinable adverbs express "once," "twice," "three times," and so on. Here is a list of the major examples:

semel	once	**octiēs**	eight times
bis	twice	**noviēs**	nine times
ter	three times	**deciēs**	ten times
quater	four times	**vīciēs**	twenty times
quinquiēs	five times	**centiēs**	one hundred times
sexiēs	six times	**mīliēs**	one thousand times
septiēs	seven times		

Nouns of Limited Form and Variable Meaning

Some nouns are normally used only in the singular, or only in the plural, and some have a different meaning in the singular from the one they have in the plural.

Nouns that exist only in the singular: some abstract nouns, like "beauty" or "wisdom," most names of places, and most uncountable substances, like "milk" or "iron," fall into this category. For example:

insānia, insāniae fem. 1	madness
sapientia, sapientiae fem. 1	wisdom
stultitia, stultitiae fem. 1	stupidity
Ēlysium, Ēlysiī neut. 2	the home of the happy dead
nōbilitās, nōbilitātis fem. 3	nobility, the upper class
plebs, plēbis fem. 3	the lower class of citizens
quiēs, quiētis fem. 3	rest, quiet

Latin has many nouns that have only plural forms: some of them, like "spoils" and "remains," are also plural in English. For example:

Athēnae, Athēnārum fem. 1	Athens
dīvitiae, dīvitiārum fem. 1	riches
exsequiae, exsequiārum fem. 1	funeral rites
minae, minārum fem. 1	threats
reliquiae, reliquiārum fem. 1	remains
līberī, līberōrum masc. 2	children
arma, armōrum neut. 2	arms, weapons
exta, extōrum neut. 2	entrails
spolia, spoliōrum neut. 2	plunder, spoils
mānēs, mānium masc. 3	the souls of the dead
penātēs, penātium masc. 3	household gods
moenia, moenium neut. 3	city walls

Other nouns that have plural forms in Latin are translated in English with a singular noun. For example:

insidiae, insidiārum fem. 1	ambush, trap
nuptiae, nuptiārum fem. 1	marriage(-ceremony)
tenebrae, tenebrārum fem. 1	darkness

A special group of nouns have one meaning in the singular and another meaning in the plural. For example:

	SINGULAR	PLURAL
cōpia, cōpiae fem. 1	abundance, amount	military forces
grātia, grātiae fem. 1	favor	thanks
littera, litterae fem. 1	letter of the alphabet	letters of the alphabet, epistle, literature
lūdus, lūdī masc. 2	game, school	games (in the circus, amphitheater etc.)
castrum, castrī neut. 2	fort	camp
fīnis, fīnis masc. 3	end	territory
mōs, mōris masc. 3	custom	character
aedēs, aedis fem. 3	temple	house
vīs, - fem. 3	force	strength (*see below*)

Vocabulary Notes

grātiae: "To give thanks to" or "to thank" is expressed in Latin with *grātiās agere* (not *dare*) and the dative of the person thanked.

The noun **aedēs** belongs in the small group of third declension masculine and feminine nouns with a genitive plural in *-ium*; see the list in Chapter 8 (*cīvis*, *ars*, etc.).

vīs: The 3rd declension feminine noun *vīs* is one of the very few irregular Latin nouns. In the **singular** it means "[violent] force" and is found only in the nominative, accusative, and ablative. In the **plural**, which has a different stem, it means "strength," "[military] resources," and is found in all cases.

	SINGULAR	PLURAL
NOMINATIVE	vīs	vīrēs
GENITIVE	—	vīrium
DATIVE	—	vīribus
ACCUSATIVE	vim	vīrēs
ABLATIVE	vī	vīribus

Prōlūsiōnēs

Parse the words in bold.

barbarī ferōcēs **omnibus** cum cōpiīs trans **flūmen** parvum in fīnēs Rōmānōrum vēnerant. "tempus est" exclāmāvit sacerdōs "virtūtem nostram hostibus monstrāre! deī animum dīvīnum **Rōmānīs** dabunt. sī fortēs erimus, Rōma **incolumis** erit." ergō **cīvium** multitūdō, tria mīlia **mīlitum**, **arma** statim cēpit et contrā castra hostium **exībat**. sed in insidiās subitō **cecidērunt** mīlitēs nostrī. hominēs mille ducentīque equī periērunt, nam dux noster audax sed stultus erat. ā corporibus mīlitum miserōrum spolia **ingentia** cēpērunt barbarī.

Complete the following equations.

1. tria + quattuor = _____
2. duo + undecim = _____
3. octō + sex = _____
4. novem + duodēvīgintī = _____
5. vīgintī ūnum + _____ = centum duo
6. quinque + quindecim = _____
7. decem + nōnāgintā = _____
8. centum tria + undēvīgintī = _____
9. sescentī trīgintā + trecentī septuāgintā = _____
10. CXII + _____ = CC
11. DCCVI + M = _____
12. mille porcī + duo mīlia porcōrum = _____

Translate.

1. omnēs cīvēs ad lūdōs īre volunt, sed discipulī in lūdō manēbunt.
2. cōpiīs nostrīs magnam cōpiam argentī dedit dux potens.
3. Venus est in caelō, nōn in aede; nam dea caelestis est.
4. Rōmānī, tenebrās noctis nōlīte timēre.
5. terrēbant hostēs tenebrae mānēsque volucrēs.

6. in aedibus dominī meī penātēs māne laudāmus omnēs—dominus uxorque cum octō līberīs, tribus puerīs et quinque puellīs, et omnī servōrum familiā, hominum vīgintī.

7. sī in silvā manent lupī, pastōrēs omnibus deīs grātiās agunt.

8. post exsequiās celebrēs frātris meī cūr aquam, nōn vīnum, bibere māvultis?

9. ante fīnem bellī in fīnēs hostium celeriter ībunt Rōmānī, nec barbarōrum insidiās metuent.

10. vim cōpiārum nostrārum semper timēbunt barbarī, sed minae hostium inānēs mentēs mīlitum nostrōrum numquam terrēbunt.

11. Rōmulus, prīmus rex Rōmānōrum, dux celeber fortisque erat et spolia ingentia in aede deī ter posuit.

12. quamquam rex septimus malus ac turpis fuit, plebs Rōmāna mōrēs bonōs semper habēbat.

13. reliquiās tristēs urbis nostrae flammae crūdēlēs rapuērunt, quoniam nec moenia magna nec portae altae hostēs repellere potuerant.

14. cūr diū molliter dormīre vult discipulus piger, sī somnus mortī nōn dissimilis est? nonne quiētem in Ēlysiō omnibus mortālibus post mortem dabunt deī caelestēs?

15. quamquam difficile erat castra cottīdiē aedificāre, mīlitēs miserī labōrem nec levem nec mollem ferēbant; nam sī mīles piger ōtium māvult, tēla hostium in tergō mox accipit.

16. The unhappy shepherd's seven pigs, a small herd, fell into the two fierce wolves' trap.

17. My father had always praised his household gods.

18. I will write two letters to my sister tomorrow.

19. While all the citizens are watching your father's sad funeral, the humble farmer wants to show his three children the walls of Athens again.

20. The lazy soldier does not want to carry the greedy leader's spoils from the Romans' camp.

21. Without good character you will not be able to live happily in the territory of our people.

22. All the immortals wished to come to the wedding of the beautiful goddess.

23. Although the king and queen were old and ugly, they had four strong children, seven little dogs, and three huge horses.

24. Had the old sailor's savage dog been able to see the fat, warm entrails of the bull on the huge altar?

25. The tired soldiers have found a large amount of gold and silver under a huge tree, for the two ugly pirates did not wish to sail away from Italy with all the riches of our city.

Lectiōnēs Latīnae

Lege, Intellege

Roman Victories in the Second Century BC

Aemilius Paulus septuāgintā cīvitātēs Ēpirī, quae rebellābant, cēpit, praedam mīlitibus distribuit. Rōmam ingentī pompā rediit in nāve rēgis Perseī. triumphāvit autem magnificentissimē in currū aureō cum duōbus fīliīs. ductī sunt ante currum duo rēgis fīliī et ipse Perseus, XLV annōs nātus. post eum etiam Anīcius dē Illyriīs triumphāvit. Gentius cum frātre et fīliīs ante currum ductus est. ad hōc spectāculum rēgēs multārum gentium Rōmam vēnērunt; inter aliōs vēnērunt etiam Attalus atque Eumenēs, Asiae rēgēs, et Prūsiās Bithyniae. magnō honōre exceptī sunt et dōna in Capitōliō posuērunt. Prūsiās etiam fīlium suum Nīcomēdēn senātuī commendāvit.

—Eutropius, *Breviārium* 4.8

autem conj. but, and

1. Who were led in front of Anicius' triumphal chariot?
2. Who took seventy rebellious cities in Epirus?
3. Who accompanied Paulus in his triumphal chariot?
4. Name three kings who came to see Anicius' triumph.
5. Where did these kings place their gifts?

Ars Poētica

Ovid's Love Poetry IV

Identify the case of the words in bold.

1. *mīlitat* **omnis** *amans et habet sua* **castra** *Cupīdō.*
   Every lover is a soldier and Cupid has his own camp.

2. *quid geminās, Erycīna, meōs sine* **fīne** *dolōrēs?*
   Venus, why do you endlessly double my sorrows?

3. *in mediā pāce quid* **arma** *timēs?*
   Why do you fear arms in the midst of peace?

4. **tria** *vīpereō fēcimus ōra canī.*
   We invented three heads for the snaky dog. [Poets invented Cerberus, who guards the entrance to the Underworld.]

5. *fēcimus Enceladon iaculantem* **mille** *lacertīs.*
   We [the poets] invented Encelados [one of the Giants] throwing spears with his thousand arms.

6. ***centum*** *fronte oculōs, centum cervīce gerēbat*
   Argus—et hōs ūnus saepe fefellit Amor.
   Argus had a hundred eyes on his forehead and a hundred on his neck—and Cupid often deceived them, though there was only one of him.

7. ***duās ūnō*** *tempore turpis amō.*
   To my shame, I love two women at one time.

8. *coniugibus bellī causa* ***duōbus*** *erat.*
   She was a cause of war for two husbands.

Erycīna, -ae fem. 1 a cult title for Venus, who had a shrine on Mt. Eryx in western Sicily

Enceladon a Greek acc. sing. masc.

Aurea Dicta

1. *ad nova hominēs concurrunt, ad nōta nōn veniunt.* (Seneca the Elder)
2. *aurum et opēs, praecipuae bellōrum causae.* (Tacitus)
3. *fortūna opēs auferre potest, nōn animum.* (Seneca the Younger)
4. *frequens imitātiō transit in mōrēs.* (Quintilian)
5. *in servitūtem cadere dē regnō grave est.* (Seneca the Younger)
6. *incerta prō certīs, bellum quam pācem mālēbant.* (Sallust)
7. *iūs est ars bonī et aequī.* (Justinian's *Dīgesta*)
8. *iūs summum saepe summa est malitia.* (Terence)

opēs, opum fem. 3 resources, wealth

praecipuus, -a, -um foremost, particular

Hōrologia Latīna

1. *brevis hominum vīta.*
   The life of mankind is short.

2. *certa mihi mors, incerta est fūneris hōra.*
   Death is certain for me, the hour of death is uncertain.

3. *heu, heu, praeteritum nōn est revocābile tempus!*
   Alas, alas, time that has passed cannot be called back!

4. *sōl omnibus lūcet.*
   The sun shines for everyone.

5. *tempus breve est.*
   Time is short.

Lūsūs

Thēsaurus Verbōrum

English changes the *-us, -a, -um* inflection of many adjectives that end in *-īvus, -īva, -īvum* to a silent *-e*. For example:

accusātīvus[1]
adoptīvus
captīvus
dēfinītīvus
dēmonstrātīvus

festīvus
fugitīvus
furtīvus
nātīvus
passīvus

Vīta Rōmānōrum

The Origins of Words

The Romans were intensely curious about the origin of their language. We know from writers such as Quintilian that etymology was part of the curriculum in schools. Philosophers, especially the Stoics, and grammarians speculated on the subject; several treatises and handbooks with lists of possible etymologies have survived, most importantly Varro's *Dē Linguā Latīnā*, Festus' *Dē Verbōrum Significātū*, and Isidore's *Etymologiae Sīve Orīginēs*. Poets played endlessly with etymologies, as a way of displaying the sophistication, *doctrīna*, of their poetry.

The science of comparative linguistics is relatively modern; before the late eighteenth century, no one even realized that there was such a thing as the Indo-European family of languages, to which Latin and English belong. The Romans thought wrongly that Latin came from Greek; still, the associations they made between the two languages were often correct.

Many of the principles that the Romans used to determine the derivation of words now seem bizarrely unscientific. They often linked words for arbitrary or superficial reasons. For example:

- night is dangerous, therefore the Romans thought *nox, noctis* fem. 3 "night" came from *noceō, nocēre, nocuī, nocitum* 2 "to be harmful";

- triumphing generals wore a laurel crown, therefore *laurus, -ī* fem. 2 "laurel" was thought to come from *laus, laudis* fem. 3 "praise";

---

1. Likewise the names of all the other cases, and the term *adiectīvus* itself.

- anger makes a person act abnormally, therefore *īra, -ae* fem. 1 "anger" was thought to come from *īre ā sē* (3rd pers. reflexive pronoun [see Chapter 17]) "to go away from oneself";

- old people tend to be forgetful, therefore *senex, senis* masc. 3 "old man" supposedly came from *sē nescīre* (*sē* 3rd pers. reflexive pronoun [see Chapter 17], *nesciō, nescīre, nescīvī* 4) "not to know oneself."

The Romans often used this kind of association even when other explanations were readily available. Everyone knew that *barbarus* was not a purely Latin word, since it existed in Greek also. Nevertheless, some suggested that a barbarian was someone with a beard (*barba, -ae* fem. 1) who lived an unsophisticated life in the countryside (*rūs, rūris* neut. 3).

Sometimes words were explained as combinations of Greek and Latin elements: *thēsaurus, -ī* masc. 2 "treasure" is a Greek word (as the *th-* indicates), but it was explained as a "place (Greek *thes-*) for gold" (Latin *aurum, -ī* neut. 2).

These false etymologies are based on a supposed similarity in meaning, but the Romans also had the idea, inherited from the Greeks, that words with completely opposite meanings might still be related. Groves are shady and dark, therefore the origin of *lūcus, -ī* masc. 2 "grove" was *lux, lūcis* fem. 3 "light." School is a place for work, not play, therefore the origin of *lūdus, -ī* masc. 2 "school" was *lūdo, lūdere, lūsī, lūsum* 3 "play." (You will find more etymologizing *ē contrāriō* in Chapter 27.)

It may be that these etymologies were not always intended to be taken seriously. For example, the word for dagger is *sīca, -ae* fem. 1, which was generally thought to come from *secō, secāre, secuī, sectum* 1 "cut." Suetonius, however, tells the following story: "A gladiator was sent out to fight, but his sword got bent out of shape. Someone ran up to straighten it, but the gladiator said '*sīc hā pugnābō* (Oh, I'll fight like this)' and that is how the *sīca* came to be so called."

From now on, each chapter in this book will include a group of etymologies, usually related in theme. Some will give insights into the way the Romans thought, some will simply be amusing, **but only a minority will actually be true.** The following account of how Nigidius Figulus explained the origins of personal pronouns in the middle of the first century BC is culturally revealing (you'll learn these pronouns in Chapter 17):

In his *Notes on Grammar*, Publius Nigidius Figulus shows that nouns and verbs were not formed through chance attribution, but through a natural and rational impulse. Philosophers frequently discuss whether words occur naturally or are simply invented. Nigidius gives many arguments as to why words may seem to be natural rather than arbitrary. The following one struck me as particularly neat and appealing: "When we say *vōs* ["you" pl.], we employ a movement appropriate to the meaning of the word itself, gradually protruding our lips and directing our breath toward those with whom we are speaking. On the other hand, when we say *nōs* ["we," "us"], we do not pronounce the word with a strong impulse of the voice nor with our lips protruding; we keep our breath and our lips, as it were, within ourselves. The same applies to *tū* ["you" sing.], *ego* ["I"], and *tibi* ["for you" sing.] and *mihi* ["for me"]. Just as, when we nod in agreement or disagreement, the movement of our head or eyes corresponds to the nature of the subject, so there is a natural gesture in our mouth and breathing when we say these things. The same principle applies for both the Greek and the Latin words."

—Aulus Gellius, *Noctēs Atticae* 10.4

CHAPTER 11
Fourth and Fifth Declension Nouns

Fourth Declension Nouns

The fourth declension is small. Almost all the nouns in it are masculine and decline like *portus*, *portūs* "port," "harbor":

	SINGULAR	PLURAL
NOMINATIVE	port**us**	port**ūs**
GENITIVE	port**ūs**	port**uum**
DATIVE	port**uī**	port**ibus**
ACCUSATIVE	port**um**	port**ūs**
ABLATIVE	port**ū**	port**ibus**

A very few nouns in the fourth declension are neuter. They decline like *cornū*, *cornūs* "horn":

	SINGULAR	PLURAL
NOMINATIVE	corn**ū**	corn**ua**
GENITIVE	corn**ūs**	corn**uum**
DATIVE	corn**ū**	corn**ibus**
ACCUSATIVE	corn**ū**	corn**ua**
ABLATIVE	corn**ū**	corn**ibus**

Fifth Declension Nouns

The fifth declension is by far the smallest. All the nouns in it are feminine except *diēs*, *diēī* "day," and the compound *merīdiēs*, *-diēī* "midday" (*medius + diēs*). *merīdiēs* is always masculine, but *diēs* itself, for reasons that we do not now fully understand, is sometimes masculine and sometimes feminine.

All fifth declension nouns decline like *diēs*, except that, if the nominative singular has only one syllable, like **rēs**, the *e* in the genitive and dative singular ending is short (compare the genitive/dative **reī** with the genitive/dative **diēī**):

	SINGULAR	PLURAL
NOMINATIVE	di**ēs**	di**ēs**
GENITIVE	di**ēī**	di**ērum**
DATIVE	di**ēī**	di**ēbus**
ACCUSATIVE	di**em**	di**ēs**
ABLATIVE	di**ē**	di**ēbus**
VOCATIVE	di**ēs**	di**ēs**

	SINGULAR	PLURAL
NOMINATIVE	rēs	rēs
GENITIVE	reī	rērum
DATIVE	reī	rēbus
ACCUSATIVE	rem	rēs
ABLATIVE	rē	rēbus
VOCATIVE	rēs	rēs

VOCABULARY

Fourth Declension Nouns

Masculine

currus, currūs	chariot
equitātus, equitātūs	cavalry
exercitus, exercitūs	army
fluctus, fluctūs	wave
fructus, fructūs	fruit
impetus, impetūs	rush, onset
magistrātus, magistrātūs	magistrate, official
metus, metūs	fear
portus, portūs	port, harbor
senātus, senātūs	Senate
versus, versūs	verse
vultus, vultūs	face

Feminine

domus, domūs	house
manus, manūs	hand

Neuter

cornū, cornūs	horn, wing (of battle line)
gelū, gelūs	frost
genū, genūs	knee

Fifth Declension Nouns
Feminine

aciēs, aciēī	battle line
diēs, diēī (sometimes masculine; see above)	day
faciēs, faciēī	face
fidēs, fidēī	trust
rēs, reī	thing
speciēs, speciēī	form, appearance
spēs, speī	hope, expectation

Third Declension Nouns
Masculine

Caesar, Caesaris	Caesar
consul, consulis	consul
gladiātor, gladiātōris	gladiator
imperātor, imperātōris	commander, emperor
iuvenis (=*juvenis*), **iuvenis**	young man
pēs, pedis	foot
sanguis, sanguinis	blood

Feminine

lībertās, lībertātis	freedom
ōrātiō, ōrātiōnis	speech
pietās, pietātis	piety
senectūs, senectūtis	old age
vēritās, vēritātis	truth

Neuter

iter, itineris	journey
lītus, lītoris	shore
mūnus, mūneris	gift
ōmen, ōminis	omen
scelus, sceleris	crime

Adverbs

forte	by chance
sponte	spontaneously
vērō	truly

Vocabulary Notes

Apart from **domus** and **manus**, there are very few feminine nouns in the fourth declension. Many of the others are names of trees. *domus* is irregular; its abl. sing. is *domō*, not "domū," and its locative (see Chapter 15) is *domī*.

Prōlūsiōnēs

Parse the words in bold.

in **faciē** miserā magistrātūs **aegrī** spemque metumque vidēre poterant nautae **audācēs**. nam, quamquam minās **fluctuum** altōrum timēbat, tamen lūmina **portūs** parvī iam vidēbat. Rōmānīs semper rēs **gravis** erat domum penātēsque relinquere. ergō deīs immortālibus dōnum magnum, exta porcī **pinguis**, iam dederat **magistrātus**, namque in **portū** incolumis ē nāve **ingentī** exīre cupiēbat.

Change from singular to plural or vice versa, and then translate.

1. currus rēgis barbarī magnus est.
2. turpe fuit scelus iuvenis pulchrī.
3. dēforme est equī meī genū.
4. gladiātōrēs vultūs crūdēlēs habēbant.
5. fructūs ingentēs in manūs avārās magistrātuum pauperum dē arboribus ceciderant.
6. fluctus ingens ad lītus insulae vēnerat.
7. cornū potens taurī veteris metuistī.
8. consulis pinguis dē rē gravī ōrātiōnem longam nūper audīvī.
9. cum brevis est nox, tunc est diēs longa.
10. ante āram lūmen magnum, ōmen nōn leve, vīdit exercitūs Rōmānī imperātor.

Translate.

1. dum nāvēs in portū sunt, fluctūs maris nautās fortēs nōn terrent.
2. omnēs nāvēs ē portibus Ītaliae iam exierant, at Caesar trans fluctūs maris sine metū nāvigāvit.
3. quandō rosās dulcēs exercituī nostrō sponte dabitis, puellae?
4. pastōrem, porce dulcis, fēlīcem faciēs, nam faciēs tua tristis nōn est.

5. vultisne vultūs porcōrum meōrum dulcium māne spectāre?

6. cornua taurōrum sunt magna, at cornua porcī nōn habent.

7. faciem ingentem dulcemque habent porcī, sed sine cornibus; genuane habent?

8. gelū frīgidum nōn amant porcī, quoniam sanguinem calidum habent.

9. longa ferox mōvit, triste ōmen, cornua taurus.

10. dux exercitūs Rōmānī currūs hostium numquam timēbit.

11. ad parvum portum porcum pinguem portāre poteritis, puellae pigrae?

12. in aciē stāre rēs bona nōn est; nonne līberōs uxōrēsque vidēre mālunt mīlitēs?

13. ab aciē abīre nōn bonum est; num in hostium manibus urbem nostram vidēre vultis?

14. aciem Rōmānam impetus equitātūs nostrī paene frēgerat.

15. num sine spē victōriae currūs equitātusque hostium contrā mīlitēs nostrōs ācriter pugnāre poterunt?

16. The sad priestess placed lovely flowers softly onto the bull's horns.

17. I was unwilling to read the rich poet's shameful verses, because he always writes bad poems.

18. By chance all the magistrates were listening happily to the fat consul's short speech in the Senate.

19. Rex, my little dog, has a sweet face, but the faces of not all the Roman emperors were sweet.

20. Although the barbarians' customs are cruel, they praise many virtues of the Roman people, especially piety and trust and truth.

21. For a long time there was peace in our territory, but the Romans recently broke our hopes of freedom.

22. After many years, old age will come to the handsome young man, but wisdom will give a happy appearance to his old face.

23. Today is indeed a happy day, for the consul, a man like a heavenly god, has given sweet freedom to all the slaves.

24. You will be able to see anger on the cruel magistrate's stupid face, because the Senate is always empty when he wishes to warn the consuls about the truth of my speech.

25. Although he is fierce, the citizens will endure neither the king's stupidity nor his shameful crimes.

Lectiōnēs Latīnae

Lege, Intellege

Pliny the Elder (Gaius Plinius Secundus; c. AD 23–79) was the author of the *Historia Nātūrālis*, a thirty-seven-book encyclopedia, outstandingly influential for 1,500 years as the greatest single collection of ancient knowledge and thought. This is how Pliny himself defined the contents: *nātūra, hōc est vīta, narrātur* "Nature, that is to say life, is my theme." In fact, about one-third of the work is devoted to medicine and magical charms. Pliny's earlier works on history, language, and rhetoric, as well as a monograph on javelin-throwing written for cavalrymen, have not survived. While serving as commander of the fleet, he rowed across the Bay of Naples to investigate the eruption of Vesuvius, so he died in the interests of science.

Crocodiles

crocodīlum habet Nīlus, quadrupēs malum et terrā pariter ac flūmine infestum. ūnum hōc animal terrestre linguae ūsū caret, ūnum superiōre mōbilī maxillā imprimit morsum. magnitūdine excēdit plērumque duodēvīgintī cubita. parit ōva quanta anserēs, nec aliud animal ex minōre orīgine in maiōrem crescit magnitūdinem. unguibus armātus est, et contrā omnia vulnera cute densā. diēs in terrā agit, noctēs in aquā, tepōris utrumque ratiōne. hunc saturum cibō piscium et in lītore somnō datum parva avis, quae trochilos ibi vocātur, rex avium in Ītaliā, invītat ad hiandum pābulī suī grātiā, ōs prīmum eius adsultim repurgans, mox dentēs et faucēs quam maximē hiantēs; in quā voluptāte somnō pressum conspicātus ichneumōn, per faucēs ut tēlum immissus, ērōdit alvum.

—Pliny the Elder, *Historia Nātūrālis* 8.89

ūsū caret "lacks the use"	*avis, avis* fem. 3 bird
anser, anseris masc./fem. 3 goose	*ad hiandum* "to open its mouth wide"
tepor, tepōris masc. 3 heat	*ichneumōn, -ōnis* masc. 3 mongoose

1. What is the name in Italy for the little bird that cleans the crocodile's teeth?
2. What animal gnaws its way out of the crocodile's stomach?
3. Is the crocodile more formidable on land or in the river Nile?
4. Why does the crocodile spend its nights in the water?
5. Can the crocodile move its upper jaw?

Ars Poētica

Ovid's Love Poetry V
Identify and explain the case of the nouns in bold.

1. *festa **diēs** Veneremque vocat **cantūs**que merumque.*
   A holiday calls for Venus and songs and unmixed wine.

2. *carmina sanguineae dēdūcunt **cornua** lūnae.*
   Songs draw down the horns of the bloody moon.

3. *purpureus lūnae sanguine **vultus** erat.*
   The face of the moon was bright with blood.

4. *candida seu tacitō vīdit mē fēmina vultū,*
     *in **vultū** tacitās arguis esse notās.*
   Or if a fair woman has looked at me with a silent face, you claim that there are silent signs in her face.

5. *ad mea formōsōs **vultūs** adhibēte, puellae, carmina.*
   Turn your lovely faces to my songs, girls.

6. *timor ūnus erat, **faciēs** nōn ūna timōris.*
   There was one fear, but not just one appearance of fear.

Aurea Dicta

1. *avāritia et luxuriēs omnia magna imperia ēvertērunt.* (Livy)

2. *crēdula rēs amor est.* (Ovid)

3. *iuvenīle vitium est, regere nōn posse impetum.* (Seneca the Younger)

4. *lūdit in hūmānīs dīvīna potentia rēbus.* (Ovid)

5. *māter omnium bonārum rērum sapientia.* (Cicero)

6. *mīlitāris sine duce turba corpus est sine spīritū.* (Quintus Curtius)

7. *mīlitiae speciēs amor est.* (Ovid)

8. *nōlīte, quod pigrī agricolae faciunt, mātūrōs fructūs per inertiam āmittere ē manibus.* (Quintus Curtius)

Hōrologia Latīna

1. *ad occāsum tendimus omnēs.*
   We are all heading to sunset.

2. *sīcut umbra diēs nostrī.*
   Our days are as a shadow.

3. *sōlis et umbrae concordia.*
   The agreement of sun and shadow.

4. *tempus fugit velut umbra.*
   Time flies like a shadow.

5. *tenēre nōn potes, potes nōn perdere diem.*
   You cannot hold the day back, but you can avoid wasting it.

Lūsūs

Thēsaurus Verbōrum

Here are some adjectives in *-idus, -ida, -idum* that have survived in English without the endings *-us, -a, -um*:

āridus	languidus	putridus	stolidus
avidus	limpidus	rabidus	stupidus
candidus	liquidus	rancidus	tepidus
fervidus	līvidus	rapidus	timidus
flaccidus	lūcidus	rigidus	torridus
flōridus	lūridus	solidus	turbidus
frīgidus	morbidus	sordidus	turgidus
horridus	pallidus	splendidus	validus
intrepidus	placidus	squālidus	vapidus

Etymologiae Antīquae

In his *Institūtiō Ōrātōria* (1.6.31), Quintilian introduces the study of etymology with these examples of familiar proper names:

> *unde Brūtī, Publicolae, Pythicī? cūr Latium, Ītalia, Beneventum? quae Capitōlium et collem Quirīnālem et Argīlētum appellandī ratiō?*

> Where do the names Brutus, Publicola, Pythicus come from? Why Latium, Italy, Beneventum? What is the reason for the Capitol, the Quirinal Hill, the Argiletum being so called?

***Brūtus**, -ī* masc. 2. *brūtus, -a, -um* means "stupid." Lucius Junius accepted this taunting *cognōmen* (nickname) so that he would not seem to pose a threat to the last king of Rome, Tarquinius Superbus, and could bide his time, waiting for an opportunity to overthrow the monarchy.

***Publicola**, -ae* masc. 1. Publius Valerius worked to overthrow the monarchy, was consul four times in the early years of the Republic, and was given this *cognōmen* because he cultivated (*colō, -ere, coluī, cultum* 3) the support of the people (*populus, -ī* masc. 2).

***Pythicus**, -ī* masc. 2. If this is a Roman *cognōmen*, we don't know its precise significance. It may be associated with the Pythian shrine of Apollo at Delphi, and there were several different explanations for the name of the shrine. According to one account, Apollo killed a snake there that was so vast that the Delphians could not remove its corpse, which rotted (Greek πύθεσθαι [*puthesthai*]) in the sun.

For ***Latium*** and ***Ītalia***, see pp. 188 and 189.

***Beneventum**, -ī* neut. 2. This town in southern Italy was called *Maleventum* by its Greek founders, but that sounded like an ill-omened name to Latin speakers ("badly come"). Similarly, it was said that the founder of Rome, Aeneas, had originally given the name *Egesta* to a Sicilian city. The name was supposedly changed because it sounded too much like the Latin word *egestās, -ātis* fem. 3 "destitution," and the city became *Segesta*.

For the ***Capitol*** and ***Quirinal*** Hills, see p. 174.

***Argīlētum**, -ī* neut. 2. The Argiletum was a street that entered the Forum near the Senate-house. The most plausible explanation of the name connects it with *argilla, -ae* fem. 1 "clay," for the clay pits that supposedly once existed there. It was also said to commemorate the death (*lētum, -ī* neut. 2) of a certain Argus, killed there in pre-Roman times, or of a senator named Argillus, torn to pieces in the Senate for suggesting that the Romans should negotiate a peace with Carthage after the Battle of Cannae in 216 BC.

Vīta Rōmānōrum

Modern Decadence

Seneca the Younger (4 BC–AD 65) somehow managed to be both a committed Stoic philosopher and a prominent advisor to the young emperor Nero. As you read the following diatribe, one of his many denunciations of contemporary society, bear in mind that Seneca was among the wealthiest men in the world at the time. Here, however, he is preaching what he practiced: the historian Tacitus records that, when Nero forced Seneca to commit suicide, his frugal diet had weakened him so much that he had difficulty bleeding himself to death.

> The requirements of the body are very slight: it needs shelter from cold, and nourishment to allay hunger and thirst. Any desires beyond that cater to our vices, not to our needs. It is not necessary to scour the depths of every sea nor to burden our bellies by slaughtering animals, nor to dig out shellfish from the farthest shores of unknown seas: may the gods and goddesses damn those whose decadence even passes the boundaries of the empire that already makes others hate us! They want game caught beyond the river Phasis [which flows into the Black Sea] to supply their pretentious kitchens, and they are not ashamed to seek birds from the Parthians [longtime enemies of Rome in western Asia]. . . . From every quarter they import everything that may tickle a fastidious palate. Things that their stomachs, ruined by rich food, can scarcely tolerate are imported from the farthest ocean. They vomit to eat; they eat to vomit, and the banquets they search for through the whole world they do not deign to digest. If a man despises such things, what harm can poverty do him? If he does desire them, poverty is actually a benefit to him, for he is cured against his will. . . . Caligula, whom Nature seems to have produced so as to show the effect of combining the extremes of vice and power, spent ten million sesterces on a single dinner; although assisted by the ingenuity of all his companions, he had difficulty finding a way to turn the tribute of three provinces into that one dinner. What wretches, whose palates are excited only by expensive dishes! It is not the dishes' exquisite flavor nor their appeal to the taste which makes them expensive, it is their rarity and the difficulty in obtaining them. . . . I should like to ask these people: "Why launch your ships? Why arm your hands against both wild beasts and your fellow men? Why rush to and fro in such a frenzy? Why pile riches upon riches? Will you not give a thought to how puny your bodies are? Is it not madness and the most extreme delusion to desire so much when you can hold so little?"

—Seneca the Younger, *Dē Consōlātiōne ad Helviam Mātrem* 10. 2–6

Comparative and Superlative Forms of Adjectives and Adverbs

Adjectives

Adjectives have three degrees, the **positive**, the **comparative**, and the **superlative**. So far, the only one of these we have seen is the positive, which simply modifies a noun by giving it a particular quality: for example, "Cupid is cruel."

Positive: Cupid is **cruel**, but **small**.
Comparative: Cupid is **more cruel** than any other god, but **smaller**.
Superlative: Cupid is **the most cruel** of all the gods, but **the smallest**.

As these examples show, to form regular comparative and superlative adjectives in English you add "more" and "the most" or the suffixes -*er* and -*est*. For most Latin adjectives, you add suffixes to the basic positive form. **These suffixes are the same for both groups of adjectives, whether first/second declension or third.**

Here is the declension of the comparative *cārior, -ius,* "dearer." You will notice that the basic stem is *cārior,* which is the same as the nominative (and vocative) singular form for both masculine and feminine. The neuter nominative/vocative and accusative singular is a special form: *cārius.* In the other neuter forms, you add to *cārior* the same endings used for neuter third declension nouns like *carmen, carminis.*

	SINGULAR	PLURAL
Masc. and Fem.		
NOMINATIVE	cārior	cāriōrēs
GENITIVE	cāriōris	cāriōrum
DATIVE	cāriōrī	cāriōribus
ACCUSATIVE	cāriōrem	cāriōrēs
ABLATIVE	cāriōre	cāriōribus
Neuter		
NOMINATIVE	cārius	cāriōra
GENITIVE	cāriōris	cāriōrum
DATIVE	cāriōrī	cāriōribus
ACCUSATIVE	cārius	cāriōra
ABLATIVE	cāriōre	cāriōribus

You use the same procedure to form the comparative of regular third declension adjectives, such as *dulcis* and *fēlix*: dulc**ior**, dulc**iōris**, etc., "sweeter," and fēlīc**ior**, fēlīc**iōris**, etc., "happier."

To construct the superlative forms of almost all adjectives, add the suffixes *-issimus*, *-issima*, *-issimum* to the base of the positive. These superlative forms will then decline like any first/second declension adjective of the type *cārus, -a, -um*. The declension of *cārissimus, -issima, -issimum* "dearest," "very dear," is as follows:

	SINGULAR	PLURAL
NOMINATIVE	cārissimus, -a, -um	cārissimī, -ae, -a
GENITIVE	cārissimī, -ae, -ī	cārissimōrum, -ārum, -ōrum
DATIVE	cārissimō, -ae, -ō	cārissimīs, -īs, -īs
ACCUSATIVE	cārissimum, -am, -um	cārissimōs, -ās, -a
ABLATIVE	cārissimō, -ā, -ō	cārissimīs, -īs, -īs

You use the same procedure to form the superlative of regular third declension adjectives, such as *dulcis* and *fēlix*: dulc**issimus**, etc., "sweetest," "very sweet," fēlīc**issimus**, etc., "happiest," "very happy."

Exceptional Superlative Forms

All adjectives ending in *-er*, whether first/second declension, like *miser, misera, miserum* and *pulcher, pulchra, pulchrum*, or third declension, like *ācer, ācris, ācre*, construct their comparative forms in the normal way. The distinction remains between adjectives that keep the *-er* ending, like *miser* (*miserior*, etc.), and those that drop the *-e*, like *pulcher* and *ācer* (*pulchrior*, etc., *ācrior*, etc.).

In the superlative, however, all of these adjectives keep the full *-er* ending. They all take the superlative endings *-rimus*, *-rima*, *-rimum*, rather than *-issimus*, *-issima*, *-issimum*.

miser, misera, miserum	miserior, -ius	miser**rimus**, -a, -um
pulcher, pulchra, pulchrum	pulchrior, -ius	pulcher**rimus**, -a, -um
ācer, ācris, ācre	ācrior, -ius	ācer**rimus**, -a, -um

Six adjectives, *facilis, difficilis, gracilis, humilis, similis*, and *dissimilis*, also form their comparatives in the normal way, but their superlative endings are *-limus, -lima, -limum*.

facilis, facile	facilior, facilius	facil**limus**, -a, -um
humilis, humile	humilior, humilius	humil**limus**, -a, -um

facilis, facile	easy
difficilis, difficile	difficult
gracilis, gracile	thin
humilis, humile	humble
similis, simile + gen. or dat.	like, similar to
dissimilis, dissimile + gen. or dat.	unlike

Irregular Comparative and Superlative Forms of Adjectives

There are a few irregular comparative and superlative adjectives, but you need to learn only their irregular stem or stems. Then you combine the stem with the regular endings, in exactly the same way as for *cārus*, *dulcis*, and *fēlix*. Some of these adjectives have no positive form.

bonus, melior, optimus	good, better, best
———, **dēterior, dēterrimus**	———, worse, worst
———, **exterior, extrēmus**	———, outer, farthest
———, **inferior, infimus**	———, lower, lowest
———, **interior, intimus**	———, interior, innermost
magnus, maior, maximus	big, bigger, biggest
malus, peior, pessimus	bad, worse, worst
———, **posterior, postrēmus**	———, later, last
———, **prior, prīmus**	———, former, first
———, **propior, proximus**	———, nearer, nearest
———, **superior, suprēmus**	———, higher, highest
———, **ulterior, ultimus**	———, farther, farthest

maior (= *major*) gives us the word "major" and sounds like "my-or," with the letters *a* and *i* forming a very unusual diphthong. Similarly, **peior** sounds like "pay-or."

The comparative and superlative of *multus* and *parvus* are special cases.

multus, plūs, plūrimus	much, more, most
parvus, minor (minus), minimus	small, smaller, smallest

minor is not very irregular; it uses the normal comparative endings, but without the *-i*.

The comparative *plūs* is more irregular. In the singular, it only exists as a neuter noun. In the plural, it is an adjective:

	NEUT. SING.	MASC./FEM. PL.	NEUT. PL.
NOMINATIVE	plūs	plūrēs	plūra
GENITIVE	plūris	plūrium	plūrium
DATIVE	plūrī	plūribus	plūribus
ACCUSATIVE	plūs	plūrēs	plūra
ABLATIVE	plūre	plūribus	plūribus

Since the plural forms are adjectives, they simply agree with the noun they modify. Since the singular is a noun, it is usually accompanied by another noun in the genitive. In practice, this means that the singular will be used with **uncountable nouns** such as *amor* and *potentia*, while the plural will be used with **countable nouns** such as *equus* and *carmen*. For example:

NEUT. SING.	MASC./FEM. PL.	NEUT. PL.
plūs potentiae	plūrēs equī	plūra carmina
plūris potentiae	plūrium equōrum	plūrium carminum
plūrī potentiae	plūribus equīs	plūribus carminibus
plūs potentiae	plūrēs equōs	plūra carmina
plūre potentiae	plūribus equīs	plūribus carminibus

Adverbs

As we saw in Chapters 6 and 9, to form the positive adverb, regular adjectives of the first/second declension add the ending *-ē* to the base, while regular adjectives of the third declension add *-iter* to the base.

Adjective		Adverb	
cārus, -a, -um	dear	*cārē*	dearly
pulcher, pulchra, pulchrum	beautiful	*pulchrē*	beautifully
miser, misera, miserum	wretched	*miserē*	wretchedly
gravis, -e	heavy	*graviter*	heavily
fēlīx, fēlīcis	happy	*fēlīciter*	happily
celer, celeris, celere	swift	*celeriter*	swiftly

You need to know the following common **irregular adverbs**:

Adjective		Adverb	
bonus	good	**bene**	well
facilis	easy	**facile**	easily
magnus	big	**magnopere**	greatly
malus	bad	**male**	badly
multus	many	**multum**	much
parvus	small	**parum**	not much

magnopere means literally "with great work," formed with the ablative of the noun *opus, operis* neut. 3.

Only the short final *e* makes *male* irregular.

Comparative and Superlative Adverbs

Like adjectives, adverbs have three degrees, positive, comparative, and superlative, but, unlike adjectives, they have only one form for each degree. For their comparative form, almost all adverbs use the neuter accusative singular of the comparative of the adjective. They construct their superlative by substituting *-ē* for the *-us, -a, -um* endings of the superlative form of the adjective.

Positive	*Comparative*	*Superlative*
cārē	cārius	cārissimē
pulchrē	pulchrius	pulcherrimē
graviter	gravius	gravissimē
fēlīciter	fēlīcius	fēlīcissimē
bene	**melius**	**optimē**
facile	facilius	facillimē
male	**peius**	**pessimē**

You will need to learn the following adverbs separately, however, because they are strongly irregular:

Positive	*Comparative*	*Superlative*
magnopere greatly	**magis** more	**maximē** most
multum much	**plūs** more	**plūrimum** most
parum little	**minus** less	**minimē** least
———	**prius** before	**prīmō** at first
		prīmum first

Adverbs Not Related to Adjectives

Many adverbs are not derived from adjectives at all. You have already seen the adverbs of time *crās, diū, herī, hodiē, mox, numquam, nunc, nūper, saepe, semper, tum*; the adverbs of place *circā/-um, procul, prope*; and the numerical adverbs *semel, bis, ter*, and so on. Here are some more adverbs that are not derived from adjectives. Their meaning restricts most of them to the positive degree—it is not likely that we would want to say "more everywhere" or "very meanwhile."

A substantial group of adverbs end in *-im* (you will recognize several that are now English words):

furtim	stealthily	**interim**	meanwhile
ōlim	at some time	**partim**	partly
passim	everywhere	**paulātim**	gradually
statim	immediately	**verbātim**	word for word

The following adverbs are related to the pronouns *hīc* "this" and *ille* "that" (see Chapter 17).

hīc	here	**illīc**	there
hinc	from here	**illinc**	from there
hūc	to here	**illūc**	to there

Most Latin prepositions were originally adverbs, and some later retained that function. For example, the following words can be either adverbs **or** prepositions that take the accusative case:

circā/-um	around	**intrā**	inside
extrā	outside	**prope**	near(by)
infrā	below	**suprā**	above

Special Meanings of the Comparative and Superlative

In Latin the comparative and superlative forms of adjectives and adverbs have additional meanings that these forms do not have in English. These meanings are highlighted below.

Comparative

Amor crūdēlior est	Cupid is more cruel [than other gods]. Cupid is **rather cruel**. Cupid is **too cruel**.
Amor hominēs crūdēlius tangit	Cupid affects people more cruelly [than other gods]. Cupid affects people **rather cruelly**. Cupid affects people **too cruelly**.

If you think about them, these special meanings still involve an implicit comparison; Cupid is/acts more/rather/too cruel(ly) **in comparison to others**.

Superlative

Amor crūdēlissimus est	Cupid is the cruellest [of all the gods]. Cupid is **very cruel**.
Amor hominēs crūdēlissimē tangit	Cupid affects people in the cruelest way. Cupid affects people in a **very cruel** way.

quam with the Comparative and Superlative

In comparative statements, the two terms being compared are linked by the comparative form of the adjective (*dulcior, cārior, peior*, etc.) followed by *quam*, and **both are in the same case**:

*equus **maior quam** porcus est.*	A horse is **bigger than** a pig.
*equum **maiōrem quam** porcum meum videō.*	I see a horse **bigger than** my pig.
*porcō meō **maiōrī quam** equō cibum dō.*	I give food to my pig (which is) **bigger than** a horse.

quam may also be placed directly before a superlative adjective or adverb to express the idea "as . . . as possible":

canis dominō quam cārissimus est.	The dog is as dear as possible to its owner.
librum quam difficillimum discipulō dedit magister.	The teacher gave the student the most difficult book possible.
equus quam gravissimē cecidit.	The horse fell as heavily as could be.

The Ablative of Comparison

Another way to express comparison is to put the second term being compared in the ablative, **provided that the first term is in the nominative, vocative, or accusative**. For example:

*equus **porcō** maior est.*   A horse is bigger **than a pig**.
*equum **porcō meō** maiōrem videō.*   I see a horse bigger **than my pig**.

Perhaps you can see why the ablative of comparison won't work with, for example, the dative case. A noun in the dative (as an indirect object, for instance) will often look exactly like an ablative, so that it would be impossible to tell which noun is bigger (or more sacred or fiercer, etc.), and which noun is an ablative of comparison. "porcō meō maiōrī [dat.] equō [abl.] cibum dō" is not Latin for "I give food to my pig [which is] bigger than a horse"; the meaning might as easily be "I give food to a horse [which is] bigger than my pig."

Prōlūsiōnēs

Parse the words in bold.

templa **plūrima** aedificāvērunt ōlim Rōmānī, sed omnibus **deīs potentior** erat Iuppiter **Optimus Maximus**. dōna quam **pulcherrima** ad arcem urbis **suprēmam** ferēbant sacerdōtēs. exta calida pecudis **minōris** deō potentissimō saepe dabant, sed taurum, animal **fortissimum** et **ācerrimum**, caedere mālēbant.

Translate, then change the adjectives first to comparative, then to superlative forms.

1. pastōrī parvō cārī sunt porcī.
2. aprī sunt animālia audācia.
3. lupī sunt magnī.
4. ācris est mens porcī.
5. pigrum porcum nōn amō.
6. humilis est casa pastōris miserī.
7. aprī malī sunt et ferōcēs.
8. agnus gracilis mātrī pinguī dissimilis est.
9. gladiātōrēs tristēs an magistrum bonum vidēre māvīs?
10. rēs gravis est turpem amīcum habēre.

Translate.

1. Iūnō est dea pulchra, Minerva pulchrior, sed Venus omnium deārum pulcherrima.
2. num verba Veneris, ventō leviōra volucerrimō, audīre voluit pastor?
3. avārior lupō est pīrāta, sed nōbilitātis Rōmānae mōrēs dēteriōrēs sunt.
4. casā arbor altior est, arbore mons.
5. nonne facilius est agrum cum taurō quam cum porcō, animālī humiliōre, arāre?
6. scelus peius est magistrātūs Rōmānōs quam hostium rēgem caedere.
7. porcus prīmus casam bonam aedificāvit, secundus meliōrem, sed tertius optimam.
8. agricolae fīlia agnam minimam, nōn porcōs agnā maiōrēs, amābat.
9. dulciōrēs sunt fructūs arborum meārum quam tuārum.
10. quamquam vīta morte dulcior est, tamen prō amīcīs perīre quam dulcissimum est.
11. officium Mercuriī est cīvēs fortissimōs post mortem in Ēlysium, mānium domum fēlīcem, dūcere.
12. plūs pecūniae habet consul avārissimus quam agricolae pauperrimī, quod maximam aurī cōpiam in intimā parte domūs meae nūper invēnit.
13. si cibum porcōrum gracillimōrum abstulit canis pessimus lupīsque omnibus audācior, ūvās plūrēs gregī miserrimō iam fer, serve stultissime!
14. in extremam Ītaliae partem cōpiās trans flūmen humillimum Caesar, vir dēterrimus, ācriter transmīsit; ergō bellum quam pessimum contrā senātum Rōmānum incēpit.
15. Iuppiter, rex deōrum, omnibus mortālibus fortior est, sed Venus omnibus mortālibus dea cārissima est, quamquam dea crūdēlissima plūs dolōris quam amōris hominibus dat.

16. Is the first day of our life the happiest?
17. The king of the very large city has more gold, but the farmers have more pigs.
18. Surely the king is not happier than the farmers?
19. The very bad teacher was unwilling to give more books to his best students.
20. The biggest chariot is carrying the very brave leader as quickly as possible out of the enemy camp, because he wishes to fight against our battle line.
21. If you are not a very good man, you will never be the leader of our army.
22. Why are you not bringing water back from the very cold river, you most wretched slave?
23. The lambs on the higher mountains are sweeter, but in the fields near the city they are bigger and sleep more softly.
24. I do not wish to give more food to the fat pigs, for they will be heavier than my cows.
25. Although the enemy have longer weapons than the Romans, it is not very easy to take our city, for it has very high walls.

Lectiōnēs Latīnae

Lege, Intellege

Advice for Generals I

Vegetius' *Excerpta Dē Rē Mīlitārī* is the only complete surviving Roman manual on warfare. It was probably written in the late fourth century AD, but it draws on earlier, classical models. The following maxims are selected from the conclusion of his third and final book.

> aut inōpiā aut terrōre melius est hostem domāre quam proeliō, in quō plūs solet fortūna
>   potestātis habēre quam virtūs.
> dēbēmus id sōlum agere, quod nōbīs ūtile iūdicāmus.
> exercitus labōre prōficit, ōtiō consenescit.
> mīlitēs timor et poena in castrīs corrigit, in expedītiōne spēs ac praemia faciunt meliōrēs.
> paucōs virōs fortēs nātūra prōcreat, bonā institūtiōne plūrēs reddit industria.
> quī frūmentum necessāriaque nōn praeparat, vincitur sine ferrō.
> quī pauciōrēs infirmiōrēsque habēre sē nōvit, ex ūnō latere aut montem aut cīvitātem
>   aut mare aut fluvium aut aliquod dēbet habēre subsidium.
> quī sinistram ālam fortissimam habēre sē nōvit, dextram ālam hostis invādere dēbet.

inōpia, -ae fem. 1 shortage of supplies

frūmentum, -i neut. 2 grain

quī pauciōrēs infirmiōrēsque habēre sē nōvit "[A general] who knows that he has fewer and weaker troops"

latus, lateris neut. 3 side

sinister, sinistra, sinistrum on the left

āla, -ae fem. 1 wing

1. Where should a general use fear and punishment to control his troops?

2. What geographical or other features should a commander exploit if he knows his troops are outnumbered or weaker than the enemy?

3. If his own left wing is very strong, which part of the enemy line should a general attack?

4. Why is it better to overcome the enemy by cutting his supplies and intimidating him rather than by engaging in an actual battle?

5. What is the effect of idleness on an army?

Ars Poētica

Ovid's Love Poetry VI
Parse the words in bold.

1. *damnōsus pecorī curris, damnōsior **agrīs**.*
   [speaking to a river in flood]: You run [and are] ruinous to the flock, more ruinous to the fields.

2. ***fertilior** seges est aliēnīs semper in agrīs,*
   *vīcīnumque pecus **grandius** ūber habet.*
   The crop is always more fertile in other people's fields, and the neighboring flock has larger udders.

3. *monte **minor** collis, campīs erat altior aequīs.*
   There was a hill smaller than a mountain, but higher than the level plains.

4. *quid magis est saxō dūrum, quid **mollius** undā?*
   What is more hard than a rock, what is softer than a wave?

5. *mē nova sollicitat, mē tangit **sērior** aetās;*
   *haec **melior**, speciē corporis illa placet.*
   A young age attracts me, a more mature age touches me; the latter is better, but the former pleases with the appearance of her body.

6. *plūra sunt semper **dēteriōra** bonīs.*
   There are always more worse things than good things.

7. *omnia fēmineā sunt ista libīdine mōta;*
   *ācrior est nostrā, plūsque **furōris** habet.*
   All those things were caused by women's lust; it is fiercer than ours, and has more madness.

fertilis, -e fertile
grandis, -e large
sērus, -a, -um late
furor, furōris masc. 3 madness

Aurea Dicta

1. *ācerrima proximōrum odia sunt.* (Tacitus)
2. *etiam prūdentissimī peccant.* (Seneca the Younger)
3. *famēs ac frīgus miserrima mortis genera.* (Livy)
4. *fortūna miserrima tūta est, nam timor ēventūs dēteriōris abest.* (Ovid)
5. *in līberō populō imperia lēgum potentiōra sunt quam hominum.* (Livy)

6. *inertia atque torpēdō plūs dētrīmentī facit quam exercitiō.* (Cato)

7. *melle dulcī dulcior tū es.* (Plautus)

8. *ūsus efficācissimus rērum omnium magister.* (Pliny the Elder)

peccō 1 sin, make a mistake

tūtus, -a, -um safe

mel, mellis neut. 3 honey

Hōrologia Latīna

1. *aetās citō pede praeterit.*
   Time goes by with swift foot.

2. *cum sōl abest obmutescō.*
   When the sun is absent, I am dumb.

3. *eō breviōrēs, quō grātiōrēs.*
   The more welcome [the hours], the shorter [they are].

4. *sōl mē, vōs umbra regit.*
   The sun rules me, my shadow rules you.

5. *umbrās umbra regit, pulvis et umbra sumus.*
   The shadow rules shadows, we are dust and shadow.

Lūsūs

Thēsaurus Verbōrum

English changes the final *-a* of many first declension Latin nouns ending in *-ūra* to a silent *-e*; for example, "capture" is derived from *captūra, -ae*, "censure" from *censūra, -ae*.

creātūra	fractūra	pictūra
cultūra	iunctūra (*junctūra*)	statūra
cūra	mixtūra	structūra
figūra	nātūra	textūra

Etymologiae Antīquae

Deī Rōmānī I

Since the Romans believed that understanding the origin of a word gave insights into its essential meaning, they were especially interested in the names of gods and goddesses. Although *deus* itself was generally considered to be the same word as the Greek θεός (*theos*), some proposed other etymologies: perhaps most interesting is the idea that *deus* came from δέος (*deos*) "fear," indicating that the Romans did not see the gods as completely benign.

Apollō, Apollinis masc. 3. The only one of the great Olympian gods whose name the Romans preserved in its Greek form (᾽Απόλλων) without proposing a Latin etymology. Apollo is linked for various reasons with the verb ἀπόλλυναι (*apollunai*) "destroy": his splendor, as sun god, destroys vegetation and is itself destroyed when the sun sets; as god of medicine, he destroys living creatures by means of diseases. As sun god, he brandishes (ἀποπάλλειν [*apopallein*]) the rays of the sun. As god of medicine, he drives away (ἀπελαύνειν [*apelaunein*]) diseases. He also, because of his importance, stands apart from others (ἀπ᾽ ἄλλων [*ap' allon*]) or from the masses (ἀ-πολλῶν [*a – pollon*]).

Cerēs, Cereris fem. 3. Ceres brings (*gerō, -ere, gessī, gestum* 3) crops.

Diāna, -ae fem. 1. As goddess of hunting, Diana seeks out lonely woods far from roads (*dēvius, -a, -um*). As goddess of the moon, she makes the night like day (*diēs, diēī* masc./fem. 5). As goddess of childbirth, she brings children to the light of day. A similar etymology, from *lux, lūcis* fem. 3 light, was current for Lucina, identified sometimes with Diana, sometimes with Juno.

Dīs, Dītis masc. 3. The god of the Underworld is rich (*dīves, dīvitis*) because all things arise from the earth and return to it. See also p. 348.

Iūnō, Iūnōnis fem. 3 and *Iuppiter, Iovis* masc. 3, the queen and king of the gods, both help (*iuvō, -āre, iūvī, iūtum* 1) mankind.

Līber, Līberī masc. 2. The god of wine frees (*līberō* 1) us from our cares. See also p. 348.

Vīta Rōmānōrum

Trades and Professions

The wealth of Rome's political and social èlite was for centuries largely generated by their vast estates. Since they did not need to work for a living, they could afford to hold influential but unpaid political and judicial positions. As a very rich landowner in his hometown of Arpinum, not far from Rome, Cicero was a *domī nōbilis*, "a man of distinction at home." At the same time, he was a *novus homō*, "a new man," the first member of his family to reach senatorial rank. Members of the old patrician (that is, aristocratic) families probably regarded him as an upstart, but he adopted their snobbish attitude to working for a living:

As regards which trades and other means of livelihood are to be considered proper for a gentleman and which are to be considered sordid, here is the conventional wisdom. First of all, those occupations which make people dislike a man are frowned upon: for example, tax-collecting and money-lending. The occupation of any hired workman is unworthy of a gentleman, for it involves selling labor, not skill. A hired workman's payment is just a recompense for slavery. Those who buy from merchants for immediate retail sale are also to be thought vulgar, for they cannot make a profit without telling lies, and there is nothing more shameful than deceit. All craftsmen engage in a vulgar occupation, for there can be nothing refined about a workshop. The least respectable occupations are those which cater to the sensual pleasures: "fishmongers, butchers, cooks, sellers of poultry, fishermen," as Terence says [*Eunuch* 257]. You may wish to add perfumers, dancers, the whole performing troupe. Professions which require greater intelligence or which are particularly beneficial—for example, medicine, architecture, teaching the liberal arts—these are respectable for those whose social class makes them suitable. Trade is to be thought vulgar, if it is on a small scale. If, however, it is on a large scale, importing many different wares from many different places and distributing them to many people without deceit, it is not to be much disparaged. Such business actually deserves strong commendation if those who engage in it, when they are not gorged but satisfied with their profits, make their way from the harbor to an estate in the country, just as they have often made their way from the deep sea into the harbor. But, of all the ways to make a living, nothing is better, nothing is more productive, nothing sweeter, nothing more worthy of a free man than agriculture.

—Cicero, *Dē Officiīs* 1.150–51

CHAPTER 13
Correlative Adjectives and Adverbs, Irregular Adjectives

Correlative Adjectives and Adverbs

In Chapter 4 you learned how to use *et . . . et . . .* "both . . . and . . ." and *nec . . . nec . . .* "neither . . . nor . . ." to construct a relation between words or clauses. Similarly, certain adjectives and adverbs can work in pairs or "correlatively," in order to construct a comparison between the two parts of a complex sentence. The comparison usually involves quantity or size. The following pairs are particularly important. Their similar "rhyming" forms will help you remember them.

Adj./ Adv.		Correlative	
tam adv.	so, as	**quam** adv.	how, as
tālis, -e adj.	of such a sort	**quālis, -e** adj.	what sort of, as
tantus, -a, -um adj.	so much/great	**quantus, -a, -um** adj.	how much/great, as
tot indecl. adj.	so many	**quot** indecl. adj.	how many, as
totiens adv.	so often	**quotiens** adv.	how often, as

In sentences structured in this way, the second term (*quam, quālis* etc.), regardless of its literal meaning, is almost always equivalent to "as." For example:

porcus nōn tam ferox est quam aper.	A pig is not as fierce as a wild boar.
porcus nōn tālis est quālis aper.	A pig is not of such a sort as a wild boar.
porcus corpus nōn tantum habet quantum aper.	A pig does not have as big a body as does a wild boar.
in silvā nōn sunt tot porcī quot aprī.	In the wood there are not as many pigs as wild boars.
in silvā porcōs nōn totiens vidēmus quotiens aprōs.	In the wood we do not see pigs as often as wild boars.

tam, tālis, and so on can also be used on their own, in statements, exclamations, or questions. For example:

aprī sunt tam ferōcēs!	Wild boars are so fierce!
tālēs porcōs nōn timeō.	I am not afraid of such pigs.
in silvā aprōs totiens vidēmus!	We see wild boars in the wood so often!

quam, quālis, and so on can be used on their own, too, introducing either exclamations or questions. For example:

quam ferox est aper!	How fierce the wild boar is!
quam ferox est aper?	How fierce is the wild boar?
quot aprōs in silvā vidēmus!	How many wild boars we see in the wood!
quot aprōs in silvā vidēmus?	How many wild boars do we see in the wood?

Notā Bene

Be careful to distinguish *quam* ("how," in the sense "to what an extent or degree") from *quōmodo* ("how," in the sense "by what means").

quam dulcia sunt somnia!	How sweet dreams are!
quōmodo somnia dulcia vidēbō?	How will I see sweet dreams?

You can express another kind of correlative balance, meaning "not only ... but also ...," with the idiom **cum ... tum ...** :

cum corpus magnum tum caput parvum habet porcus.

A pig has not only a large body but also a small head.

Another way to say "not only ... but also ..." is with **nōn modo (sōlum, tantum) ... sed etiam ...** :

vīnum nōn tantum in casam tulerat servus sed etiam biberat.

The slave had not only brought the wine into the house, but he had also drunk it.

nōn modo Gallōs sed etiam Britannōs vīcit Caesar.

Caesar defeated not only the Gauls but also the Britons.

In sentences that DON'T involve correlation, the adverbs **modo, sōlum,** and **tantum** mean "only" or "just":

duōs tantum porcōs frātrī meō dā.	Give my brother just two pigs.

Without correlation, the particle **etiam** can mean "also" or "even":

etiam pīrātae līberōs amant.	Even pirates love their children.

Finally, the combination **nē ... quidem** means "not even." The word that is emphasized is placed between *nē* and *quidem*:

nē agnōs quidem terrēbat lupus tam parvus.	Such a small wolf did not terrify even the lambs.

Irregular Adjectives

These nine adjectives are exceptional because of their declension and, in some cases, their meaning.

ūnus, -a, -um	one
nullus, -a, -um	no
ullus, -a, -um	any
sōlus, -a, -um	only, alone
neuter, neutra, neutrum	neither
alius, -a, -ud	another
uter, utra, utrum	which (of two), either
tōtus, -a, -um	whole
alter, altera, alterum	the other (of two)

You have already met *ūnus* in Chapter 10. As the following layout shows, the rest of these adjectives decline like *ūnus* in the singular, and like regular adjectives of the first/second declension type (*cārī, cārae, cāra*) if they occur in the plural. (Some, because of their sense, have no plural forms.) The only minor exception is *alius*, which has *-ud*, not *-um*, as its nominative and accusative neuter singular ending.

	SINGULAR	PLURAL
NOMINATIVE	null**us**, **-a**, **-um**	null**ī**, **-ae**, **-a**
GENITIVE	null**ius**, **-īus**, **-īus**	null**ōrum**, **-ārum**, **-ōrum**
DATIVE	null**ī**, **-ī**, **-ī**	null**īs**, **-īs**, **-īs**
ACCUSATIVE	null**um**, **-am**, **-um**	null**ōs**, **-ās**, **-a**
ABLATIVE	null**ō**, **-ā**, **-ō**	null**īs**, **-īs**, **-īs**

Notā Bene

Be careful to distinguish the gen. sing. of these adjectives (e.g., *ūnīus*) from the nom. sing. masc. of first/second declension nouns and adjectives (e.g., *fīlius*), and the dat. sing. (e.g., *ūnī*) from the gen. sing. masc. and neut. and from the nom. and voc. pl. masc. (e.g., *cārī*). The following sentences use examples of the genitive and dative singular.

***neutrīus agricolae** frātrem amō.*	I love the brother of neither farmer.
***alterīus consulis** exercitum dēlēvit Hannibal.*	Hannibal destroyed the army of the other consul.
***nullī servō** lībertātem dedit dominus crūdēlis.*	The cruel owner gave freedom to no slave.
*"**tōtī Ītaliae** lībertātem dabō" clāmāvit Hannibal.*	Hannibal shouted, "I will give freedom to all Italy."

Some Uses of These Irregular Adjectives

The meaning of *alius*, "another," is quite different from that of *alter*, "the other one [of two]." Because of its meaning, *alter* is used almost exclusively in the singular. In order to express the plural meaning, "the others," you must use *cēterī, -ae, -a* or *reliquī, -ae, -a*, both regular first/second declension adjectives:

alium porcum terruit lupus.	The wolf terrified another pig.
alterum porcum terruit lupus.	The wolf terrified the other pig.
cēterōs porcōs terruit lupus.	The wolf terrified the other pigs.

The following idioms using *alter* and *alius* are also important:

alter . . . alter . . .	(the) one . . . the other . . .
alius/aliī . . . alius/aliī . . .	one/some . . . another/others . . .
alter agricola porcōs habet, alter vaccās.	One farmer has pigs, the other cows.
aliī flōrēs amant, aliī animālia.	Some people like flowers, others like animals.

nonnullus, -a, -um is a pronominal adjective and pronoun made up of *nōn* and *nullus*, and it means "some" or "not a few." Because of its meaning, it is found mostly in the plural.

multī puerī lūdunt, sed nonnullī librōs legunt.	Many children are playing, but some are reading books.
gladiātōribus nonnullīs lībertātem spectātōrēs dare volēbant.	The spectators wanted to give freedom to some gladiators.

The pronoun **nēmō** "no one" borrows some of its forms from *nullus*:

NOMINATIVE	nēmō
GENITIVE	nullīus
DATIVE	nēminī
ACCUSATIVE	nēminem
ABLATIVE	nullō

Prōlūsiōnēs

Parse the words in bold.

pauperiōrum vērō cīvium turba Caesaris virtūtem celeberrimam passim laudābat, nam hostēs tam saevōs **celeriter** vīcerat. sed "lībertātem paulātim perdit populus Rōmānus" clāmābant senātōrēs plūrimī, "iam **rēgī** nōn dissimilis est Caesar." uxor "**stultissimē** faciēs," miserrimē exclāmāverat "vir **stultissime**, sī hodiē ad senātum ībis. cūr nē ūnum quidem diem **incolumis** carpēs? namque cum amīcōs tuōs tum ōmina quam īnfēlīcissima **multum** timēre dēbēs." etiam epistula sacerdōtis veteris Caesarem dē īnsidiīs senātōrum monēbat. **statim** tamen circum Caesarem stetērunt Brūtus et Cassius aliīque senātōrēs. **quot** cīvium sanguinem passim per viās Rōmae fūdērunt!

Translate, then change the adjectives and adverbs to the comparative and superlative forms.

1. male labōrant servī pigrī.
2. parvī canēs ferōciter pugnant.
3. taurī fortēs terram āridam lentē arant.
4. porcī gracilēs lupōs magnōs facile audiunt.
5. cum porcīs pinguibus puella pulchra pigrē pugnat.

Translate.

1. tam bonum est vīnum, sed melius est aquam tantum bibere.
2. agnōs minimōs ab agrō ad casam humillimam retulit pastor incolumēs.
3. magnopere amābat canem dulcissimum puella cum tristis tum optima.
4. lībertātem magis quam vītam habēre vult consul Rōmānus.
5. quotiēns ā porcō minōre cibum rapuistis, lupī ferīs omnibus ferōciōrēs!
6. tot aprī quot lupī per silvam altam cum puellā pulcherrimā ambulāvērunt.
7. quam pulchrae sunt tōtīus silvae arborēs! nē in Ēlysiō quidem tot flōrēs carpunt animae fēlīcēs.
8. iter tāle fēcērunt barbarōrum familiae quāle exercitus Rōmānus.
9. contrā lupum crūdēlissimum diū pugnāvērunt et intrā mūrōs hortī et extrā nōn modo porcī sed etiam agnī.
10. nē lūnam quidem in caelō nigrō vidēre poterātis.
11. alter pastor porcōs multum amat, sed equōs magis.

12. mons altissimus Eurōpae in Galliā est, sed in Asiā plūrimī altius surgunt.

13. fons et mons et pons paucās litterās habent, fontēs montēsque et pontēs plūrēs, sed fontium, montium, pontium litterae plūrimae sunt.

14. ante pedēs rēgis tertiae fīliae, puellae dulciōris quam sorōrum, rosās quam pulcherrimās sponte dēposuit nauta.

15. quamquam Caesar quam celerrimē per viās lātissimās mīlitēs dūxerat, tamen lentius quam alter exercitus ad portum in extrēmā Ītaliae parte advēnit.

16. cum templa multa deōrum tam potentium tum tot aedēs cīvium dīvitum deīsque potentibus tam similium crās vidēbimus.

17. mīles alter nulla arma habet, alter nē ūnam quidem manum; neuter igitur cēterōs cīvēs iuvāre poterit.

18. Rōmam totiens vīdī quotiens Athēnās, sed nēminem tam fēlīcem vīdī quam pastōrem veterem, patris meī servum, quamquam sōlus in montibus vīvit.

19. pater meus nōn tam dīves est quam tuus, sed paucī plūs pecūniae rēge nostrō dēterrimō habent.

20. cum tālī exercitū quālem ōlim dūcēbat Caesar quot hostēs vincere poterimus!

21. I have found so many pigs, food for the whole army.

22. No one will truly praise the lonely sailor's gift.

23. Fight against our enemies as bravely as possible, soldiers!

24. Why did your mother give flowers to the one girl but not to the other?

25. If the king seizes their wealth so often, not even the richest citizens can live easily.

26. Some of my friend's poems are very good, others are very bad.

27. While I am standing in the harbor, I can see the ships of the whole fleet.

28. Give food to the very thin pig, shepherd, not to the other animals!

29. How many pigs are sitting under the big tree?

30. Without the light of the moon, the broad plain was blacker than the inmost part of a very big cave.

31. The very fierce wolf had terrified not only the lambs but also the horses.

32. Although the wolves are coming stealthily into the garden, the pigs are meanwhile running as quickly as possible into the teacher's house.

33. To which of the king's two daughters did the sailor give such rich gifts?

34. Why does the other girl not show my books to the lonely farmer of her own accord if he wants to read the poems of so great a poet?

35. There is no one in the humble town, but we can all see the bodies of so many brave soldiers everywhere in the fields, not only near the river but also under the tall trees.

Lectiōnēs Latīnae

Lege, Intellege

Vegetius, *Advice for Generals* II

saepe plūs iuvat locus quam virtūs.
occāsiō in bellō plūs iuvat quam virtūs.
melius est post aciem plūra servāre praesidia quam lātius mīlitem spargere.
difficile vincitur quī vērē potest dē suīs et dē adversāriī cōpiīs iūdicāre.
plūs iuvat virtūs quam multitūdō.
quī hostem inconsultē sequitur, adversāriō vult dare victōriam quam ipse accēperat.
quī habet exercitātissimōs mīlitēs, in utrōque cornū pariter proelium dēbet incipere.
quī levem armātūram optimam regit, utramque ālam hostis invādere dēbet.

ipse "he himself"

praesidium, -iī neut. 2 guard post

1. Bravery is worth more than location: true or false?
2. Bravery is worth more than a large army: true or false?
3. Bravery is worth more than opportunity: true or false?
4. Under what circumstances should a general attack both enemy wings simultaneously?
5. What are the consequences of pursuing the enemy rashly?

Ars Poētica

Ovid's Love Poetry VII

Parse the words in bold.

1. *haec [oscula], quam docuī,* **multō meliōra** *fuērunt.*
    These [kisses] were much better than [the ones that] I taught you.

2. *lūmina Gorgoneō* **saevius** *igne micant.*
    Her eyes flash more savagely than the Gorgon's fire.

3. **alterius**que sinūs **aptē** *subiecta fovēbis?*
    Will you warm the other man's bosom, snugly cuddled up?

4. **lentē** *currite, noctis equī!*
    Run slowly, horses of the night!

5. *nec mea vōs* **ūnī** *damnat censūra puellae.*
    Nor does my censorship condemn you to just one girl.

6. *cui peccāre licet, peccat* **minus**; *ipsa potestās*
    sēmina nēquitiae **languidiōra** *facit.*
    Someone who is permitted to sin sins less; opportunity itself makes the seeds of misbehavior more sluggish.

7. *nostra tamen iacuēre velut praemortua membra,*
    turpiter *hesternā* **languidiōra** *rosā.*
    But my limbs lay as if prematurely dead, drooping more shamefully than yesterday's rose.

iacuēre = iacuērunt "they lay"

Aurea Dicta

1. *ad summōs honōrēs aliōs scientia iūris, aliōs ēloquentia, aliōs glōria mīlitāris prōvexit.* (Livy)

2. *genus est mortis male vīvere.* (Ovid)

3. *in īnfāmiā plūs poenae quam in morte.* (Quintilian)

4. *lingua malī pars pessima servī.* (Juvenal)

5. *magis malitia pertinet ad virōs quam ad mulierēs.* (Plautus)

6. *minus habeō quam spērāvī, sed fortasse plūs spērāvī quam dēbuī.* (Seneca the Younger)

7. *modicē et modestē melius est vītam vīvere.* (Plautus)

8. *nihil est tam fallax quam vīta hūmāna, nihil tam īnsidiōsum.* (Seneca the Younger)

prōvehō, -ere, -vexī, -vectum 3 carry forward

Hōrologia Latīna

1. *dā mihi sōlem, dabō tibi hōram.*
    Give me sun, I will give you the hour.

2. *homō humus, fāma fūmus, fīnis cinis.*
    Mankind is earth, fame is smoke, the end is ashes.

3. *omnia sōl temperat.*
    The sun controls everything.

4. *semper amīcīs hōra.*
    There is always time for friends.

5. *umbra dēmonstrat lūcem.*
    The shadow shows the light.

Lūsūs

Thēsaurus Verbōrum

Many English nouns are exactly the same as the nominative singular of the third decl. masc. nouns from which they are derived; for example, "actor" is derived from *actor, actōris* and "auditor" from *audītor, audītōris*. This principle applies more consistently with the American spelling of such words; British forms such as "colour," "favour," "labour" are influenced by Norman French.

candor	favor	odor	stupor
censor	fervor	pallor	tenor
clāmor	furor	pastor	terror
color	horror	possessor	torpor
competītor	iānitor (= *jānitor*)	rigor	tremor
crēditor	inventor	rūmor	tumor
cursor	labor	sector	tūtor
decor	languor	splendor	victor
error	liquor	sponsor	vigor

Etymologiae Antīquae

Deī Rōmānī II

Mars, Martis masc. 3. Wars are fought by men (*mās, maris* masc. 3) and bring death (*mors, mortis* fem. 3). In its variant form *Māvors, Māvortis*, the god's name was linked with overthrowing great things (*magna vertō, -ere, vertī, versum* 3). Mars' alternative name *Grādīvus, -ī* masc. 2 suggests his striding (from the deponent verb *gradior, gradī, gressus sum* 3 *i*-stem; see Chapter 15) hither and thither on the battlefield. See also p. 348.

Mercurius, -iī masc. 2. Mercury is god of trade (from the deponent verb *mercor* 1). As messenger god, he runs in the middle (*medius currō, -ere, cucurrī, cursum* 3), between heaven and earth.

Minerva, -ae fem. 1. As goddess of war, Minerva destroys (*minuō, -ere, minuī, minūtum* 3) and threatens (from the deponent verb *minor* 1). As goddess of handicrafts, she gives mankind the gift of various skills (*mūnus artium variārum*).

Neptūnus, -ī masc. 2. Neptune veils (*obnūbo, -ere* 3) the sea and land with clouds (*nūbēs, -is* fem. 3). Another theory was that his name came from swimming (*nō* 1), but Cicero objected that if you could rely on a single letter you could make any sort of etymology. He says to the proponent of this explanation, "You seemed to me to be floundering more than Neptune himself" (*magis tū mihi natāre vīsus es quam ipse Neptūnus*).

Sāturnus, -ī masc. 2. Saturn is the father, so metaphorically the "sower" (*sator, -ōris* masc. 3) of all the gods. Being old, he is saturated (*saturō* 1) with years.

Venus, Veneris fem. 3. Love comes (*veniō, -īre, vēnī, ventum* 4) to all things, and Venus is quick to grant pardon (*venia, -ae* fem. 1), perhaps an allusion to the belief that lovers who break oaths will not be punished by the gods.

Vesta, -ae fem. 1. The goddess of the hearth (Greek ἑστία [*hestia*]) is also associated with the earth, which is clothed (*vestiō, -īre, vestiī, vestītum* 4) in plants and stands firm by its own strength (*suā vī stat*).

Vulcānus, -ī masc. 2. Vulcan is named from the violence (*violentia, -ae* fem. 1) of fire, and he flies (*volō* 1) through the air.

Vīta Rōmānōrum

Farming

By the classical period, the Romans had come to idealize the simplicity of their earlier way of life, when they were unsophisticated farmers. Not many of those who had the leisure for such nostalgia were actually tempted to perform physical agricultural labor themselves; that was for slaves and peasants.

> When Cato the Elder was asked what he thought was the most profitable way of exploiting one's resources, he replied, "Grazing livestock successfully"; what second to that, "Grazing livestock fairly successfully"; what third, "Grazing livestock unsuccessfully"; what fourth, "Raising crops." When his questioner asked, "What about moneylending?" Cato replied, "What about murder?"
>
> —Cicero, *Dē Officiīs* 2.89

Whenever I think how shamefully widespread is the abandonment of our rural ways, I fear they may seem unbecoming or even beneath the dignity of free men. But I am reminded by so many writers that rural life was a matter of pride to our ancestors. This was the background of Quintius Cincinnatus, who was called from his plow to the dictatorship to save a besieged consul and his army [in 458 or 439 BC]; laying down his symbols of his office, which he relinquished after his victory more quickly than he had taken it up on assuming command, he returned to the same oxen on his small ancestral farm of four *iūgera* [= *jūgera*, about two and a half acres]. The same is true of Gaius Fabricius Luscinus and Manius Curius Dentatus; the former, when he had expelled Pyrrhus from Italy, the latter, when he had conquered the Sabines, took seven *iūgera* of captured land as a reward like every other man in the army, and cultivated them with an energy equal to the bravery with which they had won them. I need not discuss individual cases now; that would be inappropriate, given that I can observe so many other memorable Roman commanders who were happy with this twofold task of both defending and cultivating their land, whether they had inherited it or won it through conquest. I understand that the old manly way of life does not appeal to our modern extravagant sophistication. As Varro complained already in our grandfathers' day, we have all abandoned our sickles and plows and come creeping with our families inside the walls of the city, and use our hands to applaud in the circuses and theaters rather than for tending our crops and vineyards, and we gaze in wonder at the posturings of effeminate men, who trick the eyes of the spectators as they counterfeit with their womanish gestures a sex denied to men by nature. Then, so that we can be ready for our gluttonous eating, we steam out our daily indigestion in Greek baths, sucking the moisture from our bodies to stimulate thirst. We waste our nights in licentious drunkenness, our days playing games and sleeping. We think ourselves fortunate that "we see the sun neither when it rises nor when it sets" [a saying of Cato the Elder]. This lazy lifestyle leads to health problems. The bodies of our young people are so flabby and out of condition that death seems unlikely to change them at all.

—Columella, *Dē Agricultūrā* Preface 13–17

CHAPTER 14
The Passive Voice of Verbs

So far you have learned the active voice of the indicative mood of verbs. In this chapter you will learn the other voice of Latin verbs, the passive. When a **transitive verb**—a verb that takes a direct object—is used in the passive voice, the direct object of the active verb becomes the grammatical subject of the passive verb. For example:

Active	**Passive**
The farmer kills the pig.	The pig is killed by the farmer.
The soldiers will attack the city.	The city will be attacked by the soldiers.
I have done the work.	The work has been done by me.

Each of the six active tenses has a passive counterpart. These six passive tenses are easy to learn because they are so predictable.

Present (I am loved, etc.)

	1st CONJ.	**2nd CONJ.**
1st sing.	am**or**	mon**eor**
2nd sing.	am**āris**	mon**ēris**
3rd sing.	am**ātur**	mon**ētur**
1st pl.	am**āmur**	mon**ēmur**
2nd pl.	am**āminī**	mon**ēminī**
3rd pl.	am**antur**	mon**entur**
Infinitive	am**ārī**	mon**ērī**

	3rd CONJ.	**4th CONJ.**	**3rd CONJ.** *i*-stem
1st sing.	mitt**or**	aud**ior**	cap**ior**
2nd sing.	mitt**eris**	aud**īris**	cap**eris**
3rd sing.	mitt**itur**	aud**ītur**	cap**itur**
1st pl.	mitt**imur**	aud**īmur**	cap**imur**
2nd pl.	mitt**iminī**	aud**īminī**	cap**iminī**
3rd pl.	mitt**untur**	aud**iuntur**	cap**iuntur**
Infinitive	mitt**ī**	aud**īrī**	cap**ī**

Imperatives

SINGULAR	am**āre**	mon**ēre**	
PLURAL	am**āminī**	mon**ēminī**	
SINGULAR	mitt**ere**	aud**īre**	cap**ere**
PLURAL	mitt**iminī**	aud**īminī**	cap**iminī**

No doubt because of its awkward meaning ("be loved!," "be listened to!," etc.), the passive imperative is rare in Latin, except in the case of deponent verbs, which you will learn in the next chapter. The fact that the forms are ambiguous perhaps also discouraged their use: *amāre*, for example, is identical to the present active infinitive, *amāminī* is identical to the second person plural present passive indicative, "you are loved."

Future (I will be loved, etc.)

	1st CONJ.	**2nd CONJ.**
1st sing.	amābor	monēbor
2nd sing.	amāberis	monēberis
3rd sing.	amābitur	monēbitur
1st pl.	amābimur	monēbimur
2nd pl.	amābiminī	monēbiminī
3rd pl.	amābuntur	monēbuntur

	3rd CONJ.	**4th CONJ.**	**3rd CONJ.** *i*-stem
1st sing.	mittar	audiar	capiar
2nd sing.	mittēris	audiēris	capiēris
3rd sing.	mittētur	audiētur	capiētur
1st pl.	mittēmur	audiēmur	capiēmur
2nd pl.	mittēminī	audiēminī	capiēminī
3rd pl.	mittentur	audientur	capientur

Notā Bene

The length of the *e* is the only difference between the future form *mittēris* "you will be sent" and the present *mitteris* "you are being sent."

Imperfect (I was loved, etc.)

	1st CONJ.	**2nd CONJ.**
1st sing.	amābar	monēbar
2nd sing.	amābāris	monēbāris
3rd sing.	amābātur	monēbātur
1st pl.	amābāmur	monēbāmur
2nd pl.	amābāminī	monēbāminī
3rd pl.	amābantur	monēbantur

	3rd CONJ.	**4th CONJ.**	**3rd CONJ.** *i*-stem
1st sing.	mittēbar	audiēbar	capiēbar
2nd sing.	mittēbāris	audiēbāris	capiēbāris
3rd sing.	mittēbātur	audiēbātur	capiēbātur
1st pl.	mittēbāmur	audiēbāmur	capiēbāmur
2nd pl.	mittēbāminī	audiēbāminī	capiēbāminī
3rd pl.	mittēbantur	audiēbantur	capiēbantur

The Perfect System

To construct any form in the perfect passive system, you need to know the verb's fourth principal part, the perfect passive participle, which would be translated "having been loved," "having been warned," etc. For regular verbs in the first conjugation, this participle is formed by adding -*ātus*, -*āta*, -*ātum* to the present stem: for example, *amātus, amāta, amātum* "having been loved." For the other conjugations, you need to learn the fourth principal part separately but, as with the third principal part, you can use patterns to group certain verbs together for ease of memorization.

The perfect passive tenses simply combine the fourth principal part or perfect passive participle with the appropriate form of *esse*.

amātus sum	I have been loved, I was loved
monitī erant	They had been warned
missae erunt	They will have been sent

Keep in mind that the participle adds the "perfect" element of "have been," "had been," "will have been." In other words, the forms in the examples above CANNOT be translated as "I am loved," "they were warned," and "they will be sent."

You remember that predicate adjectives are used with the verb "to be" and agree with the subject. Since the perfect passive participle functions like a predicate adjective, it must agree in number, case, and gender with the subject. For example:

amātus est porcus.	The pig has been loved/was loved.
amātī sunt porcī.	The pigs have been loved/were loved.
amāta erit puella.	The girl will have been loved.
amātae erunt puellae.	The girls will have been loved.
amātum erat carmen puellae.	The girl's poem had been loved.
amāta erant carmina puellae.	The girl's poems had been loved.

Perfect (I have been loved, I was loved, etc.)

1st sing.	am**ā**tus, -a, -**um sum**
2nd sing.	am**ā**tus, -a, -**um es**
3rd sing.	am**ā**tus, -a, -**um est**
1st pl.	am**ā**tī, -ae, -**a sumus**
2nd pl.	am**ā**tī, -ae, -**a estis**
3rd pl.	am**ā**tī, -ae, -**a sunt**
Infinitive	am**ā**tus, -a, -**um esse**

Future Perfect (I will have been loved, etc.)

1st sing.	am**ā**tus, -**a**, -**um erō**
2nd sing.	am**ā**tus, -**a**, -**um eris**
3rd sing.	am**ā**tus, -**a**, -**um erit**
1st pl.	am**ā**tī, -**ae**, -**a erimus**
2nd pl.	am**ā**tī, -**ae**, -**a eritis**
3rd pl.	am**ā**tī, -**ae**, -**a erunt**

Pluperfect (I had been loved, etc.)

1st sing.	am**ā**tus, -**a**, -**um eram**
2nd sing.	am**ā**tus, -**a**, -**um erās**
3rd sing.	am**ā**tus, -**a**, -**um erat**
1st pl.	am**ā**tī, -**ae**, -**a erāmus**
2nd pl.	am**ā**tī, -**ae**, -**a erātis**
3rd pl.	am**ā**tī, -**ae**, -**a erant**

Here is a list of most of the verbs you have seen so far, with all their principal parts written out in full. Be sure to review especially the fourth principal part of each. Some verbs, such as *ambulāre*, do not have a fourth principal part, because they are intransitive. Other intransitive verbs, such as *venīre*, do have a fourth principal part, because they are used in the impersonal passive construction, which you will meet in Chapter 28. Finally, some transitive verbs, such as *bibere* and *discere*, lack a perfect passive participle for some unknown reason.

First Conjugation

aedificō, aedificāre, aedificāvī, **aedificātum**	build
ambulō, ambulāre, ambulāvī	walk
amō, amāre, amāvī, **amātum**	love
arō, arāre, arāvī, **arātum**	plow
clāmō, clāmāre, clāmāvī, **clāmātum**	shout
dō, dare, dedī, **datum**	give
dōnō, dōnāre, dōnāvī, **dōnātum**	give
iuvō, iuvāre, iūvī, **iūtum**	help
labōrō, labōrāre, labōrāvī, **labōrātum**	work
laudō, laudāre, laudāvī, **laudātum**	praise
līberō, līberāre, līberāvī, **līberātum**	free
monstrō, monstrāre, monstrāvī, **monstrātum**	show
portō, portāre, portāvī, **portātum**	carry
pugnō, pugnāre, pugnāvī, **pugnātum**	fight
spectō, spectāre, spectāvī, **spectātum**	watch

stō, stāre, stetī, **statum**	stand
tolerō, tolerāre, tolerāvī, **tolerātum**	tolerate
vītō, vītāre, vītāvī, **vītātum**	avoid
vocō, vocāre, vocāvī, **vocātum**	call

Second Conjugation

dēbeō, dēbēre, dēbuī, **dēbitum**	owe, ought to, must, should
doceō, docēre, docuī, **doctum**	teach
fleō, flēre, flēvī, **flētum**	weep
habeō, habēre, habuī, **habitum**	have
maneō, manēre, mansī	remain
moneō, monēre, monuī, **monitum**	warn
moveō, movēre, mōvī, **mōtum**	move
rīdeō, rīdēre, rīsī, **rīsum**	laugh
sedeō, sedēre, sēdī, **sessum**	sit
teneō, tenēre, tenuī, **tentum**	hold
terreō, terrēre, terruī, **territum**	frighten
timeō, timēre, timuī	fear
videō, vidēre, vīdī, **vīsum**	see

Third Conjugation

addō, addere, addidī, **additum**	add
agō, agere, ēgī, **actum**	drive, do, spend (of time)
bibō, bibere, bibī	drink
cadō, cadere, cecidī	fall
caedō, caedere, cecīdī, **caesum**	cause to fall, kill
carpō, carpere, carpsī, **carptum**	pluck
claudō, claudere, clausī, **clausum**	close
cōgō, cōgere, coēgī, **coactum**	gather, force
dīcō, dīcere, dixī, **dictum**	say
discō, discere, didicī	learn
dūcō, dūcere, duxī, **ductum**	lead
frangō, frangere, frēgī, **fractum**	break
fundō, fundere, fūdī, **fūsum**	pour
laedō, laedere, laesī, **laesum**	harm
legō, legere, lēgī, **lectum**	choose, read
lūdō, lūdere, lūsī, **lūsum**	play

metuō, metuere, metuī	fear
mittō, mittere, mīsī, **missum**	send
ostendō, ostendere, ostendī, **ostentum**	show
pascō, pascere, pāvī, **pastum**	feed
pellō, pellere, pepulī, **pulsum**	drive, repel
perdō, perdere, perdidī, **perditum**	lose, destroy
petō, petere, petiī (*or* -īvī), **petītum**	seek
pōnō, pōnere, posuī, **positum**	place
relinquō, relinquere, relīquī, **relictum**	leave
scrībō, scrībere, scripsī, **scriptum**	write
surgō, surgere, surrexī, **surrectum**	rise
tangō, tangere, tetigī, **tactum**	touch
vincō, vincere, vīcī, **victum**	conquer
vīvō, vīvere, vixī, **victum**	live

Fourth Conjugation

aperiō, aperīre, aperuī, **apertum**	open
audiō, audīre, audīvī, **audītum**	hear
dormiō, dormīre, dormīvī, **dormītum**	sleep
reperiō, reperīre, repperī, **repertum**	find
veniō, venīre, vēnī, **ventum**	come

Third Conjugation *i*-stem

capiō, capere, cēpī, **captum**	take
accipiō, -ere, accēpī, **acceptum**	accept
incipiō, -ere, incēpī, **inceptum**	begin
cupiō, cupere, cupīvī, **cupitum**	wish, desire
faciō, facere, fēcī, **factum**	do, make
rapiō, rapere, rapuī, **raptum**	seize

Notā Bene

vincere and *vīvere* have the same fourth principal part, but context prevents confusion.

Irregular Verbs and the Passive Voice

sum, *possum*, *volō*, *nōlō*, and *mālō* have no passive forms.

The intransitive verb *eō* is only rarely used passively (you will see examples in Chapter 28). Some of its compounds are transitive, though, and form their fourth principal part with *-itum*; for example, *transitum*, literally "having been gone across," that is, "having been crossed."

ferō conjugates almost exactly like regular third conjugation verbs such as *mittor* in the present passive system: pres. *feror*, fut. *ferar*, imperf. *ferēbar*, etc. The only irregular passive forms in the present system are the second and third pers. pres. sing. pass. ind. *ferris*, *fertur*, and the pres. pass. inf. *ferrī*. *ferō* has no passive imperative forms. The fourth principal part is very irregular, *lātum*, but it is used in the perfect passive tenses in the regular way. For example, *ad urbem lātī erant porcī* "The pigs had been carried to the city."

Since the prefixes in some compounds of *ferre* are so variable, you should learn them individually:

afferō, afferre, attulī, allātum	carry to
auferō, auferre, abstulī, ablātum	carry from
conferō, conferre, contulī, collātum	bring together
dēferō, dēferre, dētulī, dēlātum	bring down
differō, differre, distulī, dīlātum	disperse, postpone
efferō, efferre, extulī, ēlātum	bring out of
inferō, inferre, intulī, illātum	bring into
offerō, offerre, obtulī, oblātum	offer
perferō, perferre, pertulī, perlātum	bring through, endure
referō, referre, retulī, relātum	bring back
sufferō, sufferre, sustulī, sublātum	bring under, endure

The Ablative of the Agent and of Means

We saw earlier that, when a transitive verb is used in the passive voice, the direct object of the active verb becomes the grammatical subject of the passive verb, even though it is still the recipient of the action.

To indicate the **agent** (person, god, or animal) responsible for the action, Latin uses the **ablative with *ā/ab***.

To indicate the **means** (inanimate) by which the action was accomplished, Latin uses the **ablative on its own**.

For example:

Agent
rex ā mīlitibus interfectus est.
The king was killed /has been killed **by the soldiers**.

porcus ā lupō territus erat.
The pig had been terrified **by the wolf**.

Means
rex armīs mīlitum interfectus est.
The king was killed /has been killed **by the soldiers' weapons**.

porcus dentibus lupī territus erat.
The pig had been terrified **by the wolf's teeth**.

In addition, *ā/ab* may be used with collective nouns that imply animate agents. For example:

urbs ab exercitū Rōmānō (= *ā mīlitibus Rōmānīs*) *dēlēbitur.*
The city will be destroyed by the Roman army.

lupus ā grege ferōcī porcōrum (= *ā porcīs ferōcibus*) *territus est.*
The wolf was frightened by the fierce herd of pigs.

Vocabulary

Verbs

fugō 1	put to flight
superō 1	conquer
vulnerō 1	wound
dēleō, dēlēre, dēlēvī, dēlētum 2	destroy
iaceō (= *jaceō*), **iacēre, iacuī** 2	lie down
iubeō (= *jubeō*), **iubēre, iussī, iussum** 2	order
dēfendō, dēfendere, dēfendī, dēfensum 3	defend
invādō, invādere, invāsī, invāsum 3	invade
fugiō, fugere, fūgī 3 *i*-stem	flee
iaciō (= *jaciō*), **iacere, iēcī, iactum** 3 *i*-stem	throw
interficiō, interficere, -fēcī, -fectum 3 *i*-stem	kill

Nouns

galea, galeae fem. 1	helmet
hasta, hastae fem. 1	spear
pugna, pugnae fem. 1	battle
gladius, gladiī masc. 2	sword
scūtum, scūtī neut. 2	shield
socius, sociī masc. 2	ally
centuriō, centuriōnis masc. 3	centurion
eques, equitis masc. 3	horseman
pedes, peditis masc. 3	foot soldier
victor, victōris masc. 3	victor
legiō, legiōnis fem. 3	legion
agmen, agminis neut. 3	column (esp. of soldiers)
vulnus, vulneris neut. 3	wound

Prōlūsiōnēs

Parse the following words.

1. iacientur.
2. terrēris.
3. cōgēmur.
4. mittēbar.
5. captae sunt.

6. laudābāmur.
7. tactus eris.
8. vīsum erat.
9. aperītur.
10. mōtī estis.

Express the following sentences in the passive voice and then translate.

For example:
exercitum Rōmānum dēlent hostēs.
exercitus Rōmānus ab hostibus dēlētur.
The Roman army is being destroyed by the enemy.

1. pastor porcōs dūcēbat.
2. pastor porcōs duxit.
3. gladiī nostrī hostēs saevōs pepulērunt.
4. urbem dēfenderat dux fortis.
5. dentēs lupī porcōs interfēcērunt.
6. terruerant porcī lupōs.
7. terruērunt nautās fluctūs maris.
8. nauta in manūs puellae rosās fundēbat.
9. num porcus librōs laudāvit?
10. multa bona deus mortālibus dat.

Translate.

1. galeā bene dēfensum est ducis nostrī caput.
2. hostium agmen ā peditibus nostrīs facile fugātum erat.
3. tot equitēs subitō dē superiōre parte collis quam celerrimē rediērunt.
4. sociī hastās iēcērunt, et nunc passim per agrōs iacent corpora hostium.

5. quamquam barbarī sine galeīs, hastīs, gladiīs fortius quam Rōmānōrum sociī pugnāvērunt, tandem tamen ā Caesare victī sunt.

6. dē monte suprēmō fūgērunt porcī, namque ā lupīs territī erant.

7. dē virtūte liber ab amīcō Caesaris scriptus est.

8. nec lupus nec aper ā pastōribus facile captus erat.

9. servīs tāle vīnum ā dominō dabitur quāle amīcīs.

10. peditēs ā centuriōnibus in aciem contrā barbarōrum cōpiās dūcēbantur.

11. nec virtūte nec armīs oppidum dēfendī potest sī tam humilia sunt moenia.

12. quam fortiter pugnābat centuriō legiōnis quintae! forte tamen barbarī ducis gladiō vulnerātus erat.

13. Karthāgō ā Rōmānīs superāta est, et mox ā victōribus dēlēbitur.

14. quamquam sine spē erāmus, equitēs ā duce iussī sunt hostium aciem invādere.

15. postquam contrā hostēs pugnāvimus, dulce est arma dēpōnere et sub arbore cum amīcīs iacēre.

16. Wolves are loved by no one.

17. The pig will be frightened neither by wild boars nor by wolves.

18. When was the shepherd being killed slowly by the bull's cruel horns?

19. Many poems had been written by the happy poet.

20. Both the king and the queen were being praised by all the citizens.

21. Why has the citadel of neither city been besieged by the enemy?

22. Surely the wall has not been destroyed gradually by the huge rocks?

23. The soldier's head had been defended by his helmet, and his body by his shield, but he was wounded by a centurion of the ninth legion.

24. The gates of the towers have been closed by the soldier, but they will soon be opened by a few citizens.

25. How was the king killed? Was bad fruit given stealthily to the foolish man by the soft hand of his cruel wife?

Lectiōnēs Latīnae

Lege, Intellege

War with Hannibal

decimō annō postquam in Ītaliam vēnerat, Hannibal usque ad quartum mīliārium urbis accessit, equitēs eius usque ad portam. mox ad Campāniam rediit. in Hispāniā ā frātre eius Hasdrubale ambō Scīpiōnēs, quī per multōs annōs victōrēs fuerant, interficiuntur, exercitus tamen integer mansit; cāsū enim magis erant quam virtūte dēceptī. ā consule

Marcellō Siciliae magna pars capta est, quam tenēre Afrī coeperant, et nōbilissima urbs Syrācūsāna; praeda ingens Rōmam perlāta est. Laevīnus in Macedoniā cum Philippō et multīs Graeciae populīs et rēge Asiae Attalō amīcitiam fēcit, et ad Siciliam profectus Hannōnem, Afrōrum ducem, cēpit Rōmamque cum captīvīs nōbilibus mīsit. XL cīvitātēs in dēditiōnem accēpit, XXVI expugnāvit. ita omnis Sicilia recepta et Macedonia fracta; ingentī glōriā Rōmam regressus est. Hannibal in Ītaliā Gnaeum Fulvium consulem subitō aggressus cum octō mīlibus hominum interfēcit.

—Eutropius, *Breviārium* 3.14

usque adv. all the way

cāsus, cāsūs masc. 4 fall, chance

coepī, coepisse 3 began (see p. 226)

1. How close did Hannibal's cavalry come to the gates of Rome?
2. How many men died with the consul Fulvius when Hannibal suddenly attacked him?
3. Who killed the two Scipios in Spain?
4. Which consul captured Syracuse?
5. How long after his arrival in Italy did Hannibal come as close to Rome as the fourth milestone?

Ars Poētica

Virgil (Publius Vergilius Maro 70–19 BC) was the greatest and most influential of all Roman poets. He wrote the *Eclogues*, a collection of ten pastoral poems; the *Georgics*, a poem in four books on farming; and the *Aeneid*, his masterpiece, unfinished at his death, a twelve-book epic on the wanderings and wars of Aeneas and his band of Trojans.

Identify the person, number, and tense of the verbs in bold in the following quotations from Virgil.

1. ***panditur*** *extemplō foribus domus ātra revulsīs*
   abstractaeque bovēs abiūrātaeque rapīnae
   caelō ***ostenduntur***, *pedibusque informe cadāver*
   prōtrahitur.
   Immediately the dark house is opened, with its doors torn off, and the stolen cattle and the plunder he swore that he had not taken are shown to the sky, and the shapeless corpse is dragged out by the feet.

2.   *huic cervixque comaeque* ***trahuntur***
   per terram, et versā pulvis ***inscrībitur*** *hastā.*
   Both his neck and his hair are dragged along the ground, and the dust is marked by his spear turned backward.

3. *ecce **trahēbātur** passīs Priamēia virgō*
   crīnibus ā templō Cassandra.
   Look! Cassandra, the virgin daughter of Priam, was being dragged from the temple by her flowing hair.

4. *at rēgīna gravī iamdūdum saucia cūrā*
   *vulnus alit vēnīs et caecō **carpitur** ignī.*
   But the queen [Dido of Carthage], long since afflicted with a serious anxiety, nourishes a wound in her veins and is consumed by a blind flame.

5. *"**frangimur** heu fātīs" inquit "**ferimur**que procellā!"*
   "Alas!" he said. "We are being broken by the fates and carried off by the storm."

6. *aut hōc inclūsī lignō **occultantur** Achīvī,*
   *aut haec in nostrōs **fabricāta est** māchina mūrōs.*
   Either there are Greeks hidden, shut up in this wooden thing, or this device has been constructed to harm our walls.

Aurea Dicta

1. *ā cane nōn magnō saepe tenētur aper.* (Ovid)
2. *carmina laudantur, sed mūnera magna petuntur.* (Ovid)
3. *contrā verbōsōs nōlī contendere verbīs; sermo datur cunctīs, animī sapientia paucīs.* (Ps.-Cato)
4. *maxima dēbētur puerō reverentia.* (Juvenal)
5. *monēre et monērī proprium est vērae amīcitiae.* (Cicero)
6. *nātūra mūtārī nōn potest.* (Cicero)
7. *nihil rectē sine exemplō docētur aut discitur.* (Columella)
8. *nōn potest amor cum timōre miscērī.* (Seneca the Younger)

Hōrologia Latīna

1. *ab hōc mōmentō pendet aeternitās.*
   Eternity hangs from this moment.

2. *nihil cum umbrā, sine umbrā nihil.*
   With shadow, nothing, without shadow, nothing.

3. *sī sōl silet, sileō.*
   If the sun is silent, I am silent.

4. *sōl generat umbrās.*
   The sun produces shadows.

5. *vulnerant omnēs, ultima necat.*
   Every hour wounds, the final one kills.

Lūsūs

Thēsaurus Verbōrum

Many English adjectives ending in *-able* and *-ible* come from Latin adjectives in *-ābilis, -e* and *-ibilis, -e*, with the final *-ilis, -e* replaced by *-le*.

culpābilis	crēdibilis
habitābilis	flexibilis
mūtābilis	horribilis
observābilis	legibilis
reparābilis	plausibilis
sociābilis	sensibilis
stābilis	terribilis
tolerābilis	vīsibilis

Etymologiae Antīquae

Famous Romans

Whereas most of the ancient etymologies in other chapters are false, many of those given here are likely to be true. They are still interesting.

The origin of most *nōmina* (family or clan names) is lost to us, but some are clearly rooted in the agricultural past. It seems reasonable to assume that the ancestors of the poet **Ovid** were sheep-herders (*ovis, -is* fem. 3 "sheep") in his native Abruzzi, an area still noted for sheep farming. Ovid's stepdaughter married Publius **Suillius** Rufus, who became consul in AD 43 or 45. *Rūfus* means "red-haired," but his family may also have made their money from pigs (*sūs, suis* masc./fem. 3 "pig," and *suīle, -is* neut. 3 "pigsty"). The family of Marcus **Porcius** Cato, a great statesman and writer, presumably had a similar background in pig farming. Other such *nōmina* suggesting a family involvement in animal husbandry are **Asinius** (*asinus, -ī* masc. 2 "donkey"; e.g., Gaius Asinius Pollio, an early patron of Virgil), **Hirtius** (*hircus, -ī* masc. 2 "billy goat"; e.g., Aulus Hirtius, consul in 43 BC), **Vitellius** (*vitellus, -ī* masc. 2 "calf"; e.g., Aulus Vitellius, who was emperor for several weeks in AD 69).

Some *cognōmina* (additional names, nicknames) were honorific; for example: **Corvīnus**, esp. Marcus Valerius Messalla Corvinus, a general under Augustus and a patron of Ovid. One of his ancestors was helped by a raven (*corvus, -ī* masc. 2) when he fought a duel with a Gaul. **Torquā-tus**, esp. Titus Manlius Imperiosus Torquatus: this fourth-century member of the Manlius clan stripped a necklace or torque (*torquēs*, *-is* masc. 3) from the body of a Gaul whom he had killed in a duel, and wore it, still bloody, around his own neck.

Many other *cognōmina* point bluntly to physical characteristics: an ancestor of the triumvir Marcus Licinius **Crassus** was presumably fat (*crassus, -a, -um*); someone in the family of Publius Ovidius **Nāsō** must have had a big nose; a relative of Quintus Horatius **Flaccus** had floppy ears; an ancestor of Publius Quinctilius **Vārus**, the general who lost three legions in the Teutoburg disaster of AD 9, was bowlegged (*vārus, -a, -um*).

No *cognōmen*, however, was as evocative as **Caesar**. Some said that an early member of the family had been born by Caesarean section (*caedō, -ere, cecīdī, caesum* 3 "cut"), or had singlehandedly killed an elephant in battle (*casai* being Moorish or *caesa* Punic for "elephant"), or had eyes of a particular gray-blue color (*caesius, -a, -um*), or was born with a full head of hair (*caesariēs, caesariēī* fem. 5). Julius Caesar may have been particularly pleased by this last explanation, for he himself was practically bald, a fact that he took pains to disguise by wearing a laurel wreath on all possible occasions. (It was said that, of all the honors bestowed on him by the Senate and the people, the right to wear this wreath gratified him the most.) A modern theory is that the name actually comes from the Etruscan city of Caere (in Etruscan *Caesre*).

Vīta Rōmānōrum

Medicine

Many doctors in Rome were Greek freedmen (former slaves) and enjoyed little social prestige. In view of the prejudices displayed by Pliny in this discussion of the medical profession, it is not surprising that the Romans contributed very little to the expansion of medical knowledge.

> Our ancestors did not condemn medicine *per sē*, but rather the medical profession, and they especially disliked the idea of making money in payment for saving lives. That is said to be why they built the temple of Aesculapius [the god of medicine] outside the walls of the city, even when they were accepting him as a god. . . . It is also why doctors were included in the expulsion of Greeks from Italy which took place long after Cato's time. [Cato the Elder disapproved strongly of doctors.] Here is further support for our ancestors' wisdom. Medicine is the only one of the Greek arts which serious-minded Romans do not yet practice. Very few of our fellow citizens have touched it, despite the great profits to be made, and those who have become doctors immediately start behaving like Greeks. Indeed, to write about medicine other than in Greek commands no respect even from those who are ignorant and know no Greek. When it comes to health matters, people have less confidence if they know what is going on. That is why, by Hercules, anyone who claims to be a doctor is trusted straightaway. Medicine is the only profession in which this happens, even though there is no other profession in which lying is more dangerous. But we pay no heed to that danger, for everyone finds the sweetness of wishful thinking so seductive. Moreover, there is no law to punish someone whose ignorance costs lives, and no precedent for compensating the victims.

Doctors learn by endangering our lives, conducting experiments which lead to people's deaths. Only doctors have total immunity when they kill people. In fact, the criticism is transferred to the patient, who is faulted for self-indulgence: those who die are actually held to be responsible for their own death.

—Pliny the Elder, *Historia Nātūrālis* 29.16–18

CHAPTER 15
Deponent and Semi-Deponent Verbs, Expressions of Time and Place

Deponent Verbs

Deponent verbs are passive in form, with the same passive forms as verbs that you have already learned, but they are active in meaning. Because they are active in meaning, they can take a **direct object**, as long as they are transitive. For example, *sequor, sequī, secūtus sum* 3 "follow" and *mīror, mīrārī, mīrātus sum* 1 "admire":

porcus pastōrem sequitur.	The pig follows the shepherd.
porcum pastōrēs mīrātī sunt.	The shepherds admired the pig.

Because deponent verbs are active in meaning, however, they cannot be used to express a passive meaning. For example, you can't use *sequor* to translate "The shepherd is followed by the pig" or *mīror* to translate "The pig was admired by the shepherds."

You saw in Chapter 14 that passive imperatives are used only rarely. Since deponent verbs have an active meaning, however, their imperative forms are used as frequently as those of verbs with active forms. You need to distinguish singular imperative forms of deponents, such as *mīrāre*, "Admire!" and *sequere*, "Follow!" from present active infinitives such as *amāre* and *mittere*.

The following are some of the most commonly used deponent verbs:

First Conjugation

arbitror, arbitrārī, arbitrātus sum	think
cōnor, cōnārī, cōnātus sum	try
hortor, hortārī, hortātus sum	exhort
mīror, mīrārī, mīrātus sum	admire
moror, morārī, morātus sum	delay
precor, precārī, precātus sum	pray

Second Conjugation

fateor, fatērī, fassus sum	confess
mereor, merērī, meritus sum	deserve
polliceor, pollicērī, pollicitus sum	promise
reor, rērī, ratus sum	think
vereor, verērī, veritus sum	fear
videor, vidērī, vīsus sum	be seen, seem

Third Conjugation

adipiscor, adipiscī, adeptus sum	obtain
amplector, amplectī, amplexus sum	embrace
lābor, lābī, lapsus sum	slip
loquor, loquī, locūtus sum	speak
nascor, nascī, nātus sum	be born
proficiscor, proficiscī, profectus sum	depart
queror, querī, questus sum	complain
sequor, sequī, secūtus sum	follow
ulciscor, ulciscī, ultus sum	avenge, take vengeance upon

Fourth Conjugation

mentior, mentīrī, mentītus sum	tell a lie
orior, orīrī, ortus sum	arise

Third Conjugation *i*-stem

gradior, gradī, gressus sum	stride
morior, morī, mortuus sum	die
patior, patī, passus sum	suffer

Vocabulary Notes

moror is used both transitively ("Having delayed the Etruscans for a long time, Horatius retreated") and intransitively ("Having delayed for a long time, Caesar crossed the Rubicon").

videor is the passive of *videō*, so it can mean both "I am seen" and "I seem." Contrast *porcus in agrō vidētur* "The pig is seen in the field" with *porcus in agrō esse vidētur* "The pig seems to be in the field."

nascor means "be born," a passive sense in English. Contrast "Rhea bore two sons, Romulus and Remus" with "Romulus and Remus were born in the eighth century BC." *nascor* has no active form; "to give birth" is *pariō, parere, peperī, partum* 3 *i*-stem (hence "parent," *post partum*).

ulciscor: context will usually show which of the two related meanings is intended. Contrast *Antōnius Octāviānusque mortem Caesaris ultī sunt* "Antony and Octavian avenged the death of Caesar" with *Antōnius Octāviānusque Brūtum ultī sunt* "Antony and Octavian took vengeance upon Brutus."

gradior is not very common, but it has many important compounds: *aggredior, aggredī, aggressus sum* "attack," *ēgredior* "go out," *ingredior* "go into," *prōgredior* "go forward," *regredior* "go back."

mortuus: this form is exceptional; in the final principal part of all other verbs, the stem ends with *s, t,* or *x*.

Semi-Deponent Verbs

A small number of verbs have active forms in some tenses but passive forms in others. They are therefore called **semi-deponent**. Three common semi-deponent verbs are:

audeō, audēre, ausus sum 2   dare

gaudeō, gaudēre, gāvīsus sum 2   rejoice

soleō, solēre, solitus sum 2   be accustomed

These verbs are active throughout their present system, but they use passive forms in their perfect system, like deponent verbs. For example:

Present system	**Perfect system**
porcum laudāre audeō.	*porcum laudāre ausus sum.*
I dare to praise the pig.	I dared to praise the pig.
mare vidēre gaudēbant puellae.	*mare vidēre gāvīsae erant puellae.*
The girls used to rejoice to see the sea.	The girls had rejoiced to see the sea.
lupī ad urbem venīre solēbunt.	*lupī ad urbem venīre solitī erunt.*
The wolves will be accustomed to come to the city.	The wolves will have been accustomed to come to the city.

The irregular verb *fīō*, "be made," "become," is used for the present passive system of *faciō*, which has no present passive system of its own:

Present Tense of *fīō*

1st sing.	fī**ō**
2nd sing.	fī**s**
3rd sing.	fī**t**
1st pl.	fī**mus**
2nd pl.	fī**tis**
3rd pl.	fī**unt**
Infinitive	**fierī**

fīō conjugates like *mittō* in the future and imperfect, that is, *fīam, fīēbam,* and so on. (These tenses are written out in full in Appendix 2.)

Just as *fīō* supplies the present passive system of *faciō, fīō* has no perfect system of its own but shares that of *faciō.* For example:

Present	**Perfect**
dulcior fit fructus.	*dulcior factus est fructus.*
The fruit is becoming sweeter.	The fruit has become/been made sweeter.

Like the English "become," *fīō* is intransitive and therefore takes a predicate, not a direct object. For example:

> *Caesar rex fierī volēbat.*   Caesar wanted to become king.

fīō, fierī, factus sum is semi-deponent, in that its present system, except for the present infinitive, is active in form, whereas its present infinitive and its perfect system are passive in form.

Expressions of Time and Place

In expressions of time and place, the meaning usually depends entirely on the case that is used, with no guidance from prepositions. Many more such idioms will be introduced in Chapter 16.

Accusative and Ablative of Time

Nouns denoting a period of time are used in the accusative to express **how long an event or situation lasts,** in the ablative to express the **time when,** or the period of **time within which,** an event occurs. For example:

> <u>*tertiō diē*</u> *mātrem vidēbimus.*   We will see our mother <u>on the third day</u>.
> <u>*tribus diēbus*</u> *mātrem vidēbimus.*   We will see our mother <u>within three days</u>.
> <u>*trēs diēs*</u> *mātrem vidēbimus.*   We will see our mother <u>for three days</u>.

ante and *post* deserve particular attention.

> *ante trēs annōs* and *tribus ante annīs* both mean "three years earlier."
>
> *post trēs annōs* and *tribus post annīs* both mean "three years later."

With the accusative, *ante* and *post* are prepositions; that is, "before/after three years"; with the ablative, they are adverbs, and the ablative expresses **time by how long;** that is, "before/afterward by three years."

abhinc is an adverb, meaning "ago." It is usually constructed with the accusative of a noun referring to a period of time, but sometimes the ablative is found.

> *abhinc annōs/annīs quinque* means "five years ago."

The nouns most frequently used in these constructions are the following:

tempus, temporis neut. 3	time
hōra, hōrae fem. 1	hour
diēs, diēī masc./fem. 5	day
nox, noctis fem. 3	night
mensis, mensis masc. 3	month
annus, annī masc. 2	year
vēr, vēris neut. 3	spring
aestās, aestātis fem. 3	summer
autumnus, autumnī masc. 2	fall
hiems, hiemis fem. 3	winter

Accusative, Ablative, and Locative of Place

You already know how to use constructions such as *Caesar <u>ad urbem</u> venit, Caesar <u>ab urbe</u> venit, Caesar <u>in urbe</u> est*. Prepositions are used in this way with common nouns referring to place (*urbs, oppidum, villa*, etc.). **Prepositions are not used, however, with the names of towns and small islands. Instead, the accusative alone is used for <u>motion toward</u> and the ablative alone for <u>motion from</u>.** For example:

Caesar <u>Rōmam</u> venit.	Caesar is coming <u>to Rome</u>.
Caesar <u>Rōmā</u> venit.	Caesar is coming <u>from Rome</u>.
Caesar <u>Lesbum</u> venit.	Caesar is coming <u>to Lesbos</u>.
Caesar <u>Lesbō</u> venit.	Caesar is coming <u>from Lesbos</u>.

Sicily, Corsica, Sardinia, Crete, Cyprus, Britain, Ireland, and the mysterious Thule—which may refer to the Orkneys, the Shetlands, or Iceland—are the only islands normally considered too large for this construction.

Towns and small islands use a different case for <u>position in which</u>: the **locative. For singular nouns of the first and second declension, the locative is identical to the genitive. Otherwise it is almost always identical to the ablative.** Here are some examples using Rome and the important cities *Londinium, Londiniī* neut. 2; *Athēnae, -ārum* fem. pl. 1; *Karthāgō, Karthāginis* fem. 3:

Caesar <u>Rōmae</u> est.	Caesar is <u>in Rome</u>.
Caesar <u>Londiniī</u> est.	Caesar is <u>in London</u>.
Caesar <u>Athēnīs</u> est.	Caesar is <u>in Athens</u>.
Caesar <u>Karthāgine</u> est.	Caesar is <u>in Carthage</u>.

Three common nouns referring to places, *domus, domūs* fem. 4 "home," *humus, humī* fem. 2 "ground," and *rūs, rūris* neut. 3 "countryside," also omit *ad* and *ā/ab* and use the locative case. *domus* has an irregular locative, *domī*, and an irregular ablative, *domō*, while the locative of *rūs* is either *rūrī* or, less frequently, *rūre*. For example:

domum eō.	I am going <u>home</u>.
domī maneō.	I am staying <u>at home</u>.
domō Rōmam vēnī.	I came to Rome <u>from home</u>.
mīles humum cecidit.	The soldier fell <u>to the ground</u>.
mīles humī iacēbat.	The soldier was lying <u>on the ground</u>.
mīles humō ortus est.	The soldier rose <u>from the ground</u>.
puella rūs adit.	The girl is going <u>to the countryside</u>.
puella rūrī/rūre est.	The girl is <u>in the countryside</u>.
puella rūre revenit.	The girl is coming back <u>from the countryside</u>.

Prōlūsiōnēs

Parse the following words.

1. ultus erat.
2. orientur.
3. fiet.
4. loquēbāmur.
5. moriēminī.
6. movēminī.
7. adeptae eritis.
8. patiēris.
9. audientur.
10. ausae sumus.

Translate and then change to the plural.

1. exercitus ducem mīrātur.
2. exercitus ducem diū secūtus est.
3. frāter meus exercitūs ducem sequī ausus erat.
4. consul Rōmānus moriētur.
5. gladiātor pinguis hodiē fēlix esse nōn vidētur.
6. ē silvā ēgressa erat lupa ferōcissima.
7. pastōrem, porce, sequere!
8. num gravem gladium mīlitis verēbāris?
9. dux noster turpis contrā exercitum barbarum herī nōn profectus est.
10. cum exercitū magnō consul Rōmānus in urbem parvam ingressus est.

Translate.

1. cōnāminī ducem sequī, mīlitēs, et urbem nostram dēfendite!

2. cōnābiminī cum duce vestrō loquī, mīlitēs?

3. porcī pastōrem breve tempus secūtī erant.

4. multa crūdēlia passa est ōlim māter mea.

5. multōs annōs in agrōs capellās agēbat pastor, sed abhinc quinque mēnsēs Rōmam regressus est.

6. tot mīlia mīlitum audācium mors rapuit, nec corpus ducis omnibus Rōmānīs cārī humō orīrī poterit!

7. quotiens dē mōribus cīvium querēbātur Augustus, prīmus Rōmānōrum imperātor!

8. prīmā noctis hōrā magistrātūs omnēs prope flūmen celere morābuntur stellāsque mīrābuntur.

9. post nuptiās fīliae meae domī manēre mālēbam, quamquam Athēnīs multōs annōs vīxerāmus.

10. tertiō annī novī diē gāvīsa est plebs tōta, quod rex nēminī cārus mortuus est.

11. abhinc sex mēnsēs domum regredī ausa est amīca frātris tuī.

12. quotiens dīvitiās iuvenis miser puellae crūdēlī pollicitus est!

13. servī infēlīcēs dē sceleribus dominī turpis querī numquam poterant.

14. orta est lūna sed stellae ē caelō lapsae sunt.

15. nēmō Rōmae hodiē gaudet, namque in senātū Caesar ab amīcīs crūdēliter interfectus est.

16. octāvō diē mensis ultimī nātus est puer deīs cārus; post multōs annōs poēta celeber erat, amīcus Vergiliī, poētae meliōris.

17. quamquam multōs annōs rūrī pastor vīxerat fēlīciter, breve tempus Rōmam Athēnāsque vidēre cupiēbat.

18. īte domum, capellae meae, nam lupī nocte villam dominī aggredī solent.

19. abhinc duōs annōs dē mūrō lapsa sunt ingentia saxa.

20. nēmō, nē rex quidem hostium nostrōrum, tot annōs dolōrēs tantōs patī merētur.

21. The queen was afraid of Octavianus and wished to return home with her whole fleet.

22. The emperor was not made happy by the poet's little book.

23. A poor man will never obtain money without shameful crimes.

24. Surely the barbarians did not dare to invade Italy four years ago?

25. Big dogs suddenly came out of the shepherd's humble house.

26. The sad slave was born under a large tree, but he will die in a huge city.

27. The wretched man embraced his sick sister's thin body.

28. The sick dog tried to go back to the city, but the three little pigs dared to stay in the countryside.

29. The pigs had obtained food at the sixth hour of the day, partly from the shepherds and partly from the farmer.

30. Why do you wish to become famous soldiers, boys? It is the duty of the commanders of the whole army to go away from Rome for a long time.

31. At the first hour, Caesar, you will die, although many good men admire not only your bravery but also your speeches.

32. For five years the citizens complained about the great man, for he had more power than the other leaders of the Roman people.

33. Caesar slipped to the ground in front of the statue of my great father on the fifteenth day of the third month.

34. Caesar has been carried into the Forum by a crowd of wretched citizens; while the flames seize the sad remains of his body, he is being praised by his friend, a brave general.

35. Listen to my words, citizens! I have come to my friend's funeral, but the Roman people will have to avenge his cruel death within a few months.

Lectiōnēs Latīnae

Lege, Intellege

The Emperor Domitian

Domitiānus mox accēpit imperium, frāter Titī iūnior, Nerōnī aut Caligulae aut Tiberiō similior quam patrī vel frātrī suō. prīmīs tamen annīs moderātus in imperiō fuit, mox ad ingentia vitia prōgressus libīdinis, īrācundiae, crūdēlitātis, avāritiae multum in sē odium concitāvit. nōbilissimōs interfēcit senātōrēs. dominum sē et deum prīmus appellārī iussit. nullam sibi nisi auream et argenteam statuam in Capitōliō passus est pōnī. superbia quoque in eō execrābilis fuit. expeditiōnēs quattuor habuit, ūnam adversum Sarmatās, alteram adversum Cattōs, duās adversum Dācōs. dē Dācīs Cattīsque duplicem triumphum ēgit, dē Sarmatīs triumphālēs tantum honōrēs ūsurpāvit.

—Eutropius, *Breviārium* 7.23

1. Which three emperors did Domitian resemble more than he resembled his father Vespasian and his brother Titus?

2. How many military expeditions did Domitian undertake?

3. By what titles did Domitian insist on being addressed?

4. Of what materials were statues of him to be made?

5. Were Domitian's lust, cruelty, anger, and greed evident right from the start of his rule?

Ars Poëtica

Virgil II

Give the person, tense, and number of the verbs in bold.

1. *magnus ab integrō saeclōrum* **nascitur** *ordō.*
   The great order of the centuries is being born again.

2. *Assyrium vulgō* **nascētur** *amōmum.*
   Assyrian balsam will grow everywhere.

3. *sterilēs* **nascuntur** *avēnae.*
   Sterile oats grow up.

4. *ter* **sunt cōnātī** *impōnere Pēliō Ossam.*
   Three times they [the Giants] tried to place Ossa on Pelion.

5. *bis* **cōnātus erat** *cāsūs effingere in aurō.*
   Twice he had tried to model his misfortunes in gold.

6. **ūritur** *infēlix Dīdō tōtāque* **vagātur**
   urbe furens.
   Unhappy Dido is consumed [with love] and wanders madly through the whole city.

7. *pars stupet innuptae dōnum exitiāle Minervae*
   et mōlem **mīrantur** *equī; prīmusque Thymoetēs*
   dūcī *intrā mūrōs* **hortātur** *et arce* **locārī.**
   Some are amazed at the deadly gift of unmarried Minerva and they wonder at the size of the horse; and Thymoetes first urges that it be led inside the walls and placed in the citadel.

8. *sīc* **fātur** *lacrimans, classīque immittit habēnās*
   et tandem Euboicīs Cūmārum **adlābitur** *ōrīs.*
   Thus he speaks, weeping, and gives rein to the fleet, and glides at last to the Euboean shores of Cumae [near Naples, the home of the Sibylline oracle].

Aurea Dicta

1. *aequat omnēs cinis: imparēs nascimur, parēs morimur.* (Seneca the Younger)

2. *bonum ex malō nōn fit.* (Seneca the Younger)

3. *bonum sine ratiōne nullum est; sequitur autem ratiō nātūram.* (Seneca the Younger)

4. *Catō esse quam vidērī bonus mālēbat.* (Sallust)

5. *dulce et decōrum est prō patriā morī.* (Horace)

6. *et facere et patī fortiter Rōmānum est.* (Livy)

7. *ingenium rēs adversae nūdāre solent, cēlāre secundae.* (Horace)

8. *nātūrāle est magis nova quam magna mīrārī.* (Seneca the Younger)

cinis, cineris 3 masc. ash

pār, paris equal

autem conj. but, and

cēlō 1 hide (trans.)

secundus, -a, -um favorable

Hōrologia Latīna

1. *ā sōlis ortū vītam hominis umbra notat.*
   From the rising of the sun, my shadow records mortal life.

2. *ēheu, quam festīnant diēs!*
   Alas, how the days hurry!

3. *mē lūmen, vōs umbra regit.*
   The light rules me, my shadow rules you.

4. *nulla sine sōle umbra.*
   There is no shadow without the sun.

5. *vix orimur et occidimus.*
   We scarcely rise and we set.

Lūsūs

Thēsaurus Verbōrum

Many of these masculine third declension nouns ending in *-ātor, -ātōris*, referring to men engaged in particular activities, have been adopted in English.

amātor	lover	ōrātor	(public) speaker
arātor	plowman	piscātor	fisherman
creātor	creator	senātor	senator
dictātor	dictator	spectātor	spectator
gladiātor	gladiator	vēnātor	hunter
mercātor	merchant	viātor	traveler

Etymologiae Antīquae

The Hills of Rome

Aventine Several etymologies were suggested for this name; one claimed that it came from *avis, avis* fem. 3 "bird," another that it came from Aventinus, a local pre-Roman king.

Caelian So called after Caeles Vibenna, an Etruscan who came to the aid of one of the kings of Rome.

Capitoline The smallest of the seven hills, but the most important, because it contained the *arx* (citadel) and the temple of Jupiter Optimus Maximus. It was so called because workers digging the foundations of Jupiter's temple found a human head, which was taken as a sign that Rome would be *caput orbis*, the capital city of the world. Criminals were executed by being thrown from the *saxum Tarpeium* on the Capitol, named after the Vestal Virgin Tarpeia, who agreed to betray the citadel to the Sabines in return for what they wore on their left arms: she hoped for gold bracelets, but the Sabines killed her by dropping their shields on her.

Esquiline Some thought that the Esquiline's name came from the *excubiae* (*-ārum* fem. 1 "watch-towers") set up there when Rome was ruled by kings. Another explanation was that the hill was cultivated (*colō, colere, coluī, cultum* 3) with oak trees (*aesculus, -ī* fem. 2). We don't know the true derivation, but since the Esquiline lay outside the original city wall, one theory is that, in contrast to *inquilīnī, -ōrum* masc. 2 ("inhabitants," from *in + colō*), those who lived outside the walls may have been called *exquilīnī*.

Palatine So called after Pallas, the grandfather of Evander, the leader of the people who were living on the site when Aeneas arrived. Another suggested derivation was from *bālātus, -ūs* masc. 4 "bleating," the Romans having originally been herders. In commemoration of Rome's simple beginnings, a *casa Rōmulī* "hut of Romulus" was preserved there (as also on the Capitoline). Since Augustus and later emperors lived there, the name of the hill evolved into our word "palace."

Quirinal Named either after the Sabine town Cures, which was incorporated into Rome, or after the god Quirinus, who was identified with Romulus.

Viminal So called from the osiers (*vīmen, vīminis* neut. 3) that originally grew there.

Two other hills, both on the other (right) bank of the Tiber, should also be mentioned. The *Janiculum* is named after Janus, the god of beginnings and entrances. One of the suggested derivations for the name of the *Vatican* very appropriately, given its modern function, linked it with *vātēs, vātis* masc./fem. 3 "priest(ess)."

Vīta Rōmānōrum

Rēs Gestae Dīvī Augustī

Shortly before his death in AD 14, at the age of seventy-five, Augustus had an account prepared of his achievements, his *rēs gestae*. It was the last of his many acts of propaganda. It was presumably inscribed on monuments throughout the empire, but it survives best in a copy found at Ankara in Turkey, so it is sometimes known as the *monumentum Ancyrānum*.

The deeds of the divine Augustus, by which he brought the world under the control of the Roman people, and the expenses he incurred on behalf of the state and the Roman people, have been inscribed on two bronze pillars set up in Rome. A copy is set out below.

1. At the age of nineteen, on my own responsibility and at my own expense, I raised an army with which I restored the state to liberty when it had been oppressed by the tyranny of a faction. The Senate therefore inducted me into its ranks through decrees in my honor, in the consulship of Gaius Pansa and Aulus Hirtius [43 BC], granting me the right to give my opinion among those of consular rank, and giving me *imperium*. The Senate ordered me as *prōpraetor* [a senior magistrate] to work with the consuls to see that the state suffered no harm. In the same year, since both consuls had fallen in war, the people appointed me consul and triumvir to organize the state.

2. Those who butchered my father I drove into exile, exacting vengeance for their crime with legal judgments, and afterward I defeated them twice in battle when they made war on the state.

3. I waged frequent civil and foreign wars by land and sea through the whole world, and as victor I spared all citizens who sought mercy. Foreign peoples who could safely be pardoned I preferred to spare rather than to annihilate. About five hundred thousand Roman citizens were under military allegiance to me. I settled more than three hundred thousand of these in colonies or sent them back to their townships after their period of service, and I assigned land to them all or gave them money as a reward for their military service. I captured six hundred ships, not including those smaller than triremes.

—Augustus, *Rēs Gestae* 1–3

CHAPTER 16
Particular Uses of Cases

The nominative is used as the subject or predicate of a clause, the vocative only in addressing someone, the locative only to denote location. All the other cases are used in a wide range of idioms. So far, you have seen:

- the **genitive** denoting possession and sometimes quantity
- the **dative** as the indirect object of verbs and with certain adjectives, such as *cārus*, *sacer*, and *similis*
- the **accusative** as the direct object of transitive verbs, with prepositions, and expressing time and place
- the **ablative** with prepositions; in comparisons; and expressing means, time, and place

In this chapter, you will learn other idiomatic uses of these cases. The following words will appear in the examples and exercises, and you may find it useful to review them now.

Verbs

aestimō 1	estimate
rogō 1	ask
emō, emere, ēmī, emptum 3	buy
vendō, vendere, vendidī, venditum 3	sell
faciō, facere, fēcī, factum 3 *i*-stem	in the sense "to value"
sum, esse, fuī irreg.	in the sense "to be worth"

Nouns

causa, -ae fem. 1	cause
grātia, -ae fem. 1	sake
floccus, -ī masc. 2	tuft of wool
nihilum, nihilī neut. 2	nothing
as, assis neut. 3	the smallest Roman coin

Adjectives

ignārus, -a, -um	ignorant
memor, memoris	mindful
plēnus, -a, -um	full

Adverbs (used as nouns)

satis	enough
nimis	too much
parum	too little

Uses of the Genitive

- Partitive Genitive
- Subjective and Objective Genitive
- Genitive of Description
- Genitive of Characteristic
- Genitive of Value
- Genitive with Certain Adjectives

Partitive Genitive

You remember from Chapters 10 and 12 that *mīlia* and *plūs* take a genitive of the noun that depends on them, as in *duo mīlia porcōrum* and *plūs pecūniae*.

These are actually examples of the partitive genitive. In this idiom, words for a <u>part</u> of a group or entity are used with a genitive form of the <u>whole</u> of that group or entity. The partitive genitive is particularly frequent with such adverbs as *satis* "enough," *nimis* "too much," and *parum* "too little," which are used as indeclinable nouns.

<u>*satis pecūniae*</u> *fīliō numquam dat nauta.*	The sailor never gives his son <u>enough money</u>.
<u>*parum virtūtis*</u> *habet dominus noster.*	Our owner has <u>too little virtue</u>.

Subjective and Objective Genitive

These two complementary idioms express an active and a passive interpretation of the genitive. The objective use of the genitive involves nouns denoting feelings, qualities, or actions, where the genitive signals that these are in fact directed toward the "possessor," not felt or carried out by him or her. As a result, the best translation is often "for" or "to" rather than "of." So the phrase *odium Caesaris* would mean "hatred toward Caesar."

<u>*cūram hominum*</u> *nullam habent deī.*	The gods have no <u>care for humans</u>.
vir bonus est et <u>*amōrem deī*</u> *magnum habet.*	He is a good man and has a great <u>love for god</u>.

The subjective genitive involves these nouns, too, but is often nearly indistinguishable from the genitive of possession; here *odium Caesaris* would mean the hatred Caesar feels for something or someone.

<u>*cūrae hominum*</u> *multae sunt.*	<u>The cares of humans</u> are many.
<u>*amor deī*</u> *virum bonum contrā perīcula omnia dēfendit.*	<u>The love of god</u> defends a good man against all dangers.

Genitive of Description

A noun in the genitive, modified by an adjective, is attached to another noun in order to indicate the degree to which it possesses a quality.

uxor nautae fēmina <u>maximae stultitiae</u> erat.	The sailor's wife was a woman <u>of very great stupidity</u>.
canem <u>magnī labōris</u> habēbat pastor.	The shepherd had a <u>hard-working</u> dog (lit. a dog of hard work).

Genitive of Characteristic

Up until now you have seen predicates that are used with the verbs *esse* and *fierī* always in the same case—the nominative—as the noun they referred to: for example, *lupus ferox est.*

In the genitive of characteristic, the genitive of a noun is used as a predicate, and here also the verb is usually *esse.* In translating, you should insert a phrase such as "it is characteristic" or "it is a mark."

<u>*lupōrum*</u> *est agnōs terrēre.*	It is <u>characteristic of wolves</u> to frighten lambs.
<u>*magistrī bonī*</u> *est discipulōs laudāre.*	It is <u>the mark of a good teacher</u> to praise his students.

Genitive of Value

The genitive of the neuter singular form of adjectives denoting quantity, such as *magnī, parvī, plūris, tantī* ("so much"), is used to refer to an indefinite <u>value</u>. The genitive of some nouns signifying worthlessness—for example, *as, assis* neut. 3 "as" (the smallest Roman coin), *floccus, -ī* masc. 2 "tuft of wool," *nihilum, nihilī* neut. 2 "nothing"—is used in the same way. Verbs used in this idiom include *aestimō* 1 "estimate," *faciō,* and *sum.*

magistrum meum nōn <u>floccī</u> faciō. *magistrum meum <u>floccī</u> faciō.*	My teacher isn't worth/is worth [only] a *floccus* to me (i.e., I don't value my teacher at all.)
pastōrī nōn est <u>tantī</u> Rōmam vidēre.	It is not <u>of so much</u> (value) to the shepherd to see Rome. (i.e., The shepherd does not care so much about seeing Rome.)

You remember that *plūs, plūris,* "more," is a neuter singular noun. Its genitive is the form used in the genitive of value.

<u>*plūris*</u> *porcōs quam agnōs facit pastor.*	The shepherd makes his pigs <u>of more</u> (value) than his lambs. (i.e., The shepherd values his pigs more highly than his lambs.)

Genitive with Certain Adjectives

Some adjectives are constructed with a genitive. For example:

pastor <u>porcōrum nōn memor</u> est.	The shepherd is <u>not mindful of his pigs</u>.
<u>plēnum aquae</u> est flūmen.	The river is <u>full of water</u>.
Caesar <u>ignārus bellī</u> nōn erat.	Caesar was not <u>ignorant of war</u>.
<u>avārōs glōriae</u> nōn laudō.	I do not praise those who are <u>greedy for glory</u>.
porcus <u>aprī</u> [or dat. *<u>aprō</u>*] *<u>similis</u> est.*	A pig is like a wild boar.

Uses of the Dative

- Dative of Possession
- Dative of Reference
- Predicate Dative

Dative of Possession

Particularly in combination with the verb *esse*, the dative can be used to indicate <u>possession</u>. For example:

<u>pastōrī</u> multī porcī sunt.	The shepherd has many pigs. (lit. There are <u>to the shepherd</u> many pigs.)
nōmen <u>rēgī</u> est Tarquinius.	The king's name is Tarquin. (lit. The name <u>to the king</u> is Tarquin.)

Dative of Reference

The dative is often used to indicate who is <u>affected by</u>, or <u>interested in</u>, the action or idea. Compare these two sentences:

Genitive
<u>pastōris</u> porcōs omnēs interfēcērunt lupī.

Dative of Reference
<u>pastōrī</u> porcōs omnēs interfēcērunt lupī.

Both sentences express the idea that the wolves killed all the shepherd's pigs, but the genitive *pastōris* indicates only the ownership of the pigs, while the dative *pastōrī* emphasizes the effect of the event on the shepherd. Similarly, compare these sentences:

Adjective
Hannibal exercitum <u>Rōmānum</u> dēlēre voluit.
Hannibal wished to destroy the Roman army.

Dative of Reference
Hannibal <u>Rōmānīs</u> exercitum dēlēre voluit.
Hannibal wished to destroy the army to do harm to the Romans.

The dative of reference can also indicate that an action benefits someone or is intended to do so:

pastōrī lupōs omnēs interfēcit dominus noster.   Our owner killed all the wolves <u>for the shepherd</u>.

It can also indicate someone's attitude or opinion:

patrī meō Tiberius vir optimus est.   <u>In my father's opinion</u> Tiberius is a very good man.

Predicate Dative

Many nouns, most of them abstract nouns such as "use" and "disgrace," are used in the dative singular to express <u>purpose</u> or <u>result</u>. The person or thing affected will also be in the dative; this is a dative of reference. In this "double dative" construction, the dative expressing purpose or result is rarely modified by any adjective other than *magnus* and *parvus*.

Dative of Reference			**Predicate Dative**	
mors	*tua*	*omnibus*	*dolōrī magnō*	*erit.*

Your death will be <u>a source of great sorrow</u> (lit. for great sorrow) to everyone.

Here are some more examples of the "double dative" construction:

gladius mīlitī ūsuī est.	A sword is <u>useful</u> (lit. for use) to a soldier.
porcī gracilēs agricolīs maximō dēdecorī sunt.	Skinny pigs are <u>a very great disgrace</u> (lit. for a very great disgrace) to farmers.
labor dūrus amōrī infēlīcī remediō est.	Hard work is <u>a cure</u> (lit. for a cure) for unhappy love.
virtūs ducis mīlitibus omnibus exemplō esse dēbet.	The general's courage should be <u>an example</u> (lit. for an example) to all his soldiers.
pastōribus perīculō minimō sunt lupī, porcīs exitiō maximō.	Wolves are <u>no great threat</u> (lit. for a very small danger) to shepherds, but <u>very dangerous</u> (lit. for a very great destruction) to pigs.

Among the nouns most frequently used in the double dative construction are the following:

auxiliō (auxilium, auxiliī neut. 2)	help
cūrae (cūra, cūrae fem. 1)	care
damnō (damnum, damnī neut. 2)	injury
decorī (decus, decoris neut. 3)	adornment
dēdecorī (dēdecus, dēdecoris neut. 3)	disgrace
dolōrī (dolor, dolōris masc. 3)	pain
exemplō (exemplum, exemplī neut. 2)	example

exitiō (exitium, exitiī neut. 2)	destruction
glōriae (glōria, glōriae fem. 1)	glory
honōrī (honor, honōris masc. 3)	honor
impedīmentō (impedīmentum, impedīmentī neut. 2)	hindrance
laudī (laus, laudis fem. 3)	glory
lucrō (lucrum, lucrī neut. 2)	profit
odiō (odium, odiī neut. 2)	hatred
onerī (onus, oneris neut. 3)	burden
perīculō (perīculum, perīculī neut. 2)	danger
pudōrī (pudor, pudōris masc. 3)	shame
remediō (remedium, remediī neut. 2)	cure
salūtī (salūs, salūtis fem. 3)	deliverance
sōlāciō (sōlācium, sōlāciī neut. 2)	comfort
timōrī (timor, timōris masc. 3)	fear
ūsuī (ūsus, ūsūs masc. 4)	use

Uses of the Accusative

- Accusative of Exclamation
- Accusative of Respect
- Accusative of Extent
- Double Accusative

Accusative of Exclamation

Exclamations typically consist of a noun or pronoun in the accusative, accompanied by an adjective in agreement with it.

stultās hominum spēs!	Oh, the foolish hopes of mankind!
ō diem fēlīcem!	What a lucky day!

Accusative of Respect

This idiom uses the accusative to indicate the part of the body <u>affected</u> by an action or condition.

<u>caput</u> pīrāta graviter vulnerātus est.	The pirate was severely wounded in the head (lit. <u>with respect to his head</u>).
agnus <u>faciem</u> dulcis est.	The lamb has a pleasant face (lit. is pleasant <u>with respect to its face</u>).

Accusative of Extent

Especially with the adjectives *altus*, *lātus*, and *longus*, the accusative is used to express measurement.

flūmen multōs pedēs altum est.	The river is <u>many feet</u> deep.
mare multa mīlia pedum lātum est.	The sea is <u>many thousands of feet</u> wide.

Double Accusative

Especially with verbs such as *rogō* 1 "ask" and *doceō, docēre, docuī, doctum* 2 "teach," Latin can use the accusative for both the person asked or taught, and the thing they are asked for or taught.

pastōrem porcōs agricola rogat.	The farmer asks the shepherd for pigs.
litterās puerōs magister docet.	The teacher teaches the alphabet to the boys.

Uses of the Ablative

- Ablative of Manner
- Ablative of Description
- Ablative of Cause
- Ablative of Price

Ablative of Manner

The ablative is used to indicate the <u>manner in which</u> something is done. The noun in the ablative may stand alone, but more often it is modified by an adjective.

virtūte pugnant mīlitēs.	The soldiers are fighting <u>with courage</u>.
summā virtūte pugnant mīlitēs.	The soldiers are fighting <u>with the utmost courage</u>.

A frequent alternative to the ablative of manner is *cum* and the ablative. If the noun is modified by an adjective, then *cum* often comes between them.

cum virtūte pugnant mīlitēs.	The soldiers are fighting <u>with courage</u>.
magnā cum virtūte pugnant mīlitēs.	The soldiers are fighting <u>with great courage</u>.

Ablative of Description

A noun in the ablative modified by an adjective can express a <u>quality</u> possessed by the noun on which it depends. This idiom is often interchangeable with the genitive of description.

uxor nautae fēmina maximā stultitiā erat.	The sailor's wife was a woman <u>of very great stupidity</u>.
canem tribus capitibus cēpit Herculēs.	Hercules captured a dog <u>with three heads</u>.

Ablative of Cause

The ablative is used for the <u>reason</u> for which something is done or happens.

victōriā tuā gāvīsī sunt cīvēs.	The citizens rejoiced <u>at (because of) your victory</u>.
lībertātis amōre urbem dēfendent cīvēs.	The citizens will defend the city <u>for (because of) love of freedom</u>.

Two examples of this construction became idioms in their own right. The ablative of *causa, -ae* fem. 1 "cause" was used with a noun in the genitive to mean "for the cause of." The ablative of *grātia, -ae* fem. 1 "sake" modified by a pronominal adjective ("my," "your," etc.) was used to mean "for the sake of."

cīvēs lībertātis causā pugnāvērunt.	The citizens fought <u>for the cause of liberty</u>.
meā grātiā rosās mātrī dedit frāter.	My brother gave roses to our mother <u>for my sake</u>.

Ablative of Price

The ablative is used to indicate the <u>price</u> of something. You will find this usage particularly with the verbs *vendō, vendere, vendidī, venditum* 3 "sell" and *emō, emere, ēmī, emptum* 3 "buy."

ducentīs porcīs casam ēmerāmus.	We had bought the house <u>for two hundred pigs</u>.
urbem hostibus multō aurō vendidit.	He sold the city to the enemy <u>for much gold</u>.

Prōlūsiōnēs

Parse the words in bold.

ante bellum Actiacum sīc **Rōmae** dē Marcō Antōniō querēbātur Octāviānus Caesar: "**plūris** Antōniō est amor **Cleopatrae**, fēminae **mōribus** barbarīs, quam salūs populī Rōmānī. ō **hominem** turpissimum! multōs vērō abhinc annōs patrī meō **auxiliō** fuit. nunc tamen **Rōmae** perīculō est, nōn praesidiō, namque exercitum Rōmānum nōn floccī facit, et iam tōtum **annum** cum rēgīnā tempus stultē perdit. num **imperātōris** Rōmānī est piscēs **rūrī** capere?"

Parse the words in bold and translate the sentence.

1. num Iūlius Caesar, vir summae **nōbilitātis**, rex fierī cōnātus est?
2. Augustō mōrēs fīliae, nōmine Iūliae, magnō **dolōrī** erant.
3. **sanguine** tot cīvium Tiberius ōtium turpe ēmit.
4. **Caligulae** vērum nōmen erat Gaius Iūlius Caesar Augustus Germānicus.
5. **Claudiō** mōrēs maiōrum per tōtam vītam exemplō erant.
6. Nerōnis statua tantōs **pedēs** alta paucīs annīs humum cecidit.
7. legiōnēs Galbae, virō senectūte iam gravī, imperium **aurō** vendidērunt.
8. dīvitiārum **amōre** imperium adeptus est Othō.
9. Vitellius, quod currū Caligulae vulnerātus erat, **pedem** dēformis erat.
10. Vespāsiānus, vir **mōribus** optimīs, aurum tamen tantī faciēbat.
11. Titus **patrī** simillimus erat, sed frātre nōn modo maior sed etiam mōrum humiliōrum.
12. Domitiānus: ō **hominem** scelerum plēnum!
13. Nerva Narniae, nōn Rōmae, nātus est, sed senectūtis causā sēdecim tantum **mensēs** imperāvit.
14. sī fēlīcior **Augustō**, Traiānō melior es, deus ōlim fīēs.
15. **pācis** Rōmānae causā Hadriānus mūrum longum aedificāvit.

Translate.

1. dēdecorī est nautīs mare pīrātāsque timēre.
2. quintā nocte rex sociōrum crūdēlī morte periit.
3. cibusne tālis aegrō porcō remediō erit?
4. nē maximae quidem virtūtis dux tot hostēs vincere potest.
5. mīlitēs uxōrum līberōrumque causā domum redīre volēbant.
6. magnō perīculō classī Rōmānae sunt nāvēs nostrae.
7. numquam onerī discipulīs fuerat librōs legere.
8. nihilī facimus servum tuum, sī labōrāre nōn vult.
9. damnō maximō pastōribus est sī lupī porcōs tam facile interficiunt.
10. sociī nostrī, virī mōrum tam bonōrum, cīvibus auxiliō esse potuerant.
11. fructūs arboris nostrae decem pedēs altae maximō sōlāciō porcīs tuīs erant.
12. quattuor agnīs porcum ēmī, sed nōn tantī est, nam pastōrī lucrō nōn sunt porcī, sī gracilī corpore sunt.
13. caput manūsque multa vulnera passus est centuriō quartae legiōnis, vir faciē nōn pulchrā.

14. post uxōris cārae mortem consulī sōlāciō erat prō glōriā Rōmae labōrāre.

15. pīrātam nautae floccī nōn faciunt, nam homō corpore parvō pinguīque est.

16. dominō meō crūdēlī dēdecorī fuit maximō lībertātem servīs optimīs nōn dare.

17. bonī pastōrēs cum porcīs loquuntur, sed malī pastōris est porcōs in silvā relinquere.

18. dux magnae virtūtis erat Hannibal, cumque elephantōrum longō agmine vēnit ad Alpēs.

19. quamquam legiōnēs consulum duōrum ūnō diē vīcit Hannibal, tamen cīvium grātiā Rōmam post mortem tot mīlitum rediit consul ūnus, nōmine Gaius Terentius Varrō.

20. ō urbem infēlīcem! plēnae timōris sunt viae et tot cīvēs mortuī iacent, sed pācem hostium ducem rogāre Rōmānī nōlunt.

21. Neither my brother nor my sister have enough food, but I will never ask the consul, a man of very great wealth, for money.

22. Love for Cleopatra conquered both Caesar and Antonius, for she was a woman with a very beautiful face.

23. Although Antonius fought with great bravery, the queen sailed home because she placed no value on glory.

24. I place no value on my life, and am willing to buy victory with my blood.

25. Many bad things have been done by good men because of their fear of death.

26. It is a great comfort to listen to the pigs when they are lying in our owner's garden.

27. Although the river was only five feet wide, it was a great hindrance to Caesar, for he was still mindful of the laws.

28. He was greedy for power, but delayed for many days for the sake of the Roman people.

29. It is not the mark of a good commander to return to Italy with his army.

30. Oh, wretched citizens! Caesar will kill even the magistrates, men of good character.

Lectiōnēs Latīnae

Lege, Intellege

Seneca the Elder (Lucius Annaeus Seneca; c. 50 BC–c. AD 40), the father of Seneca the philosopher, wrote the *Ōrātōrum et Rhētōrum Sententiae, Dīvīsiōnēs, Colōrēs*, which was a memoir of the schools of declamation [speech-making] in the Augustan period. About half of the work has survived, five books on *contrōversiae* [speeches for legal argument] and one on *suāsōriae* [speeches of persuasion]. *contrōversiae* were essential training for a legal career, but they often dealt with far-fetched themes. As well as "Should Alexander sail the Ocean?" the *suāsōriae* include such topics as "Should the 300 Spartans retreat from Thermopylae?" and "Should Cicero beg Antony to spare his life?"

Urging Alexander the Great not to sail the Ocean

terrae quoque suum fīnem habent et ipsīus mundī aliquī occāsus est. nihil infīnītum est. modum magnitūdinī facere dēbēs, quoniam fortūna nōn facit. magnī pectoris est inter rēs secundās moderātiō. eundem fortūna victōriae tuae quem nātūrae fīnem facit: imperium tuum claudit Ōceanus. ō quantum magnitūdō tua rērum quoque nātūram supergressa est: Alexander orbī magnus est, Alexandrō orbis parvus est. etiam magnitūdinī modus est: nōn prōcēdit ultrā spatia sua caelum; maria intrā terminōs suōs agitantur. quidquid ad summum pervēnit, incrēmentō nōn relīquit locum. nōn magis quicquam ultrā Alexandrum nōvimus quam ultrā Ōceanum.

—Seneca the Elder, *Suāsōriae* 1.3

mundus, -ī masc. 2 world

pectus, pectoris neut. 3 breast, soul

eundem fortūna victōriae tuae quem nātūrae fīnem facit "Fortune sets the same limit to your victory as to your nature"

quidquid "whatever"

quicquam "anything"

spatium, -iī neut. 2 space

1. Why should Alexander impose a limit on his own greatness?
2. Are the seas infinite?
3. What marks the boundary to Alexander's empire?
4. When is there no scope for increase?
5. What sort of person is characterized by moderation in success?

Ars Poētica

Virgil III

Identify and explain the case of the words in bold.

1. *veteris memor Sāturnia* **bellī**.
   The daughter of Saturn [Juno], mindful of the old war [the Trojan war].

2. **Iovis** *omnia plēna;*
   ille colit terrās, illī mea carmina **cūrae**.
   All things are full of Jupiter; he looks after the earth, he takes care of my poems.

3. *vendidit hīc **aurō** patriam dominumque potentem*
   *imposuit; fixit lēgēs **pretiō** atque refixit.*
   This man sold his fatherland for gold and imposed a powerful master; for a price he made and unmade laws.

4. *centum errant **annōs** volitantque haec lītora circum.*
   For a hundred years they wander and flit round these shores.

5. *ō fortūnātōs . . . **agricolās**!*
   Lucky farmers!

6. *sunt mihi bis septem praestantī **corpore** Nymphae.*
   I have fourteen Nymphs with excellent bodies.

7. *saepe **diem** noctemque et tōtum ex ordine mensem*
   pascitur itque pecus longa in dēserta sine ullīs
   *hospitiīs: tantum **campī** iacet.*
   Often the flock grazes day and night and a whole month consecutively and goes into the vast desert with no shelter: so much plain lies spread out.

Aurea Dicta

1. *adulātiō quam similis est amīcitiae!* (Seneca the Younger)
2. *ampla domus dēdecorī dominō saepe fit.* (Cicero)
3. *aspiciunt oculīs superī mortālia iustīs.* (Ovid)
4. *ēmit morte immortālitātem.* (Quintilian)
5. *fraudis atque insidiārum et perfidiae plēna sunt omnia.* (Cicero)
6. *ignōrātiōne rērum bonārum et malārum maximē hominum vīta vexātur.* (Cicero)
7. *magnī animī est iniūriās despicere.* (Seneca the Younger)
8. *nihil est, mihi crēde, virtūte formōsius, nihil pulchrius, nihil amābilius.* (Cicero)

Lūsūs

Thēsaurus Verbōrum

These third declension feminine nouns ending in *-ātiō, -ātiōnis* refer mostly to abstract concepts. The English cognates just add *-n* to the nominative singular:

consōlātiō	indignātiō	prōcrastinātiō
creātiō	irritātiō	recitātiō
dominātiō	meditātiō	variātiō
duplicātiō	obligātiō	violātiō
ēducātiō	ōrātiō	vocātiō

Etymologiae Antīquae

More Place Names

***Africa**, -ae* fem. 1. Africa is sunny (*aprīcus, -a, -um*).

***Alba**, -ae **Longa**, -ae* fem. 1. The mother city of Rome (near Castel Gandolfo) was founded by Aeneas' son Ascanius on a long ridge where a white (*albus, -a, -um*) sow gave birth to thirty piglets.

***Britannia**, -ae* fem. 1. The inhabitants of Britain were thought to be stupid (*brūtus, -a, -um*).

***Campānia**, -ae* fem. 1. Campania is notable for its plains (*campus, -ī* masc. 2).

***Gallia**, -ae* fem. 1. Gaul is so called from the pale complexion of the inhabitants, γάλα (*gala*) meaning "milk" in Greek. The *Francī* were later notorious for breaking (*frangō, -ere, frēgī, fractum* 3) oaths.

***Germānia**, -ae* fem. 1. The Germans had huge (*immānis, -e*) bodies and were thought to breed (*germinō* 1) prolifically.

***Ītalia**, -ae* fem. 1. Italy was famous for its cattle (*vitulus, -ī* masc. 2 "calf").

***Karthāgō**, -inis* fem. 3. Carthage means "New City" in Punic, the Carthaginian language. Virgil plays on this when he calls Carthage *urbs antīqua* at the beginning of the *Aeneid*.

Latium, -iī neut. 2. The Romans spoke Latin because Rome is in *Latium*, a name that some derived from the verb *lateō, latēre, latuī* 2 "hide" (intrans.), either because the region lies hidden between the Alps and the Apennines, or because Saturn hid there when ousted from the throne of heaven by Jupiter.

Mediolānum, -ī neut. 2. The modern Milan. In the middle (*medius, -a, -um*) of the site where the city was to be founded, a pig with a fleece of wool (*lāna, -ae* fem. 1) appeared as an omen sent by the gods.

Neāpolis, -is fem. 3. Naples (νέα πόλις [*nea polis*]) means "New City" in Greek.

Pompeiī, -ōrum masc. 2. When he returned from Spain with the cattle he had stolen from Geryon, Hercules held a triumphant procession—the Greek for which is πομπή [*pompe*]—on the site of Pompeii. He also founded Herculaneum, the other city destined to be destroyed in the eruption of Vesuvius in AD 79.

Rōma, -ae fem. 1. *Rōma* may actually be an Etruscan tribal name, but it was a useful coincidence for Roman propaganda that the Greek form of "Rome" was identical to a word meaning "physical power."

Umbria, -ae fem. 1. The inhabitants of this region of Italy survived the rainstorms (*imber, imbris* masc. 3) of the Great Flood. (The Greeks and Romans had a legend similar to the biblical story.)

Vīta Rōmānōrum

Roman Superiority to Greece

Graecia capta ferum victōrem cēpit et artēs/intulit agrestī Latiō ("Although captured, Greece captivated its wild conqueror and brought the arts to unsophisticated Latium"). These lines by Horace express the Roman acceptance of Greek intellectual and artistic superiority. As a prolific writer and philosopher, Cicero had some basis for challenging this view, but his claim probably seemed very presumptuous when the *Tusculan Disputations* were written, in 45 BC, before Virgil and Horace had begun their careers as poets, and two years before Ovid was born.

> The system and method of instruction in all the arts that have a bearing on the proper conduct of life are bound up with wisdom, which is termed "philosophy." I thought I should illustrate this in Latin—not because philosophy cannot be learned from Greek writers and teachers, but it has always been my opinion that our fellow countrymen have been wiser than the Greeks both in the discoveries they have made for themselves and in improving what they have received from them and considered worthy of attention.

> Morality, customs, domestic affairs are all maintained by us in a better and more proper manner, and our ancestors undoubtedly devised better regulations and laws for our public life. What need I say about military matters? In that field the Romans have shown not only great valor but, more especially, discipline. In what they have achieved

through nature, not through literature, they are beyond comparison with the Greeks or any other people. Who has ever shown such seriousness, such steadfastness, greatness of mind, honesty, loyalty, such great virtue in every endeavor, as to deserve comparison with our ancestors?

Greece used to be superior to us in learning and in all branches of literature: victory was easy when there was no contest. In Greece the poets constitute the longest established literary class, given that Homer and Hesiod predate the foundation of Rome and Archilochus flourished in the reign of Romulus. We took to poetry much later. It was about 510 years after the foundation of Rome when Livius Andronicus first produced a play, in the consulship of Gaius Claudius, son of Appius Claudius Caecus, and Marcus Tuditanus [240 BC], a year before the birth of Ennius, who was older than Plautus and Naevius. So it took a long time for poets to be known and accepted in Rome. In the *Orīginēs* of Cato it is recorded that guests at banquets customarily sang songs in praise of the great deeds of famous men, to the accompaniment of a flute, but a speech by Cato states that such performances were not greatly valued; in that speech he criticizes Marcus Fulvius Nobilior for taking poets with him when he went to govern a province. (It is well known that, as consul, he had taken Ennius to Aetolia.) The less poets were valued, the less poetry was studied, and yet, whenever anyone has shown great talent in that field, he has matched the glory which the Greeks have won.

—Cicero, *Disputātiōnēs Tusculānae* 1.1–3

CHAPTER 17
Pronouns I, Intransitive Verbs with the Dative

Pronouns are words that substitute for nouns. Mostly they are used to avoid repetition. "The farmer was in the field. I saw him in it" and "I saw the farmer, who was in the field" are preferable to "The farmer was in the field. I saw the farmer in the field."

Many pronouns in Latin also serve as pronominal adjectives. In other words, they may be used not only <u>instead of nouns</u> but also <u>to modify nouns</u>. For example, *ille* by itself—that is, used as a pronoun—and *ille vir* both mean "that man." *ipse* by itself (as a pronoun) and *ipse vir* both mean "the man himself."

Demonstrative Pronouns/Demonstrative Pronominal Adjectives: *hīc, ille, iste, is, īdem, ipse*

hīc means "this," both as a pronoun and as a pronominal adjective. For example, *agricola nautaque hanc amant* and *agricola nautaque hanc fēminam amant* both mean "The farmer and the sailor love this woman."

hīc, haec, hōc

	MASC.	FEM.	NEUT.
Singular			
NOMINATIVE	hīc	haec	hōc
GENITIVE	huius	huius	huius
DATIVE	huic	huic	huic
ACCUSATIVE	hunc	hanc	hōc
ABLATIVE	hōc	hāc	hōc
Plural			
NOMINATIVE	hī	hae	haec
GENITIVE	hōrum	hārum	hōrum
DATIVE	hīs	hīs	hīs
ACCUSATIVE	hōs	hās	haec
ABLATIVE	hīs	hīs	hīs

Pronunciation Note: The first two vowels of *huius, eius,* and *cuius* (see Chapter 18) are pronounced as a diphthong, and the final *u* is short; compare the pronunciation of the word "colloquium" in English. Similarly, the vowels in the dative singular forms *huic* and *cui* (see Chapter 18) are also pronounced as a diphthong; compare "weak" and "queen."

ille and **iste** both mean "that," but with subtle differences. *ille* tends to be complimentary, "I admire that swift horse," whereas *iste* tends to be disparaging, "I despise that drunken sailor." **is** is the least emphatic of the three, often best translated as "he," "she," "it," and so on.

ille, **iste**, and **is** can all be used both as pronouns and as pronominal adjectives. For example, *agricola nautaque illam amant* and *agricola nautaque illam fēminam amant* both mean "The farmer and the sailor love that woman."

ille*, *illa*, *illud

	MASC.	FEM.	NEUT.
Singular			
NOMINATIVE	ille	illa	illud
GENITIVE	illīus	illīus	illīus
DATIVE	illī	illī	illī
ACCUSATIVE	illum	illam	illud
ABLATIVE	illō	illā	illō
Plural			
NOMINATIVE	illī	illae	illa
GENITIVE	illōrum	illārum	illōrum
DATIVE	illīs	illīs	illīs
ACCUSATIVE	illōs	illās	illa
ABLATIVE	illīs	illīs	illīs

iste, **ista**, **istud** declines like *ille*, *illa*, *illud*.

is*, *ea*, *id

	MASC.	FEM.	NEUT.
Singular			
NOMINATIVE	is	ea	id
GENITIVE	eius	eius	eius
DATIVE	eī	eī	eī
ACCUSATIVE	eum	eam	id
ABLATIVE	eō	eā	eō
Plural			
NOMINATIVE	eī	eae	ea
GENITIVE	eōrum	eārum	eōrum
DATIVE	eīs	eīs	eīs
ACCUSATIVE	eōs	eās	ea
ABLATIVE	eīs	eīs	eīs

īdem, eadem, idem

The word *īdem* means "the same" and, again, is used as both a pronoun and an adjective. For example, *agricola nautaque eandem amant* and *agricola nautaque eandem fēminam amant* both mean "The farmer and the sailor love <u>the same woman</u>." You can easily see that *īdem, eadem, idem* is a compound of *is, ea, id* with the suffix *-dem*. Notice that *m* changes to *n* in some forms to make pronunciation easier (e.g., *eundem* for *eumdem*).

	MASC.	**FEM.**	**NEUT.**
Singular			
NOMINATIVE	īdem	eadem	idem
GENITIVE	eiusdem	eiusdem	eiusdem
DATIVE	eīdem	eīdem	eīdem
ACCUSATIVE	eundem	eandem	idem
ABLATIVE	eōdem	eādem	eōdem
Plural			
NOMINATIVE	eīdem	eaedem	eadem
GENITIVE	eōrundem	eārundem	eōrundem
DATIVE	eīsdem	eīsdem	eīsdem
ACCUSATIVE	eōsdem	eāsdem	eadem
ABLATIVE	eīsdem	eīsdem	eīsdem

ipse, ipsa, ipsum

This is an intensive demonstrative pronoun/adjective, with the emphatic meaning of "he himself (and not anyone else)." For example, *agricola ipse porcum interficit* means "The farmer himself kills the pig," and *ipse porcum interficit* means "He himself kills the pig."

	MASC.	**FEM.**	**NEUT.**
Singular			
NOMINATIVE	ipse	ipsa	ipsum
GENITIVE	ipsīus	ipsīus	ipsīus
DATIVE	ipsī	ipsī	ipsī
ACCUSATIVE	ipsum	ipsam	ipsum
ABLATIVE	ipsō	ipsā	ipsō
Plural			
NOMINATIVE	ipsī	ipsae	ipsa
GENITIVE	ipsōrum	ipsārum	ipsōrum
DATIVE	ipsīs	ipsīs	ipsīs
ACCUSATIVE	ipsōs	ipsās	ipsa
ABLATIVE	ipsīs	ipsīs	ipsīs

The Personal Pronouns *ego, tu*

Personal pronouns are words such as "I," "you," "him," and "them." The first person, *ego*, and the second person, *tū*, are used for all genders alike. (The third person is supplied by forms of *is*, so it does vary with the gender of the person it refers to.) Since the ending of a conjugated verb tells you if the person is first, second, or third, you normally do not need the nominative of the personal pronoun. It is used only to avoid ambiguity, or when particular emphasis is intended, or when a verb form has been omitted for the sake of style.

You remember Julius Caesar's question to his friend Brutus, which we used as an example of the second declension vocative singular: *et tū, Brūte?* Caesar's question is also an example of how personal pronouns can be used for emphasis.

et tū, Brūte?	*You* also, Brutus?
ego nautam amō, tū agricolam.	*I* love the sailor, *you* love the farmer.
sī hostēs timētis, fugite, mīlitēs! nōs tamen mortem pulchram petēmus.	If you fear the enemy, run away, soldiers! *We,* however, will seek a glorious death.

First Person Pronouns

	SINGULAR	PLURAL
NOMINATIVE	ego	nōs
GENITIVE	meī	nostrum, nostrī
DATIVE	mihi	nōbīs
ACCUSATIVE	mē	nōs
ABLATIVE	mē	nōbīs

Second Person Pronouns

	SINGULAR	PLURAL
NOMINATIVE	tū	vōs
GENITIVE	tuī	vestrum, vestrī
DATIVE	tibi	vōbīs
ACCUSATIVE	tē	vōs
ABLATIVE	tē	vōbīs

In Chapter 16 you learned the partitive and objective genitives. *nostrum* and *vestrum* are partitive genitives, while *nostrī* and *vestrī* are objective genitives:

duo mīlia nostrum.	Two thousand of us.
memor sum vestrī.	I am mindful of you.

Reflexive vs. Non-Reflexive

At this point we need to consider the distinction between reflexive and non-reflexive pronouns and adjectives. The first aspect of this distinction that we'll look at is the difference between "his

[own]" and "his": the first is **reflexive**, because it emphasizes the subject of the sentence or clause as the possessor of whatever is being talked about, while the second is **non-reflexive**, referring to someone other than the subject of the sentence or clause. When you are translating "his," "her," and "their," if the possessive refers back to the subject of the sentence or clause, you will use *suus*, *-a, -um*, the reflexive third person pronominal adjective. If it refers back to someone else, you will use the genitive forms *eius*, *eōrum*, and *eārum*, meaning "of him/her/it," "of them [masc. and neut.]," and "of them [fem.]." You have to use these genitive forms of *is, ea, id* because Latin has no non-reflexive third person pronominal adjective corresponding to *suus, -a, -um*.

Possessive refers back to the subject
*dux Rōmānus fīlium **suum** interfēcit.*
The Roman commander killed his own son.

Possessive refers to another person
*Rōmānī Sabīnōs vīcērunt, fīliāsque **eōrum** rapuērunt.*
The Romans defeated the Sabines, and carried off their daughters.

*agricola nautam timet sed uxōrem **suam** amat.*
The farmer fears the sailor but loves his [his own] wife.

*agricola nautam timet sed uxōrem **eius** amat.*
The farmer fears the sailor but loves his [the sailor's] wife.

This seems more complicated than English, but it has the advantage of avoiding ambiguity when two people of the same gender are being referred to in a single sentence or clause. As you learned in Chapter 2, however, if there is no need to emphasize the identity of the possessor, you can usually omit any word for "his," "her," or "their."

The Reflexive Personal Pronouns *meī, tuī, suī*

Reflexive pronouns refer back to the subject of the sentence or clause: "I kill myself," "You wash yourself," "She gives herself no credit," "They talk to themselves." These pronouns can serve as a direct/indirect object, or appear in a prepositional phrase, or perform some other function within the sentence or clause, but **they never stand alone as the subject of the sentence or clause. Therefore, they have no nominative case.** For the first and second persons, their forms are identical to those of the non-reflexive personal pronouns, but with no nominative. In the third person, singular and plural share one set of forms, again with no nominative.

As with non-reflexive personal pronouns, the forms *nostrum/vestrum* and *nostrī/vestrī* are partitive and objective genitives.

First Person Reflexive Pronouns

	SINGULAR	PLURAL
NOMINATIVE	—	—
GENITIVE	meī	nostrum, nostrī
DATIVE	mihi	nōbīs
ACCUSATIVE	mē	nōs
ABLATIVE	mē	nōbīs

Second Person Reflexive Pronouns

	SINGULAR	PLURAL
NOMINATIVE	—	—
GENITIVE	tuī	vestrum, vestrī
DATIVE	tibi	vōbīs
ACCUSATIVE	tē	vōs
ABLATIVE	tē	vōbīs

Third Person Reflexive Pronouns

	SING. and PL.
NOMINATIVE	—
GENITIVE	suī
DATIVE	sibi
ACCUSATIVE	sē
ABLATIVE	sē

Using Reflexive Pronouns

Compare these pairs of sentences. Those on the left use nouns or non-reflexive pronouns as direct objects, indirect objects, or objects of a preposition; those on the right use reflexive pronouns with the same grammatical function:

pastor porcum in flūmen iacit.
The shepherd throws the pig into the river.

porcus sē in flūmen iacit.
The pig throws <u>itself</u> into the river.

pastor puellam amat. ergō porcum eī emit.
The shepherd loves the girl. Therefore he buys a pig <u>for her</u>.

pastor sibi porcum emit.
The shepherd buys a pig <u>for himself</u>.

pastor porcōs multōs habet. cum eīs ad urbem venit.
The shepherd has many pigs. He is coming <u>with them</u> to the town.

pastor sēcum porcōs ad urbem affert.
The shepherd is taking the pigs with <u>him</u> (i.e., <u>himself</u>) to the town.

Notice the form *sēcum* meaning "with him(self)" in the last sentence. The preposition *cum* is always added as a suffix when used with the personal pronouns *mē, nōbīs, tē, vōbīs,* and *sē.* Other examples are:

venī mēcum ad senātum, Caesar.   Come with me to the Senate, Caesar.

ad lūdum nōbīscum adiit lupus.   The wolf went to school with us.

You also need to distinguish between reflexive pronouns and the intensive pronoun *ipse*, *ipsa*, *ipsum*, which we saw earlier. Even though both are translated with "myself," "himself," and so on, they are used quite differently.

ipse	*sē*
agricola <u>ipse</u> porcum interficit.	*agricola <u>sē</u> interficit.*
The farmer <u>himself</u> kills the pig.	The farmer kills <u>himself</u>.
<u>ipse ego</u> puellam amō.	*florēs <u>mihi</u> emō.*
<u>I myself</u> love the girl.	I buy flowers for <u>myself</u>.
puellam <u>ipsam</u> amō.	*puella <u>sē</u> amat.*
I love the girl <u>herself</u>.	The girl loves <u>herself</u>.
pastor puellae <u>ipsī</u> porcum emit.	*pastor <u>sibi</u> porcum emit.*
The shepherd buys a pig for the girl <u>herself</u>.	The shepherd buys a pig for <u>himself</u>.

Vocabulary Notes

As you already know, when two adjectives modify the same noun, they are usually connected by *et* or *-que*. You also know that pronominal adjectives (such as *meus* and *tuus*) are an exception. The pronominal adjectives introduced in this chapter and Chapter 18 do not require *et* or *-que* either.

porcum <u>magnum dulcemque</u> spectō.	I am watching the big, sweet pig.
porcum <u>meum dulcem</u> spectō.	I am watching my sweet pig.
<u>ipsum hunc</u> porcum <u>dulcem</u> spectō.	I am watching this sweet pig itself.

hīc, the adverb meaning "here" that you met in Chapter 12, has the same form as the nom. sing. masc. of the pron./pronom. adj. meaning "this." Context will usually make clear which is intended. For example, *porcī meī omnēs hīc sunt* can only mean "All my pigs are here," and *hīc porcus procul abest* can only mean "This pig is far away."

Intransitive Verbs with the Dative

Many verbs that are used transitively in English and other modern languages have their nearest Latin equivalent in intransitive verbs that take a different case, most frequently the dative. For example:

fortūna fortibus favet.	Fortune favors (= is favorable to) the brave.
lupī porcīs nocent.	Wolves harm (= are harmful to) pigs.
rūs tibi placet.	The countryside pleases (= is pleasing to) you.

Since these verbs are intransitive and have no direct objects, they cannot be used passively in the normal way. For example, *porcō parcō* means "I spare the pig," but "porcus ā mē parcitur" is not the

Latin for "The pig is spared by me," since *parcere* doesn't have a direct object that can become the subject of the passive form.

The idiom that most often raises this issue is the dative of reference, which you learned in Chapter 16. It is not always easy, however, to define the type of dative being used with these verbs; you just need to learn them as verbs that take the dative. These are the most common verbs that take the dative:

appropinquō 1	approach
imperō 1	order
faveō, favēre, fāvī, fautum 2	favor
indulgeō, indulgēre, indulsī, indultum 2	be lenient to
invideō, invidēre, invīdī, invīsum 2	envy
medeor, medērī 2	heal
noceō, nocēre, nocuī, nocitum 2	harm
placeō, placēre, placuī, placitum 2	please
displiceō, displicēre, displicuī, displicitum 2	displease
studeō, studēre, studuī 2	study
suādeō, suādēre, suāsī, suāsum 2	urge
dissuādeō, -ēre, dissuāsī, dissuāsum 2	dissuade
persuādeō, -ēre, persuāsī, persuāsum 2	persuade
crēdō, crēdere, crēdidī, crēditum 3	trust, believe (a person)
fīdō, fīdere, fīsus sum 3	trust
diffīdō, diffīdere, diffīsus sum 3	distrust
ignoscō, ignoscere, ignōvī, ignōtum 3	forgive
īrascor, īrascī, īrātus sum 3	be angry with
nūbō, nūbere, nupsī, nuptum 3	marry (of a woman)
obsequor, obsequī, obsecūtus sum 3	obey
parcō, parcere, pepercī, parsum 3	spare
resistō, resistere, restitī 3	resist
serviō, servīre, servīvī, servītum 4	serve

Vocabulary Notes

The verbs **fīdō** and **diffīdō** are semi-deponent; see Chapter 15.

nūbō is used only of women. *puella pulchra nautae nupsit* means "The beautiful girl married the sailor," but *puellam pulchram nauta in mātrimōnium duxit* means "The sailor married the beautiful girl."

Prōlūsiōnēs

Parse the words in bold.

1. nōmen **ipsum** Hannibalis, **illīus** ducis tam fortis, Rōmānī timēbant.
2. **tē**cum sub arbore **eādem** sedēre voluī.
3. **sibi** nimium placēbat poēta **iste**.
4. semper carmina **eius** legō, **mea** numquam.
5. **huic** puerō ego dōna dabō, **tibi** puellae illae.

Change to the singular and then translate.

1. illī agricolae hōs porcōs nōbīs dabunt.
2. in agrīs istīs eōs vīdistis?
3. vōbīs, agricolae, sunt haec animālia cāra.
4. eōrundem agricolārum porcīs vōs illīc medēbāminī.
5. istōrum rēgum urbēs capientur.
6. hōs ducēs fortēs sequiminī!
7. hōrum mīlitum hastae in lupōrum eōrum corporibus sunt.
8. rēgēs istī ā vōbīs ipsīs, puellae, in hīs urbibus vīsī sunt.
9. eīsdem porcīs illās rosās date!
10. illī ā nōbīs ipsīs laudātī erant.

Change to the plural and then translate.

1. puer ipse eī puellae displicēbat.
2. in aquā sē vīdit iuvenis, et ā sē vīsus est.
3. sē semper laudābat et sibi dōnum dare volēbat.
4. cūr mihi librum istum nōn monstrās?
5. haec eadem puella hunc canem ipsa vocābit.
6. iste puer sē dē summō saxō iacere nōn vult.
7. hōc rēgī ipsī difficillimum nōn est, sed id tibi facere nōn poterit.
8. tibi ipsī hanc eandem vaccam nōn dabit ille.
9. eiusdem pastōris porca hāc in silvā est.
10. ducem eum hūc ipse sequere!

Translate.

1. dominō eīdem semper serviēmus annōn?
2. nōs amāmus porcōs tuōs, sed hīc equōs illōs.
3. nōs amant porcī tuī, sed hīc equōs illōs numquam vīdī.
4. porcus et corpus eīsdem sex litterīs scrībuntur.
5. īdem equus sē amat, nōn eum porcum.
6. huic iuvenī invidēmus omnēs, quia tot tantāsque urbēs ipse vīdit.
7. cum porcī tum taurī meī aegrī erant, nec eīs medērī poterat deus ipse.
8. nē mātrī quidem suae ignōvit magistrātus iste tam crūdēlis.
9. nōn modo sociōrum pars magna sed etiam legiōnēs ipsae prīmō barbarōrum impetū fugātae sunt.
10. haec puella fīlium illīus agricolae amāverat et eīdem puerō id dōnum dabit.
11. fīliō ipsīus nautae mare nōn placet; num nauta suum fīlium interficiet?
12. mortuus est dominus ipse, sed porcīs eius venēnum idem nōn nocēbit, namque tālem cibum eīs cottīdiē dare solet hīc pastor.
13. quamquam in spēluncam lupōrum totiens ingressa est agna illa tam parva, ferae istae eī numquam nocuērunt.
14. sē interfēcit dux noster infēlix quod mūrīs ipsīs huius urbis appropinquābant istae hostium cōpiae.
15. quamquam tam saevae faciēī erant barbarī istī, trans hōc flūmen, octō tantum pedēs lātum, in fīnēs nostrōs venīre numquam ausī sunt.

16. Obey your teacher, students, and study this new book!
17. This woman loves those pigs, but those women love this bull.
18. How many wild boars were wounded so easily by the same young man's spear?
19. Perhaps my brother and your friend will give the same presents to the same girl.
20. That handsome young man went with us to the cruel king.
21. That centurion will not be angry with us; he will harm not even the laziest soldiers.
22. Run away, soldiers, toward the furthest part of those high mountains! Do not resist the barbarians' swift charge!
23. First he wounded the bull with his sword and then he fled with that lovely daughter of the same magistrate.
24. The enemy did not themselves kill our soldiers; many Romans killed themselves of their own accord.
25. Believe me, citizens! The gods favor us, for tomorrow the queen of the barbarians herself will marry that brave king.

Lectiōnēs Latīnae

Lege, Intellege

Justinian ruled the eastern Roman empire from Constantinople (the modern city of Istanbul) from AD 527 till 565. One of his earliest acts as emperor was to commission a comprehensive reform of the laws. His *Cōdex*, *Institūtiōnēs*, and *Dīgesta* ensured the lasting influence of Roman law in much of the Western world.

Legal Definitions

iūs nātūrāle est quod nātūra omnia animālia docuit. nam iūs istud nōn hūmānī generis proprium est, sed omnium animālium, quae in caelō, quae in terrā, quae in marī nascuntur. iūs autem cīvīle vel gentium ita dīviditur: omnēs populī quī lēgibus et mōribus reguntur partim suō propriō, partim commūnī omnium hominum iūre ūtuntur: nam quod quisque populus ipse sibi iūs constituit, id ipsīus proprium cīvitātis est vocāturque iūs cīvīle: quod vērō nātūrālis ratiō inter omnēs hominēs constituit, id apud omnēs populōs peraequē custōdītur vocāturque iūs gentium. et populus itaque Rōmānus partim suō propriō, partim commūnī omnium hominum iūre ūtitur. nātūrālia quidem iūra, quae apud omnēs gentēs peraequē servantur, dīvīnā quādam prōvidentiā constitūta, semper firma atque immūtābilia permanent: ea vērō quae ipsa sibi quaeque cīvitās constituit, saepe mūtārī solent vel tacitō consensū populī vel aliā posteā lēge lātā.

—Justinian, *Institūtiōnēs* 1.2

ūtor, ūtī, ūsus sum 3 (+ abl.; see Chapter 18) use

quisque, quaeque, quidque/quodque adj., pron. each

gens, gentis fem. 3 tribe, nation

1. What sort of law has nature taught to all animals?
2. What sort of law is particular to a specific community?
3. What sort of law is observed by all peoples alike?
4. Can laws established by divine providence be changed?
5. How may a community change its laws?

Ars Poētica

Catullus (Gaius Valerius Catullus; 84?–54? BC) was the central figure in the so-called neoteric group of Roman poets, who wrote just before Virgil's time and were influenced by the post-classical or "Hellenistic" Greek poets. The works of the other neoterics have been almost entirely lost.

Parse the words in bold in the following quotations from Catullus.

1. ***ego*** *gymnasī fuī flōs, ego eram decus oleī:*
   mihi *iānuae frequentēs, mihi līmina tepida,*
   mihi flōridīs corollīs redimīta domus erat.
   I was the flower of the gymnasium, I was the glory of the olive oil [i.e., of the wrestling ring, because wrestlers anointed themselves with oil]; for me the doors were thronged, for me the doorsteps were warm, for me the house was hung with flowery crowns.

2. *vōs ego saepe, meō **vōs** carmine compellābō.*
   ***tē**que adeō eximiē taedīs fēlīcibus aucte,*
   *Thessaliae columen Pēleu, cui Iuppiter **ipse**,*
   ipse suōs dīvum genitor concessit amōrēs;
   ***tē**ne Thetis tenuit pulcherrima Nērēīnē?*
   tēne suam Tēthys concessit dūcere neptem.
   You, I will often address you with my song. And you indeed, excellently adorned with lucky garlands, Peleus, the support of Thessaly, to whom Jupiter himself, the father of the gods himself yielded his own beloved; Did Thetis the very beautiful Nereid [sea nymph] hold you? Did Tethys [the sea goddess] grant that you should marry her granddaughter?

3. *ipse valēre optō et taetrum **hunc** dēpōnere morbum.*
   I myself wish to be strong and to lay aside this disgusting disease.

4. *tam gaudet in **sē** tamque **sē** ipse mīrātur.*
   He rejoices so much in himself and admires himself so much.

5. ***tū** mea tū moriens frēgistī commoda, frāter;*
   ***tē**cum ūnā tōta est nostra sepulta domus.*
   You, my brother, when you died you broke my happiness; together with you our whole house has been buried.

Aurea Dicta

1. *decorī est ovibus sua lāna.* (Ovid)
2. *errāre mālō cum Platōne quam cum istīs vēra sentīre.* (Cicero)
3. *frangitur ipsa suīs Rōma superba bonīs.* (Propertius)
4. *hominēs vitia sua et amant simul et ōdērunt.* (Seneca the Younger)
5. *idem velle atque idem nolle, ea dēmum firma amīcitia est.* (Sallust)
6. *in eādem rē ūtilitās et turpitūdō esse nōn potest.* (Cicero)
7. *ipse alimenta sibi maxima praebet amor.* (Propertius)
8. *mea mihi conscientia plūris est quam omnium sermō.* (Cicero)

ovis, ovis fem. 3 sheep

lāna, -ae fem. 1 wool

sentio, -īre, sensī, sensum 4 feel, perceive

dēmum finally, after all

praebeō, -ēre, praebuī, praebitum 2 provide

Lūsūs

Thēsaurus Verbōrum

These feminine nouns of the third declension ending in *-itūdō, -itūdinis* refer mostly to abstract concepts; English changes the final *-ō* of the nominative singular to a silent *-e*.

altitūdō	longitūdō	sōlitūdō
fortitūdō	magnitūdō	turpitūdō
lātitūdō	multitūdō	vicissitūdō

Etymologiae Antīquae

Landmarks

campus, *-ī* masc. 2 "plain." People first took (*capiō, -ere, cēpī, captum* 3 *i*-stem) crops from flat ground.

collis, *-is* masc. 3 "hill." When people began to cultivate (*colō, -ere, coluī, cultum* 3) the higher ground, they called those places *collēs*.

humus, *-ī* fem. 2 "ground." The ground is moist (*hūmidus, -a, -um*). *hominēs* are born from the ground, and humble [*humilis, -e*] people are close to the ground.

insula, *-ae* fem. 1 "island." Islands are in the sea (*salum, -ī* neut. 2).

lacus, *-ūs* masc. 4 "lake." A lake is a place (*locus, -ī* masc. 2) full of water.

lītus, lītoris neut. 3 "shore." Waves play on the shore (*lūdo, -ere, lūsī, lūsum* 3) and are broken (*ēlīdō, -ere, ēlīsī, ēlīsum* 3) there.

mare, maris neut. 3 "sea." Seawater is bitter (*amārus, -a, -um*).

mons, montis masc. 3 "mountain." Mountains stand out (*ēmineō, -ēre, -uī* 2).

oppidum, -ī neut. 2 "town." An *oppidum* is so called either because it is full (*opplētus, -a, -um*) of people, or because people keep their wealth (*opēs, opum* fem. 3) there, or because of its opposition (*oppositiō, -ōnis* fem. 3) of walls to the enemy, or because the inhabitants give each other help (*ops, opis* fem. 3).

rūs, rūris neut. 3 "countryside." To get crops again (*rursus*), the same work has to be done again every year.

solum, -ī neut. 2 "(surface of the) ground." Only (*sōlus, -a, -um*) the surface of the ground can be trodden. The ground can bear the weight of everything, because it is solid (*solidus, -a, -um*).

stagnum, -ī neut. 2 "pool." The water in a pool stands (*stō, stāre, stetī, statum* 1) still.

tellūs, tellūris fem. 3 "earth." We lift (*tollō, -ere, sustulī, sublātum* 3) crops from the earth.

terra, -ae fem. 1 "earth." The earth is rubbed away (*terō, -ere, trīvī, trītum* 3) by the footsteps of people going hither and thither.

urbs, urbis fem. 3 "city." An *urbs* is so called because its limits are marked out in a circle (*orbis, orbis* masc. 3) by a plow.

Vīta Rōmānōrum

How to Write Poetry

The Roman poets of the Augustan Age, such as Horace and Virgil, were extremely subtle and painstaking, showing the pervasive influence of sophisticated and learned Hellenistic Greek poets such as Callimachus of Cyrene, who lived in Alexandria in the first half of the third century BC.

> Lucilius [180?–101? BC; Horace's predecessor as a satirist] was witty, with a nose for satire, but rough in composing his verses. This was his weakness: often, just to show off, he'd compose two hundred verses in an hour, standing on one leg. While he was flowing muddily along, there was stuff you'd like to remove. He was garrulous and too lazy to bother with the effort of writing, of writing properly. I'm not impressed by the quantity of his output. Look, Crispinus is betting me at very long odds: "Pick up your writing tablets, please, and I'll pick up mine; set a place, a time, and referees. Let's see who can write more." The gods have done well in molding me with a poor and feeble intellect, speaking rarely and very little.

> —Horace, *Sermōnēs* 1.4.1–18

They say that, when Virgil was writing the *Georgics*, his daily practice was to dictate a large number of verses in the morning, and work on them throughout the day, reducing them to a very small number. He said rather appropriately that he produced his poem the way a she-bear produces her cubs, gradually licking them into shape. [The Romans thought that newborn bears were shapeless lumps.] He wrote a prose version of the *Aeneid* first, dividing it into twelve books, and only then did he start composing the poem section by section, just as he fancied, in no particular order. So that nothing might stop his progress, he left some parts unfinished, others he buttressed, so to speak, with very lightweight words, which he jokingly said he was inserting as "props" to support the structure till the solid columns arrived.

—Suetonius, *Vīta Vergiliī* 22–24

CHAPTER 18

Pronouns II, Intransitive Verbs with the Genitive or Ablative

The Relative Pronoun *quī*

Relative pronouns introduce a subordinate clause that refers to a noun or pronoun in another clause and provides further information about it. For example:

> I love the girl <u>who</u> lives here.
>
> I love the girl <u>whom</u> you see here.
>
> I love the girl <u>whose</u> pig has run away.

You will see patterns in the forms of the pronouns/pronominal adjectives introduced in this chapter that will remind you of *hīc*, *ille*, and so on. These similarities should help you learn the new forms and focus on the small but crucial variations between the cases and genders of the relative pronouns/pronominal adjectives.

	MASC.	FEM.	NEUT.
Singular			
NOMINATIVE	quī	quae	quod
GENITIVE	cuius	cuius	cuius
DATIVE	cui	cui	cui
ACCUSATIVE	quem	quam	quod
ABLATIVE	quō	quā	quō
Plural			
NOMINATIVE	quī	quae	quae
GENITIVE	quōrum	quārum	quōrum
DATIVE	quibus	quibus	quibus
ACCUSATIVE	quōs	quās	quae
ABLATIVE	quibus	quibus	quibus

So far you have learned adjectives that agree in number, gender, and case with the noun they modify, and also appositional and predicate nouns that may differ in number and gender from the noun to which they refer, but always agree in case at least.

Relative pronouns take their number and gender from the noun or pronoun they stand for, but they are very likely to be in a different case. This is because their case is determined by their function in the relative clause they introduce. For example:

*magistrum laudō **quī in lūdō est**.*　　　　　　I praise the teacher **who is in the school**.

quī is masculine and singular, because it refers to *magistrum. magistrum* is in the accusative, because it is the direct object of *laudō*, but *quī* is in the nominative, because it is the subject of its own clause, the relative clause.

puellae, **cuius porcī in silvā sunt***, flōrēs dat nauta.*   The sailor gives flowers to the girl **whose pigs are in the wood**.

cuius is feminine and singular, because it refers to *puellae. puellae* is in the dative, because it is the indirect object of *dat*, but *cuius* is in the genitive, because it indicates possession of the pigs mentioned in the relative clause.

agnam, **quam amābat fīlia pastōris***, interfēcērunt lupī.*   The wolves killed the lamb **that the shepherd's daughter loved**.

quam is feminine and singular, because it refers to *agnam. agnam* is in the accusative because it is the direct object of *interfēcērunt*, but *quam* is in the accusative because it is the direct object of *amābat*, the verb in the relative clause. So, *agnam* and *quam* are in the same case, but for different reasons; *quam* does not derive its case from *agnam*.

The following two Latin sentences have different meanings but can be translated in the same way:

lūcem astrōrum vidēmus, **sine quibus** *trans mare nāvigāre nōn possumus.*

lūcem astrōrum vidēmus, **sine quā** *trans mare nāvigāre nōn possumus.*

We see the light of the stars, **without which** we cannot sail across the sea.

In the English sentence, the relative pronoun, "which," is ambiguous. Does it refer to the light or to the stars? The Latin sentences avoid this ambiguity. In the first Latin sentence, *quibus* is neuter and plural, and it refers to *astrōrum*, but it is ablative, not genitive, because it is governed by the preposition *sine*. In the second sentence, *quā* is feminine and singular, and it refers to *lūcem*, but it is ablative, not accusative, because it is governed by the preposition *sine*.

Occasionally, the noun or pronoun to which the relative pronoun refers may not be explicitly stated. In a sentence like this, the relative clause quite often comes before the clause on which it depends. English frequently omits the relative pronoun ("The girl I love is beautiful"), but the pronoun is never omitted in Latin.

pulchra est, quam amō and *quam amō, pulchra est*

both mean

The girl (whom) I love is beautiful.

The Interrogative Pronoun *quis* and the Interrogative Adjective *quī*

Interrogative pronouns are used to introduce questions:

quis hōc carmen scrīpsit?	Who wrote this poem?
quid faciunt porcī?	What are the pigs doing?

The singular forms of the interrogative pronoun are the same as those of the relative pronoun, except:

- the nom. sing. masc. is *quis* (not *quī*)

- the nom. and acc. sing. neut. is *quid* (not *quod*)

- the feminine shares the masculine forms throughout the singular.

	MASC./FEM.	NEUT.
Singular		
NOMINATIVE	quis	quid
GENITIVE	cuius	cuius
DATIVE	cui	cui
ACCUSATIVE	quem	quid
ABLATIVE	quō	quō

In the plural, interrogative pronouns have exactly the same forms as relative pronouns.

Interrogative adjectives perform the same function as interrogative pronouns, but with a specific noun. They decline exactly like relative pronouns in both the singular and the plural, but you can easily distinguish them since their grammatical function is so different.

Interrogative pronoun	**Interrogative adjective**
quis porcum interfēcit?	*quī mīles porcum interfēcit?*
Who killed the pig?	Which soldier killed the pig?
quem amās?	*quam puellam amās?*
Whom do you love?	Which girl do you love?
cuius porcum in silvīs vīdimus?	*cuius agricolae porcum in silvīs vīdimus?*
Whose pig did we see in the woods?	Which farmer's pig did we see in the woods?

The Indefinite Pronouns/Pronominal Adjectives *aliqui(s)* and *quīdam*

aliquis/aliquī is the most common indefinite pronoun/pronominal adjective meaning "some(one)," "some(thing)." The pronoun declines like the interrogative *quis*, except that it has separate feminine forms in the singular as well as in the plural, and the neut. pl. nom. and acc. is *aliqua*, not *aliquae*. The pronominal adjective differs from the pronoun only in that it has *aliquī*, not *aliquis*, as the masc. sing. nom., *aliquod*, not *aliquid*, as the neut. sing. nom. and acc.

	MASC.	FEM.	NEUT.
Singular			
NOMINATIVE	aliquis (adj. **aliquī**)	aliqua	aliquid (adj. **aliquod**)
GENITIVE	alicuius	alicuius	alicuius
DATIVE	alicui	alicui	alicui
ACCUSATIVE	aliquem	aliquam	aliquid (adj. **aliquod**)
ABLATIVE	aliquō	aliquā	aliquō
Plural			
NOMINATIVE	aliquī	aliquae	**aliqua**
GENITIVE	aliquōrum	aliquārum	aliquōrum
DATIVE	aliquibus	aliquibus	aliquibus
ACCUSATIVE	aliquōs	aliquās	**aliqua**
ABLATIVE	aliquibus	aliquibus	aliquibus

The indefinite pronoun/pronominal adjective *quīdam, quaedam, quiddam/quoddam* is a compound of the relative pronoun *quī, quae, quod* and the suffix *-dam*, and it means "a certain (person/thing)," or "some (one/thing)." It is to some extent synonymous with *aliqui(s)*, but is in general the more definite of the two terms: if "someone" is known, but not named, *quīdam* is the word more frequently used. Notice that the neut. sing. nom. and acc. is *quiddam* for the pronoun and *quoddam* for the adjective, and that *m* changes to *n* before *d* to make pronunciation easier, just as in the declension of *īdem*.

	MASC.	FEM.	NEUT.
Singular			
NOMINATIVE	quīdam	quaedam	quiddam (adj. **quoddam**)
GENITIVE	cuiusdam	cuiusdam	cuiusdam
DATIVE	cuidam	cuidam	cuidam
ACCUSATIVE	quendam	quandam	quiddam (adj. **quoddam**)
ABLATIVE	quōdam	quādam	quōdam
Plural			
NOMINATIVE	quīdam	quaedam	quaedam
GENITIVE	quōrundam	quārundam	quōrundam
DATIVE	quibusdam	quibusdam	quibusdam
ACCUSATIVE	quōsdam	quāsdam	quaedam
ABLATIVE	quibusdam	quibusdam	quibusdam

Notā Bene

In Chapter 13 you learned the correlating idiom *aliī . . . aliī . . .*; for example, *aliī flōrēs amant, aliī animālia*, "Some people like flowers, others like animals." *aliquī*, *quīdam*, and *nonnullī* are not used in this idiom.

Intransitive Verbs with the Genitive or Ablative

In Chapter 17 we saw that some intransitive verbs take the **dative**. Here are some of the most common intransitive verbs that take the **genitive** or **ablative**:

Genitive

meminī, meminisse 3	remember
oblīviscor, oblīviscī, oblītus sum 3	forget
potior, potīrī, potītus sum 4	take possession of

Ablative

careō, carēre, caruī 2	lack
egeō, egēre, eguī 2	lack
fīdō, fīdere, fīsus sum 3	trust
fruor, fruī, fructus sum 3	enjoy
fungor, fungī, functus sum 3	perform
potior, potīrī, potītus sum 4	take possession of
ūtor, ūtī, ūsus sum 3	use
vescor, vescī defective (no perfect system) 3	feed on

Vocabulary Notes

The verb **meminī** is defective. The only forms it has are those of the perfect system, but these forms have the meanings of present system forms. Hence *hodiē meminī* "Today I remember," *crās meminerō* "Tomorrow I will remember," *herī memineram* "Yesterday I remembered." Like **oblīviscor**, *meminī* sometimes takes the accusative. Its imperative forms are **mementō** and **mementōte**.

egeō generally implies a stronger need than **careō** does. For example, *vīnō caret, sed nōn eget, quia aqua pūra eī placet*, "He is without wine, but he does not feel the lack of it, since he likes pure water." *egeō* sometimes takes the genitive.

The verb **fīdō**, but not **diffīdō**, takes either the dative or the ablative, and **potior** takes either the genitive or the ablative.

Prōlūsiōnēs

Parse the words in bold.

1. puerō **eī quem** amās porcī sunt odiō.
2. ā puerō **istī** porcī ad urbem **eandem** agentur.
3. **cuius** pastōris porcī in **eō** agrō sunt?
4. pastōrem **quendam cui** porcī cārī sunt in agrō videō.
5. **quās** vaccās in agrō vidēs **ipse**?

Change from singular to plural, or vice versa, and then translate.

1. quīdam amīcī dominōrum nostrōrum mortuī sunt.
2. quī sunt puerī istī?
3. cui puellae dōnum idem dare dēbeō?
4. carmen aliquod ā puerō hōc lectum est.
5. ā quibus interfectī sunt hī cīvēs?
6. puellam quandam amō quae mē nōn amat.
7. porcōsne aliquōs in nostrōs agrōs duxērunt pastōrēs illī?
8. quōrum porcōs ex eīs agrīs rapuērunt hī lupī?
9. cui dabis librum illīus puellae?
10. in istīs pugnīs ducēs aliquōs interfēcērunt hī mīlitēs.
11. cuius puellae est liber iste cui studēs?
12. nonne vōbīscum hōc officiō functus est cīvis ille?
13. quārum fīliās amābant mīlitēs ipsī?
14. quārum puellārum patrēs ingentibus sub arboribus sedēbant?
15. quem amat deus, celeriter moritur.
16. iuvenis aliquī, quī hanc amat, gladiō suō vulnerātus est.
17. porcī, quōs pascēbant pastōrēs illī, fēlīcēs sunt.
18. mūnera aliqua, quibus nautae ūtuntur, rēgēs hī nōbīs dederant.
19. quō cibō vescuntur porcī, sī pastōre egent?
20. porcīs illīs, quōrum corpora pinguia sunt, fructūs istōs date!

21. ā porcīs, quī in hīs montibus erant, dēlētī sunt hī mūrī.
22. quī discipulus mēcum ad templum illud ībit?
23. quī gladiātōrēs sē interficere voluērunt?
24. discipulīsne quibusdam librōs eōs dedērunt ipsī magistrī?
25. quem porcum illī agricolae, quem in agrō vīdī, dedistī?

Translate.

1. ā tē ipsō dōnum aliquod accēpit eadem puella?
2. quibus puellīs dōnum istud dabō?
3. quī deōs nōn laudat mente bonā caret.
4. puellae, quibus dōnum dabō, pulchrae sunt.
5. quem amās? num puellam istam?
6. quō in templō mūnera illa pōnēmus?
7. quōs amant deī celerius moriuntur quam hominēs mōrum malōrum.
8. quis stultitiae tuae oblīviscī poterit?
9. imperātor quī sibi fīdit victōriā potītur.
10. iuvenis quīdam, ā quō haec amātur, gladiō eius nautae vulnerātus est.
11. porcōs, quibus frūctūs eōs dabant pastōrēs aliquī, in eīsdem agrīs nōn vidēmus.
12. amābat illa rēgem cuius exsequiārum nēmō oblīvīscētur.
13. puellam quandam, cuius amōre pereō, nauta iste pessimus interficere cupit.
14. discipulae alicui dedit librum illum magister īdem, nōn istī amīcō.
15. Aenēās, vir ille fortis, cuius māter dea amōris erat et quī ā Vulcānō, deō ignis, arma nova et immortālia accēperat, glōriā magnā brevī tempore potītus est.

16. Whose bull did those soldiers kill?
17. Did you want to feed on some farmer's best pig, centurion?
18. Believe me, no one who lacks piety can be a good priest.
19. What animals use both poison and their teeth when they defend themselves?
20. It is characteristic of a fool to use his money badly.
21. Without the boy she loves, what girl can truly enjoy life?
22. Which teacher can be angry with students who study these books well?
23. Will the citizens avenge my friend, whose wife has been wounded by some barbarian?
24. The girl herself prefers to praise some silly sailor, whose ship has gone to Italy.
25. Those same pirates, by whom our harbor has already been destroyed, will soon seize the whole city very easily.

Lectiōnēs Latīnae

Lege, Intellege

In addition to his historical works, Tacitus (Publius? Cornelius Tacitus; c. AD 56–c. 120), the greatest Roman historian, wrote the *Agricola*, a biography of his father-in-law, Gnaeus Julius Agricola, governor of Britain; the *Germānia*, an ethnographical treatise; and the *Dialogus Dē Ōrātōribus*, on the decline in modern oratory. All that we have of the *Historiae* is about a third of the whole work, treating the particularly eventful years AD 69–70. (Rome had five emperors between June 68 and December 69.) The *Annālēs*, which covers the reigns of Tiberius, Gaius, Claudius, and Nero, was his masterwork, but little more than half of its original sixteen or eighteen books have survived.

Cicero as an Orator

ad Cicerōnem veniō, cui eadem pugna cum aequālibus suīs fuit, quae mihi vōbīscum est. illī enim antīquōs mīrābantur, ipse suōrum temporum ēloquentiam antepōnēbat; nec ullā rē magis eiusdem aetātis ōrātōrēs praecurrit quam iūdiciō. prīmus enim excoluit ōrātiōnem, prīmus et verbīs dīlectum adhibuit et compositiōnī artem, locōs quoque laetiōrēs attemptāvit et quāsdam sententiās invēnit, utīque in eīs ōrātiōnibus, quās senior iam et iuxtā fīnem vītae composuit, id est, postquam magis prōfēcerat ūsūque et experimentīs optimum dīcendī genus didicerat. nam priōrēs eius ōrātiōnēs nōn carent vitiīs antīquitātis: lentus est in principiīs, longus in narrātiōnibus, ōtiōsus circā excessūs; tardē commovētur, rārō incalescit; paucī sensūs aptē et cum quōdam lūmine terminantur.

—Tacitus, *Dialogus dē Ōrātōribus 22*

dīlectus, -ūs masc. 4 choice, discrimination

adhibeō, -ēre, adhibuī, adhibitum 2 apply

utīque adv. at least, definitely

iuxtā adv., prep. + acc. near

prōficiō, -ere, prōfēci, prōfectum 3 *i*-stem improve

optimum dīcendī genus "the best style of speaking" (see Chapter 20)

1. Cicero was a better orator in his old age than at the beginning of his career: true or false?
2. Unlike his contemporaries, Cicero preferred oratory in earlier times: true or false?
3. Cicero excelled his contemporaries in judgment: true or false?
4. Cicero was careful in his choice of words: true or false?
5. Cicero could be boring and long-winded: true or false?

Ars Poētica

Catullus II

Parse the words in bold.

1. ***cui*** *dōnō lepidum novum libellum?*
   To whom do I give this smart new little book?

2. *passer mortuus est meae puellae,*
   passer, dēliciae meae puellae,
   quem *plūs illa oculīs suīs amābat.*
   nam mellītus erat suamque nōrat
   ipsam tam bene quam puella mātrem,
   *nec **sēsē** ā gremiō **illius** movēbat.*
   My girl's sparrow is dead, her sparrow, my girl's delight, that she loved more than her own eyes. For he was honey sweet and knew his mistress as well as a girl knows her mother, and he did not move from her lap.

3.   ***illa*** *multa cum iocōsa fīēbant,*
   quae *tū volēbās nec puella nōlēbat,*
   *fulsēre vērē candidī **tibī** sōlēs.*
   *nunc iam **illa** nōn vult: tū quoque impotens nōlī,*
   *nec **quae** fugit sectāre, nec miser vīve,*
   sed obstinātā mente perfer, obdūrā.
   valē puella, iam Catullus obdūrat,
   *nec **tē** requīret nec rogābit invītam.*
   at tū dolēbis, cum rogāberis nulla.
   *scelesta, vae tē, **quae** tibī manet vīta?*
   quis *nunc tē adībit? cui vidēberis bella?*
   quem *nunc amābis? **cuius** esse dīcēris?*
   *quem bāsiābis? **cui** labella mordēbis?*
   When those many playful things were happening, which you wanted and the girl did not refuse, truly suns shone bright for you. Now she does not want them: since you are powerless, refuse as well, do not pursue a girl who runs away, don't live in misery, but bear up, be hard, and keep a stubborn mind. Farewell, girl, now Catullus is hard, and he won't look for you nor ask you since you are unwilling. But you will suffer, when you are not asked at all. Too bad for you, wicked girl, what life is left for you? Who will come near you now? To whom will you seem pretty? Whom will you love now? Whose will you be said to be? Whom will you kiss? Whose lips will you nibble?

4. *Caelī, Lesbia nostra, Lesbia **illa**,*
   *illa Lesbia, **quam** Catullus ūnam*
   *plūs quam **sē** atque suōs amāvit omnēs,*
   nunc in quadriviīs et angiportīs
   glūbit magnanimī Remī nepōtēs.
   Caelius, my Lesbia, that Lesbia, that Lesbia, the one girl whom Catullus loved more than himself and all his family, now at crossroads and in alleys she strips the descendants of great-minded Remus.

Aurea Dicta

1. *caelum, nōn animum, mūtant quī trans mare currunt.* (Horace)
2. *deus quaedam mūnera ūniversō hūmānō generī dedit, ā quibus exclūditur nēmō.* (Seneca the Younger)
3. *dīligitur nēmō, nisi cui fortūna secunda est.* (Ovid)
4. *ea molestissimē ferre hominēs dēbent quae ipsōrum culpā contracta sunt.* (Cicero)
5. *ego eadem nōn volō senex quae puer voluī.* (Seneca the Younger)
6. *fēlix quī potuit rērum cognoscere causās.* (Virgil)
7. *leve fit, quod bene fertur, onus.* (Ovid)
8. *nōlīte velle quod fierī nōn potest.* (Cicero)

dīligō, -ere, dīlexī, dīlectum 3 like, love

senex, senis masc. 3 old man

Lūsūs

Thēsaurus Verbōrum

These third decl. fem. nouns ending in *-i(e)tās, -i(e)tātis* refer mostly to abstract concepts. English changes the final *-ās* of the nominative singular to a *-y*.

anxietās	loquācitās	satietās
auctoritās	mortālitās	simplicitās
brevitās	nōbilitās	sobrietās
commoditās	pietās	societās
extrēmitās	probitās	tenācitās
facilitās	proprietās	urbānitās
fēlīcitās	quālitās	varietās
garrulitās	quantitās	vēlōcitās
levitās	rusticitās	vīvācitās

Etymologiae Antīquae

Body Parts I

artēria, *-ae* fem. 1 "artery." The circulatory system was not understood in antiquity. The veins (*vēna*, *-ae* fem. 1) were regarded as the "path of swimming blood" (*via natantis sanguinis*), but since the arteries of a corpse are empty, the Romans thought they must be either passages for air (*āēr*, *āeris* masc. 3) or narrow (*artus*, *-a*, *-um*) passages for the vital spirit. Galen (AD 129–after 205), who was physician to the emperor Marcus Aurelius, disproved the notion that arteries were air vessels (but he thought that the purpose of breathing was to regulate body temperature).

cervix, *cervīcis* fem. 3 "(nape of the) neck." The neck is the *cerebrī* (*cerebrum*, *-ī* neut. 2) *via*, the path by which the brain sends messages to the spine.

collum, *-ī* neut. 2 "neck." The neck is rigid and round, like a pillar (*columna*, *-ae* fem. 1).

costa, *-ae* fem. 1 "rib." The ribs guard (*custōdiō*, *-īre*, *-īvī*, *-ītum* 4) the internal organs.

crūs, *crūris* neut. 3 "leg." Legs are for running (*currō*, *-ere*, *cucurrī*, *cursum* 3).

gena, *-ae* fem. 1 "cheek" and *genū*, *-ūs* neut. 4 "knee" were thought to be related, because of their proximity when a child is still in its mother's womb.

mamilla, *-ae* fem. 1 "breast." Breasts are round, like apples (*mālum*, *-ī* neut. 2).

pellis, *-is* fem. 3 "skin." The skin repels (*pellō*, *-ere*, *pepulī*, *pulsum* 3) harm from the body by covering it.

Vīta Rōmānōrum

How Ovid Wrote Poetry

Even while I was still a boy, the divine rites of poetry pleased me, and the Muse stealthily drew me toward her task. My father [an old country gentleman, who wanted Ovid to be a lawyer] often said: "Why are you trying a useless pursuit? Homer himself died penniless." I was persuaded by what he said, and abandoned Helicon [the Muses' mountain] completely, and tried to write words free of meter. But my poetry used to fall into meter of its own accord, and whatever I tried to write was a verse.

—Ovid, *Tristia* 4.10.19–26

The last sentence may have inspired a wonderful but apocryphal anecdote. Once, when his father was beating him for persisting with his poetry, Ovid cried out, "Spare me, father, and I'll never write verses again!" (*parce mihī; numquam versificābo, pater!*). Even this promise, however, is in one of the meters that Ovid used in his poetry.

Ovid was not unaware of the flaws in his poetry; in fact, he cherished them. Here is proof of that. His friends once asked him to remove three lines from his poetry. He agreed, on condition that he could select three lines that they couldn't touch. The stipulation seemed fair; his friends secretly wrote down the three which they wanted removed, and he wrote down the ones he wanted to preserve. The same verses were on both tablets. . . . It is clear from this that Ovid, a man of the greatest genius, recognized the excesses of his poems; he simply didn't want to control them. He used to say sometimes that a face was the more attractive if it had a mole on it.

—Seneca the Elder, *Contrōversiae* 2.2.12

A participle is an adjective formed from a verb. In English there are two basic participles:

Present active participle	**Leading** his legions, Caesar conquered Gaul.
Past passive participle	**Led** by Caesar, the Roman legions conquered Gaul.

Latin has three participles:

- the present active
- the future active
- the perfect passive

English can construct other participles by compounding: "being led," "being about to lead," "being about to be led," "having led," "having been led." Latin does not do this.

The Present Active Participle

To form the present active participle of all verbs of all conjugations, start with the present stem and add the endings *-ns*, *-ntis*, and so on, with the appropriate linking vowel(s), as if they were third declension adjectives of the type *fēlix, fēlīcis*. Here is the declension of *amans, amantis* "loving," which you should learn; the other conjugations, such as *monens, monentis* "warning," *mittens, mittentis* "sending," *audiens, audientis* "hearing," and *capiens, capientis* "capturing," will all follow the same paradigm.

	MASC./FEM.	NEUT.
Singular		
NOMINATIVE	ama**ns**	ama**ns**
GENITIVE	ama**ntis**	ama**ntis**
DATIVE	ama**ntī**	ama**ntī**
ACCUSATIVE	ama**ntem**	ama**ns**
ABLATIVE	ama**ntī** (or ama**nte**)	ama**ntī** (or ama**nte**)

	MASC./FEM.	NEUT.
Plural		
NOMINATIVE	ama**ntēs**	ama**ntia**
GENITIVE	ama**ntium**	ama**ntium**
DATIVE	ama**ntibus**	ama**ntibus**
ACCUSATIVE	ama**ntēs**	ama**ntia**
ABLATIVE	ama**ntibus**	ama**ntibus**

As in the case of nearly all third declension adjectives, the forms for masculine and feminine present participles are the same.

Notā Bene

am**antī**/am**ante**: The ablative singular form *amantī* occurs mostly when the participle is used like an adjective. The form *amante* is used when the participle is equivalent to a noun (as well as in the ablative absolute construction, which you will learn in this chapter).

Participle as adjective
*porcus ā pastōre **amantī** dēfenditur.*
The pig is protected by the loving shepherd.

Participle as noun
*Cleopatra ab **amante** dēfenditur.*
Cleopatra is protected by her lover (lit. by the loving man).

This distinction is sometimes ignored, especially in poetry.

The Future Active Participle

To form the future active participle, add *-ūrus, -ūra, -ūrum* to the stem of the fourth principal part. For example:

amātūrus, -ūra, -ūrum	being about to love
monitūrus, -ūra, -ūrum	being about to warn
missūrus, -ūra, -ūrum	being about to send
audītūrus, -ūra, -ūrum	being about to listen
captūrus, -ūra, -ūrum	being about to take

We have already met some verbs that have no fourth principal part. Some of these do, however, have a future active participle:

ambulāre	*ambulātūrus, -ūra, -ūrum*
cadere	*cāsūrus, -ūra, -ūrum*
esse	*futūrus, -ūra, -ūrum*
manēre	*mansūrus, -ūra, -ūrum*

Others do not have a future active participle in Classical Latin: *bibere, discere, metuere, timēre, posse, velle, nolle,* and *malle.*

The Perfect Passive Participle

You met the perfect passive participle in Chapter 1, when you began to learn principal parts, and you met it again in Chapter 14, as part of the perfect passive system. For example:

amātus, -a, -um	having been loved
monitus, -a, -um	having been warned
missus, -a, -um	having been sent
audītus, -a, -um	having been heard
captus, -a, -um	having been taken

This chart summarizes the forms of the three participles of most regular transitive verbs:

	ACTIVE	**PASSIVE**
Present	present stem + linking vowel + *-ns, -ntis* *amans, amantis*: loving	X
Future	stem of 4th principal part + *-ūrus, -ūra, -ūrum* *amātūrus, -ūra, -ūrum*: being about to love	X
Perfect	X	4th principal part *amātus, -a, -um*: having been loved

Participles of Deponent Verbs

Deponent verbs form their participles in the same way as other verbs, **but their perfect participle has an active meaning**. Compare the translation of the perfect participles here:

amō	**mīror**	**sequor**	**audeō**
amans, amantis loving	*mīrans, -antis* admiring	*sequens, -entis* following	*audens, -entis* daring
amātūrus, -ūra, -ūrum being about to love	*mīrātūrus, -ūra, -ūrum* being about to admire	*secūtūrus, -ūra, -ūrum* being about to follow	*ausūrus, -ūra, -ūrum* being about to dare
amātus, -a, -um **having been loved**	***mīrātus, -a, -um*** **having admired**	***secūtus, -a, -um*** **having followed**	***ausus, -a, -um*** **having dared**

mīlitēs ducem in silvam secūtī lupōs interfēcērunt.	The soldiers, having followed (or: who had followed) their general into the wood, killed the wolves.
mīlitēs ducem in silvam secūtōs lupī interfēcērunt.	The wolves killed the soldiers who had followed their general into the wood.

Notā Bene

morior, morī 3 *i*-stem "die" has the irregular perfect participle *mortuus, -a, -um*. Its future participle, *moritūrus, -ūra, -ūrum* "being about to die," does not use the same stem.

Participles of Irregular Verbs

The irregular verbs you have learned do not always have the full range of participles, and some (*possum, mālō*) have none at all.

	ferō	**sum**	**eō**	**volō**	**nōlō**	**fīō**
Present Active	*ferens, ferentis*		*iens, euntis*	*volens, volentis*	*nōlens, nōlentis*	*fīens, fīentis*
Future Active	*lātūrus, -a, -um*	*futūrus, -a, -um*	*itūrus, -a, -um*			
Perfect Passive	*lātus, -a, -um*					*factus, -a, -um*

Notā Bene

fīens, fīentis, the present participle of *fīō*, is very rare. Its perfect passive participle, *factus, -a, -um*, means "having become" or, since the form comes from *faciō*, "having been made."

Translating Participles

Participles are often used in Latin where English might more naturally use a clause with a conjugated verb. For example, *puellae porcum dūcentī dōnum dō* means "I give a gift to the girl leading the pig," but you may often prefer to translate it in one of the following ways, depending on the context:

> I give a gift to the girl <u>who</u> is leading the pig.
>
> I give a gift to the girl <u>when</u> she is leading the pig.
>
> I give a gift to the girl <u>since</u> she is leading the pig.
>
> I give a gift to the girl <u>although</u> she is leading the pig.
>
> I give a gift to the girl <u>if</u> she is leading the pig.

The unit *porcum dūcentī* functions basically as an adjective describing the girl, literally, "I give a gift to the pig-leading girl." But as you can see from the above translations, the meaning can be more than merely descriptive. The broader context will usually help you choose between, for example, "<u>since</u> she is leading the pig" or "<u>although</u> she is leading the pig," two clauses that have opposite implications.

Keeping all these alternatives in mind when you are translating participles can also bring out the important fact that the tense of a participle is not **absolute** but **relative**. The following groups of sentences show how the same participle can refer to different times, depending on the tense of the main verb in the sentence:

> Were people happy, **living** in caves?
>
> Are people happy, **living** in tiny apartments?
>
> Will people be happy, **living** on the moon?

> Were people happy, even though they **lived** in caves?
>
> Are people happy, even though they **live** in tiny apartments?
>
> Will people be happy, even though they **will be living** on the moon?

> **Being about to die**, gladiators saluted the emperor.
>
> **Being about to die**, gladiators salute the emperor.
>
> **Being about to die**, gladiators will salute the emperor.

> When they **were** about to die, gladiators saluted the emperor.
>
> When they **are** about to die, gladiators salute the emperor.
>
> When they **are** about to die, gladiators will salute the emperor.

> Carthage **having been destroyed**, Rome was safe.
>
> Carthage **having been destroyed**, Rome is safe.
>
> Carthage **having been destroyed**, Rome will be safe.

> Since Carthage **had been** destroyed, Rome was safe.
>
> Since Carthage **has been** destroyed, Rome is safe.
>
> Since Carthage **will have been destroyed**, Rome will be safe.

Changing the participle to an abstract noun is often a useful solution when a literal translation would sound awkward in English. For example, in the sentence *porcī mortuī pastōribus dolōrī erant*, since the emphasis is not on the pigs but rather on what happened to them, "The death of the pigs was a grief to the shepherds" seems the best translation. Similarly, *pudor auxiliī nōn lātī* means literally "shame of help not brought" but might best be translated as "shame at their failure to bring help."

The following passage shows how point of view, context, and style affect how you can translate a participle:

> prope flūmen **ambulans**, hippopotamum in aquā **iacentem** vīdī. "hippopotame in aquā **iacens**, dentēs sanguine **maculātōs** leōnis per herbam **venientis** nōn timēs?"

hippopotamus, aurēs minūtōs **habens**, ā mē **monentī** nōn **turbātus** est, sed, corpus vastum **habens**, leōnī famē **furentī** cēna numquam erit.

Walking by the river, I saw a hippo, **wallowing** in the water. "Hippo **wallowing** in the water," I cried, "are you not afraid of the **blood-stained** teeth of the lion **coming** through the grass?" The hippo, **having** very small ears, **was not disturbed** by me **warning** it, but, **having** a vast body, it will never be a meal for the lion **slavering** with hunger.

When I **was walking** by the river, I saw a hippo, **which was wallowing** in the water. "Hippo, you there, **the one that is wallowing** in the water," I cried, "are you not afraid of the teeth of the lion **if it comes** through the grass, **although they are stained with blood**?" The hippo, **because it had** very small ears, **was not disturbed** by me **when I warned it**, but, **because it has** a vast body, it will never be a meal for the lion **no matter how he slavers** with hunger.

Participles as Nouns

Since adjectives may be used as nouns (remember examples such as *ferōcēs crūdēlia faciunt* "Fierce people do cruel things") and participles are adjectival forms of verbs, participles can also be used as nouns. For example: *amans, -antis* masc./fem. 3 "lover," *sapiens, -entis* masc. 3 "philosopher" (*sapiō, sapere, sapiī* 3 *i*-stem "have taste/sense"), *serpens, -entis* fem. "snake" (*serpō, serpere, serpsī* 3 "creep"), *advocātus, -ī* masc. 2 "lawyer" (a man called [to help in court]), *dictum, -ī* neut. 2 "saying," *factum, -ī* neut. 2 "fact," "feat."

The Ablative Absolute

In the ablative absolute, **an action or situation that is <u>grammatically</u> unconnected with the action or situation in the main clause** is set apart (*absolūtus* "freed from" the main clause). At its simplest, this phrase consists of a noun or pronoun in the ablative and a participle in agreement with it.

duce mortuō, hostēs fūgērunt.	Because/when their leader had died, the enemy fled. (lit. Their leader having died, the enemy fled.)
duce moriente, hostēs fūgērunt.	Because/when their leader was dying, the enemy fled. (lit. Their leader dying, the enemy fled.)
duce moritūrō, hostēs fūgērunt.	Because/when their leader was going to die, the enemy fled. (lit. Their leader being about to die, the enemy fled.)

The lack of connection between the action referred to in the ablative absolute and that in the main clause is strictly grammatical. There will usually be a causal or temporal link; the death of their leader may well have a decisive effect on the enemy's action, but there is nothing in the wording of the main clause to connect it to the ablative absolute. To emphasize this point, we can contrast the ablative absolute with a relative clause. By definition, a relative clause creates a grammatical relation between two clauses, so an ablative absolute can NEVER be converted into a relative clause.

In the following table, you have examples of sentences using the ablative absolute, along with sentences that use participles in other constructions. The sentences using participles in other constructions CAN be converted into sentences containing relative clauses; the sentences using the ablative absolute CANNOT.

Sentence using a participle	Can we convert it using a relative clause?
lupum captum pastor interfēcit.	*lupum, quem cēperat, pastor interfēcit.* The shepherd killed the wolf which he had caught.
lupō captō, pastor rīsit. When the wolf had been caught, the shepherd laughed.	NO, this is an ablative absolute.
rēgī dormientī quid dixistī?	*rēgī, quī dormiēbat, quid dixistī?* What did you say to the king who was sleeping?
rēge dormiente, quid mīlitibus dixistī? What did you say to the soldiers when the king was sleeping?	NO, this is an ablative absolute.
Rōmulō moenia Rōmae aedificātūrō invidet Remus.	*Rōmulō, quī moenia Rōmae aedificābit, invidet Remus.* Remus envies Romulus, who will build the walls of Rome.
Rōmulō moenia Rōmae aedificātūrō, abībit Remus? When Romulus is about to build the walls of Rome, will Remus go away?	NO, this is an ablative absolute.
mīles Rōmam regressus uxōrem vītāvit.	*mīles, quī Rōmam regressus erat, uxōrem vītāvit.* The soldier who had returned to Rome avoided his wife.
mīlitem Rōmam regressum uxor vītāvit.	*mīlitem, quī Rōmam regressus erat, uxor vītāvit.* His wife avoided the soldier who had returned to Rome.
mīlitī Rōmam regressō carmen cecinimus omnēs.	*mīlitī, quī Rōmam regressus erat, carmen cecinimus omnēs.* We all sang a song for the soldier who had returned to Rome.

mīlite Rōmam regressō, carmen cecinimus omnēs.

The soldier having returned to Rome, we all sang a song.

NO, this is an ablative absolute.

The Ablative Absolute and *esse*

As you saw in the chart of irregular verbs, *esse* has no present participle, a remarkable deficiency. Often, however, a noun or pronoun in combination with a predicate noun or adjective is used as an ablative absolute, as if a present participle of *esse*, meaning "being," were assumed. For example:

Tarquiniō rēge, cīvēs infēlīcēs erant. — Tarquin (being) king, the citizens were unhappy.

pastōre fessō, porcus fūgit. — The shepherd (being) tired, the pig ran away.

Translating the Ablative Absolute

An ablative absolute may be translated using a participle, sometimes with the addition of "because of," "despite," or "with." Very often, however, you will want to change the phrasing for a more idiomatic and precise English translation. For example:

- you may change the ablative absolute to a clause introduced by a word such as "when," "since," "although," "if"

- you may replace a passive construction with an active one

- you may transform the expression completely, using, for instance, an abstract noun instead of the participle

Here are two sentences with some possible English translations:

pastōre abeunte, fēlix porcus erat.

(With) the shepherd going away, the pig was happy.

Although the shepherd went away, the pig was happy.

The pig was happy in spite of the shepherd's departure.

Rōmānīs victīs, Hannibal Rōmam prōgredī dēbuit.

(With) the Romans defeated, Hannibal should have advanced on Rome.

Having defeated the Romans, Hannibal should have advanced on Rome.

Hannibal should have advanced on Rome after defeating the Romans.

Hannibal should have advanced on Rome after he had defeated the Romans.

Hannibal should have advanced on Rome after the Roman defeat.

Vocabulary

ardeō, ardēre, arsī 2	burn (intrans.)
augeō, augēre, auxī, auctum 2	increase (trans.)
accendō, accendere, accendī, accensum 3	set on fire
canō, canere, cecinī 3	sing
cēdō, cēdere, cessī, cessum 3	yield
colō, colere, coluī, cultum 3	cultivate, worship
contemnō, -ere, contempsī, contemptum 3	despise
crescō, crescere, crēvī, crētum 3	increase (intrans.)
currō, currere, cucurrī, cursum 3	run
vertō, vertere, vertī, versum 3	turn
aspiciō, -ere, aspexī, aspectum 3 *i*-stem	look at

Note also the following group of three defective verbs, which over time lost all forms based on the present stem.

coepī, coepisse 3	began
meminī, meminisse 3	remember
ōdī, ōdisse 3	hate

In the case of **ōdī** and **meminī**, which you have already met in Chapter 18, the perfect is used for the present, the future perfect is used for the future, and the pluperfect is used for the imperfect (occasionally for the perfect). **coepī** lacks a present system, both in form and in meaning.

discipulī librum legere coepērunt.	The students began to read the book.
puellam istam semper ōderō.	I will always hate that girl.
dōnum mihi dare nōn meminerat.	She did not remember to give me a gift.

These verbs simply do not have equivalents for the full range of tenses of English verbs. As a result, in translating, you will need to use alternatives. Here are some possibilities.

I will begin to fear wolves.	*lupōs timēre incipiam.*
I had always hated that girl.	*puella ista semper odiō mihi fuerat.*
She had not remembered to give me a gift.	*dōnum mihi dare oblīta erat.*

Prōlūsiōnēs

Parse the words in bold.

Gnaeō Pompeiō et Marcō Crassō **consulibus** nātus est Publius Vergilius Marō, omnium poētārum Rōmānōrum **celeberrimus**. prīmō dē vītā pastōrum scrīpsit, tum dē agricultūrā, postrēmō dē **factīs** Troiānōrum quī Aenēā viam **monstrante** ex urbe **ardentī** fūgerant. **Caesare** mortuō bellum cīvīle rursus ortum est. Augustō pācem imperiō **tōtī** dare **cōnantī** magnō **auxiliō** erant carmina Vergiliī, quī **victūrum** per omne tempus nōmen habet.

Translate.

Ovidium carmina amātōria scrībentem laudābant amīcī. sed, carmina amātōria scrībente eō, Augustus Rōmam urbem magnam facere cupiēbat. malīs carminibus malōs cīvēs facientibus, poētam Augustus in exilium mīsit. Augustō imperātōre, Ovidius multōs annōs in exiliō victūrus erat. Ovidius Augustō imperātōrī epistulam longam mīsit, sed ille verba poētae in Ītaliam regredī cupientis nōn audiēbat. morte Augustī audītā, Ovidius gāvīsus est, sed ā Tiberiō, novō imperātōre, nōn revocātus est.

Translate, turning the participial phrases into clauses with conjugated verbs.

For example, *agricolā fessō, porcī cibum nōn habēbant.*

When the farmer was tired, the pigs did not have food.

   or

Since the farmer was tired, the pigs did not have food.

   or

If the farmer was tired, the pigs did not have food.

1. mīlitēs, barbarum nōbīs viam monstrantem sequī dēbēmus.
2. num porcī in agrum itūrī lupum contemnent?
3. Rōmānīs urbem accendentibus territī sunt cīvēs.
4. ā Rōmānīs urbem invādentibus territī sunt cīvēs.
5. Rōmānōs urbem invādentēs ōderant cīvēs.
6. Caesare duce Rōmānī hostium metūs semper augēbant.
7. vōcibus lupōrum per tenebrās noctis procul audītīs, metus noster semper crescēbat.
8. porcō in agrum īre volentī portam nōn aperuit pastor.
9. Caesarem hostium cōpiās regredī cōgentem aspexerāmus.

10. mīlitēs multa vulnera passī passim per campum iacent.
11. corpus mīlitis multa vulnera passī in campō iacet.
12. mīlitī vulnera gravia passō aquam dedit puella.
13. mīlitibus multīs crūdēlia vulnera passīs paulātim ē pugnā cessērunt agmina nostra.
14. deō nōbīs bona nōn semper dantī cūr dōna damus? cūr templum eius colimus?
15. vel capellā vel porcō vel agnō ā lupīs interfectō, pastor domum recurrere nōlet.
16. caelum procul habitans, mortālēs nec ōdit nec amat rex deōrum.
17. cīvī illī bonō aut lībertātem aut mortem habēre volentī mortem crūdēlem dedērunt hostēs.
18. Sāturnō caelī rēge, quam bene vīvēbant hominēs! illō deō imperium caeleste tenente, arborēs sine labōre fructūs hominibus dabant.
19. Sāturnō ē caelō expulsō, Iuppiter rex deōrum factus est.
20. aut Cupīdine aut Venere mentēs hominum vertente, vīta nostra difficillima est dolōrēsque nostrī sine fine crescunt.

Translate.

1. When they had seen their brother the girls began to sing.
2. The wolves killed the soldiers forced by our leader to go into the forest.
3. Listening to the poem, the boys gradually became very unhappy.
4. Do not despise the poems written by this poet.
5. I saw a wolf walking through the streets of the whole city inside the walls.
6. Running into the wood, I saw the wolf.
7. When they were about to see their brother, the girls became happier.
8. When he was giving a rose to the girl, the boy was happy.
9. Having given a rose to the girl, the boy began to run out of the house.
10. With the trees giving fruit to the little farmer, we have enough food.
11. Did you see the soldier lying dead near the river?
12. When Romulus was king, the Romans worshipped the gods every day.
13. When the soldier was lying dead near the swift river, his father and mother were at home, weeping with their other son.
14. Surely gladiators were not forced to praise Caesar when they were going to die?
15. When they had killed the soldiers, the enemy rejoiced and sang songs to their savage god.

Lectiōnēs Latīnae

Lege, Intellege

The *Dē Virīs Illustribus* (On Famous Men) attributed to the fourth-century AD historian Aurelius Victor is a collection of eighty-six brief biographies, mostly of Romans.

Hannibal

Hannibal, Hamilcāris fīlius, novem annōs nātus, ā patre āris admōtus odium in Rōmānōs perenne iūrāvit. exinde mīles in castrīs patris fuit. mortuō eō causam bellī quaerens Saguntum, cīvitātem Rōmānīs foederātam, intrā sex mensēs ēvertit. tum Alpibus patefactīs in Ītaliam trāiēcit. Publium Scīpiōnem apud Ticinum, Semprōnium Longum apud Trebiam, Flāminium apud Trasimēnum, Paullum et Varrōnem apud Cannās superāvit. castra ad tertium ab urbe lapidem posuit sed, tempestātibus repulsus, prīmum ā Fabiō Maximō frustrātus, deinde ā Valēriō Flaccō repulsus, ā Gracchō et Marcellō fugātus, in Africam revocātus, ā Scīpiōne superātus, ad Antiochum rēgem Syriae confūgit eumque hostem Rōmānīs fēcit; quō victō ad Prūsiam rēgem Bithyniae concessit; tum Rōmānā legātiōne repetītus venēnō, quod sub gemmā ānulī habēbat, absumptus est.

—[Aurelius Victor], *Dē Virīs Illustribus* 42

1. How old was Hannibal when his father made him swear eternal hatred of Rome?
2. Why did Hannibal attack the Spanish city of Saguntum?
3. Where did Hannibal win his two great victories after Ticinus and Trebia?
4. Who defeated Hannibal in Africa?
5. How did Hannibal die?

exinde adv. subsequently

patefaciō, -ere, -fēcī, -factum 3 *i*-stem reveal, open up

trāiciō, -ere, trāiēcī, trāiectum 3 *i*-stem throw across, cross

apud prep. + acc. at, in the home of

lapis, lapidis masc. 3 stone, milestone

ānulus, -ī masc. 2 ring

Ars Poētica

Martial (Marcus Valerius Martialis; AD c. 38–c. 103) was the author of more than 1,500 epigrams (short satirical poems). As he himself acknowledges, some are better than others, but they present a vivid picture of contemporary life in Rome.

Parse the words in bold in the following quotations from Martial.

1. *et **stantī** legis et legis **sedentī**,*
   *currentī legis et legis **canentī**.*
   *ad cēnam properō: tenēs **euntem**.*
   ad cēnam veniō: fugās sedentem.
   *fessus dormiō: suscitās **iacentem**.*

   You read to me when I'm standing and you read to me when I'm sitting, you read to me when I'm running and you read to me when I'm singing. I'm hurrying to dinner: you hold me back when I'm going. I'm coming to dinner: you scare me off when I'm sitting down. I'm tired and sleeping: you wake me up as I lie there.

2. *effugere nōn est, Flacce, bāsiātōrēs.*
   nec labra pinguī dēlibūta cērātō
   *nec **congelātī** gutta prōderit nāsī.*
   *et **aestuantem** bāsiant et algentem,*
   *et nuptiāle bāsium **reservantem** . . .*
   *febrīcitantem bāsiābit et **flentem**,*
   *dabit oscitantī bāsium **natantīque**,*
   *dabit **canentī**.*

   It isn't possible, Flaccus, to escape from kissers. Neither lips smeared with greasy ointment nor a dripping frozen nose will do you any good. They kiss you when you're hot and when you're cold, and when you're saving a kiss for the bride . . . He'll kiss you when you have a fever and when you're weeping, he'll give you a kiss when you're yawning and when you're swimming, he'll give you one when you're singing.

3. ***flentibus** Hēliadum rāmīs dum vīpera rēpit,*
   *   fluxit in **obstantem** sūcina gutta feram:*
   quae dum mīrātur pinguī sē rōre tenērī,
   *   concrētō riguit vincta repente gelū.*

   While a viper was crawling on the weeping branches of the Heliades [the sisters of Phaethon who were turned into poplar trees that "wept" amber sap when he fell from the Sun-god's chariot], an amber drop flowed onto the creature when it was in its path: while it was marveling that it was being held by the rich dew, it suddenly grew stiff bound by the hardened glue.

Aurea Dicta

1. *audentēs deus ipse iuvat.* (Ovid)
2. *aurum omnēs, victā iam pietāte, colunt.* (Propertius)
3. *dūcunt volentem fāta, nōlentem trahunt.* (Seneca the Younger)
4. *facta mea, nōn dicta, vōs sequī volō.* (Livy)
5. *flūmine vīcīnō stultus sitit.* (Petronius)

6. *Graecia capta ferum victōrem cēpit.* (Horace)
7. *ignōrātiō futūrōrum malōrum ūtilior est quam scientia.* (Cicero)
8. *iniūriam quī factūrus est iam fēcit.* (Seneca the Younger)

trahō, -ere, traxī, tractum 3 drag

vīcīnus, -a, -um neighboring, close at hand

sitiō, -īre 4 be thirsty

Lūsūs

Thēsaurus Verbōrum

Most English words ending in *-ant* and *-ent* that come from Latin present participles are adjectives; for example:

benevolent	ignorant	tolerant
cogent	permanent	triumphant
consequent	resurgent	urgent
dominant	sentient	vacant
hesitant	significant	vigilant

Many are used also, or solely, as nouns; for example:

agent	militant	rodent[1]
constant	occupant	serpent
continent	orient	servant
ingredient	patient	stimulant
inhabitant	repellent	student

---

1. From *rōdō, -ere, rōsī, rōsum* 3 "gnaw."

Etymologiae Antīquae

Body Parts II

corpus*, *corporis neut. 3 "body." The body is subject to corruption (*corrumpō, -ere, corrūpī, corruptum* 3).

cadāver*, *cadāveris neut. 3 "corpse." Dead bodies fall (*cado, -ere, cecidī* 3).

caput*, *capitis neut. 3 "head." Our senses and nerves take (*capiō, -ere, cēpī, captum* 3 *i*-stem) their origin in the head.

carō*, *carnis fem. 3 "flesh." Our flesh falls (*cado, -ere, cecidī* 3) when it lacks (*careō, -ēre, caruī* 2) life. It is also created (*creō* 1) and dear (*cārus, -a, -um*) to us.

musculus*, *-ī masc. 2 "muscle." Muscles rippling under the skin were compared to little mice (*mūs, mūris* masc. 3). The muscles in the upper arm (*lacertus, -ī* masc. 2) were compared, in the same fanciful way, to lizards (*lacerta, -ae* fem. 1).

oculus*, *-ī masc. 2 "eye." The eyes are covered (*occulō, -ere, occuluī, occultum* 3) by the eyelids.

palpebra*, *-ae fem. 1 "eyelid." Our eyelids quiver (*palpitō* 1).

pēnis*, *-is masc. 3 "penis." The penis hangs down (*pendeō, -ēre, pependī* 2).

Vīta Rōmānōrum

Leopards and Hippopotamuses

The Romans had an insatiable love for watching wild beasts fight in the arena. When Trajan celebrated his triumph over the Dacians [who lived in the lower Danube region] in AD 107, he had eleven thousand animals killed in spectacles lasting 123 days. Such slaughter reduced or exterminated many species within and beyond the empire. Already in 50 BC, Cicero, as governor of Cilicia [southeastern Turkey], wrote to Marcus Caelius Rufus, who was preparing to put on games, a recognized way to gain political popularity:

> As regards the leopards, the matter is being handled diligently by the usual hunters in accordance with my instructions. But there is a surprising shortage, and they say that such leopards as are still here are complaining bitterly that they alone in my province are being hunted, and apparently they have decided to leave for Caria.

> —Cicero, *Epistulae ad Familiārēs* 2.11.2

By the time Pliny wrote the following passage, in the mid-first century AD, extremely exotic animals (rhinoceroses, tigers, giraffes, polar bears) had been put on show in Rome, but he clearly does not really know what a hippopotamus looks like. The notion that the hippopotamus is crafty enough to escape hunters by walking backward and to perform surgery on itself hints at the paradoxical sentimentality (despite the butchery in the amphitheater) the Romans felt toward animals. Compare, for example, the story of Androclus, spared in the Circus Maximus by a lion from whose paw he had extracted a thorn in Africa, or of the elephant so ashamed of its slowness in learning tricks that it would go out alone at night to practice them. For a similarly clever self-surgery by beavers, see Chapter 21 *Etymologiae*, under *castor*.

> The Nile produces another animal even bigger than the crocodile, namely, the hippopotamus, which has cloven hooves like those of an ox; the back, mane, and whinny of a horse; a short snout; the tail of a wild boar and also its curved tusks (though they are not as harmful). Its hide provides impenetrable material for shields and helmets except when soaking wet. It grazes on crops, reputedly marking out a certain amount for each day in advance by walking backward, leaving tracks that seem to lead out of the field so that no trap will be set for it when it comes back. A hippopotamus was first shown at Rome, along with five crocodiles, in an artificial stream, by Marcus Aemilius Scaurus during the games which he gave as superintendent of public works [in 58 BC]. The hippopotamus has even distinguished itself as a master of one branch of medicine. When it has become too fat through constant eating, it goes out onto the bank to look for places where rushes have recently been cut. Where it sees a very sharp stalk, it presses its body against it. By this bloodletting it unburdens its body, which would otherwise be likely to become diseased; then it covers the wound over again with mud.

—Pliny the Elder, *Historia Nātūrālis* 8.95–96

Chapter 20
Gerunds and Gerundives, the Supine

The **gerund** is a verbal noun. In English, it is formed in the same way as the present active participle, by adding "-ing" to the present stem of the verb, for example, "loving." Such ambiguity does not occur in Latin, since the gerund is formed quite differently from the present active participle. Even so, before considering the form and functions of the Latin gerund, it is important to distinguish the functions of the two parts of speech in English.

The gerund, unlike the participle, can be replaced by another noun or by an infinitive, or governed by a preposition. Contrast

Seeing is **believing** = Sight is belief = To see is to believe = Through **seeing** we come to **believing**
with
Seeing his bees **leaving** their hive, the farmer was sad.

The Latin **gerundive** is a passive verbal adjective, usually translated as "being -ed" or "to be -ed." This brief description will make the gerundive seem to be much the same as a passive participle, but it is used rather differently.

The gerund is **active** and the gerundive is **passive**, but in Latin you can often use either form to express the same idea. Since it has a clear equivalent in English, you will first learn how to use the gerund. Then you will learn how the gerund and the gerundive can be used to express the same idea. Finally, you will learn idioms involving the gerundive alone.

Forming the Gerund

The Latin gerund has only what are called the **oblique cases**, meaning all cases except the nominative and vocative. Its endings are those of a second declension neuter singular noun. You form it by adding each conjugation's characteristic vowel(s) to the present stem, and then adding *-ndī*, *-ndō*, *-ndum*, *-ndō*. For example:

NOMINATIVE	—	—	—
GENITIVE	am**andī**	aud**iendī**	sequ**endī**
DATIVE	am**andō**	aud**iendō**	sequ**endō**
ACCUSATIVE	am**andum**	aud**iendum**	sequ**endum**
ABLATIVE	am**andō**	aud**iendō**	sequ**endō**

Of the irregular verbs you know, only *īre* and *ferre* have gerunds: *eundī*, which is irregular, and *ferendī*, which is regular.

Forming the Gerundive

The gerundive is formed in the same way as the gerund, but **it has all cases in both singular and plural in all genders**.

Singular

NOMINATIVE	am**andus, -a, -um**	aud**iendus, -a, -um**	sequ**endus, -a, -um**
GENITIVE	am**andī, -ae, -ī**	aud**iendī, -ae, -ī**	sequ**endī, -ae, -ī**
DATIVE	am**andō, -ae, -ō**	aud**iendō, -ae, -ō**	sequ**endō, -ae, -ō**
ACCUSATIVE	am**andum, -am, -um**	aud**iendum, -am, -um**	sequ**endum, -am, -um**
ABLATIVE	am**andō, -ā, -ō**	aud**iendō, -ā, -ō**	sequ**endō, -ā, -ō**
VOCATIVE	am**ande, -a, -um**	aud**iende, -a, -um**	sequ**ende, -a, -um**

Plural

NOMINATIVE	am**andī, -ae, -a**	aud**iendī, -ae, -a**	sequ**endī, -ae, -a**
GENITIVE	am**andōrum, -ārum, -ōrum**	aud**iendōrum, -ārum, -ōrum**	sequ**endōrum, -ārum, -ōrum**
DATIVE	am**andīs, -īs, -īs**	aud**iendīs, -īs, -īs**	sequ**endīs, -īs, -īs**
ACCUSATIVE	am**andōs, -ās, -a**	aud**iendōs, -ās, -a**	sequ**endōs, -ās, -a**
ABLATIVE	am**andīs, -īs, -īs**	aud**iendīs, -īs, -īs**	sequ**endīs, -īs, -īs**
VOCATIVE	am**andī, -ae, -a**	aud**iendī, -ae, -a**	sequ**endī, -ae, -a**

Of the irregular verbs you have met, *ferre* is the only one whose gerundive is often found: *ferendus*, *-a*, *-um*, which is regular.

The Gerund as a Noun

Because the gerund has no nominative case, the infinitive is used instead, as if it were a neuter noun. For example:

cantāre dulce est. Singing is pleasant.

The gerund is used as a noun in all the other cases. For example:

Gen.	*ars **cantandī** difficilis est.*	The art **of singing** is difficult.
Dat.	***cantandō** operam dedit.* [Note this use of *opera*, *-ae* fem. 1]	He paid attention **to singing**.
Acc.	*cum amīcīs **ad cantandum** abiit.*	He went off with his friends **for the purpose of singing/to sing**.
Abl.	***cantandō** uxōrī placuit.*	**By singing** he pleased his wife.

The **genitive** of the gerund can also express purpose (which is most frequently conveyed in English by an infinitive), with the ablative of *causā* or *grātiā* (meaning "for the sake of") usually coming after the gerund.

> *cum amīcīs cantandī causā/grātiā abiit.*
>
> He went off with his friends **for the sake of singing** (= to sing).

The **accusative** of the gerund is used only with prepositions, most often with *ad* to express purpose (*ad cantandum*).

The Gerund as a Verbal Form

Because the gerund is a verbal form, it has an active meaning, and if the verb in question is transitive, the gerund can take a direct object, which usually comes immediately before it. This chart shows you the same sentences as before, but now with *carmina* as the direct object:

***carmina cantāre** difficile est.* [Infinitive as subject.]	Singing songs is difficult.
*ars **carmina cantandī** difficilis est.*	The art of singing songs is difficult.
***carmina cantandō** operam dedit.*	He paid attention to singing songs.
*cum amīcīs **ad carmina cantandum** abiit.*	He went off with his friends for the purpose of singing songs/to sing songs.
***carmina cantandō** uxōrī placuit.*	By singing songs he pleased his wife.

Although the gerund is a noun, **it can't be modified by adjectives**. Reflecting its verbal nature, however, it can be modified by adverbs or phrases that function like adverbs. For example:

***bene** cantandō uxōrī placuit.*	By singing **well** he pleased his wife.
*carmina **tōtum diem** cantandō uxōrī nōn placuit.*	By singing songs **all day long** he did not please his wife.

The Gerundive as an Equivalent to the Gerund

Because it is an adjectival form, the gerundive is almost always used to modify a noun or pronoun, which usually comes immediately before it.

If the gerund is used with a direct object in the accusative case, it is possible to express the same idea with a gerundive. Simply put the accusative object of the gerund into the case that the gerund was in (the case required by the syntax of the sentence), and then make the gerundive agree with that noun, just as any adjective would do. For example:

Gerund

*ars **carmina cantandī** difficilis est.*
The art of singing songs is difficult.

***carmina cantandō** operam dedit.*
He paid attention to singing songs.

*cum amīcīs **ad carmina cantandum** abiit.*
He went off with his friends for the purpose of singing songs.

***carmina cantandō** uxōrī placuit.*
By singing songs he pleased his wife.

Gerundive

*ars **carminum cantandōrum** difficilis est.*
The art of song-singing is difficult.

***carminibus cantandīs** operam dedit.*
He paid attention to song-singing.

*cum amīcīs **ad carmina cantanda** abiit.*
He went off with his friends for the purpose of song-singing.

***carminibus cantandīs** uxōrī placuit.*
By song-singing he pleased his wife.

Notā Bene

The translation "song-singing" is used simply to emphasize the way in which the gerundive forms a unit with the noun it modifies; "singing songs" is an equally good translation.

When either the gerund or the gerundive is possible, nearly all Roman writers preferred to use the gerundive, except when this would require long chains of nouns and adjectives in the same case as the gerundive. For example, most people would agree that

in hortum exiī hōs duōs flōrēs meōs pulchrōs carpendī causā

is less awkward than

in hortum exiī hōrum duōrum flōrum meōrum pulchrōrum carpendōrum causā

as a translation of "I went out into the garden to pick these two beautiful flowers of mine."

The Gerundive of Obligation

In this very frequent idiom, also known as the **passive periphrastic**, the gerundive is combined with a form of *esse*, to mean that something needs to be done or must be done. There is a comparable English expression in, for example, "The pigs are <u>to be kept</u> in the field. They are not <u>to be allowed</u> into the wood." English has adopted numerous Latin gerundive forms to convey a sense of necessity. For example:

addenda	things to be added
agenda	things to be done
Amanda	a woman to be loved
corrigenda	things to be corrected
memorandum	a thing to be remembered
Miranda	a woman to be admired
propaganda	things to be spread
referendum	a thing to be referred (to the voters etc.)

With the gerundive of obligation, **the agent of the action is put into the dative**. Contrast the use of the ablative of the agent with the preposition *ā/ab*. For example:

porcus mihi pascendus est.	I must feed the pig. (lit. The pig is to be fed by me.)
lupī agricolae fortī interficiendī sunt.	The brave farmer must kill the wolves. (lit. The wolves are to be killed by the brave farmer.)

You can use the gerundive of obligation impersonally, in the neuter nominative singular, with no subject expressed. For example:

nōbīs fortiter pugnandum est, mīlitēs.	We must fight bravely, soldiers. (lit. It must be fought by us bravely, soldiers.)
Rōmam tibi quam celerrimē eundum est.	You must go to Rome as quickly as possible. (lit. It must be gone by you to Rome as quickly as possible.)

The Supine

The supine is a fourth declension verbal noun, which is used almost exclusively in the accusative and ablative. These cases are formed by adding *-um* or *-ū* to the perfect passive stem; for example, *dictum* and *dictū*, *vīsum*, and *vīsū*. The translation of the supine varies according to the case and the particular construction.

The accusative of the supine is used in two constructions, to form the future infinitive passive (which you will meet in Chapter 21) and, with a verb of motion, to express purpose. As a verb, the supine has an active meaning in the accusative and may therefore take an object. For example:

Rōmam vēnimus templa vīsum.	We have come to Rome to see the temples.
Rōmam iī lūdōs spectātum.	I went to Rome to watch the games.

The ablative of the supine is not common. It is used mostly to modify a very limited number of adjectives, and it never takes an object, because it has a passive meaning. For example:

per omnēs viās (horribile vīsū!) iacēbant corpora cīvium.
The citizens' bodies were lying along all the streets, a horrible sight to see (lit. "to be seen")!

omnēs discipulī (mīrābile dictū!) librō bene studuerant.
The students had all studied their book well, an amazing thing to say (lit. "to be said")!

fīlius maior nātū patrem amābat.
The elder (lit. "greater in being born") son loved his father.
(*nātū* is related to *nascor, nascī, nātus sum* 3 be born)

Prōlūsiōnēs

Parse the words in bold.

1. **dandum** semper est tempus: vēritātem diēs aperit. (Seneca the Younger)
2. dispār **vīvendī** ratiō est, mors omnibus ūna. (Ps.-Cato)
3. **vīvendō** vīcī mea fāta. (Virgil)
4. **exaequanda** facta dictīs. (Sallust)
5. fortitūdō contemptrix **timendōrum** est. (Seneca the Younger)
6. nēmō est cāsū bonus; **discenda** virtūs est. (Seneca the Younger)
7. aliud **agendī** tempus, aliud quiescendī. (Cicero)
8. omnia hominī, dum vīvit, **spēranda** sunt. (Seneca the Younger)
9. nec mihi iam patriam antīquam spēs ulla **videndī**. (Virgil)
10. scrībitur historia ad **narrandum**, nōn ad probandum. (Quintilian)

Change the gerunds in the following sentences to gerundives, or vice versa, and then translate.

1. ad templa omnium deōrum mīrandum Rōmam vēnī.
2. amor pecūniam petendī malus est.
3. ad porcōs miserōs interficiendum ē silvā vēnērunt lupī.
4. porcī ingentis videndī grātiā rūs vēnit dominus meus.
5. librīs legendīs sapientior fīō.

Rephrase the following sentences with a gerundive, and then translate.
For example, *Caesarem laudāre dēbeō. Caesar mihi laudandus est.* I must praise Caesar.

1. exercitus tōtus urbem fortiter dēfendere dēbet.
2. dēbēs, pastor, lupōs ex agrīs agere.
3. Hannibal Rōmānōs celeriter vincere dēbet.
4. fortem ducem, mīlitēs, sequī dēbētis.
5. quis hanc epistulam scrībere dēbet?

239

hae sententiae aut Anglicē aut Latīnē tibi vertendae sunt.

1. nonne pastōrī Rōmam hodiē eundum est?

2. ipse ego (mīrābile dictū!) porcīs videndīs humilis fīō.

3. porcōs interficiendī causā ē silvā vēnērunt lupī.

4. porcīs meīs tot mensēs carēre maximō mihi dolōrī est.

5. discipulōs docendō discit multa magister, sed porcus meus librīs legendīs operam nullam dat.

6. magistrātus ille veterrimus "dēlenda nōbīs est Karthāgō" cottīdiē inquit.

7. hinc profectī sunt Rōmānī Karthāginis dēlendae causā, nōn deōs nostrōs laudātum.

8. Karthāgine dēlendā Rōmānī dīvitiōrēs factī sunt.

9. quamquam tot iuvenēs tōtum annum lūdōrum spectandōrum causā Rōmae mansērunt, nōs tamen ipsī gaudēmus rūrī porcōs taurōsque videntēs.

10. tōtī populō Rōmānō sociīsque omnibus laudandus es, Caesar, namque exercitū tam celeriter contrā hostium aciem dūcendō fīnēs nostrōs auxistī.

11. spem domum regrediendī habēmus nullam; pīrātae enim ad insulae ōram spolia rapiendī causā nāvem iam vertērunt.

12. gladiōs, hastās, scūta barbarīs vendendō sacerdōs quīdam, vir mōrum pessimōrum, urbem nostram perdidit.

13. floccī nōn faciendus est magister, sī dīvitiārum tantum memor est et pecūniae adipiscendae causā ad lūdum venit.

14. deōs aurum rogāre virō bonō dēdecorī est; multō melius est labōrandō dīvitiās petere.

15. crēde mihi, nē optimōrum quidem hominum memorēs sunt deī, neque sceleribus nostrīs ad īram movērī solent. num igitur exta taurōrum, mūnera cum cāra tum inānia, in ārīs eōrum mortālibus pōnenda sunt?

16. By killing the wolves, the farmer defended his pigs.

17. The hope of seeing my friends was sweet to me.

18. I gave the pirates more money to free my sick brother.

19. The sailors laughed and asked the priest, "Why do you have so great a fear of sailing?"

20. You mustn't drink more wine today, if you wish to go with us to watch the games.

21. Surely this poet is very stupid, for he pays no attention to reading the books of the other poets?

22. We ourselves must force the big bad wolf to return to its cave, because the shepherd has gone away to see the Roman consul.

23. If you love freedom, soldiers, you must leave the citadel to fight against the barbarians.

24. Sitting under the tree, you caught the falling fruit, boys, but I was sitting under the huge rock to catch the falling pigs.

25. By running away from the battle line so shamefully, the Roman consul was a disgrace to the whole army, for he paid no attention to defending our city.

Lectiōnēs Latīnae

Lege, Intellege

Caesar in Action

Caesarī omnia ūnō tempore erant agenda: signum tubā dandum; ab opere revocandī mīlitēs; quī paulō longius frūmentī reperiendī causā prōcesserant, arcessendī; aciēs instruenda; mīlitēs cōhortandī. quārum rērum magnam partem temporis brevitās et incursūs hostium impediēbant. hīs difficultātibus duae rēs erant auxiliō, scientia atque ūsus mīlitum, quod superiōribus proeliīs exercitātī nōn minus commodē ipsī sibi prae-scrībere quam ab aliīs docērī poterant, et quod ab opere singulīsque legiōnibus sin-gulōs legātōs Caesar discēdere nisi mūnītīs castrīs vetuerat. hī propter propinquitātem et celeritātem hostium Caesaris imperium nōn exspectābant, sed per sē quae facienda esse vidēbantur administrābant.

—Caesar, *Dē Bellō Gallicō* 2.20

arcessō, -ere, arcessīvī, arcessītum 3 summon

ūsus mīlitum "the soldiers' experience"

nisi mūnītīs castrīs "unless the camp had been fortified"

propter prep. + acc. on account of

1. What were the two factors which most impeded preparations for battle?
2. Why had some of the soldiers gone slightly too far from camp?
3. What had to be completed before individual legionary commanders were allowed to leave their posts?
4. What were the two factors that most assisted the Romans in such crises?
5. Why did Caesar's legionary commanders decide for themselves what needed to be done without waiting for his orders?

Ars Poētica

Horace (Quintus Horatius Flaccus; 65–8 BC) was the author of *Satires*, *Epodes*, *Odes*, and *Epistles*. He fought for the assassins of Julius Caesar at Philippi but soon became, through his patron, Gaius Maecenas, one of Augustus' leading propagandists.

Which of the forms in these quotations from Horace are gerunds, and which are gerundives?

1. *mōvit Amphīōn lapidēs* **canendō**.
   Amphion [one of the builders of Thebes] moved stones with his singing.

2. *omnēs ūna manet nox*
   et **calcanda** *semel via lētī.*
   One night awaits everyone and the path of death must be trod just once.

3. *nunc est* **bibendum**, *nunc pede līberō*
   pulsanda *tellūs.*
   Now we should drink, now we should strike the ground with free foot.

4. *quem Venus arbitrum*
   dīcet **bibendī**?
   Whom will Venus name as master of ceremonies for our drinking?

5. **vīsendus** *āter flūmine languidō*
   Cōcytos errans.
   We must see dark Cocytus [one of the rivers of the Underworld] wandering with its languid stream.

6. **linquenda** *tellūs et domus et placens*
   uxor.
   You must leave your land and your home and your pleasing wife.

7. *rēgum* **timendōrum** *in propriōs gregēs,*
   rēgēs in ipsōs imperium est Iovis.
   [The power of] fearsome kings is over their own herds; Jupiter's power is over the kings themselves.

8.   *neque tē silēbō,*
   Līber, et saevīs inimīca virgō
   bēluīs, nec tē, **metuende** *certā*
       Phoebe sagittā.
   Nor will I be silent about you, Liber [another name for Bacchus], nor you, virgin hostile to savage beasts [Diana], nor you, Phoebus [Apollo], fearsome with your sure arrow.

Aurea Dicta

1. *amō lībertātem loquendī.* (Cicero)

2. *aut bellō vincendum est aut meliōribus pārendum.* (Livy)

3. *beātos putō quibus deōrum mūnere datum est aut facere scrībenda, aut scrībere legenda; beātissimōs vērō quibus utrumque.* (Pliny the Younger)

4. *bellum nec timendum nec prōvocandum.* (Pliny the Younger)

5. *claudendae sunt aurēs malīs vōcibus.* (Seneca the Younger)

6. *disce legendō.* (Ps.-Cato)

7. *legendī semper occāsiō est, audiendī nōn semper.* (Pliny the Younger)

8. *nihil agendō hominēs male agere discunt.* (Columella)

pāreō, -ēre, pāruī, pāritum 2 (+ dat.) obey

Lūsūs

Thēsaurus Verbōrum

Many English adjectives ending in *-acious* are derived from third declension Latin adjectives in *-ax*. For example:

audax	loquax	sagax
capax	mendax	tenax
efficax	pugnax	vīvax
fallax	rapax	vorax

Etymologiae Antīquae

Domestic Animals

***agnus**, -ī* masc. 2 "lamb." Lambs are particularly good at recognizing (*agnoscō, -ere, agnōvī, agnitum* 3) their mothers.

anas, anatis fem. 3 "duck." Ducks swim (*nō, nāre, nāvī, nātum* 1).

ariēs, arietis masc. 3 "ram." Rams are aggressive, like Ares, the (Greek) god of war. They are also sacrificed on altars (*āra, -ae* fem. 1).

canis, canis masc./fem. 3 "dog." Dogs sing (*canō, -ere, cecinī* 3); specifically, they sing out a warning by their barking when danger approaches.

caper, caprī masc. 2 "goat." Goats take (*capiō, -ere, cēpī, captum* 3 *i*-stem) and eat all sorts of vegetation.

equus, -ī masc. 2 "horse." When horses are yoked to chariots, it is important to ensure that they are well matched (*aequus, -a, -um* equal).

iuvencus, *-ī* masc. 2 "bullock." Bullocks help (*iuvō*, *-āre*, *iūvī*, *iūtum* 1) with plowing, and they are sacrificed to Jupiter (*Iuppiter*, *Iovis* masc. 3).

mulus, *-ī* masc. 2 "mule." Mules are used to turn millstones (*mola*, *-ae* fem. 1).

porcus, *-ī* masc. 2 "pig." Pigs wallow in mud and are therefore dirty (*spurcus*, *-a*, *-um*).

Vīta Rōmānōrum

Comic Characters

The only examples of Roman comedy that survive are the plays of Plautus and Terence. Comedy featured stock characters: young men in love, beautiful slave girls, irascible fathers, cunning slaves, unscrupulous pimps, and so on. Plautus' Peniculus, from the *Menaechmī*, which provided Shakespeare with the basic plot for *A Comedy of Errors*, is a fine example of the "parasite," a man who gets free meals by flattering rich men who give dinner parties.

> The young men have given me the name Peniculus [Little Brush], because I sweep the tables clean when I eat. People who bind captives with chains and put fetters on runaway slaves act very foolishly in my opinion. For, if a wretched man has bad treatment added to his misfortune, his desire to run away and get into mischief just gets stronger. For they free themselves from their fetters somehow; when they are chained up, they wear away a link with a file or knock out the nail with a stone; that's easy. A person you wish to keep securely so he doesn't run away should be bound with food and drink; tie the fellow's mouth to a full table. So long as you provide him every day with all he wants to eat and drink, for sure he'll never run away, even if he has committed a capital offense; you'll keep him easily, so long as you bind him with those chains. Chains of food are extremely pliable: the more you stretch them, the more tightly they bind. I'm going here to Menaechmus' house; I have been sentenced for a long time now to come here, and I'm coming of my own accord, so that he can chain me. For Menaechmus doesn't just feed people, he nourishes them and restores their strength; no one administers medicine more pleasantly. This young man's like that; he's an abundant food supply, and he gives dinners fit for Ceres, the way he heaps the tables up, and sets out such vast piles of dishes that you have to stand up on your couch if you want to get something from the top. But I've been away from here for many days now, living it up at home all this time with my own dear ones—for everything I eat or buy is very dear. Since our dear ones desert us when they are well provided for, I'm now paying Menaechmus a visit. But his door is opening; look, I see him coming out.

> —Plautus, *Menaechmī* 77–109

Compare these three sentences:

> The pig is singing.
> The farmer says, "The pig is singing."
> The farmer says that the pig is singing.

The first two are both examples of **direct statements**. The first is the original direct statement. The second simply quotes that direct statement in its original form. The third, however, is an example of **indirect statement**, in which the original statement is not quoted but **reported**.

In Latin, as you might expect, the two direct statements would be expressed as *porcus canit* and *agricola "porcus canit" ait*. **An indirect statement, however, uses the infinitive in the appropriate tense, and puts the subject of the original statement in the accusative:**

> *agricola porcum canere dīcit.*   The farmer says that the pig is singing.

To translate an indirect statement involving the negative of "say" or an equivalent verb, *nōn* is rarely used; rather, you use the verb *negō*, literally, "I deny":

> *agricola porcum canere negat.*   The farmer says that the pig is not singing.

What happens, though, if the verb in the indirect statement takes a direct object?

> *agricola porcum carmen canere dīcit.*   The farmer says that the pig is singing a song.

In this sentence, both the subject (*porcum*) and the object (*carmen*) of the infinitive are in the accusative case. You cannot use case here to determine which is the subject and which is the direct object, but common sense and context usually prevent confusion.

Infinitives

In indirect statement, you can use a wide range of tenses of the infinitive: present, future, and perfect, both active and passive.

You have already seen the present and perfect infinitives, active and passive:

amāre	to love
amārī	to be loved
amāvisse	to have loved
amātus, -a, -um esse	to have been loved

The future active infinitive is formed by combining the future active participle with *esse*:

amātūrus, -ūra, -ūrum esse	to be about to love

The future passive infinitive is formed by combining the accusative form of the supine, which is identical to the neuter nominative singular of the perfect passive participle, with *īrī*, the present passive infinitive of *eō, īre, iī/īvī, itum* "go." Since *īre* is an intransitive verb, the form *īrī* seems illogical and difficult to translate on its own, but Latin often uses intransitive verbs passively in idioms that have no equivalent in English; Chapter 28 gives more examples. For the model verbs of the five conjugations, the forms of the future passive infinitive are:

amātum īrī	to be about to be loved
monitum īrī	to be about to be warned
missum īrī	to be about to be sent
audītum īrī	to be about to be heard
captum īrī	to be about to be captured

Deponent verbs DO NOT HAVE this future passive infinitive form. In Chapter 19 you saw that deponent verbs form their future participle in the same way as do other verbs, by adding *-ūrus, -ūra, -ūrum* to the perfect passive/deponent stem. They form their future infinitive by combining this future participle with *esse*:

mīrātūrus, -ūra, -ūrum esse	to be about to admire

Agreement in Indirect Statement

Since participles are adjectival forms of verbs, they must agree in number, gender, and case with the nouns to which they refer. When the future active infinitive and the perfect passive infinitive are used in an indirect statement, the participle must agree with the accusative subject of the infinitive, as in these examples:

sacerdōs dīcit <u>puellam</u> deōs <u>amātūram</u> esse.	The priest says that the girl will love the gods.
sacerdōs dīcit puellam <u>deōs</u> <u>amātūrōs</u> esse.	The priest says that the gods will love the girl.
agricola dīcit <u>porcum</u> ā lupīs <u>interfectum</u> esse.	The farmer says that the pig has been killed by the wolves.
agricola dīcit <u>lupōs</u> ā porcō <u>interfectōs</u> esse.	The farmer says that the wolves have been killed by the pig.

This issue of agreement does not arise with the future passive infinitive, because **the form of the supine never changes and therefore cannot agree with the subject-accusative**:

pastor dixit <u>porcōs</u> ad insulam <u>missum</u> īrī.	The shepherd said that the pigs would be sent to the island.
rex dixit <u>urbēs</u> nostrās <u>captum</u> īrī.	The king said that our cities would be captured.

Simply because of its meaning, the future passive infinitive is not very common, and it does not even exist for deponent verbs. In any case, as you will see in Chapter 28, the Romans seem to have avoided using this infinitive.

Here is a complete summary of the infinitive forms for regular transitive verbs:

Present Active	*Future Active*	*Perfect Active*
amāre	amātūrus, -ūra, -ūrum esse	amāvisse
monēre	monitūrus, -ūra, -ūrum esse	monuisse
mittere	missūrus, -ūra, -ūrum esse	mīsisse
audīre	audītūrus, -ūra, -ūrum esse	audīvisse
capere	captūrus, -ūra, -ūrum esse	cēpisse

Present Passive	*Future Passive*	*Perfect Passive*
amārī	amātum īrī	amātus, -a, -um esse
monērī	monitum īrī	monitus, -a, -um esse
mittī	missum īrī	missus, -a, -um esse
audīrī	audītum īrī	audītus, -a, -um esse
capī	captum īrī	captus, -a, -um esse

Infinitives of Irregular Verbs

As you can see from the following chart, not all irregular verbs have the entire range of infinitives.

	sum	*possum*	*eō*	*ferō*	*volō*	*nōlō*	*mālō*
Present Active	esse	posse	īre	ferre	velle	nolle	malle
Future Active	futūrus, -a, -um esse		itūrus, -a, -um esse	lātūrus, -a, -um esse			
Perfect Active	fuisse	potuisse	iisse/ īvisse	tulisse	voluisse	nōluisse	māluisse
Present Passive			īrī	ferrī			
Future Passive				lātum īrī			
Perfect Passive				lātus, -a, -um esse			

The verb *fīō* has only the present infinitive *fierī*: it borrows the forms *factum īrī* and *factus, -a, -um esse* from *faciō*.

Translating Indirect Statements

Since Latin does not have, for example, a pluperfect infinitive or an infinitive that would distinguish "that he **would** praise" from "that he **will** praise," and since the perfect in Latin has two possible translations depending on the context (e.g., "he **praised**," "he **has praised**"), the same indirect statement may often be translated in more than one way. For example:

*discipulus **dīcit** magistrum porcōs **laudāre**.*	The student **says** that the teacher **praises** pigs.
*discipulus **dīcit** magistrum porcōs **laudāvisse**.*	The student **says** that the teacher **praised/has praised/had praised** pigs.
*discipulus **dīcit** magistrum porcōs **laudātūrum esse**.*	The student **says** that the teacher **will praise/would praise** pigs.
*discipulus **dixit** magistrum porcōs **laudāre**.*	The student **said** that the teacher **praises/praised** pigs.
*discipulus **dixit** magistrum porcōs **laudāvisse**.*	The student **said** that the teacher **praised/has praised/had praised** pigs.

*discipulus **dixit** magistrum porcōs **laudātūrum esse**.* — The student **said** that the teacher **will praise/would praise** pigs.

*discipulus **dīcet** magistrum porcōs **laudāre**.* — The student **will say** that the teacher **praises** pigs.

*discipulus **dīcet** magistrum porcōs **laudāvisse**.* — The student **will say** that the teacher **praised/has praised/had praised** pigs.

*discipulus **dīcet** magistrum porcōs **laudātūrum esse**.* — The student **will say** that the teacher **will praise/would praise** pigs.

Pronouns and Indirect Statement

In Chapter 17 you learned how to avoid ambiguity by using the reflexive pronominal adjective *suus, -a, -um* or the genitive forms of the demonstrative pronoun *eius, eōrum,* and *eārum* in translating a sentence such as "The farmer hates the sailor but loves his wife." You would translate "his" with either the reflexive *suam* (the farmer's wife) or with the non-reflexive *eius* (the sailor's wife).

At the beginning of this chapter, you saw that in an indirect statement, both the subject and the direct object are in the accusative:

> *agricola dīcit porcum carmen canere.* — The farmer says that the pig is singing a song.

But what if the indirect statement involves pronouns instead of nouns? If the subject-accusative is the same as the third person subject of the main verb, you use the reflexive pronoun *sē*; if the two subjects are not the same, you use one of the demonstrative pronouns: *eum, eam, id, eōs, eās,* or *ea*.

> *mīles dīcit **sē** fortem esse.* — The soldier says that he (himself) is brave.
> *mīles dīcit **eum** fortem esse.* — The soldier says that he (someone else) is brave.

Now look at how the use of reflexive forms can, to the extent possible, avoid ambiguity in indirect statement. When a pronoun or adjective is **reflexive**, it and the noun it refers to are in bold.

agricola pastōrem iuvat et porcum eius pascit.

The farmer helps the shepherd and feeds his [the shepherd's] pig.

agricola dīcit eum [pastōrem] bonum esse.
The farmer says that he [the shepherd] is good.

agricola *pastōrem amat sed porcum **suum** pascit.*
The farmer loves the shepherd but feeds his own pig.

agricola *dīcit **sē** bonum esse.*
The farmer says that he [himself] is good.

agricola dixit *sē* porcum eius [*pastōris*] pāvisse.
The farmer said that he [the farmer] had fed his [the shepherd's] pig.

agricola dixit eum [*pastōrem*] porcum eius pāvisse.
The farmer said that he [the shepherd] had fed his/her pig [referring to someone other than the farmer or the shepherd].

agricola dixit *sē* porcum **suum** pāvisse.
The farmer said that he [the farmer] had fed his own pig.

agricola dixit eum [*pastōrem*] porcum **suum** [*agricolae*] pāvisse.
The farmer said that he [the shepherd] had fed his [the farmer's] pig.

agricola dixit **eum** [*pastōrem*] porcum **suum** [*pastōris*] pāvisse.
The farmer said that he [the shepherd] had fed his own pig.

Notā Bene

Since the form *eius* is both masculine and feminine, there is a lingering ambiguity in the sentence *agricola dixit eum porcum eius pāvisse*; the unnamed third person may be either a man or a woman. The sentence *agricola dixit eum porcum suum pāvisse* simply has two possible meanings; only context can eliminate this ambiguity.

Vocabulary

Verbs that commonly introduce indirect speech include:

First Conjugation

arbitror	think		**narrō**	tell
cantō	sing		**negō**	deny
exclāmō	exclaim		**nuntiō**	announce
existimō	think		**putō**	think
ignōrō	be unaware		**spērō**	hope
monstrō	show		**susurrō**	whisper

Second Conjugation

fateor, fatērī, fassus sum	confess
polliceor, pollicērī, pollicitus sum	promise
reor, rērī, ratus sum	think
respondeō, respondēre, respondī, responsum	reply
videō, vidēre, vīdī, vīsum	see

Third Conjugation

cano, canere, cecinī	sing
crēdō, crēdere, crēdidī, crēditum	believe
dīcō, dīcere, dixī, dictum	say
discō, discere, didicī	learn
intellegō, intellegere, intellexī, intellectum	understand
noscō, noscere, nōvī, nōtum	find out
oblīviscor, oblīviscī, oblītus sum	forget
prōmittō, prōmittere, prōmīsī, prōmissum	promise
scrībō, scrībere, scripsī, scriptum	write

Fourth Conjugation

audiō, audīre, audīvī, audītum	hear
nesciō, nescīre, nescīvī	do not know
sciō, scīre, scīvī	know
sentiō, sentīre, sensī, sensum	feel
ait defective, found mostly in this form	he (she, it) says or said
inquit defective, found mostly in this form	he (she, it) says or said
meminī, meminisse defective	remember

Prōlūsiōnēs

Parse the words in bold.

quis nescit sociōs Aenēae multōs **annōs** mala multa **passōs esse**? Troiā **dēlētā**, Apollō, deus ōrāculī, dixerat **Troiānōs** novam patriam in Ītaliā inventūrōs esse, Latīnumque, rēgem Latiī, Aenēae **Lāvīniam**, fīliam **suam**, esse datūrum. sed Turnus, rex Rutulōrum, **sē** Lāvīniam in mātrimōnium ductūrum esse spērābat, et Iūnō, **cui** Troiānī omnēs odiō erant, pollicita est sē eī contrā Troiānōs **pugnantī** auxiliō **futūram esse**.

Change the following direct statements to indirect statements by adding the words *puella dixit* **and then translate.**

For example:
fēlix sum.
puella dixit mē fēlīcem esse. The girl said that I was lucky.

1. rex hostium ferox est.
2. servī, miserī estis.
3. hostēs urbem nostram dēlēbunt.
4. urbs nostra ab hostibus dēlēbitur.
5. lupī ē silvā vēnērunt.
6. lupī ē silvā vēnerant.
7. pastor piger porcōs in agrum ēgit.
8. porcī pigrī ā pastōribus in agrum agentur.
9. agnī omnēs ā pastōre ad casam portātī sunt.
10. agna aegra ā pastōre ad casam portābitur.

Translate.

Given the various ways in which an indirect statement can be translated, and given the imprecision in the use of pronouns, both in Latin and in English, you should expect sometimes to find more than one correct translation.

1. dixit soror mea sē ā populō laudātam esse.
2. putō mīlitēs ducem secūtūrōs esse.
3. noctem diem secūtūram esse reor.
4. rēgem quī rēgīnam amābat bonum esse dīcimus.
5. deus rēgem illum respondet Rōmānōs vincere posse.
6. puellae dulcī nauta vōce humilī susurrābat sē eam amāre.
7. crēdisne puellam sē nautam amāre dictūram esse?
8. polliceor mē tuam fīliam semper amātūrum esse.
9. quis rēgī nostrō dixit hostēs in arcem urbis nostrae vēnisse?
10. pollicentur rex et rēgīna sē bonōs semper futūrōs esse.
11. Caesarem Gallōs victūrūm esse quis putāverat?
12. Gallōs ā Caesare victum īrī quis putābat?
13. cuius porcōs tē ex agrīs nostrīs ēgisse fatēris?
14. respondit consul sē in senātū numquam mentītum esse.
15. spērābat puer sē pīrātam futūrum esse, sed negābat pater fīlium sē ad portum missūrum esse.

16. meminī mē iuvenem dulcem fuisse, sed nē māter quidem idem dīcere audet.

17. nautam plūs pecūniae sed minus virtūtis quam mīlitem habēre arbitrātus est agricola.

18. lupōs in agrum vēnisse nesciēbant porcī, quamquam vōcēs ferārum totiens audīverant.

19. magistrātus dīves, quī venēnum biberat, nōn sēnsit sē proximō diē esse moritūrum.

20. quam trīste carmen cecinit sacerdōtis veteris fīlius, in quō narrāvit tōtum porcōrum gregem saevīs sub fluctibus maris asperī periisse!

21. I saw that the pigs had remained in the field for the whole night.

22. The shepherd whispered to the farmer that the pigs seemed to be in the field.

23. Since the wolves are coming out of the wood, I hope that the pigs will be safe in this cave with me.

24. If you think that the wolves are in the field, take your two biggest dogs with you immediately.

25. Good teachers have shown us so often that money is a very shameful thing, but not even a fool thinks that he can live without money.

26. The dying soldier announced to the other citizens that we had defeated the barbarians.

27. Augustus thinks that all his own poems are bad, but I myself know that the emperor has written a very good poem.

28. My father has written to the Roman magistrate that our laws are better than the Roman laws.

29. I hope that my son will be consul, although he admits that it is difficult to study such big books.

30. I used to think that the teacher was a bad person, for I know that he had been cruel to many students for many years.

Lectiōnēs Latīnae

Lege, Intellege

Livy (Titus Livius; 59 BC–AD 17) is the author of the *Ab Urbe Conditā*, a history of Rome from the foundation to 9 BC. Books 1–10 and 21–45 have survived, as well as summaries and a few fragments of the others.

The Romans and the Sabines Fight for Control of Rome

ad veterem portam Pālātiī Rōmulus turbā fugientium āctus, arma ad caelum tollēns, "Iuppiter, tuīs" inquit "iussus ōminibus hīc in Pālātiō prīma urbis fundāmenta iēcī.

arcem iam Sabīnī habent; inde hūc armātī superātā mediā valle tendunt; at tū, pater deōrum hominumque, hinc saltem prohibē hostēs; dēme terrōrem Rōmānīs fugamque turpem siste. hīc ego tibi templum voveō." haec precātus, "hīc, Rōmānī," inquit "Iuppiter Optimus Maximus resistere atque iterāre pugnam iubet." restitērunt Rōmānī tamquam caelestī vōce iussī: ipse ad prīmōrēs Rōmulus prōvolat. dux Sabīnōrum, Mettius Curtius, ab arce dēcucurrerat et effūsōs ēgerat Rōmānōs per tōtum forum. nec procul iam ā portā Palātiī erat, clāmitans "vīcimus perfidōs hospitēs, imbellēs hostēs; iam sciunt longē aliud esse virginēs rapere, aliud pugnāre cum virīs." in eum haec glōriantem cum globō ferōcissimōrum iuvenum Rōmulus impetum facit.

—Livy, *Ab Urbe Conditā* 1.12

tollō, -ere, sustulī, sublātum 3 raise

tendō, -ere, tetendī, tentum 3 stretch, proceed

saltem adv. at least

dēmō, -ere, dēmī, demptum 3 (+ acc. + dat.) take away

tamquam conj. as if

prīmōrēs, -um masc. front-rank soldiers

globus, -ī masc. 2 sphere, group

1. Who had run down from the citadel and driven the scattered Romans through the whole Forum?
2. What did Romulus pray to Jupiter to do for the Romans?
3. To where was Romulus driven by the crowd of people who were running away?
4. Where did Romulus lay the first foundations of the city?
5. What did the Sabine leader shout?

Ars Poētica

Martial II
Explain the case of the words in bold.

1. *esse negās coctum* **leporem** *poscisque flagella.*
   māvīs, Rūfe, cocum scindere quam **leporem**.
   You deny that the hare is cooked and call for the whips. You prefer, Rufus, to cut up your cook rather than the hare.

2. *nullōs esse deōs, ināne* **caelum**
   affirmat Segius: probatque, quod **sē**
   factum, dum negat **haec**, *videt beātum.*
   Segius affirms that there are no gods, that heaven is empty: and he proves it because he sees himself made prosperous while denying these things.

3. *quī recitat lānā faucēs et colla revīnctus,*
    *hīc **sē** posse loquī, posse tacēre negat.*
    A person who recites with his throat and neck wrapped in wool says that he can't speak and that he can't be quiet.

4. *scrībere mē quereris, Vēlox, **epigrammata** longa.*
    ipse nihil scrībis: tū breviōra facis.
    You complain, Velox, that I write long epigrams. You yourself write nothing: you compose ones that are too short.

5. *dīcis amōre **tuī** bellās ardēre puellās,*
    quī faciem sub aquā, Sexte, natantis habēs.
    You say that pretty girls are burning with love for you, Sextus, you who have the face of someone swimming underwater.

6. ***versiculōs** in mē narrātur scrībere Cinna.*
    *nōn scrībit, **cuius** carmina nēmo legit.*
    Cinna is said to be writing silly verses against me. A person whose poems no one reads doesn't write anything.

7. *consule **tē Brūtō** quod iūrās, Lesbia, nātam,*
    mentīris. nāta es, Lesbia, rēge Numā?
    sīc quoque mentīris. namque, ut tua saecula narrant,
    ficta Promēthēō dīceris esse lutō.
    When you say that you were born when Brutus was consul, Lesbia, you're lying. Were you born, Lesbia, when Numa was king? Even so you are lying. For, as your centuries declare, you are said to have been formed from Promethean mud [that is, at the dawn of creation].

Aurea Dicta

1. *antīquum poētam audīvī scrīpsisse in tragoediā, mulierēs duās peiōrēs esse quam ūnam: rēs ita est.* (Plautus)
2. *crēdēbās dormientī haec tibi confectūrōs deōs?* (Terence)
3. *dixit nōn esse consuētūdinem populī Rōmānī, ullam accipere ab hoste armātō condiciōnem.* (Caesar)
4. *infirmī animī est nōn posse dīvitiās patī.* (Seneca the Younger)
5. *māluit sē dīligī quam metuī.* (Cornelius Nepos)
6. *nescīs longās rēgibus esse manūs?* (Ovid)
7. *nescit amor magnīs cēdere dīvitiīs.* (Propertius)
8. *nihil mihi vidētur turpius quam optāre mortem.* (Seneca the Younger)

consuētūdō, -inis fem. 3 custom

Lūsūs

Thēsaurus Verbōrum

Diminutive forms of nouns and adjectives, expressing affection, familiarity, or contempt, were very widespread in spoken Latin, and we find many such forms in the written language also. The most common diminutive suffixes are *-ellus* (*-a, -um*) and *-ulus* (*-a, -um*).

agellus, -ī masc. 2 little field	ager, agrī masc. 2 field
bellus, -a, -um pretty	bonus, -a, -um good[1]
libellus, -ī masc. 2 booklet	liber, librī masc. 2 book
porcellus, -ī masc. 2 piglet	porcus, -ī masc. 2 pig
puella, -ae fem. 1 girl	puera, -ae fem. 1 girl[2]
capella, -ae fem. 1 she-goat	capra, -ae fem. 1 she-goat
adulescentulus, -ī masc. 2 young man	adulescens, -entis masc. 3 young man
calculus, -ī masc. 2 pebble	calx, calcis masc. 3 limestone
Graeculus, -ī masc. 2 little Greek	Graecus, -ī masc. 2 Greek
parvulus, -a, -um tiny	parvus, -a, -um small
rēgulus, -ī masc. 2 little king	rex, rēgis masc. 3 king
caligula, -ae fem. 1 little military boot	caliga, -ae fem. 1 military boot
capsula, -ae fem. 1 jar	capsa, -ae fem. 1 book-basket
formula, -ae fem. 1 formula	forma, -ae fem. 1 shape
sportula, -ae fem. 1 basket	sporta, -ae fem. 1 basket[3]
ungula, -ae fem. 1 hoof, claw	unguis, -is fem. 3 fingernail[4]

Etymologiae Antīquae

Wild Animals I

aper, aprī masc. 2 "wild boar." Wild boars live in rough places, *in locīs asperīs*.

---

1. Both the Romans and the Greeks were prone to equate good looks and good morals.

2. *puera* is rare in Classical Latin, as is the masculine diminutive *puellus*. The doubly diminutive form *puellula* is found occasionally.

3. The *sportula* was the dole of food given to clients by their patrons.

4. Here, the diminutive form refers to the larger object!

apis, *apis* fem. 3 "bee." Bees are born without feet (*a* + *pēs, pedis* masc. 3).

arānea, *-ae* fem. 1 "spider." Spiders are worms (*sic*) that hang in the air (*āēr, āeris* masc. 3), from which they get their nourishment.

avis, *avis* fem. "bird." Birds are able to fly over places away from the road (*ā viā*).

castor, *-oris* masc. 3 "beaver." Beavers' testicles are used in medicine. When a beaver senses that a hunter is near, it chews off its testicles and runs away, saving its life by castrating (*castrō* 1) itself.

fera, *-ae* fem. 1 "wild animal." Wild animals carry (*ferō, ferre, tulī, lātum* irreg.) themselves on all their limbs, going wherever they wish to go.

formīca, *-ae* fem. 1 "ant." Ants carry (*ferō, ferre, tulī, lātum* irreg.) crumbs (*mīca, -ae* fem. 1).

lepus, *leporis* masc. 3 "hare." Hares are light (*levis, -e*) on their feet (*pēs, pedis* masc. 3). Eating hare bestows charm (*lepos, lepōris* masc. 3).

lupus, *-ī* masc. 2 "wolf." Wolves have feet (*pēs, pedis* masc. 3) like those of a lion (*leō, leōnis* masc. 3).

mustēla, *-ae* *fem.* 1 "weasel." Just as a missile (*tēlum, -i* neut. 2) is thrown "from a distance" (Greek ἀπὸ τοῦ τηλόθεν [*apo tou tēlothen*]), so a weasel is a sort of long mouse (*mūs, mūris* masc. 3).

vulpēs, *-is* fem. 3 "fox." Foxes fly (*volō* 1) with their feet (*pēs, pedis* masc. 3), which they are always turning (*volvō, -ere, volvī, volūtum* 3) in different directions.

Vīta Rōmānōrum

Sayings of Julius and Augustus Caesar (from Suetonius' *Dē Vītā Caesarum*)

Julius Caesar

When he caught up with his cohorts at the river Rubicon, the boundary to his province [which he could not legally cross with his army], he stopped for a little while. Pondering the enormity of what he was undertaking, he turned to those who were near him and said, "Even now we can turn back, but if we cross this little bridge, everything will have to be done with weapons.... Let us go on, where the signs from the gods and our enemies' unjust actions are calling us. The die has been cast."

Sometimes, after a major victory, he granted his troops relief from their duties and allowed them to celebrate however they pleased. He used to say that his soldiers could fight well even when reeking of perfume.

When he was asked why he had divorced his wife, he replied, "Because I believe members of my family must be free no less from suspicion than from guilt."

In a conversation about the best way to die which arose at dinner on the day before he was killed, he said that he would prefer a sudden and unexpected death.

Augustus Caesar

After the Teutoburg massacre [three legions were annihilated in the German forest in AD 9], he used to bash his head against a door, shouting, "Quinctilius Varus, give me back my legions!"

He used to say that whatever was done well enough was done quickly enough.

He used to say that he was leaving as a city of marble the city of brick which he had taken over [because of all the temples and other buildings he had constructed].

He was keen to reintroduce the ancient style of dress. Once, when he saw a crowd of people in dark garments in the assembly, he cried out in indignation, "Look at them, 'the Romans, the rulers of the world, and the people who wear the toga' [*Rōmānōs, rērum dominōs gentemque togātam* (Virgil, *Aeneid* 1.282)]," and he ordered the magistrates not to allow anyone to appear in or around the Forum except in a toga and without a cloak.

He started composing a tragedy with great enthusiasm, but, since the style seemed unsuccessful, he rubbed it out. When his friends asked him how his *Ajax* was coming along, he replied that he had fallen on his sponge. [The mythical hero Ajax had fallen on his sword. Augustus had presumably been writing on papyrus, from which writing could be wiped off with a wet sponge.]

On the prospect of Tiberius succeeding him: "Alas for the Roman people, which will be ground up by such slow-moving jaws."

CHAPTER 22
The Subjunctive Mood of Verbs in Main Clauses

You have already learned all the forms and most uses of three of the four moods of the Latin verb, the indicative, imperative, and infinitive.

To understand the use of the fourth mood, the **subjunctive**, you first need to contrast it with the **indicative**.

Actual events or circumstances	**Hypothetical, doubtful, unreal events or circumstances**
The pig is happy.	I wonder if the pig is happy.
The pig will be happy.	I gave the pig food in order that it might be happy.
The pig was happy.	I was afraid that the pig was not happy.
The pig had been happy, etc.	May the pig be happy!
	Should a pig be happy? etc.

In Latin any verb referring to actual events or circumstances will be in the indicative; any verb referring to what is hypothetical, doubtful, or unreal will be in the subjunctive.

Very often the subjunctive will be in a subordinate clause, and the subject of the subjunctive verb may or may not be the same as the subject of the main clause. This chapter, however, will explain constructions **where the subjunctive verb is the main verb of the sentence**. This chapter also presents the paradigms of the forms of the subjunctive for you to learn.

The subjunctive has only four active and four passive tenses (whereas there are six active and six passive indicative tenses):

- present
- imperfect
- perfect
- pluperfect

As with the indicative, you will see obvious similarities when you look at how the conjugations form the tenses of the subjunctive.

PRESENT ACTIVE: combine the present stem (without the linking vowel, if there is one), with -**e**- (for the 1st conj.), -**ea**- (for the 2nd conj.), -**a**- (for the 3rd conj.), -**ia**- (for the 4th conj. and 3rd conj. *i*-stem), then add the personal endings -**m**, -**s**, -**t**, -**mus**, -**tis**, -**nt**

    e.g., **amem, moneās, mittat**

IMPERFECT ACTIVE: add the personal endings **-m, -s, -t, -mus, -tis, -nt** to the present active infinitive

e.g., **amārem, monērēs, mitteret**

PERFECT ACTIVE: add the personal endings **-m, -s, -t, -mus, -tis, -nt** to the perfect active stem + **-eri-**

e.g., **amāverim, monuerīs, mīserit**

PLUPERFECT ACTIVE: add the personal endings **-m, -s, -t, -mus, -tis, -nt** to the perfect active infinitive

e.g., **amāvissem, monuissēs, mīsisset**

PRESENT PASSIVE: combine the present stem, without the linking vowel (if there is one), with **-e-** (for the 1st conj.), **-ea-** (for the 2nd conj.), **-a-** (for the 3rd conj.), **-ia-** (for the 4th conj. and 3rd conj. *i*-stem), then add the personal endings **-r, -ris, -tur, -mur, -minī, -ntur**

e.g., **amer, moneāris, mittātur**

IMPERFECT PASSIVE: add the personal endings **-r, -ris, -tur, -mur, -minī, -ntur** to the present active infinitive

e.g., **amārer, monērēris, mitterētur**

PERFECT PASSIVE: combine the perfect passive participle with the present active subjunctive of **sum**

e.g., **amātus sim, monitus sīs, missus sit**

PLUPERFECT PASSIVE: combine the perfect passive participle with the imperfect active subjunctive of **sum**

e.g., **amātus essem, monitus essēs, missus esset**

Notā Bene

The vowel before the personal ending is long in the 2nd pers. sing. and the 1st and 2nd pers. pl. of all active tenses of the subjunctive. The vowel before the personal ending is long in the 2nd and 3rd pers. sing. and the 1st and 2nd pers. pl. of the present and imperfect passive tenses of the subjunctive.

Deponent verbs form their subjunctive tenses exactly like passive verbs; for example: *mīrer, mīrārer, mīrātus sim, mīrātus essem*, and *sequar, sequerer, secūtus sim, secūtus essem*.

Present Active Subjunctive

1st sing.	am**em**	mone**am**	
2nd sing.	am**ēs**	mone**ās**	
3rd sing.	am**et**	mone**at**	
1st pl.	am**ēmus**	mone**āmus**	
2nd pl.	am**ētis**	mone**ātis**	
3rd pl.	am**ent**	mone**ant**	

1st sing.	mitt**am**	audi**am**	capi**am**
2nd sing.	mitt**ās**	audi**ās**	capi**ās**
3rd sing.	mitt**at**	audi**at**	capi**at**
1st pl.	mitt**āmus**	audi**āmus**	capi**āmus**
2nd pl.	mitt**ātis**	audi**ātis**	capi**ātis**
3rd pl.	mitt**ant**	audi**ant**	capi**ant**

From *sum* and *possum*

1st sing.	**sim**	poss**im**
2nd sing.	**sīs**	poss**īs**
3rd sing.	**sit**	poss**it**
1st pl.	**sīmus**	poss**īmus**
2nd pl.	**sītis**	poss**ītis**
3rd pl.	**sint**	poss**int**

From *volō, nōlō, mālō*

1st sing.	vel**im**	nōl**im**	māl**im**
2nd sing.	vel**īs**	nōl**īs**	māl**īs**
3rd sing.	vel**it**	nōl**it**	māl**it**
1st pl.	vel**īmus**	nōl**īmus**	māl**īmus**
2nd pl.	vel**ītis**	nōl**ītis**	māl**ītis**
3rd pl.	vel**int**	nōl**int**	māl**int**

From *fīō, eō,* and *ferō*

fi**am**, e**am**, fer**am**, conjugated like *mittam, mittās, mittat,* etc.

Imperfect Active Subjunctive

1st sing.	amār**em**	monēr**em**
2nd sing.	amār**ēs**	monēr**ēs**
3rd sing.	amār**et**	monēr**et**
1st pl.	amār**ēmus**	monēr**ēmus**
2nd pl.	amār**ētis**	monēr**ētis**
3rd pl.	amār**ent**	monēr**ent**

1st sing.	mitt**erem**	aud**īrem**	cap**erem**
2nd sing.	mitt**erēs**	aud**īrēs**	cap**erēs**
3rd sing.	mitt**eret**	aud**īret**	cap**eret**
1st pl.	mitt**erēmus**	aud**īrēmus**	cap**erēmus**
2nd pl.	mitt**erētis**	aud**īrētis**	cap**erētis**
3rd pl.	mitt**erent**	aud**īrent**	cap**erent**

From *sum* and *possum*

1st sing.	ess**em**	poss**em**
2nd sing.	ess**ēs**	poss**ēs**
3rd sing.	ess**et**	poss**et**
1st pl.	ess**ēmus**	poss**ēmus**
2nd pl.	ess**ētis**	poss**ētis**
3rd pl.	ess**ent**	poss**ent**

From *volō, nōlō, mālō*

1st sing.	vell**em**	noll**em**	mall**em**
2nd sing.	vell**ēs**	noll**ēs**	mall**ēs**
3rd sing.	vell**et**	noll**et**	mall**et**
1st pl.	vell**ēmus**	noll**ēmus**	mall**ēmus**
2nd pl.	vell**ētis**	noll**ētis**	mall**ētis**
3rd pl.	vell**ent**	noll**ent**	mall**ent**

From *fīō, eō,* and *ferō*

fi**erem**, ī**rem**, and ferr**em** conjugated like *mitterem*

Perfect Active Subjunctive

1st sing.	amāv**erim**	monu**erim**
2nd sing.	amāv**erīs**	monu**erīs**
3rd sing.	amāv**erit**	monu**erit**
1st pl.	amāv**erīmus**	monu**erīmus**
2nd pl.	amāv**erītis**	monu**erītis**
3rd pl.	amāv**erint**	monu**erint**

1st sing.	mīs**erim**	audīv**erim**	cēp**erim**
2nd sing.	mīs**erīs**	audīv**erīs**	cēp**erīs**
3rd sing.	mīs**erit**	audīv**erit**	cēp**erit**
1st pl.	mīs**erīmus**	audīv**erīmus**	cēp**erīmus**
2nd pl.	mīs**erītis**	audīv**erītis**	cēp**erītis**
3rd pl.	mīs**erint**	audīv**erint**	cēp**erint**

From *sum* and *possum*

1st sing.	fu**erim**	potu**erim**
2nd sing.	fu**erīs**	potu**erīs**
3rd sing.	fu**erit**	potu**erit**
1st pl.	fu**erīmus**	potu**erīmus**
2nd pl.	fu**erītis**	potu**erītis**
3rd pl.	fu**erint**	potu**erint**

From *volō, nōlō, mālō*

1st sing.	volu**erim**	nōlu**erim**	mālu**erim**
2nd sing.	volu**erīs**	nōlu**erīs**	mālu**erīs**
3rd sing.	volu**erit**	nōlu**erit**	mālu**erit**
1st pl.	volu**erīmus**	nōlu**erīmus**	mālu**erīmus**
2nd pl.	volu**erītis**	nōlu**erītis**	mālu**erītis**
3rd pl.	volu**erint**	nōlu**erint**	mālu**erint**

From *fīō*

factus s**im**

From *eō* and *ferō*

i**erim** (or īv**erim**), tul**erim**, conjugated like *mīserim*

Pluperfect Active Subjunctive

1st sing.	amāv**issem**	monu**issem**
2nd sing.	amāv**issēs**	monu**issēs**
3rd sing.	amāv**isset**	monu**isset**
1st pl.	amāv**issēmus**	monu**issēmus**
2nd pl.	amāv**issētis**	monu**issētis**
3rd pl.	amāv**issent**	monu**issent**

1st sing.	mīs**issem**	audīv**issem**	cēp**issem**
2nd sing.	mīs**issēs**	audīv**issēs**	cēp**issēs**
3rd sing.	mīs**isset**	audīv**isset**	cēp**isset**
1st pl.	mīs**issēmus**	audīv**issēmus**	cēp**issēmus**
2nd pl.	mīs**issētis**	audīv**issētis**	cēp**issētis**
3rd pl.	mīs**issent**	audīv**issent**	cēp**issent**

From *sum* and *possum*

1st sing.	fu**issem**	potu**issem**
2nd sing.	fu**issēs**	potu**issēs**
3rd sing.	fu**isset**	potu**isset**
1st pl.	fu**issēmus**	potu**issēmus**
2nd pl.	fu**issētis**	potu**issētis**
3rd pl.	fu**issent**	potu**issent**

From *volō, nōlō, mālō*

1st sing.	volu**issem**	nōlu**issem**	mālu**issem**
2nd sing.	volu**issēs**	nōlu**issēs**	mālu**issēs**
3rd sing.	volu**isset**	nōlu**isset**	mālu**isset**
1st pl.	volu**issēmus**	nōlu**issēmus**	mālu**issēmus**
2nd pl.	volu**issētis**	nōlu**issētis**	mālu**issētis**
3rd pl.	volu**issent**	nōlu**issent**	mālu**issent**

From *fīō*

factus ess**em**

From *eō* and *ferō*

iissem (or **īvissem**), tul**issem**, conjugated like *mīsissem*

Present Passive Subjunctive

1st sing.	am**er**	mone**ar**
2nd sing.	am**ēris**	mone**āris**
3rd sing.	am**ētur**	mone**ātur**
1st pl.	am**ēmur**	mone**āmur**
2nd pl.	am**ēminī**	mone**āminī**
3rd pl.	am**entur**	mone**antur**

1st sing.	mitt**ar**	audi**ar**	capi**ar**
2nd sing.	mitt**āris**	audi**āris**	capi**āris**
3rd sing.	mitt**ātur**	audi**ātur**	capi**ātur**
1st pl.	mitt**āmur**	audi**āmur**	capi**āmur**
2nd pl.	mitt**āminī**	audi**āminī**	capi**āminī**
3rd pl.	mitt**antur**	audi**antur**	capi**antur**

From *ferō*

fer**ar**, conjugated like *mittar*

There are no passive subjunctive forms of *sum, possum, volō, nōlō,* or *mālō*. Because it is semi-deponent, *fīō* uses the perfect and pluperfect passive forms of *faciō*.

As you saw in Chapter 21, *īrī*, the present passive infinitive of *īre*, is used in the future passive infinitive of all verbs. Otherwise, passive forms of *īre*, because it is intransitive, are rare.

Imperfect Passive Subjunctive

1st sing.	amā**rer**	monē**rer**
2nd sing.	amā**rēris**	monē**rēris**
3rd sing.	amā**rētur**	monē**rētur**
1st pl.	amā**rēmur**	monē**rēmur**
2nd pl.	amā**rēminī**	monē**rēminī**
3rd pl.	amā**rentur**	monē**rentur**

1st sing.	mitte**rer**	audī**rer**	cape**rer**
2nd sing.	mitte**rēris**	audī**rēris**	cape**rēris**
3rd sing.	mitte**rētur**	audī**rētur**	cape**rētur**
1st pl.	mitte**rēmur**	audī**rēmur**	cape**rēmur**
2nd pl.	mitte**rēminī**	audī**rēminī**	cape**rēminī**
3rd pl.	mitte**rentur**	audī**rentur**	cape**rentur**

From *ferō*

ferrer, ferrēris, ferrētur, ferrēmur, ferrēminī, ferrentur

Perfect Passive Subjunctive

1st sing.	amātus, -a, -um sim	monitus, -a, -um sim
2nd sing.	amātus, -a, -um sīs	monitus, -a, -um sīs
3rd sing.	amātus, -a, -um sit	monitus, -a, -um sit
1st pl.	amātī, -ae, -a sīmus	monitī, -ae, -a sīmus
2nd pl.	amātī, -ae, -a sītis	monitī, -ae, -a sītis
3rd pl.	amātī, -ae, -a sint	monitī, -ae, -a sint

1st sing.	missus, -a, -um sim	audītus, -a, -um sim	captus, -a, -um sim
2nd sing.	missus, -a, -um sīs	audītus, -a, -um sīs	captus, -a, -um sīs
3rd sing.	missus, -a, -um sit	audītus, -a, -um sit	captus, -a, -um sit
1st pl.	missī, -ae, -a sīmus	audītī, -ae, -a sīmus	captī, -ae, -a sīmus
2nd pl.	missī, -ae, -a sītis	audītī, -ae, -a sītis	captī, -ae, -a sītis
3rd pl.	missī, -ae, -a sint	audītī, -ae, -a sint	captī, -ae, -a sint

From *ferō*

lātus, -a, -um sim, conjugated like all other perfect passive subjunctives.

Pluperfect Passive Subjunctive

1st sing.	amātus, -a, -um essem	monitus, -a, -um essem
2nd sing.	amātus, -a, -um essēs	monitus, -a, -um essēs
3rd sing.	amātus, -a, -um esset	monitus, -a, -um esset
1st pl.	amātī, -ae, -a essēmus	monitī, -ae, -a essēmus
2nd pl.	amātī, -ae, -a essētis	monitī, -ae, -a essētis
3rd pl.	amātī, -ae, -a essent	monitī, -ae, -a essent

1st sing.	missus, -a, -um essem	audītus, -a, -um essem	captus, -a, -um essem
2nd sing.	missus, -a, -um essēs	audītus, -a, -um essēs	captus, -a, -um essēs
3rd sing.	missus, -a, -um esset	audītus, -a, -um esset	captus, -a, -um esset
1st pl.	missī, -ae, -a essēmus	audītī, -ae, -a essēmus	captī, -ae, -a essēmus
2nd pl.	missī, -ae, -a essētis	audītī, -ae, -a essētis	captī, -ae, -a essētis
3rd pl.	missī, -ae, -a essent	audītī, -ae, -a essent	captī, -ae, -a essent

From *ferō*

lātus, -a, -um essem, conjugated like all other pluperfect passive subjunctives.

Since the meaning of a subjunctive form depends on the particular construction in which it is being used, translation exercises that focus on each construction will appear in the relevant chapters, rather than here.

The Subjunctive as the Main Verb of a Sentence

Situations in which you will find the subjunctive not in a subordinate clause but in a main clause include

- exhortations
- deliberative questions
- wishes
- potential main clauses

Exhortations

In exhortations, the subjunctive expresses a command or request; "Let's go!" "Let them eat peacocks' tongues and dormice in honey!" The negative is *nē*.

Exhortations are usually found in the first and third persons of the present tense. A second person **positive** exhortation is supplied by the imperative mood. When the exhortation is **negative**, however, the second person subjunctive is frequently used. Both the **perfect** and the **present subjunctive** are used in negative exhortations/commands; the present is more common in poetry. Of course, a negative command can also be expressed using *nōlī*, as in *porcīs cibum nōlī dare*.

Positive	**Negative**
hōc faciāmus.	*hōc nē fēcerīmus/faciāmus.*
Let us do this.	Let us not do this.
exeat in agrum porcus.	*nē exierit/exeat in agrum porcus.*
Let the pig go out into the field.	Let the pig not go out into the field.
ducem sequāmur.	*ducem nē secūtī sīmus/sequāmur.*
Let us follow our leader.	Let us not follow our leader.
porcīs cibum dā.	*porcīs cibum nē dederīs/dēs.*
Give food to the pigs.	Do not give food to the pigs.

Deliberative Questions

You use the subjunctive to ask deliberative questions, that is, questions where the speaker is wondering what is to be done:

quid faciat agricola?	What is the farmer to do?
arma relinquāmus?	Should we relinquish our weapons?
hodiē labōrem?	Should I work today?
quid facerem?	What was I to do?

Deliberative questions are most often found in the first and third persons of the present active subjunctive. Questions such as "What are you to do?" are not very natural, so second person deliberative questions are uncommon. Negative deliberative questions are rare, but when they occur they use *nōn*.

Wishes

The use of subjunctive tenses in wishes is roughly parallel to correct English usage, although the forms used in English often look like indicatives. The difference in tenses between the main clause ("I wish") and the subordinate clause ("you were here") is all English has left of the subjunctive here. (American English, however, increasingly does not follow some of these rules.)

Wish for the future: present subjunctive

May you succeed/I wish you may succeed (tomorrow).

Wish for the present: imperfect subjunctive

I wish you were succeeding (today).

Wish for the past: pluperfect subjunctive

I wish you had succeeded (yesterday).

Wishes in Latin may begin with *ō sī* or *utinam* or *ō utinam* or, less frequently, *velim* (for the future) or *vellem* (for the present or past). Often, however, there is no introductory marker.

A negative wish is introduced by *nē* or *utinam nē* or, less frequently, by *nōlim* (for the future) or *nollem* (for the present or past). For example:

Wishes

diū vīvant rex et rēgīna!
Long live the king and queen!

ō sī dīves nunc essem!
If only I were rich now!

utinam consul mihi pecūniam crās det!
Oh, let the consul give me money tomorrow!

vellem servus mēcum nunc esset!
How I wish my slave were with me now!

utinam in agrō mansissent porcī!
If only the pigs had stayed in the field!

Negative wishes

nē diū vīvant hostēs!
May our enemies not live long!

utinam nē pauper semper essem!
If only I were not always poor!

nōlim consul Rōmānīs stultīs pecūniam crās det!
Oh, let the consul not give the foolish Romans money tomorrow!

nollem servus mēcum nunc esset!
How I wish my slave were not with me now!

nollem in silvam abiissent porcī!
If only the pigs had not gone away into the wood!

Potential Main Clauses

Potential main clauses use the subjunctive for what one might do, given certain circumstances that are hypothetical. They simply state what might happen, without implying any exhortation or wish. The negative is *nōn*.

If the circumstances refer to the present or future, you use the **present or perfect subjunctive**. If the circumstances could have occurred in the past (but didn't), you use **the imperfect or** (less commonly) **pluperfect subjunctive**. Here are some examples:

nōlim porcīs cibum dare.	I would not like to give food to the pigs [if the farmer happened to ask me to do so]. (Present/future)
dīcat agricola porcōs pulchrōs esse, sed ego porcōs equīs pulchriōrēs esse negem.	A farmer may say [if you happened to ask him] that pigs are beautiful, but I would say [if I were asked] that pigs are not more beautiful than horses. (Present/future)
dixerim equōs porcīs pulchriōrēs esse.	I'd say horses are more beautiful than pigs. (Present/future)
putāret frāter meus gladiātōrēs fēlīcēs esse.	My brother would have thought gladiators were lucky. (Past)
crēdidissēs porcum meum equō pulchriōrem esse.	You would have thought my pig more beautiful than a horse [if you had seen it]. (Past)

Prōlūsiōnēs

Parse the words in bold.

Turnus contrā rēgem Troiānum **pugnātūrus haec** sibi dixit: "utinam nē **tot** amīcōs Aenēae **interfēcissem**! vellem nunc **vīveret** Pallās, fīlius ille Evandrī, quī **gladiō** meō periit! ō sī Iūnō mihi auxilium **ferat**! num **patiēris**, deōrum rēgīna, mē **hīc** morī? Aenēae resistam an fugere **cōner**?"

Supply the imperfect, perfect and pluperfect subjunctive forms of the given verb in the same number, person, and voice.

For example: *amem*: *amārem, amāverim, amāvissem.*

1. pellās.
2. faciātis.
3. dent.
4. reperiāmus.
5. maneat.
6. dēbeās.
7. suādeam.
8. nūbat.
9. scrībāmus.
10. sciant.
11. amēmur.
12. sequāris.
13. oblīvīscātur.
14. videantur.
15. reātur.
16. pōnāminī.
17. fīat.
18. moriāmur.
19. gaudeāmus.
20. incipiās.

Translate.

1. huic librō studēte, puerī!
2. huic librō studeant omnēs puerī.
3. hīs librīs studeāmus?
4. hīs librīs studeāmus!
5. utinam lupī porcōs in silvam nē ēgissent!
6. quid faciat pastor, per agrum venientibus aprīs?
7. ō utinam semper mē mea māter amet!
8. quis crēderet nautam fīliam agricolae amāre?
9. quis morte rēgīnae cārae gaudeat?
10. ad senātum nē ierīs, Caesar!
11. nōlīte Caesarem interficere!
12. utinam ad senātum nē iisset Caesar!
13. incolumis sit Caesar et domum fēlix redeat!
14. utinam hostēs urbem nostram nē dēlērent!
15. utinam hostēs urbem nostram nē dēleant!
16. ō sī hostēs urbem nostram nē dēlēvissent!
17. Marcus Porcius Catō dīcit dēlendam esse Karthāginem.
18. hostibus tandem fugātīs deī nōbīs pācem dent!
19. dēpositīs armīs iam dulcī pāce fruēmur?
20. vellem verba magistrātūs istīus prius audīvissem!

21. Let's give food to the pigs.
22. Let's not give food to the pigs.
23. How are we to defend the city against the enemy?
24. Are we to throw stones down from the walls?
25. Will the enemy run away?
26. If only they would run away!
27. If only they were running away now!
28. I should not wish to see them in the city.
29. Let's hope that they will go away.
30. May the gods defend us!
31. If only we had spared the barbarians' brave leader!
32. If only the enemy were not in our territory now!
33. Let us attack Rome immediately!
34. "If only we had attacked Rome immediately!" Hannibal whispered to himself.
35. The Romans could not have defended the city without the legions.

Lectiōnēs Latīnae

Lege, Intellege

A Cautious Roman Commander

Quintus Titurius Sabīnus cum eīs cōpiīs quās ā Caesare accēperat in fīnēs Venellōrum pervēnit. hīs praeerat Viridovix ac summam imperiī tenēbat eārum omnium cīvitātum quae dēfēcerant, ex quibus exercitum coēgerat; atque hīs paucīs diēbus Aulercī Eburovīcēs Lexoviīque, senātū suō interfectō quod auctōrēs bellī esse nōlēbant, portās clausērunt sēque cum Viridovīce coniunxērunt; magnaque praetereā multitūdō undique ex Galliā perditōrum hominum convēnerat, quōs spēs praedae studiumque bellī ab agrī cultūrā et cottīdiānō labōre revocābat. Sabīnus castrīs sē tenēbat; Viridovix contrā eum duōrum mīlium spatiō cōnsēderat cottīdiēque cōpiās ad pugnam prōdūcēbat. ergō nōn sōlum hostibus in contemptiōnem Sabīnus veniēbat, sed etiam nostrōrum mīlitum vōcibus nōn nihil carpēbātur; magnam enim opīniōnem timōris praebuit et iam ad vallum castrōrum hostēs accēdere audēbant.

—Caesar, *Dē Bellō Gallicō* 3.17

praesum, praeesse, praefuī irreg. (+ dat.) be in command

carpō, -ere, carpsī, carptum 3 pluck, criticize

vallum, -ī neut. 2 rampart

1. From what source had Viridovix collected his army?
2. Why had the Aulerci, Eburovices, and Lexovii killed their senators?
3. Why was Sabinus suspected of cowardice?
4. What had lured desperate men from all parts of Gaul to fight against the Romans?
5. How far from the Romans did Viridovix establish his own camp?

Ars Poētica

Juvenal (Decius Iunius Iuvenalis; AD c. 55–c. 127) was the author of five books of satires. They are brilliantly critical of Roman social and political life, and they also reveal his thoroughly unappealing personality.

Explain the mood and tense of the verbs in bold in the following quotations from Juvenal.

1. *quid Rōmae* **faciam**? *mentīrī nescio.*
   What am I to do in Rome? I don't know how to tell lies.

2. *quis prōpōnere tālem / aut emere* **audēret** *piscem?*
   Who would have dared to put such a fish up for sale or buy it?

3. *utinam rītūs veterēs et publica saltem*
   hīs intacta malīs **agerentur** *sacra.*
   If only the ancient rites and the public ceremonies at least could be conducted untainted by these evils.

4. ‎   **pōnātur** *calculus, adsint*
   cum tabulā puerī; numerā sestertia quinque
   omnibus in rēbus, **numerentur** *deinde labōrēs.*
   Let the counters be set out and let the slaves be present with the abacus; count out five thousand sesterces in payment for everything, then let all my efforts be counted up.

5. *utinam hīs potius nūgīs tōta illa* **dedisset**
   tempora saevitiae, clārās quibus abstulit urbī
   illustrēsque animās impūne et vindice nullō.
   How I wish he had devoted all those times of savagery to these trifles instead, the times which, with impunity and with no one to exact revenge, he took famous and distinguished souls away from the city.

6. *citius Scyllam vel concurrentia saxa*
   Cyaneīs plēnōs et tempestātibus utrēs
   crēdiderim *aut tenuī percussum verbere Circēs*
   et cum rēmigibus grunnisse Elpēnora porcīs.
   I'd sooner believe in Scylla or the Cyanean Clashing Rocks and bags full of storms, and that Elpenor, struck by Circe's delicate whip, grunted with the pig oarsmen.

7. *maxima dēbētur puerō reverentia, sī quid*
   turpe parās, nec tū puerī **contempseris** *annōs,*
   sed peccātūrō **obstet** *tibi fīlius infans.*
   The greatest consideration is owed to your child, if you are planning something shameful. Don't show disrespect for your child's years; instead let your infant son prevent you when you are going to do wrong. [In other words, "not in front of the children."]

ergā prep. (+ acc.) concerning

nūgae, -ārum fem. 1 trivialities

vindex, -icis masc. 3 avenger

uter, utris masc. 3 leather bag

verber, verberis neut. 3 lash, whip

Circēs Greek gen. sing. of Circe, the witch goddess

rēmex, -igis masc. 3 oarsman

Elpēnora Greek masc. acc. sing. of Elpenor, one of Ulysses' companions

Aurea Dicta

1. *cēdant carminibus rēgēs rēgumque triumphī.* (Ovid)
2. *cum dignitāte potius cadāmus quam cum ignōminiā serviāmus.* (Cicero)
3. *dī mala prohibeant!* (Terence)
4. *hanc utinam faciem nōlit mūtāre senectūs!* (Propertius)
5. *hōc volo, sīc iubeō, sit prō ratiōne voluntās.* (Juvenal)
6. *maior frāter dīvidat patrimōnium, minor ēligat.* (Seneca the Elder)
7. *mālim indisertam prūdentiam quam stultitiam loquācem.* (Cicero)
8. *palleat omnis amans; hīc est color aptus amantī.* (Ovid)

ratiō, ratiōnis fem. 3 reason

indisertus, -a, -um unskilled in speaking

palleō, -ēre, palluī 2 be pale

Lūsūs

Thēsaurus Verbōrum

The adjectival ending *-ōsus, -ōsa, -ōsum* means "endowed with," "full of"; hence *formōsus, -a, -um*, from *forma, -ae* fem. 1 "shape," "beauty," means "shapely," "beautiful," and *verbōsus, -a, -um*, from *verbum, -ī* neut. 2 "word," means "talkative." Here are more examples, some of which English has adopted, with the ending changed to *-ous*:

ambitiōsus	ambitious	ambitus, -ūs masc. 4	going round (to canvass)
animōsus	brave	animus, -ī masc. 2	spirit
damnōsus	detrimental	damnum, -ī neut. 2	loss
fābulōsus	fabulous	fābula, -ae fem. 1	story
fāmōsus	famous	fāma, -ae fem. 1	fame
frondōsus	leafy	frons, frondis fem. 3	leaf
furiōsus	furious	furia, -ae fem. 1	fury
glōriōsus	glorious	glōria, -ae fem. 1	glory
herbōsus	grassy	herba, -ae fem. 1	grass
ingeniōsus	ingenious	ingenium, -ī neut. 2	genius
insidiōsus	treacherous	insidiae, -ārum fem. 1	ambush
iocōsus (= jocōsus)	witty	iocus, -ī masc. 2	joke
lūminōsus	full of light	lūmen, -inis neut. 3	light

Etymologiae Antīquae

Wild Animals II

ballaena, -ae fem. 1 "whale." Whales spout (Greek βάλλειν [*ballein*] "throw") water.

cancer, cancrī masc. 2 "crab." Crabs are shells (*concha, -ae* fem. 1) with legs (*crūs, crūris* neut. 3).

lemurēs, -um masc. 3 "ghosts." The first Europeans to see lemurs on Madagascar thought they looked like ghosts. Similarly, larvae, as the grub-form of insects, are named after *larvae, -ārum* fem. 1 "evil spirits."

panthērā, -ae fem. 1 "panther." Panthers are friendly to all (the Greek πᾶν [*pan*] means "all") other wild animals (Greek θήρ [*ther*], related to the Latin *fera*) except snakes.

pāpiliō, -ōnis masc. 3 "butterfly." No ancient source gives an etymology of this word, but the English word *pavilion*, a large and splendid tent, is derived from the name of this little bird (*sic!*).

piscis, -is masc. 3 "fish." Fish are always grazing (*pascō, -ere, pāvī, pastum* 3) for food.

sīmia, -ae fem. 1 "monkey." Monkeys are similar (*similis, -e*) to humans.

ursus, -ī masc. 2 "bear." Bears use their mouths (*ōs, ōris* neut. 3) to lick their cubs into shape.

vespertiliō, -ōnis masc. 3 "bat." Bats fly in the evening (*vesper, vesperī* masc. 2).

vīpera, -ae fem. 1 "viper." Most European vipers produce live young, so the Romans thought they gave birth (*pariō, -ere, peperī, partum* 3 *i*-stem) with violence (*vīs*, fem. 3 irreg.), the young eating their way out through their mother's sides. (*parere* is part of the true derivation, but with *vīvus, -a, -um* "living.")

Vīta Rōmānōrum

Sayings of Tiberius and Caligula (from Suetonius' *Dē Vītā Caesarum*)

Tiberius

When some of the provincial governors advised him to place a heavy tax burden on the provinces, he wrote back that it was the mark of a good shepherd to shear his sheep, not to skin them.

To set a personal example for frugality, even at formal dinners he often served up half-eaten leftovers from the day before, or just half a wild boar, declaring that it had all the qualities of a whole one.

He spoke Greek fluently, but did not do so on all occasions. He refrained from using Greek especially in the Senate.

"Let the people hate me, provided they approve my decisions."

Caligula

"Let the people hate me, provided they fear me."

He rarely allowed anyone to be put to death except slowly with many tiny wounds, and was famous for always saying, "Strike him in such a way that he knows he is dying."

When the rabble supported a charioteer from a team he did not support, he shouted out, "I wish the Roman people had just a single neck!"

At an elegant banquet, he suddenly burst into a fit of giggling. When the consuls, who were reclining next to him, politely asked him why he was laughing, he replied, "Why, because at a single nod from me, both of you could have your throats cut here and now."

[On campaign in Germany] he deployed his battle line on the shore of the Atlantic Ocean, drawing up his *ballistae* [giant rock-throwers] and other artillery. No one knew or could guess what he was going to do. Suddenly, he ordered his soldiers to gather shells and fill their helmets and the folds in their clothing with them. He called these "Spoils from the Ocean, owed to the Capitol and the Palatine."

Intending to terrify the man, he ordered a Roman knight who had caused a disturbance in the theater to go with a message for King Ptolemy in Mauretania. What the message said was "Do nothing good or bad to the man I have sent."

CHAPTER 23

The Present and Imperfect Subjunctive in Subordinate Clauses I

In this chapter you will begin learning how the subjunctive is used in subordinate clauses. Because such sentences involve a relation between two verbs—one in the main clause, one in the subordinate clause that the main clause introduces—there is a rule determining which tenses are to be used in the subordinate clause. **This rule is known as the sequence of tenses**.

Verb in main clause	Subjunctive verb in subordinate clause
If this verb is in a **primary** tense,	this verb will be either
present	**present** subjunctive
future	or
future perfect	**perfect** subjunctive
perfect that is connected to the present ("I have gone")	
If this verb is in a **secondary** tense,	this verb will be either
imperfect	**imperfect** subjunctive
pluperfect	or
perfect referring to a specific time in the past ("I went")	**pluperfect** subjunctive

You remember from Chapter 7 that the **perfect tense** in Latin can be used both for past events that can be assigned to a specific time ("I went") and also for past events that can't be so assigned, or past events that are connected to the present ("I have gone"). As you can see from the chart above, this distinction is very important for the sequence of tenses: one meaning puts the sentence into primary sequence, the other puts it into secondary sequence. You will often have to consider the context in order to be sure which meaning of the perfect is at issue.

In this chapter and the next, you will be studying sentences where the subordinate clause almost always uses

1. the present subjunctive if the main verb is in primary sequence
2. the imperfect subjunctive if the main verb is in secondary sequence

That is, if the main verb is in the **present, future, future perfect**, or **perfect with "have,"** the **present subjunctive** is used in the subordinate clause. If the main verb is in the **imperfect, perfect without "have,"** or **pluperfect**, the **imperfect subjunctive** is used in the subordinate clause.

If you think about the function of the sentences you'll study in these chapters, you can see why they use only these two tenses of the subjunctive.

- **Clauses of purpose, result, command, hindering, or preventing** logically refer to what may or may not happen AFTER the action of the main verb.

- **Clauses of characteristic** are descriptive, so they refer to the SAME TIME as the main verb.

When these clauses describe the present or look forward to the future FROM A STAND-POINT IN THE PRESENT OR THE FUTURE, they will use the present subjunctive. When they describe the present or look forward to the future FROM A STANDPOINT IN THE PAST, they will use the imperfect subjunctive. Neither the perfect nor the pluperfect subjunctive would make sense in these clauses, because those tenses refer to a time BEFORE the action of the main verb.

Purpose Clauses

A purpose clause is a subordinate clause that shows the intention of the verb in the main clause. Sometimes it is positive (intending to do something), and sometimes it is negative (intending not to do something, or intending to prevent something):

Positive	Negative
The wolves are coming **[in order] to kill** the pigs.	The shepherd is building a wall **so that the wolves do not kill** the pigs.
	The shepherd is building a wall **lest the wolves kill** the pigs.
	The shepherd is building a wall **so as not to endanger** his pigs.

English often uses the infinitive to express purpose: "I went to the garden <u>to pick</u> flowers." Classical Latin almost never does. You have already learned how to express purpose using the gerund/gerundive with *causā/grātiā* and the accusative of the supine. By far the most common method of expressing purpose, however, is to use a subordinate clause with a subjunctive verb.

You will sometimes see negative purpose clauses translated using "lest," as above; this is a little old-fashioned, but it is concise and marks the clause as clearly being in the subjunctive.

If a purpose clause is positive, it is introduced by *ut*. If it is negative, it is introduced by *nē*.

As you look at the examples in the chart that follows, remember that if the main clause is in the perfect tense, you have a special situation. When the perfect tense refers to a past action that has no specific time or that continues up to the present, the verb in the subordinate clause is in the

present subjunctive. When the perfect tense refers to a past event at a specific time, the verb in the subordinate clause is in the **imperfect subjunctive**.

Past action connected to the present	**Past action at a specific time**
vēnī ut Caesarem videam.	*vēnī herī ut Caesarem vidērem.*
I have come [and am now here] in order to see Caesar.	I came yesterday in order to see Caesar.

Notā Bene

In the following sentences, "may" is the present tense, and "might" is the past, even though American English does not always follow this rule.

Purpose clauses in primary sequence	**Purpose clauses in secondary sequence**
*pecūniam tibi **dō** ut fēlix **sīs**.*	*pecūniam tibi **dederam** ut fēlix **essēs**.*
I am giving you money so that you may be happy.	I had given you money so that you might be happy.
*pecūniam tibi **dedī** ut fēlix **sīs**.*	*pecūniam tibi **dedī** ut fēlix **essēs**.*
I have given you money so that you may be happy.	I gave you money so that you might be happy.
*fortiter **pugnāmus** nē urbs **capiātur**.*	*fortiter **pugnābāmus** nē urbs **caperētur**.*
We are fighting bravely so that the city may not be taken/lest the city be taken.	We were fighting bravely so that the city might not be taken/lest the city be taken.
*fortiter **pugnābimus** nē urbs **capiātur**.*	
We will fight bravely so that the city may not be taken/lest the city be taken.	
*fortiter **pugnāvimus** nē urbs **capiātur**.*	*fortiter **pugnāvimus** nē urbs **caperētur**.*
We have fought bravely so that the city may not be taken/lest the city be taken.	We fought bravely so that the city might not be taken/lest the city be taken.
	*fortiter **pugnāverāmus** nē urbs **caperētur**.*
	We had fought bravely so that the city might not be taken/lest the city be taken.
*ducem nostrum **sequēmur** ut hostēs **vincāmus**.*	
We will follow our leader to defeat the enemy/so that we may defeat the enemy.	
*ducem nostrum **secūtī sumus** ut hostēs **vincāmus**.*	*ducem nostrum **secūtī sumus** ut hostēs **vincerēmus**.*
We have followed our leader to defeat the enemy/so that we may defeat the enemy.	We followed our leader to defeat the enemy/so that we might defeat the enemy.

*ducem nostrum **secūtī erāmus** ut hostēs **vincerēmus**.*
We had followed our leader to defeat the enemy/so that we might defeat the enemy.

*Caesarem **interficiāmus** nē rex **fīat**!*
Let us kill Caesar lest he become king/
so that he may not become king!

*Caesarem **interfice** nē rex **fīat**!*
Kill Caesar lest he become king/so that
he may not become king!

Notā Bene

The sentences whose main clause is an exhortation or an imperative can't be put into secondary sequence, because exhortations and imperatives have no past-tense equivalent.

Result Clauses

A result clause shows the outcome or consequence of an action or circumstance that is referred to in the main clause:

Main clause	Result clause
He fed the pigs so much	that they became fat.
The pigs were so fat	that they could not walk.

You remember that if a purpose clause is positive, it is introduced by *ut*, and if it is negative, it is introduced by *nē*. **By contrast, *ut* introduces all result clauses, positive and negative. When the result clause is negative, *nōn* or some other negative term such as *nullus*, *nēmō*, or *numquam* is added.**

Positive result clause	Negative result clause
*tam bonus est **ut** hunc porcum laudet.*	*tam stultus est **ut** hunc porcum **nōn** laudet.*
He is so good that he praises this pig.	He is so stupid that he doesn't praise this pig.
*tam bonus erat **ut** omnēs eum laudārent.*	*tam stultus erat **ut nēmō** eum laudāret.*
He was so good that everyone praised him.	He was so stupid that no one praised him.

The sequence of tenses in result clauses is the same as for purpose clauses. Again, the rules for the interpretation of a perfect tense verb in the main clause are also the same.

Past action connected to the present	Past action at a specific time
tam bene pugnāvērunt gladiātōrēs ut Caesar eōs līberāre velit.	*tam bene pugnāvērunt gladiātōrēs ut Caesar eōs līberāre vellet.*
The gladiators have fought so well that Caesar is willing to free them.	The gladiators fought so well that Caesar was willing to free them.

The following words referring to degree or extent often appear in the main clause before a result clause.

adeō adv.	so, to such an extent (used mostly with verbs)
ita adv.	so (in such a way)
sīc adv.	so (in such a way)
tam adv.	so (used mostly with adjectives or other adverbs)
tālis, -e adj.	of such a sort
tantus, -a, -um adj.	so great
tot indecl. adj.	so many
totiens adv.	so often

Result clauses in primary sequence

lupōs adeō timent porcī ut omnēs moriantur.
The pigs are so afraid of the wolves that they are all dying/will all die.

sīc pugnāvit pastor ut lupō timōrī sit.
The shepherd has fought in such a way that he is a cause of fear to the wolf.

tam pigrī sunt porcī ut sub arbore semper iaceant.
The pigs are so lazy that they always lie under the tree.

tālem cibum porcīs dabit ut omnēs moriantur.
He will give the pigs food of such a kind that they will all die.

tantā virtūte pugnāvērunt mīlitēs ut hostēs fugiant.
The soldiers have fought with such great bravery that the enemy are fleeing.

tot porcī in agrō sunt ut cibum nōn habeant vaccae.
There are so many pigs in the field that the cows do not have food.

tot porcōs habet agricola ut omnibus cibum dare nōn possit.
The farmer has so many pigs that he cannot give food to them all.

porcōs sīc dēfende, pastor, ut lupus fugiat!
Defend your pigs in such a way, shepherd, that the wolf flees!

Result clauses in secondary sequence

lupōs adeō timuērunt porcī ut omnēs morerentur.
The pigs were so afraid of the wolves that they all died.

sīc pugnāvit pastor ut lupus fugeret.
The shepherd fought in such a way that the wolf fled.

tam pigrī erant porcī ut sub arbore semper iacērent.
The pigs were so lazy that they always lay under the tree.

tālem cibum porcīs dederat ut omnēs morerentur.
He had given the pigs food of such a kind that they all died.

tantā virtūte pugnāvērunt mīlitēs ut hostēs fugerent.
The soldiers fought with such great bravery that the enemy fled.

tot porcī in agrō erant ut cibum nōn habērent vaccae.
There were so many pigs in the field that the cows did not have food.

tot porcōs habēbat agricola ut omnibus cibum dare nōn posset.
The farmer had so many pigs that he could not give food to them all.

porcō totiens cibum dedistī ut nunc currere nōn possit.
You have given food to the pig so often that now it cannot run.

porcō totiens cibum dedistī ut currere nōn posset.
You gave food to the pig so often that it could not run.

Since negative purpose clauses begin with *nē*, while negative result clauses begin with *ut* followed by *nōn* or some other negative term, you can always tell them apart. POSITIVE result clauses, however, can sometimes look exactly like POSITIVE purpose clauses, because both types begin with *ut*. Words like *tam*, *tantus*, and so on in the main clause OFTEN signal a result clause, but they do not ALWAYS do so. Here are examples of Latin sentences that can be ambiguous in this way:

	As a result clause	**As a purpose clause**
tot hostēs interfēcit exercitus Rōmānus ut urbs incolumis esset.	The Roman army killed so many enemies that the city was safe.	The Roman army killed so many enemies in order that the city might be safe.
librō studēbat discipula ut multa intellegeret.	The student studied her book, so she understood many things.	The student studied her book in order that she might understand many things.

Here, context will help make the meaning clear. For instance, if the first sentence is a purpose clause, the writer may have just mentioned how many enemies the Romans killed, giving *tot* something to refer to.

Prōlūsiōnēs

Change the tense of the main verb from present to pluperfect, or vice versa, adjust the sequence of tenses accordingly, and then translate.

For example:
*pauper in forum **currit** ut scelera consulis plēbī **nuntiet**.*
*pauper in forum **cucurrerat** ut scelera consulis plēbī **nuntiāret**.*
A poor man had run into the Forum to announce the consul's crimes to the lower classes.

1. aper in spēluncam fūgerat nē vulnera plūra paterētur.
2. tot vulnera patiuntur mīlitēs nostrī ut saevīs hostium vīribus cēdant.
3. aciem barbarōrum tam celeriter frēgerant Rōmānī ut hostēs ipsī virtūtem nostram laudārent.

4. hīs librīs studuerāmus ut carmina Vergiliī legerēmus.

5. nē rex quidem tam crūdēlis oculōs aperīre ausus erat, nē poenās cīvium malōrum aspiceret.

6. nauta tot astra nōbīs monstrāverat ut nēmō omnia eōrum nōmina discere posset.

7. astra numerō carentia diū mīror ut negōtia hominum parvī aestimem.

8. aliī rūre vēnerant ut lūdōs aspicerent, aliī ut vītā et molliōre et meliōre fruerentur.

9. piscium capiendōrum causā totiens abītis, agricolae, ut porcōrum saepe oblīvīscāminī?

10. num pīrātārum minās patī voluerās ut piscēs maiōrēs in apertō marī caperēs?

Replace the gerund(ive) phrase with an *ut* clause of purpose and then translate.

For example:

num dē consulātū suō carmen compōnit Marcus Tullius Cicerō glōriae maiōris adipiscendae causā?

num dē consulātū suō carmen compōnit Marcus Tullius Cicerō ut glōriam maiōrem adipiscātur?

Surely Marcus Tullius Cicero is not composing a poem about his own consulship in order to obtain greater glory?

1. pecūniae petendae causā tot cōmoediās fēcit Titus Maccius Plautus.

2. poētārum veterum legendōrum causā Athēnās nāvigābit Publius Terentius Afer.

3. vēritātem hominibus aperiendī causā carmen dē rērum nātūrā scrīpserat Titus Lucrētius Cārus.

4. Gaiō Valēriō Catullō mille bāsia dā, puella, poētae amōris retinendī causā.

5. nonne Augustī laudandī causā carmen illud tam celebre scrīpsit Publius Vergilius Marō?

6. "scūtum humī dēpōne" sibi susurrāvit Quintus Horātius Flaccus "celerius fugiendī causā."

7. quot epistulās tristēs scrībet Publius Ovidius Nāsō Rōmam redeundī causā!

8. Claudiī mortuī stultitiae dērīdendae causā librum parvum scrībere ausus est Lūcius Annaeus Seneca.

9. carminum audiendōrum causā Gaiō Valēriō Martiālī pecūniam dēmus!

10. īrae suae dēlendae causā multa dē sceleribus hominum scrībit Decius Iūnius Iuvenālis.

Translate.

1. tanta est urbs ut ūnō diē omnia templa vidēre nōn possīmus.
2. hīs librīs studē ut magistrō, virō faciēī ita dulcis, placeās.
3. cūr aprum hastā vulnerāvistī? num ut in spēluncam recurreret?
4. prope flūmen celere stābant mīlitēs ut urbem dēfenderent.
5. tōtam per noctem tam dulcia somnia vīdī ut semper dormīre cuperem.
6. totiens in hortum ingressī erant lupī ut pastor ipse timēret.
7. ut tristis nōn sim tū tot mihi dōna dedistī.
8. tantae stultitiae est consul alter ut cīvēs paene omnēs eum contemnant.
9. uxōrēs agricolārum ad portum cottīdiē venīre solent ut piscēs emant.
10. Rōmae tot cīvēs aestāte aegrī sunt ut rūs abeat pars magna senātūs.
11. in fluctūs maris frīgidī cucurrerant canēs ut piscēs parvōs dentibus magnīs captōs dominō pigrō referrent.
12. tantā vōce clāmāvit pastor ut omnēs porcī ex agrō fugerent.
13. dominus "hodiē vōbīs labōrandum est" servīs miserrimīs ait "ut crās tōtum diem ōtiō fruāminī."
14. nautīs rēs magna est scīre astrōrum viās nē per ingentēs maris undās nāvigantēs pereant.
15. rēs ita tristis est ante oculōs līberōrum morī ut pācem hostēs rogēmus.
16. tam ferōciter pugnāvit centuriō ille parvus nē hostēs eum capere possent.
17. Rōmānī in fīnēs nostrōs vēnērunt, nōn ut pācem nōbīs offerrent sed praedae auferendae causā.
18. porcus iste magnus sub villae mūrō iacēbat aeger, quod vīnum totiens biberat.
19. bellī minīs crescentibus, moenia urbis auximus ut hostium vīribus resistere possent.
20. quis mēcum exībit ut porcōs ex hortō expellāmus?

21. The Roman army had brought ten thousand slaves to work in the fields of Italy.
22. My dog is so dear to me that he never leaves me in order to play with the wolves.
23. My owner is so stupid! Why does he give his dogs so much food that they are unwilling to catch soft little animals in the woods?
24. Die bravely, gladiator, so that you may please the Romans!
25. The wolves have killed so many pigs that the farmer is without hope.
26. Surely the wolves did not kill so many pigs to have food for themselves?
27. The farmer knew that the wolves had come out of the wood to kill the pigs.
28. The enemy general had fled so as not to be captured by our infantry.
29. Yesterday I was so happy that I sang in the Forum.
30. Because I had drunk too much wine, my voice was so rough that not even my friends were willing to listen to my song.

Lectiōnēs Latīnae

Lege, Intellege

Cato the Elder (Marcus Porcius Cato 234–149 BC) was the leading orator of his time. He was a prominent conservative politician known for opposing Greek influence. He was the first Roman to write history in Latin rather than Greek. His only surviving work is the *Dē Agricultūrā* (*On Farming*), a practical manual on how to run a medium-sized estate using slave labor.

The Duties of a Farm Manager

haec erunt vīlicī officia. disciplīnā bonā ūtātur; fēriae serventur; aliēnō manum abstineat, sua servet dīligenter; lītibus familiae supersedeat; familia nē algeat, nē ēsuriat; vīlicus sī nōlet male facere, nōn faciet; sī passus erit, dominus impūne nē sinat esse. vīlicus nē sit ambulātor; sobrius sit semper; ad cēnam nē quō eat; nē plūs censeat sapere sē quam dominum; amīcōs dominī, eōs habeat sibi amīcōs; rem dīvīnam nisi Compitālibus in compitō aut in focō nē faciat; cibāria, vīnum, oleum mūtuum dederit nēminī; duās aut trēs familiās habeat, unde ūtenda roget et quibus det, praetereā nēminī; nē quid ēmisse velit insciente dominō, neu quid dominum cēlāvisse velit; haruspicem, augurem, hariolum, Chaldaeum nē quem consuluisse velit; prīmus cubitū surgat, postrēmus cubitum eat.

—Cato, *Dē Agricultūrā* 5

fēriae, -ārum fem. 1 holidays

līs, lītis fem. 3 quarrel

familia is a broader term than "family," referring to the whole household, including the slaves

algeō, -ēre, alsī 2 feel cold

ēsuriō, -īre 4 be hungry

sinō, -ere, sīvī, situm 3 allow

quō adv. to anywhere

Compitālia, -ium neut. 3 the festival of the crossroads (*compitum, -ī* neut. 2)

cibāria, -orum neut. 2 provisions of food

haruspicēs, augurēs, hariolī, and Chaldaeans are all types of soothsayers

1. To whom might a farm manager lend equipment?
2. A farm manager should never perform religious ceremonies: true or false?
3. When was a farm manager permitted to get drunk?
4. A farm manager should never consult soothsayers: true or false?
5. What could a farm manager buy without his owner's knowledge?

Ars Poētica

Little is known about Phaedrus, who wrote Latin versions of the Greek fables of Aesop. He lived in the first half of the first century AD, and may have been a slave freed by Augustus.

In the following quotations from Phaedrus' *Fables*, which of the subjunctive verbs in bold are in purpose clauses?

1. *regnāre nōlō, līber ut nōn **sim** mihi.*
   I don't want to rule in such a way that I'm not free for myself.

2. *asellum in prātō timidus pascēbat senex.*
   is hostium clāmōre subitō territus
   *suādēbat asinō fugere, nē **possent** capī.*
   A timid old man was letting his little donkey graze in a meadow. Frightened by the sudden shouting of enemies, he started to urge the donkey to flee, lest they could be captured.

3. *"heus," inquit "linguam vīs meam praeclūdere,*
   *nē **lātrem** prō rē dominī? multum falleris.*
   namque ista subita mē iubet benignitās
   *vigilāre, **faciās** nē meā culpā lucrum."*
   "Hey," he said, "do you want to put my tongue out of action, lest I bark in defense of my owner's possessions? You are much mistaken. For that sudden generosity [being given food by an intruder] bids me be vigilant, lest you make a profit through my fault."

4. *descende, amīce; tanta bonitās est aquae,*
   *voluptās ut satiārī nōn **possit** mea.*
   Come down, my friend; the water is so good that my pleasure cannot be satiated.

5. *sīc porcellī vōcem est imitātus suā,*
   *vērum ut subesse palliō **contenderent**.*
   He imitated the voice of a piglet with his own voice in such a way that they maintained that a real pig was under his cloak.

6. *vulpem rogābat partem caudae sīmius,*
   *contegere honestē **posset** ut nūdās natēs.*
   A monkey asked a fox for part of its tail, so that it could cover its naked rump decently.

7. *canēs currentēs bibere in Nīlō flūmine,*
   *ā crocodīlīs nē **rapiantur**, trāditum est.*
   It has been said that dogs drink from the river Nile while running, lest they be snatched by crocodiles.

8. *lacerātus quīdam morsū vehementis canis,*
   tinctum cruōre pānem mīsit maleficō,
   audierat esse quod remedium vulneris.
   tunc sīc Aesōpus: "nōlī cōram plūribus
   *hōc facere canibus, nē nōs vīvōs **dēvorent**,*
   cum scierint esse tāle culpae praemium."

Someone wounded by the bite of a fierce dog threw the wrongdoer some bread dipped in his gore, because he had heard this was a way of curing the wound. Then Aesop spoke thus: "Don't do this in front of any more dogs, in case they devour us alive, when they learn that such is the reward for wrongdoing."

Aurea Dicta

1. *dīlige sīc aliōs, ut sīs tibi cārus amīcus.* (Ps.-Cato)
2. *ferās facilia, ut difficilia perferās.* (Publilius Syrus)
3. *indulget fortūna malīs, ut laedere possit.* (Ps.-Cato)
4. *ita vīxī, ut nōn frustrā mē nātum esse existimem.* (Cicero)
5. *malus bonum malum esse vult ut sit suī similis.* (Plautus)
6. *rīsit, ut audīrem, tenerā cum mātre Cupīdō.* (Ovid)
7. *sēcum, sed ut audiam, susurrat.* (Martial)
8. *ut placeās, dēbēs immemor esse tuī.* (Ovid)

Lūsūs

Thēsaurus Verbōrum

More adjectives ending in *-ōsus*:

luxuriōsus	luxurious	luxuria, -ae fem. 1	luxury
morbōsus	diseased	morbus, -ī masc. 2	disease
numerōsus	numerous	numerus, -ī masc. 2	number
odiōsus	hateful	odium, -iī neut. 2	hatred
ōtiōsus	at leisure	ōtium, -iī neut. 2	price
pretiōsus	precious	pretium, -iī neut. 2	leisure
rūgōsus	wrinkled	rūga, -ae fem. 1	wrinkle
ruīnōsus	ruinous	ruīna, -ae fem. 1	ruin
spatiōsus	spacious	spatium, -iī neut. 2	space
studiōsus	studious	studium, -iī neut. 2	study
ventōsus	windy	ventus, -ī masc. 2	wind
vitiōsus	vicious, immoral	vitium, -iī neut. 2	flaw, vice

Etymologiae Antīquae

Planets, Stars, etc.

astrum, *-ī* neut. 2 "star." The stars are the children of the Titan Astraeus.

caelum, *-ī neut.* 2 "the sky," "heaven." The sky is adorned with stars engraved (*caelō* 1) on it. Alternatively, it hides (*cēlō* 1) the stars by day.

comētēs, *-ae* masc. 1 "comet." Comets seem to be followed by trailing hair (*coma*, *-ae* fem. 1). They were thought to portend disaster, because letting one's hair down was a mourning ritual. When a comet appeared in AD 79, the emperor Vespasian (who was bald) said it must be an omen for the king of Parthia, who had long hair, and not for himself. In fact, Vespasian died that year. *comētēs* is a Greek 1st decl. masc. nom. sing. form.

lūna, *-ae* fem. 1 "moon." The moon shines (*lūceō*, *-ēre*, *luxī* 2) at night (*nox*, *noctis* fem. 3).

planēta, *-ae* masc. 1 "planet." Unlike *sīdera* and *stellae* (see below), planets wander through the sky. The Greek for "to wander" is πλανᾶσθαι [*planasthai*].

sīdus, *-eris* neut. 3 "star." Stars sit (*consīdō*, *-ere*, *consēdī* 3) in one place. They also lie in ambush (*insidiae*, *-ārum* fem. 1), to cause harm to mortals. Sailors consider (*consīderō* 1) them when navigating.

sōl, *sōlis* masc. 3 "sun." The sun shines alone (*sōlus*, *-a*, *-um*), and usually (*solitē*, an adverb from *soleō*, *-ēre*, *solitus sum* 2 "to be accustomed") rises and sets every day.

stella, *-ae* fem. 1 "star." Stars stand (*stō*, *stāre*, *stetī*, *statum* 1) in one place. Quintilian records another derivation, that stars are drops (*stilla*, *-ae* fem. 1) of light, but comments that this suggestion is so absurd that it would be unkind of him to mention the name of the scholar who proposed it. It seems to be in the same vein as the notion that the adverb *māne* "in the morning" indicates that the day then seeps (*mānō* 1) from the east.

Vīta Rōmānōrum

More Sayings of the Emperors
(from Suetonius' *Dē Vītā Caesarum*)

Nero

At the dedication of the *domus aurea* [the "Golden House," a palace that took up vast tracts of land in the center of Rome], his only approving comment was that at last he had a house in which he could live like a human being.

Galba

When a guardian poisoned his ward so as to inherit the boy's property, Galba had him crucified. The man protested that, because he was a Roman citizen, he was not subject to this degrading punishment. Pretending to show respect for the man's legal status, Galba ordered him to be transferred to a cross that had been painted white and set up much higher than the others.

Otho

He had hoped that Galba would adopt him. But after Galba preferred another candidate, Otho turned to violence. He was not motivated just by resentment but also by heavy debts. He began to declare openly that he could only survive if he were emperor, and that it did not matter whether he fell to his enemies in the battle line or to his creditors in the Forum.

Vitellius

When he visited the battlefield [at Bedriacum, where his army had defeated Otho], he had the audacity to say encouragingly to his companions, who were appalled by the decomposing corpses, that a dead enemy smelled very good, but a dead fellow citizen smelled even better.

Vespasian

He lost no opportunity to punish indiscipline. When a very young man came, smelling of perfume, to thank him for a commission which he had been granted, Vespasian tossed his head in disgust and revoked the commission, censuring him in a very stern voice: "I wish you had smelled of garlic."

When his son Titus criticized him for devising a tax on urine from public conveniences [urine was used as a bleaching agent in laundering], he put a coin from the first payment of the tax under Titus' nose and asked him if he was offended by the smell. Titus said he was not, and Vespasian commented: "But it comes from urine."

He was not interested in pomp and show. On the day of his triumph, he was so exhausted by the slow and boring procession that he could not refrain from saying: "It serves me right! What a foolish old man I was to want a triumph, as if it was something I owed to my ancestors or ever desired for myself."

Titus

When his aides warned him not to promise anyone more than he could actually give, he said that no one should go away sad from a conversation with the emperor. It once occurred to him at dinner that he had done nothing for anyone all day, and he uttered that memorable and praiseworthy comment: "My friends, I have wasted a day."

The Present and Imperfect Subjunctive in Subordinate Clauses II

Indirect Commands

You remember that the subjunctive is used when an action or event is hypothetical or problematic: it may not happen or ever have happened. So-called indirect commands are often actually more like petitions or prayers, a situation in which the result depends on the person addressed and is therefore unpredictable; this is why such sentences take the subjunctive, even when the prayer or persuasion has clearly been successful.

Indirect commands follow the rules for the sequence of tenses that you have already learned, so the examples below do not give versions in both primary and secondary sequence for each example—by now you should know how to tell which is which.

Indirect commands are usually introduced by *ut*, if they are positive. If they are negative, they are introduced by *nē*. Occasionally ***ut*** will be omitted (as in, e.g., *tē ōrō mihi parcās* "I beg you to spare me").

This is another type of expression, like purpose clauses, where English tends to use the infinitive, but Latin never does, except with particular verbs such as *iubeō* and *vetō*, which are explained in this chapter.

tē ōrō ut mihi parcās.	I beg you to spare me.
pastōrī persuāserat agricola ut porcōs pasceret.	The farmer had persuaded the shepherd to feed the pigs. The farmer had persuaded the shepherd that he should feed the pigs.
pastōrī persuāserat agricola nē porcōs pasceret.	The farmer had persuaded the shepherd not to feed the pigs. The farmer had persuaded the shepherd that he should not feed the pigs.
petīvit uxor ā Caesare nē ad senātum illō diē īret.	Caesar's wife asked him not to go to the Senate that day.
petīvit uxor ā Caesare nē ad senātum hodiē eat.	Caesar's wife has asked him not to go to the Senate today.
Caesar mīlitibus imperāvit ut sē sequantur.	Caesar has ordered the soldiers to follow him.
Caesar mīlitibus imperāvit ut sē sequerentur.	Caesar ordered the soldiers to follow him.

Verbs that introduce indirect commands include

hortor 1	urge
imperō 1 + dat.	order
ōrō 1	implore
precor 1	implore
rogō 1	ask
moneō, monēre, monuī, monitum 2	warn
persuādeō, -ēre, -suāsī, -suāsum 2 + dat.	persuade
suādeō, suādēre, suāsī, suāsum 2 + dat.	urge
petō, -ere, petiī/petīvī, petītum 3 + *ā/ab* + abl	seek, ask
quaerō, -ere, quaesīvī, quaesītum 3 + *ā/ab* + abl.	seek

Two further verbs are important because, unlike all the others we have been looking at, they DO normally take a direct object and an infinitive (as in English).

iubeō, iubēre, iussī, iussum 2	order
vetō, vetāre, vetuī, vetitum 1	forbid

These two verbs complement each other: **iubeō** is for positive commands, **vetō** for negative commands.

tē iubeō domī manēre.	I order you to stay at home.
tē vetō domī manēre.	I order you not to stay at home.

You cannot use **iubeō** to order someone NOT to do something; for that, you should use **vetō**. Notice too that, because **vetō** is negative by its meaning, you should not add *nōn* to the infinitive. Neither **iubeō** nor **vetō** can introduce another verb in the subjunctive.

Clauses of Hindering and Preventing

Here again the hypothetical or problematic nature of the subjunctive is important. Hindering and preventing imply an action that has not yet actually become real; the person who is trying to hinder or prevent an action or event wants to keep that action or event from ever happening. You can also think of them as negative purpose clauses, with the OBJECT of the main verb (the verb of hindering or preventing) as the SUBJECT of the subordinate clause.

Clauses of hindering and preventing follow the regular rules for sequence of tenses. Since clauses of hindering and preventing are about stopping someone from doing something, they are almost always negative. The negative markers that may introduce them are *nē*, *quīn*, and *quōminus*.

mūrus magnus hostēs impedit quīn in urbem veniant.	A big wall prevents the enemy from coming into the city. (lit. A big wall hinders the enemy, lest they come into the city.)
hostēs prohibēte, cīvēs, nē in urbem veniant!	Citizens, stop the enemy from coming into the city! (lit. Citizens, hinder the enemy, lest they come into the city.)
pastor lupōs dēterruit quōminus in agrum venīrent.	The shepherd deterred the wolves from coming into the field. (lit. The shepherd deterred the wolves, lest they come into the field.)
nautae interdīxerat agricola nē flōrēs fīliae daret.	The farmer had forbidden the sailor to give flowers to his daughter. (lit. The farmer had forbidden the sailor, lest he give flowers to his daughter.)

Verbs that introduce clauses of hindering and prevention include

obstō, obstāre, obstitī 1 + dat.	hinder, impede
dēterreō, dēterrēre, dēterruī, dēterritum 2	deter
prohibeō, prohibēre, prohibuī, prohibitum 2	prevent
retineō, retinēre, retinuī, retentum 2	restrain
interdīcō, interdīcere, interdīxī, interdictum 3 + dat.	forbid
resistō, resistere, restitī 3 + dat.	resist
impediō, impedīre, impedīvī, impedītum 4	hinder, impede

Relative Clauses of Characteristic

These clauses emphasize the fact that the subjunctive is less definite and more theoretical than the indicative, because they describe not a particular real person or thing, but general types of people or things.

Real individuals (indicative)
porcum habeō quī lupōs timet.
I have a pig who fears wolves.

mīlitēs quī fortēs sunt hostēs crās vincent.
The soldiers who are brave will defeat the enemy tomorrow.

Types (subjunctive)
porcus quī lupōs timeat in silvās numquam it.
A pig who fears wolves [or, the sort of pig who fears wolves] never goes into the woods.

mīlitēs quī fortēs sint hostēs semper vincent.
[The kind of] soldiers who are brave will always defeat the enemy.

mīlitēs quī fortēs erant hostēs herī vīcērunt.
The soldiers who were brave defeated the enemy yesterday.

mīlitēs quī fortēs essent hostēs semper vīcērunt.
[The kind of] soldiers who were brave always defeated the enemy.

pecūniam servō quī piger est numquam dabō.
I will never give money to the slave who is lazy.

pecūniam servō quī piger sit numquam dabō.
I will never give money to a [any] slave who is lazy.

pecūniam servō quī nōn labōrābat numquam dederam.
I had never given money to the slave who did not work.

pecūniam servō quī nōn labōrāret numquam dederam.
I had never given money to a [any] slave who did not work.

pecūniam servō quī nōn labōrāvisset numquam dedī.
I never gave money to a [any] slave who had not worked.

Relative Clauses of Purpose

In Latin you can express purpose using a subjunctive verb in a relative clause. The clause will be introduced either by a relative pronoun or by a relative adverb such as

ubi	where
quō	to where
unde	from where

These clauses are rarely, if ever, negative. The verb in the main clause tends to be a verb of motion or sending. For example:

exiērunt senātōrēs quī pācem ab hostibus petant.	Senators have gone out to seek peace from the enemy. (lit. Senators have gone out who may seek peace from the enemy.)
exiērunt senātōrēs quī pācem ab hostibus peterent.	Senators went out to seek peace from the enemy. (lit. Senators went out who might seek peace from the enemy.)
servōs mīserat agricola quī lupōs interficerent.	The farmer had sent his slaves to kill the wolves. (lit. The farmer had sent his slaves who might kill the wolves.)
ad agrōs ībit pastor unde/ā quibus agnōs redūcat.	The shepherd will go to the fields to lead back the lambs. (lit. The shepherd will go to the fields from where/which he may lead back the lambs.)
nōn habēbant lupī quō fugerent.	The wolves had nowhere to flee. (lit. The wolves did not have [a place] to which they might flee.)

Prōlūsiōnēs

Parse the words in bold.

1. Hannibal, ut Rōmam **dēlēret**, transiit Alpēs.
2. **dēleat** ut Rōmam, trans Alpēs Hannibal ībit.
3. **pugnēmus**, nostram nē **dēleat** Hannibal urbem.
4. quis tam fortis adest saevīs ut hostibus **obstet**?
5. tot peditēs aderant ut nēmo resistere **posset**.
6. Hannibalem ōrāmus nē moenia **dēleat** urbis.
7. Hannibal advēnit quī nostram **dēleat** urbem.
8. quī Rōmam **capiant** elephantōs Hannibal affert.
9. Rōmam **dēlētum** trans Alpēs Hannibal īvit.
10. Hannibalī Fabius per multōs restitit annōs,
    nē Rōmam **caperet** tōtamque incenderet urbem.

Change the following direct commands to indirect commands by adding the words *Caesar mīlitibus imperat* **and then translate.**

For example:
contrā aciem hostium currite!
Caesar mīlitibus imperat ut contrā aciem hostium currant.
Caesar orders the soldiers to run at the enemy battle line.

1. in castrīs tōtam noctem manēte!
2. mē ipsum contrā hostēs sequiminī!
3. scūtīs relictīs tēla bīna manū fortī capite!
4. insidiās barbarōrum vītāte!
5. equitum ducī obsequiminī!

Change the following direct commands to indirect commands by adding the words *magister discipulō persuāserat* **and then translate.**

For example:
Vergiliī carmina lege!
magister discipulō persuāserat ut Vergiliī carmina legeret.
The teacher had persuaded the student to read the poems of Virgil.

1. carminibus Catullī studē!
2. librum tuum tēcum cottīdiē fer!
3. nōlī tempus perdere currūs gladiātōrēsque spectandō!
4. porcum tibi tam cārum domī relinque!
5. in lūdō nē dormīverīs!

Translate.

1. rex Etruscōrum, nōmine Porsenna, cōpiās magnās Rōmam duxit quae urbem nostram caperent.
2. hostibus appropinquantibus, Horātius, vir quam fortissimus, cēterōs mīlitēs precātus est ut sēcum in alterā flūminis ōrā hostibus resistendō urbem dēfenderent.
3. diū nē ūnum quidem invēnit quī Etruscīs resistere vellet.
4. tandem tamen duōbus amīcīs persuāsit ut agminī hostium ferōcī resisterent quōminus urbem flammīs dēlērent.
5. dum trans pontem prōgrediuntur, deōs ōrant ut sibi auxiliō sint hostibusque interdīcant nē Rōmam dēleant.
6. ūsuīne urbī erit numerus mīlitum tam parvus? quōmodo tot agmina hostium prohibēre poterunt nē statim in urbem incurrant?
7. illō diē Rōmānīs fāvērunt deī caelestēs; cīvēs enim nōn habēbant quō fugerent, sed virtūs trium tantum mīlitum tot minās cōpiāsque tantās rēgis crūdēlis āvertit.
8. dum gladiīs hastīsque hostēs impediunt Horātius amīcīque quōminus flūmen transeant, cīvium turba maxima pontem in aquam dēicere cōnātur.
9. tandem petiit consul ā tribus mīlitibus ut recurrerent, nē dēlētō ponte morerentur.
10. Horātius amīcōs sēcum hostibus obstāre vetuit, et statim recēdere iussit.
11. ipse iam sōlus Porsennae obstitit quīn cōpiās trans pontem mitteret.
12. gaudet rex, nam scit sē mortem tot mīlitum suōrum iam tandem ulciscī posse, sociōrumque ducibus saevā vōce imperat ut Horātium interficiant.
13. mīlitibus īrae plēnīs prōgredientibus quī verbīs Porsennae obsequantur, Horātium tamen nōn impediunt arma quīn ante oculōs uxōris līberōrumque dē moenibus urbis aspicientium in celerēs flūminis undās sē iaceret.
14. in veterrimīs librīs legimus Horātium, pugnandō iam fessum, armīs gravibus impedītum esse quīn incolumis ad alteram flūminis ōram perveniat.
15. nēmō est quī Horātiī nōmen nesciat; virtūte enim glōriam meritus est quae numquam pereat.

16. Why do you not order the soldiers to fight against the enemy now, Caesar?
17. Caesar's wife was not able to restrain him from going to the Senate.
18. A little river has prevented the famous poet from seeing his friend.

19. The Romans never praised kings who were bad men.

20. Let us all ask the gods to take revenge on the barbarians.

21. The centurion will deter the enemy from killing our leader.

22. I like this sailor who is not a pirate.

23. Why do you forbid me to study that book, mother?

24. With soft words, the big wolf was urging the third little pig to open the door.

25. "I forbid you to listen to the wolf's words," said their mother, a large, fat pig.

26. The wolf had been prevented by the huge herd of pigs from leaving the cave.

27. Although it had big sad eyes, the wolves prevented the little lamb from running back to its mother.

28. Is there no deep cave where my lambs may escape the cruel wolves?

29. Do not spare wolves that have savage eyes full of blood.

30. Give me a bigger sword with which I may kill the wolf.

Lectiōnēs Latīnae

Lege, Intellege

Cicero (Marcus Tullius Cicero 106–43 BC) was the greatest of all Roman orators, and a leading political figure throughout the last years of the Republic. We know the titles of almost ninety of his speeches, and some fifty-eight of them survive in whole or in part. He also wrote several treatises on rhetoric (most notably *Dē Ōrātōre*, *Brūtus*, and *Ōrātor*), and numerous philosophical works (among others, the *Dē Fīnibus Bonōrum et Malōrum*, *Disputātiōnēs Tusculānae*, *Dē Nātūrā Deōrum*, *Dē Dīvīnātiōne*, *Dē Officiīs*), as well as almost forty books of letters. His voluminous writings are by far the most important source of information about the final decades of the Republic. In addition, his clear and powerful style made a unique contribution to the development of Roman thought and of the Latin language itself. He was brutally murdered in 43 BC, when Mark Antony had his name included in the proscriptions, published lists that declared the opponents of the Second Triumvirate to be outlaws with a price on their heads.

War with Mithridates

adhūc ita nostrī cum illō rēge contendērunt imperātōrēs, ut ab illō insignia victōriae, nōn victōriam reportārent. triumphāvit Lūcius Sulla, triumphāvit Lūcius Mūrēna dē Mithridāte, duo fortissimī virī et summī imperātōrēs; sed ita triumphāvērunt, ut ille pulsus superātusque regnāret. vērum tamen illīs imperātōribus laus est tribuenda quod fēcērunt, venia danda quod relīquērunt, proptereā quod ab eō bellō Sullam in Ītaliam rēs pūblica, Mūrēnam Sulla revocāvit. Mithridātēs autem omne reliquum tempus nōn ad oblīviōnem veteris bellī, sed ad comparātiōnem novī contulit: quī cum maximās aedificāvisset ornāvissetque classēs exercitūsque magnōs comparāvisset, et sē fīnitimīs suīs bellum inferre similāret, usque in Hispāniam legātōs ac litterās mīsit ad eōs ducēs quibuscum tum bellum gerēbāmus, ut, cum duōbus in locīs disiunctissimīs maximēque dīversīs ūnō consiliō ā bīnīs hostium cōpiīs bellum terrā marīque gererētur, vōs ancipitī contentiōne districtī dē imperiō dīmicārētis.

—Cicero, *Dē Imperiō Gnaeī Pompeiī* 8

proptereā quod "because"

quibuscum After the Republican period, it was not usual to attach *cum* to relative pronouns

gerō, -ere, gessī, gestum 3 bear, do, wage

ut . . . vōs ancipitī contentiōne districtī dē imperiō dīmicārētis "that you were fighting for your empire, pulled in different directions by a two-headed struggle."

1. How comprehensive were the victories of Sulla and Murena over Mithridates?
2. Who called Murena back to Italy?
3. What did Mithridates do in the period after his wars with Sulla and Murena?
4. What reason did Mithridates give for constructing huge fleets and amassing vast armies?
5. To whom did Mithridates send ambassadors?

Ars Poētica

Juvenal II
Explain the use of the subjunctive verbs in bold.

1. *ego vel Prochytam praepōno Subūrae;*
   nam quid tam miserum, tam sōlum vīdimus, ut nōn
   *dēterius **crēdās** horrēre incendia, lapsūs*
   tectōrum assiduōs ac mille perīcula saevae
   urbis et Augustō recitantēs mense poētās?
   I rank even Prochyta [an insignificant island in the Bay of Naples] higher than the Subura [an area of Rome near the Forum]; for what have we seen that is so wretched, so deserted, that you would still not think it worse to tremble at the fires, the constant collapsing of roofs and the thousand perils of the cruel city and poets reciting in the month of August?

2. *hōc agit, ut **doleās**; nam quae cōmoedia, mīmus*
   quis melior plōrante gulā? ergō omnia fīunt,
   sī nescīs, ut per lacrimās effundere bīlem
   cōgāris.
   He does this to hurt you: for what comedy, what mime, is better than a groaning gullet? So it's all done, in case you don't know, so that you may be forced to pour your bile out through your tears. [A patron enjoys humiliating a client by having him served inferior food at a dinner.]

3. *ut **spectet** lūdōs, condūcit Ogulnia vestem,*
   condūcit comitēs, sellam, cervīcal, amīcās,
   *nutrīcem et flāvam cui **det** mandāta puellam.*
   To go watch the games, Ogulnia rents an outfit, she rents companions, a carriage, a cushion, friends, a nurse, and a blonde slave-girl to whom she may give orders.

4. *prīma ferē vōta et cunctīs nōtissima templīs*
   *dīvitiae, **crescant** ut opēs, ut maxima tōtō*
   *nostra **sit** arca forō.*
   Almost always the first things prayed for, the requests most familiar at all the temples, are riches, so that our wealth should increase, so that our money chest should be the biggest in the whole Forum.

5. *quae praeclāra et prospera tantī,*
   *ut rēbus laetīs pār **sit** mensūra malōrum?*
   What fame and fortune is worth so much that the measure of your ills should be equal to your prosperity?

6. *ī, dēmens, et saevās curre per Alpēs*
   *ut puerīs **placeās** et dēclāmātio fīās.*
   Go on, you madman, run across the wild Alps, so that you can please children and become a topic for exercises in speech-making. [To Hannibal.]

7. *ōrandum est ut **sit** mens sāna in corpore sānō.*
   We should pray that our mind will be healthy in a healthy body.

8. ***expectent** ergo tribūnī,*
   ***vincant** dīvitiae, sacrō nē **cēdat** honōrī*
   nūper in hanc urbem pedibus quī vēnerat albīs.
   So let the people's representatives wait, let wealth win, don't have the man who had recently come to this city with white feet make way for their sacred office. [Slaves for sale had their feet whitened with chalk.]

9. *ardet adhūc, et iam accurrit quī marmora **dōnet**.*
   His house is still ablaze, and already someone is running up to give him marble statuary.

10. *tibi nōn committitur aurum,*
    vel, sī quando datur, custōs affixus ibīdem,
    *quī **numeret** gemmās, unguēs **observet** acūtōs.*
    You're not trusted with a gold cup, or, if ever one is given to you, a guard is placed on it right away to count the gems and keep an eye on your sharp fingernails.

Aurea Dicta

1. *cavē et dīligenter attende, nē cum homine malō loquāris.* (Seneca the Younger)

2. *dā vacuae mentī, quō teneātur, opus.* (Ovid)

3. *dēbitor nōn est sine crēditōre, nōn magis quam marītus sine uxōre aut sine fīliō pater; aliquis dare dēbet, ut aliquis accipiat.* (Seneca the Younger)

4. *dūrius in terrīs nihil est quod vīvat amante.* (Propertius)

5. *līberālitāte ūtāmur, quae prōsit amīcīs, noceat nēminī.* (Cicero)

6. *maior sum quam cui possit fortūna nocēre.* (Ovid)

7. *nēmō umquam neque poēta neque ōrātor fuit quī quemquam meliōrem quam sē arbitrārētur.* (Cicero)

8. *nīl dictū foedum vīsūque haec līmina tangat, intrā quae puer est.* (Juvenal)

prōsum, prōdesse, prōfuī irreg. (+ dat.) be advantageous

līmen, līminis neut. 3 threshold

Lūsūs

Thēsaurus Verbōrum

Adjectives with the ending *-ānus, -āna, -ānum,* and *-īnus, -īna, -īnum* signify "belonging to," "concerned with."[1] For example:

Caesariānus	(Caesar, Caesaris masc. 3)	Alpīnus	leōnīnus
hūmānus	(homō, hominis masc./fem. 3)	canīnus	lībertīnus[5]
montānus	(mons, montis masc. 3)	Capitōlīnus	marīnus
Neāpolītānus	(Neāpolis, -is fem. 3)	corvīnus[3]	mātūtīnus[6]
oppidānus	(oppidum, -ī neut. 2)	dīvīnus[4]	medicīnus
Praetōriānus	(praetōrium, -iī neut. 2)[2]	elephantīnus	ostrīnus[7]
Rōmānus	(Rōma, -ae fem. 1)	equīnus	peregrīnus[8]
urbānus	(urbs, urbis fem. 3)	fēlīnus	porcīnus
veterānus	(vetus, veteris)	fēminīnus	serpentīnus

1. There are relatively few such adjectives suffixed with *-ēnus, -ēna, -ēnum,* perhaps the commonest being *terrēnus* (from *terra*) and *aliēnus* (from *alius*).

2. The *praetōrium* was the commander's tent, later the headquarters of the Praetorian Guard in Rome.

3. From *corvus, -ī* masc. 2 "raven." *Corvīnus* is the *cognōmen* of Messalla, one of Augustus' closest colleagues.

4. From *dīvus, -ī* masc. 2, an alternative term for "god."

5. From *lībertus, -ī* masc. 2 "freedman."

6. "Of the morning," Matuta being a goddess of the dawn.

7. "Purple." Purple dye was extracted from an oyster or *ostreum, -ī* neut. 2.

8. *peregrīnī* are non-Romans living under Roman jurisdiction.

Etymologiae Antīquae

Seasons, etc.

aestās, *aestātis* fem. 3 "summer." In summer, there is heat (*aestus*, *-ūs* masc. 4).

annus, *-ī* masc. 2 "year." The seasons go round in a circle, like a ring (*ānulus*, *-ī* masc. 2).

(*annī*) *curriculum*, *-ī* neut. 2 "seasons." The seasons do not stand still; rather they run (*currō*, *-ere*, *cucurrī*, *cursum* 3).

(*annī*) *tempus*, *temporis* neut. 3 "season." The four seasons are regulated (*temperō* 1) by moisture (spring), dryness (fall), heat (summer), and cold (winter).

autumnus, *-ī* masc. 2 "autumn." In autumn, when crops are gathered from the fields, farmers' prosperity is increased (*augeō*, *-ēre*, *auxī*, *auctum* 2).

brūma, *-ae* fem. 1 "winter." In winter the days are at their shortest (*brevissimus*, *-a*, *-um*), and people have a greater desire for food (Greek βρῶμα [*broma*]).

hiems, *hiemis* fem. 3 "winter." In winter there are many rainstorms (*imber*, *imbris* masc. 3) and people's breath can be seen coming from their gaping mouths (*hiātus*, *-ūs* masc. 4).

lustrum, *-ī* neut. 2 "five-year period." At the end of every *lustrum* the censors ensure that tax debts have been discharged (*luō*, *-ere*, *luī* 3) and that the city is purified (*lustrō* 1).

mensis, *-is* masc. 3 "month." The months measure (*mētior*, *-īrī*, *mensus sum* 4) the year.

saeculum, *-ī* neut. 2 "century." A century is the longest period that an old man (*senex*, *senis* masc. 3) lives, and one century follows (*sequor*, *sequī*, *secūtus sum* 3) another.

vēr, *vēris* neut. 3 "spring." In spring, vegetation begins to be green (*vireō*, *-ēre*, *viruī* 2) and the season turns (*vertō*, *-ere*, *vertī*, *versum* 3).

Mors Rōmānōrum

Dying Words of the Emperors

The Romans thought it was very important to record a person's final words (*verba novissima*), which would ideally be spoken when he or she was dying in bed at an advanced age, surrounded by their loving family and friends. Amazingly, given what his private and public life was like, Augustus achieved this ideal. He survived bloody wars, first with the assassins of Julius Caesar and then with Antony, as well as a nearly fatal illness early in his reign, dying at the age of 75 in AD 14. On his deathbed, he asked his friends if he had acted his part well in life's play, and then he exhorted his wife: *Līvia, nostrī coniugiī memor vīve ac valē!* "Livia, live mindful of our marriage, and farewell!"

Caligula was assassinated in AD 41: Suetonius reports that "When he was lying on the ground with his limbs twitching and shouting that he was still alive, the rest of the assassins finished him off with thirty more wounds."

Claudius' last words (in AD 54) are not preserved, but a satirical account of his final moments is given by Seneca the Younger: "After he had made rather a loud noise with that part of his body with which he usually spoke more easily [than his mouth; Claudius stuttered], this was his last utterance heard among mortals: *vae mē, putō, concacāvī mē* 'Dear me, I think I've made a mess of myself.' Whether he did or not I don't know; he certainly made a mess of everything else."

Driven to suicide in AD 68, Nero, who thought himself a great singer, musician, actor, and charioteer, lamented: *quālis artifex pereō!* "What an artist I am to be dying!"

In AD 69, just before being killed and beheaded by Otho's soldiers, Galba cried out to his own men, who were deserting him: *quid agitis, commīlitōnēs? ego vester sum, et vōs meī!* "What are you doing, my fellow soldiers? I am yours, and you are mine!"

Otho survived as emperor only a few weeks in AD 69. On the last evening of his life, he said: *adiciāmus vītae et hanc noctem!* "Let us add this night also to life!" He stabbed himself at dawn the next morning.

If it is true that Caligula hastened Tiberius' death in AD 37 so that he could succeed him, this means that all the emperors after Augustus died violently until Vespasian managed to pass peacefully away in AD 79. His last words could not have been wittier: *vae, putō, deus fīō* "Oh dear, I suppose I'm turning into a god." An alternative version makes his final utterance more conventionally Roman: *imperātōrem stantem morī oportet* "It is fitting for a commander to die on his feet."

On the day before his particularly bloody assassination (in AD 96), Domitian predicted that the next day the moon would be blood-red and a deed would be done that would be talked about throughout the whole world. Then, when he scratched an ulcerous wart on his forehead, he said: *utinam hactenus!* "I hope that's as far as it [the bloodshed] goes!"

CHAPTER 25
All Subjunctive Tenses in Subordinate Clauses

So far, you have worked only with main clauses and subordinate clauses requiring the present or imperfect subjunctive. This chapter introduces constructions where the subordinate clauses can use all four tenses of the subjunctive.

Indirect Questions

To begin thinking about indirect questions, compare them to indirect statements, which you studied in Chapter 21:

	Statement	**Question**
Direct	The pig is in Rome.	Where is the pig?
	porcus Rōmae est.	*ubi est porcus?*
Quoted	The farmer said, "The pig is in Rome."	The farmer asked, "Where is the pig?"
	agricola "porcus Rōmae est" inquit.	*agricola "ubi est porcus?" rogāvit.*
Indirect	The farmer said that the pig was in Rome.	The farmer asked where the pig was.
	dixit agricola porcum Rōmae esse.	*rogāvit agricola ubi porcus esset.*

You can see immediately two important differences:

- indirect questions use the subjunctive, not the infinitive

- the subject of the indirect question is in the nominative

In most cases, the main clause introducing an indirect question uses a verb of asking or perception, such as *rogō* 1 "ask," or *sciō* 4 "know." As in English, an interrogative word will usually signal an indirect question. Some examples are:

- *cūr* why
- *num* whether
- *quid* what

- *quis* who
- *quōmodo* how
- *ubi* where

Negative indirect questions use *nōn*, or other negative terms such as *numquam* or *nēmō*.

Here are some examples of simple indirect questions in all the subjunctive tenses.

sciō ubi sint porcī.	I know where the pigs are.
sciō ubi fuerint porcī.	I know where the pigs were/have been.
sciēbam ubi essent porcī.	I knew where the pigs were.
sciēbam ubi fuissent porcī.	I knew where the pigs had been.
agricolam rogābō ubi sint porcī.	I will ask the farmer where the pigs are.
agricolam rogāvī ubi essent porcī.	I asked the farmer where the pigs were.
agricolam rogāveram ubi essent porcī.	I had asked the farmer where the pigs were.

The basic rule for the tenses used with indirect questions is:

- present or perfect in primary sequence

- imperfect or pluperfect in secondary sequence

BUT: indirect questions do not always follow the sequence of tenses as strictly as the subjunctive clauses that you have studied so far. For example:

sciō quid fēcissent porcī.	I know what the pigs had done.
sciēbam ubi porcī semper iacēre ament.	I knew where the pigs always like to lie.

Alternatives in Indirect Questions: Latin Equivalents to "Whether"

If the speaker does not know if something has happened, is happening, or will happen, the indirect question often begins with the particle *num*, equivalent to the English "whether."

nesciō num lupus porcōs interfēcerit.	I do not know **whether the wolf has killed** the pigs.
pastōrem rogābō num lupus porcōs interfēcisset.	I will ask the shepherd **whether the wolf had killed** the pigs.

Of course, in sentences like this, English can use both "if" and "whether," but this is not true of Latin: *sī* is never a possible translation of "whether."

English would also use "whether" in the indirect version of a complex question such as those discussed in Chapter 4:

I do not know whether you love **the sailor or the farmer**.

I do not know whether you love the sailor **or not**.

Latin formulates indirect questions of this type just like their direct equivalents; the only difference (apart from the mood of the verb) is that, in the indirect question, the word for "or not" is not *annōn* but *necne*.

Direct	**Indirect**
nautam amās an agricolam?	*nesciō nautam amēs an agricolam.*
utrum nautam amās an agricolam? Do you love the sailor or the farmer?	*nesciō utrum nautam amēs an agricolam.* I do not know whether you love the sailor or the farmer.
*nautamne amās **annōn**?* Do you love the sailor or not?	*nesciō nautamne amēs **necne**.* I do not know whether you love the sailor or not.

Clauses of Doubting

Expressions such as *dubitō* (1) "I doubt" and its variants, for example, *dubium est* "It is doubtful," are followed by a subjunctive clause, because they are a particular type of indirect question. If the main clause is affirmative, it is introduced by *an* or *num*; if it is either negative or interrogative, it is introduced by *quīn*.

Affirmative main clause	**Negative/interrogative main clause**
dubitō an/num porcus mē amet. I doubt whether the pig loves me.	*nōn dubitō quīn porcus mē amet.* I do not doubt that the pig loves me.
	quis dubitat quīn porcus mē amet? Who doubts that the pig loves me?

All tenses of the subjunctive are used in this idiom. The subjunctive verb in the subordinate clause is rarely negated, but when it is, the negative is *nōn*. Here are a few further examples:

Affirmative main clause	**Negative/interrogative main clause**
dubitat pastor an/num porcī fēlīcēs sint. The shepherd doubts whether/if/that his pigs are happy.	*nōn dubitat pastor quīn porcī fēlīcēs sint.* The shepherd does not doubt that his pigs are happy.
dubitō an/num porcī pigrī sint. I doubt whether/if/that pigs are lazy.	*nōn dubitō quīn porcī pigrī sint.* I have no doubt that pigs are lazy.
dubium erat an/num porcōs interfēcissent lupī. It was uncertain whether the wolves had killed the pigs.	*nōn dubium erat quīn porcōs interfēcissent lupī.* There was no doubt that the wolves had killed the pigs.
dubitāmus an/num lupī in silvam redierint. We doubt that the wolves have gone back into the wood.	*quis dubitāre possit quīn lupī in silvam redierint?* Who could doubt that the wolves have gone back into the wood?

Special meanings of *dubitāre*: In all the sentences above, *dubitāre* means "doubt," but it also frequently means "hesitate." With this meaning, *dubitāre* takes an infinitive.

Caesar Rubicōnem transīre dubitāvit.	*Caesar dubitāvit num bonum esset transīre Rubicōnem.*
Caesar hesitated to cross the Rubicon.	Caesar doubted whether it was a good thing to cross the Rubicon.

Clauses of Fearing

If a verb of fearing would take an infinitive in English, it does so in Latin as well. But if it introduces a subordinate clause, then the verb in the subordinate clause will be in the subjunctive.

Infinitive

morī timeō.
I am afraid to die.

timet pastor in silvam īre.
The shepherd is afraid to go into the wood.

Subjunctive

timeō nē moriar.
I am afraid (that) I am dying.

timet pastor nē porcī in silvam ierint.
The shepherd is afraid (that) the pigs have gone into the wood.

You are used to *ut* introducing affirmative subjunctive clauses and *nē* introducing negative clauses. With verbs of fearing, the rule is exactly the opposite: **nē is used if the clause is affirmative, *ut* or *nē nōn* if it is negative.**

Affirmative

*porcus timet **nē** veniat lupus.*
The pig is afraid that the wolf **IS** coming.

Negative

*porcus timet **ut** veniat pastor.*
The pig is afraid that the shepherd **IS NOT** coming.

This apparent contradiction is explained by the history of the Latin language. Originally, the affirmative clause and the negative clause were two quite different uses of the subjunctive. The *nē* clause was a negative exhortation in response to the fear (*porcus timet; nē veniant lupī!* The pig is afraid; may the wolves not come!). The *ut* clause was a wish in response to the fear (*porcus timet; ut veniat pastor!* The pig is afraid; may the shepherd come!).

This origin explains why clauses of fearing are constructed differently in Latin from indirect statements. English uses the same construction for "I know (that) you love pigs" and "I am afraid (that) you love pigs," but you cannot say "timeō tē porcōs amāre."

Here are some further examples of the basic uses of verbs of fearing:

Affirmative

timeō nē hōc faciat.
I am afraid that he is doing this.

timeō nē hōc fēcerit.
I am afraid that he has done this.

timēbam nē hōc faceret.
I was afraid that he was doing this.

timēbam nē hōc fēcisset.
I was afraid that he had done this.

Negative

timeō ut hōc faciat.
I am afraid that he is not doing this.

timeō ut hōc fēcerit.
I am afraid that he has not done this.

timēbam ut hōc faceret.
I was afraid that he was not doing this.

timēbam ut hōc fēcisset.
I was afraid that he had not done this.

Prōlūsiōnēs

Parse the words in bold.

Cassius et Brūtus cum magnā parte senātūs
nōn dubitāvērunt quīn Caesar **vellet** habēre
imperium rēgāle. diū nē Caesar honōrēs
dīvīnōs **caperet** metuēbant. namque potestās
tālis et ambitiō, Caesar, tam magna movēbant
insatiābiliter mentem ingeniumque tuum, rex
ut **cuperēs** fierī. sed **quae** sibi fāta **parentur**
quis videt aut quō sit moritūrus tempore? certē
territa clāmāvit Calpurnia, Caesaris uxor,
"nē **pereās** timeō!," sed persuādēre **marītō**
nōn potuit, **sēcum** ut tūtus **remanēret**. et illī
"nescīs in magnō Pompeiī, stulte, theātrō
tē peritūrum hodiē?" dīvīnō nūmine mōtus
Artemidōrus ait. sed nōn dubitāvit **adīre**
fātiferumque locum Caesar mortemque ferōcem.

Change the following direct questions to indirect questions by adding the words *puer rogat* **and then translate.**

For example:
quot librōs dē Aeneā scripserat Vergilius?
puer rogat quot librōs dē Aeneā scripsisset Vergilius.
The boy asks how many books Virgil had written about Aeneas.

1. quot librōs dē corporibus transformātīs scrībere vult Ovidius?
2. post duo mīlia annōrum omnia Catullī carmina perdita sunt annōn?
3. quae tria verba dixit Caesar moriēns?
4. quae tria verba dixerat Caesar post victōriam celerrimam?
5. utrum gladiō periit Hannibal an venēnō?
6. Rōmānīs Syrācusās dēlentibus, quid faciēbat Archimēdēs?
7. Rōmānī pontem trans Tiberim aedificātum ōlim dēlēverant?
8. Nerō tōtam urbem dēlēre cōnābitur?
9. cuius ducis magnī corpus capite carēns in lītore iacēbat?
10. cuius ducis dīvitis caput abstulērunt Parthī?

Translate.

1. quis nescit cūr Crassus, Pompeiī Caesarisque socius, exercitum contrā Parthōs duxerit?

2. Crasse, Rōmae tibi manendum est! verēmur omnēs nē tōtī populō Rōmānō exitiō magnō futūrus sīs.

3. quamquam sacerdōs vetus eum monuerat nē pugnāret, exercitum magnum collēgit cum quō rēgem Parthōrum caperet.

4. nēmō scit num sacerdōtis verba audierit necne.

5. metuēbāmus nē Crassus spem malam dīvitiārum ab hostibus rapiendārum habēret.

6. nōn dubium erat quīn deī caelestēs Crassō īrascerentur.

7. Crassus, dux stultitiae maximae, nōn intellegēbat cūr Parthī cum exercitū nostrō pugnāre nollent.

8. hostēs fūgisse sciēbās, Crasse, sed cūr fūgissent nesciēbās.

9. paucōs post diēs mīlitēs Rōmānī aquā egēbant, et timēre incipiēbant nē numquam cum uxōribus līberīsque pāce fruerentur.

10. omnibus equitibus contrā aciem nostram incurrentibus, tam fessī erant Rōmānī ut nescīrent quōmodo tēla hostium āverterent.

11. capite fīliī mortuī hastā mīlitis barbarī impositō, Crassus "dīc mihi quid faciam" clāmāvit "vel quō discēdere possim."

12. ō hominem stultum! omnēs rogant cūr crēdiderīs mortālibus aurī tam avārīs deōs fautūrōs esse.

13. nēmō verēbātur nē Parthī caput Crassī ipsīus auferrent.

14. post Crassī mortem non dubitāvit Caesar maiōrem sibi glōriam petere.

15. quis scit cūr Caesarī longiōrem quam Crassō vītam fortūna dederit?

16. After so many years we cannot know whether Caesar wanted to be king or not.

17. The queen, already dying because of the poison, asked why Augustus had been unwilling to see her.

18. There is no doubt that Tiberius has gone to his little island.

19. Tell me whether Caligula was afraid to sail across the sea or not.

20. Although he was old and sick, Claudius did not hesitate to sail across the sea.

21. Do not ask me so many times whether Nero burned Rome.

22. Do you know who was emperor after Galba but before Vitellius?

23. Do you know how many sons Vespasianus had?

24. Do you know who is Vespasianus' elder son?

25. The Roman people asked why Domitianus had dared to do so many cruel things.

Lectiōnēs Latīnae

Lege, Intellege

The *spolia opīma*

A Roman commander who personally killed an enemy leader in single combat was allowed to dedicate his fallen foe's armor and equipment, the *spolia opīma* ("choice spoils"), to Jupiter Feretrius [the origin of this title was unknown even in antiquity]. Only three commanders actually achieved this feat, the first being Romulus himself, who killed Acron, king of the Sabine town of Caenina.

> hostēs agrōs effūsē vastantēs invādit cum exercitū Rōmulus parvōque certāmine docet vānam sine vīribus īram esse. exercitum fundit fugatque, fūsum persequitur: rēgem in proeliō obtruncat et spoliat: duce hostium occīsō urbem prīmō impetū capit. inde exercitū victōre reductō, ipse cum factīs vir magnificus tum factōrum ostentātor nōn minor, spolia ducis hostium caesī gerens in Capitōlium ēscendit; ibique ea ad arborem dēposuit, simul cum dōnō dēsignāvit templō Iovis fīnēs cognōmenque addidit deō: "Iuppiter Feretrī," inquit, "haec tibi victor Rōmulus rex rēgia arma ferō, templumque hīc dēdicō, sēdem opīmīs spoliīs quae rēgibus ducibusque hostium caesīs mē auctōrem sequentēs posterī ferent." haec templī est orīgō quod prīmum omnium Rōmae sacrātum est. bīna posteā, inter tot annōs, tot bella, opīma parta sunt spolia: adeō rāra eius fortūna decoris fuit.

> —Livy, *Ab Urbe Conditā* 1.10

effūsē adv. over a wide area

certāmen, -inis neut. 3 struggle

obtruncō 1 cut down

pariō, -ere, peperī, partum 3 *i*-stem give birth, produce

1. Romulus took the city in the first onslaught after killing the enemy king: true or false?
2. The shrine of Jupiter Feretrius was the first temple dedicated in Rome: true or false?
3. Anger is a good substitute for actual strength: true or false?
4. What were the enemy doing when Romulus attacked them?
5. On which hill is the shrine of Jupiter Feretrius located?

Ars Poētica

Ovid's *Metamorphōsēs* I
Explain the use of the subjunctive verbs in bold.

1. *nōn metuam certē nē quis tua pectora, Mīnōs,*
   ***vulneret** imprūdens; quis enim tam dūrus ut in tē*
   *dērigere immītem nōn inscius **audeat** hastam?*
   I will certainly not be afraid, Minos, that someone may wound your chest without meaning to; for who is so hardened that he would dare to direct a cruel spear at you, unless he did not know what he was doing?

2.   *moderātius, ōrō,*
   curre fugamque inhibē; moderātius insequar ipse.
   *cui **placeās** inquīre tamen: nōn incola montis,*
   nōn ego sum pastor, nōn hīc armenta gregēsque
   horridus observō. nescīs, temerāria, nescīs
   *quem **fugiās**, ideōque fugis.*
   I beg you, run more slowly, and check your flight; I myself will chase you more slowly. But ask who it is that you please: I'm not a dweller on the mountain, I'm not a shepherd, I'm not a shaggy fellow watching the herds and flocks here. You don't know, you silly girl, you don't know from whom you're running away, and that's why you're running away.

3. *quid **faciat**? **repetat**ne domum et rēgālia tecta*
   *an **lateat** silvīs? pudor hōc, timor impedit illud.*
   What should he do? Should he make his way home to the royal roofs, or should he lurk in the woods? Shame prevents the one course of action, fear the other.

4. *metuitque loquī nē mōre iuvencae*
   ***mūgiat**.*
   And she was afraid to speak in case she mooed like a heifer.

5. *nē **ferar** in praeceps, Tēthys solet ipsa verērī.*
   Tethys herself [the queen of the sea] is accustomed to fear that I may be carried headlong.

Aurea Dicta

1. *cernimus ut contrā vim et metum suīs sē armīs quaeque bestia dēfendat.* (Cicero)
2. *dīcere quō pereās saepe in amōre levat.* (Propertius)
3. *ea rēs vērane an falsa sit, nōn labōrō.* (Aulus Gellius)
4. *incertum est quō tē locō mors exspectet: itaque tū illam omnī locō exspectā.* (Seneca the Younger)
5. *incrēdibile est quam facile etiam magnōs virōs dulcēdō ōrātiōnis abdūcat ā vērō.* (Seneca the Younger)
6. *nēmō est quī sē ōderit.* (Cicero)
7. *nescīs quantīs fortūna procellīs disturbet omnia?* (Seneca the Younger)
8. *nihil est quod nōn consūmat vetustās.* (Cicero)

cernō, -ere, crēvī, crētum 3 discern, see

quisque, quaeque, quidque/ quodque pron., pronom. adj. each

procella, -ae fem. 1 storm

vetustās, -ātis fem. 3 old age

Lūsūs

Thēsaurus Verbōrum

The majority of countries and other large geographical regions in the Roman world have first declension feminine names, which are used in English with little or no change; for example, *Africa, -ae* fem. 1, *Arabia, -ae* fem. 1. Note also the following:

Armenia	Germānia	Libya
Asia	Graecia	Macedonia
Britannia	Hibernia	Palaestīna
Corsica	Hispānia	Parthia
Crēta	India	Sardinia
Eurōpa	Ītalia	Sicilia
Gallia	Iūdaea (= Jūdaea)	Syria

Etymologiae Antīquae

Plants

arbor, -oris fem. 3 "tree." Trees are so called because of their strength (*rōbur, rōboris* neut. 3, which primarily means "oak tree").

asparagus, -ī masc. 2 "asparagus." Asparagus grows on rough (*asper, aspera, asperum*) bushes.

cēpa, -ae fem. 1 "onion." A *cēpa* consists of nothing but a head (*caput, capitis* neut. 3). (The English word "onion" is derived from *ūnus* by a similar thought process.)

flōs, flōris masc. 3 "flower." Flowers flow down (*dēfluō, -ere, dēfluxī, dēfluxum* 3) from trees.

frons, frondis fem. 3 "leaf." Leaves bring (*ferō, ferre, tulī, lātum* irreg.) shoots and shade.

hortus, -ī masc. 2 "garden." Plants arise (*orior, orīrī, ortus sum* 4) in gardens.

legūmen, -inis neut. 3 "vegetable." Vegetables are picked (*legō, -ere, lēgī, lectum* 3) by hand (*manus, -ūs* fem. 4).

liber, librī masc. 2 "bark of a tree." The bark is liberated (*līberō* 1) from the tree.

nux, nucis fem. 3 "nut." Nuts are so called because their juice (at least the juice of walnuts) stains one's skin dark, just as the night (*nox, noctis* fem. 3) turns the air dark, or because the shade and sap from nut trees harm (*noceō, -ēre, nocuī, nocitum* 2) nearby trees.

rādix, -īcis fem. 3 "root." Roots are fixed (*fixus, -a, -um*) with spokes (*radius, -iī* masc. 2) in the earth. This word is the origin of the English word "radish."

sēmen, -inis neut. 3 "seed." Seeds are less than half (*sēmi-*) what they later become.

spīca, -ae fem. 1 "ear of wheat." Farmers sow in hope (*spēs, speī* fem. 5) of a full harvest.

Vīta Rōmānōrum

The *Lex Oppia*

In 215 BC, the year following Hannibal's disastrous defeat of the Romans at Cannae, the *tribūnus plēbis* [representative of the non-aristocratic classes] Gaius Oppius passed a law, the *lex Oppia*, imposing strict limitations on the luxuries and privileges accorded to women. Valerius Maximus, writing in the early first century AD, seems very conservative to us, but the attitudes toward women reflected in his account of the repeal of the *lex Oppia* in 195 probably seemed quite normal at the time.

The end of the Second Punic War [201 BC] and the defeat of Philip of Macedon [at Cynoscephalae in northern Greece in 197 BC] gave Rome the opportunity to adopt a more permissive way of life. At that time the married women dared to lay siege to the house of the Bruti [who were now the *tribūnī plēbis*], who were set to veto the repeal of the *lex Oppia*. The women wanted the law repealed, because it forbade them to wear clothes of more than one color, to own more than half an ounce of gold, or to ride in a vehicle drawn by animals within a mile of the city except when attending sacrifices. They did manage to get the law repealed, after it had been in force for twenty years without a break. The men at that period did not foresee how far-reaching and how pervasive this stubborn passion for unaccustomed finery and audacity in overthrowing laws would be. If their minds had been able to envisage the way in which some new and more wasteful sophistication is added to women's finery on a daily basis, they would have stopped this unrestrained extravagance at the start. But why should I talk any more about women, seeing that the weakness of their minds and the fact that they are debarred from any opportunity for more serious pursuits encourage them to direct all their attention to dressing themselves up ever more elaborately? [Valerius goes on to denounce the decadence of men of high rank and distinguished families who should have known better.]

—Valerius Maximus, *Facta et Dicta Memorābilia* 9.1.3

CHAPTER 26
Variations in the Mood of the Verb I: Conditional Sentences

In almost all the constructions you have met so far that use the subjunctive in subordinate clauses, there is no other possibility: purpose and result clauses, indirect questions, and so on take the subjunctive and nothing else. The only exception has been in relative clauses. Relative clauses of purpose and characteristic take a subjunctive verb, while ordinary relative clauses use the indicative. In this chapter and the next, you will learn more constructions in which the verb may be either indicative or subjunctive according to the intended meaning.

Conditional Sentences

Conditional sentences consist of a main clause, the **apodosis**, and a subordinate clause, the **protasis**. The apodosis is/was/will be/would be/would have been true, if the protasis is/was/will be/had been true.

Protasis	**Apodosis**
If my pigs are happy,	I am happy.
	I will be happy.
If my pigs were not happy,	I would not be happy.
Unless my pigs were happy,	
If I had started pig-farming earlier,	I would have had a happier life.

Notā Bene

"Unless" is just a synonym for "if . . . not." In Latin, the protasis or if-clause can be introduced by *sī, nisi,* or *sī . . . nōn* (if, unless, or if . . . not).

The protasis does not have to come first, either in English or in Latin, but it generally will in the explanations and exercises in this chapter. Latin has six basic types of conditional sentence, easily divided into two groups.

The first three basic types of conditional sentence use indicative tenses in both clauses, because they refer to real or likely events.

	Protasis	**Apodosis**
Simple fact present	**present indicative**	**present indicative**
	sī lupī porcōs meōs interficiunt,	*infēlix sum.*
	If wolves are killing my pigs,	I am unhappy.
Simple fact past	**perfect** or **imperfect indicative**	**perfect** or **imperfect indicative**
	sī lupī porcōs meōs interfēcērunt,	*infēlix fuī.*
	sī lupī porcōs meōs interficiēbant,	*infēlix eram.*
	If wolves killed my pigs,	I was unhappy.
	If wolves were killing my pigs,	I was unhappy.
Future more vivid	**future** or **future perfect indicative**	**future indicative**
	sī lupī porcōs meōs interficient,	*infēlix erō.*
	sī lupī porcōs meōs interfēcerint,	*infēlix erō.*
	If wolves kill/will have killed my pigs,	I will be unhappy.

In the "future more vivid" type, the future perfect option emphasizes that the speaker will be unhappy only after the killing has taken place; the future perfect always refers to an action fully accomplished by a particular point in the future. English uses the **present** tense in this type of conditional expression.

The other three basic types of conditional sentence use the subjunctive in both clauses. The first two refer to events that are not true, and imagine what the consequences would be if they were true. As its name suggests, the future less vivid type is less definite than the future more vivid; it doesn't refer to what <u>will</u> happen if or when particular events occur, but what <u>would</u> happen if they did.

	Protasis	**Apodosis**
Contrary to fact present	**imperfect subjunctive**	**imperfect subjunctive**
	sī lupī porcōs meōs interficerent,	*infēlix essem.*
	If wolves were killing my pigs,	I would be unhappy.
	[But wolves are not killing them]	
Contrary to fact past	**pluperfect subjunctive**	**pluperfect subjunctive**
	sī lupī porcōs meōs interfēcissent,	*infēlix fuissem.*
	If wolves had killed my pigs,	I would have been unhappy.
	[But wolves did not kill them]	
Future less vivid	**present subjunctive**	**present subjunctive**
	sī lupī porcōs meōs interficiant,	*infēlix sim.*
	If wolves killed/were to kill my pigs,	I would be unhappy.
	[But wolves haven't killed them so far]	

Although these six types are the basic constructions, Latin does not always conform to them. As you read more texts you will encounter conditional sentences with different combinations of tenses and forms. For example:

sī lupī porcōs meōs herī interfēcissent, infēlix hodiē essem.	If wolves had killed my pigs yesterday, I would be unhappy today.
sī vīnum nunc bibis, crās labōrāre nōn poteris.	If you are drinking wine now, you will not be able to work tomorrow.
dā mihi flōrēs, sī mē amās.	Give me flowers, if you love me.
cui flōrēs dabō, sī nōn uxōrī meae?	To whom will I give the flowers, if not to my wife?
porcōs meōs interficiant lupī, sī tibi vērum nōn dīcō.	May the wolves kill my pigs, if I am not telling you the truth.
discipulīs librō studentibus fēlix erit magister.	If the students study their book, the teacher will be happy.
discipulīs librō studentibus fēlix fuisset magister.	If the students had studied their book, the teacher would have been happy.

Notice that the last two sentences both use the same ablative absolute, *discipulīs librō studentibus*, literally "(with) the students studying their book" as a substitute for the protasis. In translating this type of sentence, you can only tell which tense to use—"study" or "had studied"—by looking at the apodosis and applying the rule for normal conditional sentences.

sī quis/quī

You learned in Chapter 18 that the most common indefinite pronoun/pronominal adjective meaning "some(one)," "some(thing)" is *aliquis/aliquī*. After *sī* and *nisi* (that is, in conditional sentences), the prefix *ali-* is dropped. For example:

sī quis Rōmam amat, Caesarem interficiet.	If anyone loves Rome, he will kill Caesar.
sī qua puella carmen meum lēgerit, mē amābit.	If any girl reads my poem, she will love me.

The prefix *ali-* is also dropped after *num* ("whether"/"if") and *nē* (for instance, in negative purpose clauses).

pastōrem rogāvī num quis porcōs meōs interfēcisset.	I asked the shepherd whether/if anyone had killed my pigs.
dixit sē pauperem esse, nē cui pecūniam dare dēbēret.	He said he was poor, so that he would not have to give money to anyone.

Notā Bene

You remember from the last chapter that *num* can be translated as "if," but *sī* can never mean "whether."

Prōlūsiōnēs

Parse the words in bold.

1. rex eris, sī rectē **faciēs**. (Horace)

2. pudor sī **quem** nōn flectit, nōn frangit timor. (Publilius Syrus)

3. lībera sī **dentur** populō suffrāgia, quis tam perditus, ut dubitet Senecam praeferre Nerōnī? (Juvenal)

4. sī quis in hōc artem populō nōn nōvit amandī, hōc **legat** et lectō carmine doctus amet. (Ovid)

5. putō multōs potuisse ad sapientiam pervenīre, nisi **putāvissent** sē pervēnisse. (Seneca the Younger)

6. quī stultīs vidērī ērudītī volunt, **stultī** ērudītīs videntur. (Quintilian)

7. maledīcus ā maleficō nōn distat nisi **occāsiōne**. (Quintilian)

8. sī fortūna volet, **fīēs** dē rhētore consul; sī volet haec eadem, fīēs dē consule rhētor. (Juvenal)

9. sī tē ad studia revocāveris, omne vītae fastīdium **effūgeris**. (Seneca the Younger)

10. audē aliquid, sī **vīs** esse aliquid. (Juvenal)

Change the first phrase, clause, or sentence into the protasis of a conditional sentence, with the second clause or sentence as the apodosis, and then translate.

For example:
dā mihi flōrēs! fēlix erō.
sī flōrēs mihi dederis/dabis, fēlix erō.
If you give me flowers, I'll be happy.

1. utinam flōrēs mihi dedissēs! fēlix fuissem.

2. nollem mēcum hīc sedērēs. fēlix essem.

3. Caesare duce, Rōmānī vīcissent.

4. laudandō Augustī statuam, laudābitis ipsum Augustum.

5. pecūniam nullam habentēs, Rōmam nāvigāre nōn possēmus.

6. urbe dēlētā moriēmur omnēs.

7. ō sī consulī potentī abhinc trēs annōs nōn nupsisset pulchra puella! hodiē multō fēlīcior esset.

8. sine armīs pugnandō pereātis.

9. in hostium agmen fortiter currāmus! mortem pulchram merēbimur.

10. magnō numerō stellārum dē caelō cadente mortālēs timeant.

Translate.

1. sī quis dē librīs Sibyllae, mulieris pietāte et annīs gravis, discere cupit, audiat!

2. Tarquiniō, Rōmānōrum rēgī, sacerdōs veterrima "sī mihi aurum dederis" ait ōlim "hōs novem librōs, versibus sacrīs plēnōs, tibi dabō."

3. "nisi sponte abībis" respondet rex "in viam tē ēicient mīlitēs meī."

4. plūra locūta esset sacerdōs sī mīlitēs nōn timuisset.

5. sī crās revēnerit mulier ista vetus, claudite statim iānuam! interdīcite eī nē nōbīscum loquātur.

6. nēmō mentis bonae esse sacerdōtem crēdat sī proximō diē regressa trēs librōs ante oculōs Tarquiniī flammīs det.

7. rogāvit Sibylla num sex tantum librōs eādem aurī cōpiā emere vellet Tarquinius necne.

8. sī sex tantum librī remanent, cūr cōpiam aurī nōn minōrem ā mē petis?

9. quis mihi crēdat sī dīcam sacerdōtem tertiō diē trēs librōs in ignem iēcisse?

10. nunc tandem sacerdōtī aurum dā, librōs omnēs nisi perdere māvīs!

11. sī pecūniam hodiē eī nōn dabis, auxiliō deōrum semper carēbimus.

12. cōpia pecūniae sacerdōtī nunc danda est tam magna quam abhinc duōs diēs, etiam sī sex iam librī periērunt.

13. ō sī Tarquiniō, virō nimis avārō, deī persuāsissent ut prīmō diē pecūniam Sibyllae daret!

14. sī Tarquinius hōc fēcisset, novem librōs in templō positōs nunc legere possēmus.

15. sī hostēs urbī appropinquantur, hōs trēs librōs legendō Rōmānī quid deī caelestēs moneant cognoscunt.

16. Go to the Forum if you want to buy a fat pig.

17. If you see any shepherds in the fields tomorrow, ask them if they know where the wolf's cave is or not.

18. If he did not love his pigs, the farmer would have run away from the wolves' cave.

19. Would he have been so brave if he had seen the wild boar's teeth?

20. Will the citizens hate Caesar if they learn why he crossed the little river?

21. If you have led your legions into Italy in order to become king, you are worse than the barbarians.

22. The sailors would not be leaving the harbor now, sailing through the waves made so rough by the anger of the god himself, if they did not want to return home as quickly as possible.

23. If only I could become a little fish! I would not have to sit for so many days in this slow boat.

24. If you read this poet's greatest work, you will learn about many men and women who are now animals.

25. The god exclaimed to the beautiful girl, "If you run away from me more slowly, I myself will follow you more slowly."

Lectiōnēs Latīnae

Lege, Intellege

Roman Humor

cum ad poētam Ennium vēnisset eīque ab ostiō quaerentī Ennium ancilla dīxisset domī nōn esse, Nāsīca sēnsit illam dominī iussū dīxisse et illum intus esse; paucīs post diēbus cum ad Nāsīcam vēnisset Ennius et eum ad iānuam quaereret, exclāmat Nāsīca domī nōn esse, tum Ennius "quid? ego nōn cognōscō vōcem" inquit "tuam?" hīc Nāsīca "homō es impudēns: ego cum tē quaererem ancillae tuae crēdidī tē domī nōn esse, tū mihi nōn crēdis ipsī?"

—Cicero, *Dē Ōrātōre* 2.276

ostium, *ostiī* neut. 2 doorway

ancilla, *-ae* fem. 1 slave-girl

1. How did Ennius avoid seeing Nasica?
2. How did Ennius know a few days later that Nasica was at home?
3. Why did Nasica think that Ennius ought to believe that he (Nasica) was not at home?

Macrobius (Macrobius Ambrosius Theodosius) was a pagan philosopher and scholar of the late fourth and early fifth centuries AD. The *Sāturnālia* was his most important work, a rag-bag of serious and trivial subjects.

Marcus Cicerō, cum apud Damasippum cēnāret et ille, mediocrī vīnō positō, dīceret "bibite Falernum hōc, annōrum quadrāgintā est," "bene" inquit "aetātem fert." īdem, cum Lentulum, generum suum, exiguae statūrae hominem, longō gladiō accinctum vīdisset, "quis" inquit "generum meum ad gladium alligāvit?" Canīnius Revilus ūnō diē consul fuit: Cicerō dīcere nōn dēstitit "hōc consecūtus est Revilus, ut quaererētur quibus consulibus consul fuerit" et "vigilantem habēmus consulem Canīnium, quī in consulātū suō somnum nōn vīdit."

—Macrobius, *Sāturnālia* 2.3

cēnō 1 dine

Falernum [i.e., *vīnum*] Falernian [i.e., wine], from the region just south of Rome

gener, generī masc. 2 son-in-law

exiguus, -a, -um tiny

accingō, -ere, accinxī, accinctum gird up

alligō 1 tie

consequor, -sequī, -secūtus sum 3 go after, manage

quibus consulibus "in whose consulship"

1. What was Cicero's joke at his son-in-law's expense?
2. Why, according to Cicero, was Caninius such a good consul?

Ars Poētica

Ovid's *Metamorphōsēs* II
Explain the mood and tense of the verbs in bold.

1. *fūmat uterque polus! quōs sī **vitiāverit** ignis,*
   ātria vestra ruent! Atlās ēn ipse labōrat
   vixque suīs umerīs candentem sustinet axem!
   *sī freta, sī terrae **pereunt**, sī rēgia caelī,*
   in chaos antīquum confundimur!
   Both poles [of the world] are smoking! If the fire ruins them, your palace will collapse! Look! Atlas himself is in difficulties and can hardly bear the glowing axle on his shoulders! If the seas, if the earth, if the palace of heaven is perishing, we are being thrown in confusion into primeval chaos!

2. *nisi opem **tulerō**, taurōrum afflābitur ōre*
   concurretque suae segetī, tellūre creātīs
   hostibus, aut avidō dabitur fera praeda dracōnī.
   *hōc ego sī **patiar**, tum mē dē tigride nātam,*
   tum ferrum et scopulōs gestāre in corde fatēbor!
   If I don't bring help, he will be breathed on by the bulls' mouths and will have to fight with his own harvest, enemies created from the earth, or he will be given as cruel plunder to the greedy dragon. If I endure this, then I will confess that I was born of a tigress, then I will confess that I have iron and craggy rocks in my heart! [Medea is about to intervene to save Jason. The "harvest" refers to the soldiers that have just sprung from the earth after he sowed it with dragon's teeth.]

3. *crēde mihī, sī tē quoque pontus **habēret**,*
   tē sequerer, coniunx, et mē quoque pontus habēret.
   Believe me, if the sea held you also, I would follow you, my husband, and the sea would hold me also.

4. *sī tamen haec superī cernunt, sī nūmina dīvum*
   sunt aliquid, sī nōn periērunt omnia mēcum,
   quandōcumque mihī poenās dabis! ipsa pudōre
   *prōiectō tua facta loquar: sī cōpia **dētur**,*
   *in populōs veniam; sī silvīs clausa **tenēbor**,*
   implēbō silvās et conscia saxa movēbō.
   But if the gods above see these things, if the spirits of the gods are anything, if not everything has perished with me, you will pay the penalty to me sometime! I will throw away my shame and speak of what you have done; if I were to be granted the opportunity, I would come to where people live; if I am held shut up in the woods, I will fill the woods and move the rocks that know of your guilt.

5. *tē quoque, Amyclīdē, posuisset in aethere Phoebus,*
   *tristia sī spatium pōnendī fāta **dedissent**.*
   You also, Spartan boy, Phoebus [Apollo] would have placed in the sky, if the sad fates had given space to place you there.
   [*Amyclīdē* is a Greek first decl. voc. sing. masc. Amyclae was a place near Sparta. The boy is Hyacinthus, who didn't become a star but did become a flower.]

Aurea Dicta

1. *contumēliam sī dīcēs, audiēs.* (Plautus)

2. *dēsinēs timēre, sī spērāre dēsieris.* (Seneca the Younger)

3. *longa est vīta, sī plēna est.* (Seneca the Younger)

4. *meam rem nōn cūrēs, sī rectē faciās.* (Plautus)

5. *miserrimum est timēre, cum spērēs nihil.* (Seneca the Younger)

6. *nātūram sī sequēmur ducem, numquam aberrābimus.* (Cicero)

7. *nēmō ab aliō contemnitur, nisi ā sē ante contemptus est.* (Seneca the Younger)

8. *ōderō, sī poterō; sī nōn, invītus amābō.* (Ovid)

dēsinō, -ere, dēsiī, dēsitum 3 cease, stop

Lūsūs

Thēsaurus Verbōrum

Ancient Cities

Alexandrīa, -ae fem. 1	Ephesus, -ī fem. 2	Pergamum, -ī neut. 2
Antiochīa, -ae fem. 1	Herculāneum, -ī neut. 2	Pompeiī, -ōrum masc. 2
Athēnae, -ārum fem. 1	Hierosolyma, -ōrum neut. 2	Rōma, -ae fem. 1
Brundisium, -ī neut. 2	Londinium, -ī neut. 2	Syrācūsae, -ārum fem. 1
Capua, -ae fem. 1	Neāpolis, -is fem. 3	Tarentum, -ī neut. 2
Corinthus, -ī fem. 2	Ostia, -ae fem. 1	Vērōna, -ae fem. 1

Etymologiae Antīquae

Family Members

amita, ***-ae*** fem. 1 "paternal aunt." An aunt is another mother (*alia māter*).

avus, ***-ī*** masc. 2 "grandfather." Grandfathers are advanced in age (*aevum, -ī* neut. 2).

frāter, ***frātris*** masc. 3 "brother." A brother is almost a second self (*ferē alter*).

māter, ***mātris*** fem. 3 "mother." Mothers provide the material (*māteria, -ae* fem. 1) from which children are produced.

mātertera, ***-ae*** fem. 1 "maternal aunt." An aunt is a second mother (*māter altera*).

nepōs, ***nepōtis*** masc./fem. 3 "grandchild." A grandchild is born (*nātus, -a*) after (*post*) one's children. *nepōs* can also mean "spendthrift"; the Romans linked this meaning with the *nepa*, a type of scorpion that is eaten by one of its offspring, just as a spendthrift wastes his father's wealth.

pater, ***patris*** masc. 3 "father." Fathers are so called because it is evident (*pateō, -ēre, patuī* 2) that conception has taken place.

patruus, ***-ī*** masc. 2 "paternal uncle." An uncle is another father (*pater alius*).

soror, -ōris fem. 3 "sister." Sisters, when they marry, go to live apart from (*seorsum* adv.) the family into which they are born.

uxor, -ōris fem. 3 "wife." When a bride first comes to her husband's house, the doorposts are anointed (*ungō, -ere, unxī, unctum* 3). Alternatively, a wife is like a sister (*ut soror*).

Vīta Rōmānōrum

Devising a Massacre

Most people, knowing nothing about warfare, think a victory is more conclusive if they can either trap the enemy in such a tight spot or surround them with so many soldiers that they can find no way to escape. But, when men are trapped, their desperation makes them more daring, and their fear takes up arms when there is no hope. Knowing death to be inevitable, they are keen to die with their comrades. Scipio's view, that the enemy should be given a way out, has therefore been much commended. When an escape route opens up and a whole army decides to run away, they can be cut down like cattle. Their pursuers are in no danger when those who have been defeated turn away from them the very weapons with which they might have defended themselves. The greater the number of soldiers who flee like this, the easier it is to slaughter them. Numbers mean nothing once panic has set in and soldiers are only interested in escaping their pursuers' weapons. On the other hand, soldiers who are trapped, even if weak and few in number, are a match for their enemy precisely because they are desperate and have no alternative.

—Vegetius, *Excerpta Dē Rē Mīlitārī* 3.21

CHAPTER 27

Variations in the Mood of the Verb II: *cum*, *dum*, etc.

cum

The conjunction *cum* is quite separate from the preposition *cum*. The conjunction is used to introduce subordinate clauses. These clauses can be divided into two basic types, **temporal** and **causal or concessive**. In temporal *cum* clauses, *cum* means "when"; in causal or concessive *cum* clauses, it means "since" or "although." The mood and tense used and the context will help you decide which type of *cum* clause you are dealing with.

cum Meaning "When": Temporal *cum* Clauses

As a rule, temporal *cum* clauses that refer to the PRESENT or the FUTURE use the indicative:

cum in agrum eō, porcōs meōs **videō**.	When I go into the field, I see my pigs.
cum in agrum **ībō** [or **ierō**], *porcōs meōs* **vidēbō**.	When I go into the field, I will see my pigs.

Notā Bene

Don't be confused by the fact that English uses a present tense ("I go") in the second example. The reference is to the future, and Latin can only use the future or future perfect here.

Temporal *cum* clauses that refer to the PAST, however, most often use the subjunctive:

cum pastor **dormīret**, *lupī in agrum* **veniēbant**.	When the shepherd was sleeping, the wolves were coming into the field.
cum pastor **dormīret**, *lupī in agrum* **vēnērunt**.	When the shepherd was sleeping, the wolves came into the field.
cum pastor diū **dormīvisset**, *porcōs* **vocāvit**.	When the shepherd had slept for a long time, he called his pigs.

As you can see, the imperfect subjunctive is used when the two past events are simultaneous, but the pluperfect subjunctive indicates that they are consecutive. In certain situations, however, temporal *cum* clauses that refer to the PAST can use the indicative. These situations are

1. To emphasize that the *cum* clause is merely indicating the time that something happened, or what was going on when it happened, with little causal or logical relation between the two clauses.

2. When *cum* means not "when," but "WHENEVER"—that is, regularly and repeatedly. In this case the pluperfect is the tense most often used.

3. When the writer, for whatever reason, wants to make the action or event that is in the *cum* clause more prominent.

Here are some examples of how the indicative might be used in PAST temporal *cum* clauses.

cum pastor **dormiēbat**, *canis stellās* **spectābat**.	When the shepherd was sleeping, his dog was looking at the stars.
cum pastor **dormiēbat**, *canis cum agnīs* **lūsit**.	When the shepherd was sleeping, his dog played with the lambs.
cum discipulī librō bene **studuerant**, *semper fēlix* **erat** *magister*.	Whenever the students studied/had studied their book well, the teacher was always happy.
pastor dormiēbat, cum **aper canem** *interfēcit*.	The shepherd was sleeping, when a boar killed his dog.

cum Meaning "Since" or "Although": Causal or Concessive *cum* Clauses

Clauses in which *cum* means "since" or "although" are actually less complicated than temporal *cum* clauses, primarily because they ALWAYS use the subjunctive. This table presents the most common combinations of tenses in sentences with causal or concessive *cum* clauses.

cum lupī ferōcēs saepe ē silvīs **veniant**, *difficile* **est** *porcōs dēfendere*.	Since fierce wolves often come out of the woods, it is difficult to protect one's pigs.
cum lupī ferōcēs saepe ē silvīs **veniant**, [**tamen**] *pastōrēs porcōs* **dēfendunt**.	Although fierce wolves often come out of the woods, the shepherds protect their pigs.
cum lupī in agrō **essent**, *porcī* **timēbant**.	Since the wolves were in the field, the pigs were afraid.
cum lupī in agrō **essent**, [**tamen**] *porcī nōn* **timēbant**.	Although the wolves were in the field, the pigs were not afraid.
cum lupī porcōs **interfēcissent**, *pastor tristis* **erat**.	Since the wolves had killed his pigs, the shepherd was sad.
cum lupī porcōs **interfēcissent**, [**tamen**] *pastor tristis nōn* **erat**.	Although the wolves had killed his pigs, the shepherd was not sad.

You can see that exactly the same sentence can be interpreted as either CAUSAL (*cum* meaning "since") or CONCESSIVE (*cum* meaning "although"). *tamen*, "however," CAN be used at the beginning of the main clause to make it clear that a sentence is concessive, but it is completely optional. When *tamen* is not present, the only way to decide which of the two meanings is intended is to look at the context. You will remember that *tamen* is an enclitic/postpositive; after a concessive clause, however, it may appear as the first word in the main clause.

If you look back at the examples of past-tense temporal *cum* clauses using the subjunctive, it will be clear that they could also be taken as causal/concessive *cum* clauses. One sentence could then have three possible meanings:

cum pastor dormīret, lupī in agrum veniēbant.	When the shepherd was sleeping, the wolves were coming into the field.
	Since the shepherd was sleeping, the wolves were coming into the field.
	Although the shepherd was sleeping, the wolves were coming into the field.

Logic might make the third possible meaning the least likely, but only context can help you decide definitively.

dum

dum is another conjunction used to introduce subordinate clauses. As with *cum*, its meaning changes, depending on the mood and tense of the verb.

1. *dum* meaning "while"

With this meaning, *dum* always takes the present indicative, even when referring to a past situation. You have to look at the tense used in the other clause in order to decide how to translate the verb introduced by *dum*.

dum in agrō sunt porcī, sub arbore sedet pastor.	**While** the pigs **are** in the field, the shepherd **sits** under a tree.
dum in agrō sunt porcī, sub arbore frīgore fruēbātur pastor.	**While** the pigs **were** in the field, the shepherd was **enjoying** the coolness under a tree.
dum in agrō sunt porcī, arborem cadentem vītāre nōn potuit pastor.	**While** the pigs **were** in the field, the shepherd **was unable** to avoid the falling tree.

2. *dum* meaning "as long as" or "during the entire time that"

With this meaning, both clauses normally use the same indicative tense.

dum Rōmae erant, porcōs nōn vidēbant.	**As long as/while they were** in Rome, they **did not see** their pigs.
dum Rōmae erunt, porcōs nōn vidēbunt.	**As long as/while they are** in Rome, **they will not see** their pigs.

You can see that Latin uses the future tense in the second sentence where English would use the present.

As the translations suggest, the difference between the uses of *dum* in 1 and 2 is slight. In both, it is possible to translate *dum* as "while"; sense 1 refers to a period during which something else happens, and sense 2 emphasizes that it happened throughout the period.

Be careful to distinguish this second use of *dum* from its use to mean "provided that," which will be discussed next. Here we are talking about time exclusively.

3. *dum* meaning "provided that"

With this meaning, *dum* (or *dummodo*) takes the subjunctive, usually the present subjunctive. The negative is *nē*.

dum/dummodo sim tēcum, fēlix erō.	**Provided that I am** with you, **I will be** happy.
dum/dummodo lupī ē silvīs nē veniant, fēlīcēs erunt porcī.	**Provided that the wolves don't come** out of the woods, the pigs **will be** happy.

Of course, you could translate *dum/dummodo* here with "as long as," because English uses that phrase both temporally ("during the entire time that") and to express a condition ("provided that"). To avoid confusion, use a translation that makes it clear you understand the specific context.

4. *dum* meaning "until"

With this meaning, *dum* takes either the subjunctive or, less often, the indicative. With the subjunctive, it implies an intention or an expectation; with the indicative, it refers without any such implication to something that has not yet happened.

domī manēbō dum veniās.	I will wait at home until you come. (i.e., I expect you to come home, and I'll wait until you do.)
pugnāvērunt Rōmānī dum hostēs vīcissent.	The Romans fought until they had conquered the enemy. (i.e., They intended to conquer the enemy, and fought until they achieved their goal.)
deīs displicēbimus dum templum reficimus/refēcerimus.	We will displease the gods until we rebuild the temple. (i.e., We will rebuild the temple; until then, the gods will continue to be angry.)

In this last sentence, notice the use of the present indicative or future perfect indicative in the *dum* clause, where English normally uses the present tense. Latin rarely uses the future indicative in such clauses.

quod

The conjunction *quod* means "because." It takes the **indicative** when the speaker believes that the reason being given is correct. It takes the **subjunctive** when someone else is giving a reason, but the speaker can't guarantee its validity.

*mīlitem dux laudat **quod** fortis **est**.*	The general praises the soldier because he is brave.
*mīlitem dux laudat **quod** fortis **sit**.*	The general praises the soldier because (in the general's opinion) he is brave.
*pastor canibus cibum nullum dedit **quod** pigrī **erant**.*	The shepherd gave no food to his dogs because they were lazy.
*pastor canibus cibum nullum dedit **quod** pigrī **essent**.*	The shepherd gave no food to his dogs because (he felt) they were lazy.

In previous chapters you have met two other words for "because," *quia* and *quoniam*. The distinction between fact and opinion does not apply to them, since they almost always introduce facts, so they almost always take the indicative.

priusquam

The conjunction *priusquam* and its less common synonym *antequam* mean "before." When it is simply a matter of one thing coming before another, **in the present or the past**, the present and perfect indicative are used. When there is an idea of expectation or purpose, whether or not the expected event actually happens, the present subjunctive is used in primary sequence, the imperfect subjunctive in secondary sequence. For example:

Consecutive events	**Expectation/purpose**
*lupōs interficit pastor **priusquam** porcōs in silvās **mittit**.*	*lupōs interficit pastor **priusquam** porcōs **interficiant**.*
The shepherd kills the wolves before he sends his pigs into the woods.	The shepherd kills the wolves before they kill/can kill the pigs.
***priusquam** hostēs impetum **fēcērunt**, deus nōbīs ōmen mīsit.*	***priusquam** hostēs impetum **facerent**, dux portam clausit.*
Before the enemy attacked, the god sent us an omen.	Before the enemy attacked/could attack, the general closed the gate.

If the two events will take place **in the future**, *priusquam/antequam* takes the present indicative or the future perfect indicative. (The future indicative is almost never used in such clauses; compare the use of the present and future perfect with *dum* meaning "until.")

*morī nōn cupiō **priusquam** Rōmam **videō/vīderō**.*	I don't want to die before I see Rome.

Both *priusquam* and *antequam* are often separated into their component parts: the adverb *prius* or *ante* "sooner" and the conjunction *quam* "than." In this case *prius/ante* acts as an adverb in the main clause and *quam* introduces the subordinate clause. Here the *quam* clause must follow the main clause. For example:

> *dux portam* **prius** *clausit* **quam** *hostēs impetum* **facerent.**

> *morī nōn* **prius** *cupiō* **quam** *Rōmam* **vīderō.**

quamquam, quamvīs

The conjunctions *quamquam* and *quamvīs* both mean "although." Originally, *quamquam* took an indicative verb, while *quamvīs* took a subjunctive verb. By the classical period, however, this distinction was becoming blurred, so both conjunctions may be used with either mood, without any effect on the meaning.

Prōlūsiōnēs

Parse the words in bold.

Aenēān Dīdō quod **erat** tam pulcher amābat,
sed, cum rēgīnā quamvīs dux ipse manēre
oblītus **fātī cuperet**, nōn ante voluntās
est explēta Iovis quam condidit altera Troiae
moenia in Ītaliā. "cum **sīs** pulcherrima" dixit
rēgīnae Aenēās, "prohibent mē fāta deōrum
hīc tēcum in magnā **remanēre** diūtius urbe."
cum tamen ā summā Dīdō Karthāginis arce
Aenēae nāvēs sociōsque **vidēret** euntēs,
hās rēgīna precēs **moritūrā** vōce mināsque
plēna **odiī** aeternī furiōsō ē pectore fūdit:
"ō sī tū nostrā tandem **exoriāris** ab īrā,
Hannibal, ut magnum Aenēae scelus **ulciscāris**!"

Change the ablative absolute to a *cum* clause and then translate.

Bear in mind that, in some cases, more than one answer will be possible. For example,

piscibus in arbore summā inventīs, ōmen mīrātī ad templum deī cucurrimus could be rewritten in two ways:

> *cum* *piscēs in arbore summā* **invēnissēmus**, *ōmen mīrātī ad templum deī cucurrimus.*
>
> **Since/when we had found fish** at the top of a tree, we ran to the god's temple, amazed at the omen.
>
> *cum* *piscēs in arbore summā* **invēnerāmus**, *ōmen mīrātī ad templum deī cucurrimus.*
>
> **When we had found fish** at the top of a tree, we ran to the god's temple, amazed at the omen.

Only the first version can mean "since." Both could mean "when," the first as a normal temporal *cum* clause in secondary sequence, the second if the goal is to emphasize the action in the subordinate clause.

1. lupīs in agrōs ingressīs, porcī periērunt turpiter omnēs.
2. lupīs in agrōs ingressīs, pastor porcīque perībunt.
3. Caesare ipsō ante aciem nostram pugnante, hostēs tamen vix superāvimus.
4. Caesare ipsō ante aciem nostram pugnante, hostēs celeriter superābimus.
5. lupīs porcōs rapientibus, pastor in tabernā erat.
6. porcīs raptīs, tam miser erat pastor ut in tabernam īre cuperet.
7. sōle ortō, ad forum nōbīs eundum est.
8. sōle oriente, lupī in spēluncā iacēbant.

Translate.

1. cum amīcīs ad senātum iit Caesar, cum scīret sē illō diē esse moritūrum.
2. dum Rōmānī aliam partem urbis invādunt, ex arce fūgērunt hostēs quod īram mīlitum nostrōrum timērent.
3. ōderat plēbem imperātor iste dēterrimus et ipse odiō omnibus erat.
4. saepe "ōderint dum metuant" magnā vōce clāmābat iuvenis nimis potens.
5. flūmina prius ē campō in collēs recurrerint quam mīlitēs nostrī barbarīs cēdent.
6. quamvīs corporis ingentis essent puerī, cum stultī tum pigrī erant.
7. dummodo pecūniae satis mihi dēs, iter per silvam tibi monstrābō.
8. priusquam in montibus sōlis trēs deās pulchrās vīdit, fēlix erat ille pastor.
9. pastōrī bonō prius moriendum est quam lupī agnōs interficiant.

10. cum pigra sīs, soror cāra, omnēs tē mihi auxiliō futūram esse putant.

11. cum piger non essēs, rogāvērunt omnēs cūr auxiliō mihi nōn fuissēs.

12. Rōmulus frātrem minōrem nātū, nōmine Remum, interfēcit quod rex fierī cuperet.

13. multī deōs immortālēs hominum memorēs nōn esse arbitrantur quod in parte caelī hinc tam procul remōtā vīvant.

14. dum hostium minīs carēbant, fēlīciter vīvēbant cīvēs omnēs, et pauperēs et dīvitēs.

15. nigram mē fateor noctem tenebrāsque timēre, sed (mīrābile dictū!) lūna orta est antequam domum regressī sumus.

16. turba barbarōrum, cum tam fortēs esse videantur, prīmō cōpiārum nostrārum impetū facile fugābitur.

17. cum pedēs tam brevēs habēret, in silvam furtim effūgit aper priusquam agricola eum aspicere posset.

18. nōn prius rūs abībō quam pecūniam mihi det vetus iste miser; hīc nōbīs prope mūrum sedendum est dum iānua aperiātur.

19. cottīdiē deōs pācem tālibus verbīs rogābant: "dummodo sit procul hinc hostis crūdēlis, in ārīs pōnēmus vestrīs ingentia mūnera semper."

20. dum caelum stellās, piscēs dum flūmina habēbunt,
    exitiō porcīs dum lupus asper erit,
noster amor numquam dēlēbitur; aurea iunxit
    mē tibi tēque mihi tempus in omne Venus.
      aureus, -a, -um golden
      iungō, iungere, iunxī, iunctum 3 join

21. When I come to Rome, the moon is always in the sky; when I come to the city tomorrow, I'll be happy because you'll be with us.

22. Whenever he came to Rome, a beautiful city, he always wanted to go to Athens, for he thinks that city is more beautiful than all others.

23. When I was a young man, I went to Rome because I had to fight in Caesar's games.

24. When I was a young man, I was able to drink more wine, and I did not become sick, although I used to sit in the tavern for so many hours.

25. Who will feed my pigs while I am fighting against the Roman legions?

26. As long as the wolves do not kill his pigs, the farmer will become rich within a few years.

27. Although the enemy fought so fiercely, the Romans were able to defeat them very easily, because they had better weapons.

28. I am as sad as I could possibly be, because I know that my pig is unable to sing.

29. Before we sailed across the river, which is almost a hundred feet deep, I saw the farmer's daughter.

30. Before going to Rome, Hannibal had to destroy the Roman army.

Lectiōnēs Latīnae

Lege, Intellege

Hannibal's Military Genius

cum Hannibal Karthāgine expulsus Ephesum ad Antiochum vēnisset exsul, invītātus est ab hospitibus suīs, ut Phormiōnem philosophum, sī vellet, audīret; cumque is sē nōn nolle dixisset, locūtus esse dīcitur homō cōpiōsus multās hōrās dē imperātōris officiō et dē omnī rē mīlitārī. tum, cum cēterī, quī illum audīverant, vehementer essent dēlectātī, quaerēbant ab Hannibale, quid ipse dē illō philosophō iūdicāret: Poenus nōn optimē Graecē, sed tamen līberē respondisse dīcitur, multōs sē dēlīrōs senēs saepe vīdisse, sed quī magis quam Phormiō dēlīrāret vīdisse nēminem. neque mē hercule iniūriā; quid enim aut arrogantius fierī potuit quam Hannibalī, quī tot annōs dē imperiō cum populō Rōmānō omnium gentium victōre certāvisset, Graecum hominem, quī numquam hostem, numquam castra vīdisset, numquam dēnique minimam partem ullīus publicī mūneris attigisset, praecepta dē rē mīlitārī dare?

—Cicero, *Dē Ōrātōre* 2.75–76

Antiochus III (The Great), the Seleucid king of much of western Asia, not to be confused with Antioch (Antiochīa, -ae fem. 1), the city in Syria

dēlectō 1 please, entertain

Poenus, -a, -um Carthaginian

neque mē hercule iniūriā "and not without reason, by Hercules"

dēnique adv. finally, even

mūnus, mūneris neut. 3 gift, duty

1. Where did Hannibal go when he was exiled from Carthage?
2. Did Hannibal speak Greek fluently?
3. What was the subject of Phormio's speech?
4. What was Hannibal's opinion of Phormio?
5. Why did Cicero agree with Hannibal's opinion?

Ars Poētica

Ovid's *Metamorphōsēs* III
Explain the mood of the verbs in bold.

1. *tempus erit, cum dē tantō mē corpore parvam*
   *longa diēs **faciet**, consumptaque membra senectā*
   ad minimum redigentur onus.
   There will be a time when length of days will make me small, diminished from such a large body, and my limbs, used up by old age, will be reduced to very little weight.

2. *quamvīs **sint** sub aquā, sub aquā maledīcere temptant.*
   Although they are under the water, they try to curse under the water. [People turned into frogs.]

3.   *pugnat mollēs ēvincere somnōs*
   *et, quamvīs sopor **est** oculōrum parte **receptus**,*
   parte tamen vigilat.
   He struggles to overcome gentle sleep and, although sleep was let in by some of his eyes, nevertheless he stays awake with others. [The hundred-eyed Argus.]

4. *tālia nēquīquam tōtō Venus anxia caelō*
   verba iacit superōsque movet, quī rumpere quamquam
   *ferrea nōn **possunt** veterum dēcrēta sorōrum,*
   signa tamen luctūs dant haud incerta futūrī.
   In vain Venus anxiously tosses such words about in the whole of heaven and moves the gods above, who, although they cannot break the iron decrees of the aged sisters [the Fates], nevertheless give clear indications of future grief.

5. *prōnaque cum **spectent** animālia cētera terram,*
   ōs hominī sublīme dedit caelumque vidēre
   iussit et ērectōs ad sīdera tollere vultūs.
   Whereas the other animals look down at the ground, he gave an upright face to man and ordered him to see the sky and to raise his countenance directed upward to the stars.

6. *dum **volat**, arsērunt agitātī fortius ignēs,*
   nec prius āeriī cursūs suppressit habēnās,
   *quam Ciconum **tenuit** populōs et moenia.*
   As he [the North Wind] flew, the flames burned more strongly as they were stirred, nor did he check the reins of his flight through the air till he reached the Ciconian peoples and their walls.

7.   *"prius" inquit "in aequore frondēs"*
   Glaucus "et in summīs nascentur montibus algae,
   *sospite quam Scyllā nostrī **mūtentur** amōrēs."*
   Glaucus said, "Leaves will sooner grow in the sea and seaweed on the mountain tops than my love will change while Scylla is safe."

8. *ante retrō Simoīs fluet et sine frondibus Īdē*
stābit, et auxilium prōmittet Achāia Troiae,
quam, cessante meō prō vestrīs pectore rēbus,
*Aiācis stolidī Danaīs sollertia **prōsit.***
Sooner will the Simois [a river near Troy] flow backward and Ide [a mountain near Troy] stand without leaves and Greece promise help to Troy, with my brave heart hesitating to help you in your affairs, than that the intelligence of stolid Ajax should do the Greeks any good.

Aurea Dicta

1. *cum feriant ūnum, nōn ūnum fulmina terrent.* (Ovid)
2. *cum sciāmus nōs moritūrōs esse, quārē nōn vīvāmus?* (Petronius)
3. *difficile est tacēre cum doleās.* (Cicero)
4. *dum vīrēs annīque sinunt, tolerāte labōrēs: iam veniet tacitō curva senecta pede.* (Ovid)
5. *dummodo sit dīves, barbarus ipse placet.* (Ovid)
6. *magis pauper ille est quī, cum multa habeat, plūra dēsīderat.* (Minucius Felix)
7. *magnō mē metū līberābis, dummodo inter mē atque tē mūrus intersit.* (Cicero)
8. *miserum tē iūdicō, quod numquam fuistī miser.* (Seneca the Younger)

feriō, -īre 4 (defective, lacking the perfect system) strike

quārē adv. why

doleō, -ēre, doluī, dolitum 2 grieve

Lūsūs

Thēsaurus Verbōrum

Body Parts I

artēria, -ae fem. 1	windpipe, artery	nāsus, -ī masc. 2	nose
barba, -ae fem. 1	beard	nervus, -ī masc. 2	nerve
costa, -ae fem. 1	rib	oculus, -ī masc. 2	eye
gena, -ae fem. 1	cheek	pilus, -ī masc. 2	(body) hair
lingua, -ae fem. 1	tongue	stomachus, -ī masc. 2	stomach
mamma, -ae fem. 1	breast	tālus, -ī masc. 2	ankle
maxilla, -ae fem. 1	jaw	umbilicus, -ī masc. 2	navel
palma, -ae fem. 1	palm	umerus, -ī masc. 2	shoulder
rūga, -ae fem. 1	wrinkle	bracchium, -iī neut. 2	(fore)arm
spīna, -ae fem. 1	spine	cerebrum, -ī neut. 2	brain
vēna, -ae fem. 1	vein	collum, -ī neut. 2	neck
articulus, -ī masc. 2	joint	cubitum, -ī neut. 2	elbow, forearm
capillus, -ī masc. 2	hair	labium, -iī neut. 2	lip
digitus, -ī masc. 2	finger	mentum, -ī neut. 2	chin
lacertus, -ī masc. 2	upper arm	supercilium, -iī neut. 2	eyebrow
musculus, -ī masc. 2	muscle	tergum, -ī neut. 2	back

Etymologiae Antīquae

ē contrāriō

Ancient people frequently explained the origin of a word by relating it to another word that meant the opposite. This etymologizing principle is associated particularly with Stoic philosophers.

The Romans gave supernatural powers contradictory names: the Fates are called the *Parcae* (*-ārum* fem. 1) because they spare (*parcō, -ere, pepercī, parsum* 3) no one, and the spirits of the dead are called the *mānēs* (*-ium* masc. 3) because they are not at all good (*minimē bonī* [*mānus, -a, -um* being a synonym for *bonus, -a, -um* known to us almost exclusively from etymological discussions of *mānēs*]).

foedus, foederis neut. 3 "treaty." Even though treaties are excellent things, their name comes from the disgusting nature (*foeditās, -ātis* fem. 3) of the pigs sacrificed when they are ratified.

lūcus, -ī masc. 2 "grove." The dense shade of the trees meant that a grove was without light (*lux, lūcis* fem. 3).

lūdus, -ī masc. 2 "school." See p. 348.

lutum, -ī neut. 2 "mud." Mud is dirty, not washed (*lavō, -āre, lāvī, lautum* 1).

mīles, mīlitis masc. 3 "soldier." Soldiers are not soft (*mollis, -e*). Other etymologies were also current: originally each of three tribes sent one thousand (*mille*) men to make up a legion; *mīlitēs* were so called because of their large number (*multitūdō, -inis* fem. 3) or because they ward off evil (*malum, -ī neut. 2*).

sepulchrum, -ī neut. 2 "tomb." Tombs are far from beautiful (*seorsum* [adv.] *ā pulchrō*), or only half- (*sēmi-*) beautiful, because they look fine but are full of bones.

Mors Rōmānōrum

Epitaphs

Funeral inscriptions make up more than two-thirds of the many hundreds of thousands of Latin inscriptions that have survived. Some are so formulaic that they very often appear in abbreviated form, a space-saving and therefore economical device. *STTL* (*sit tibi terra levis* "May the earth be light for you") was especially common. Since spelling in inscriptions is often rather eccentric, it has been standardized in some of the following:

ulterius nihil est morte nec ūtilius.
There is nothing beyond death and nothing more useful.

haec domus aeterna est, hīc sum situs, hīc ero semper.
This is my eternal home, I am placed here, I will be here forever.

mortālēs sumus, immortālēs nōn sumus.
We are mortal, we are not immortal.

Latrō servus annōrum XII ā vīperā percussus septimō diē periit.
The twelve-year-old slave Latro was struck by a viper and died on the seventh day.

deīs inīquīs quī rapuērunt animulam tam innocuam L. Tettī Alexandrī.
To the cruel gods who snatched away the little soul, so innocent, of Lucius Tettius Alexander.

viātor, quod tū es, ego fuī, quod nunc sum, et tū eris.
Passer-by, what you are, I was, what I am now, you also will be.

cāra meīs vixī, virgō vītam reddidī.
mortua hīc ego sum et sum cinis, is cinis terra est;
sīn est terra dea, ego sum dea, mortua nōn sum.
rogō tē, hospes, nōlī ossa mea violāre.
   Mūs vixit annōs XIII.

I lived dear to my family, I gave up my life while still a virgin.
I am dead here and am ashes, those ashes are earth;
but, if the earth is a goddess, I am a goddess, I am not dead.
I beg you, stranger, do not violate my bones.
   Mouse lived for thirteen years.

hospes, quod dīcō paullum est, astā ac pellege.
hīc est sepulchrum haud pulchrum pulchrae fēminae.
nōmen parentēs nōminārunt Claudiam.
suum marītum corde dīlexit suō.
nātōs duōs creāvit. hōrum alterum
in terrā linquit, alium sub terrā locat.
sermōne lepidō, tum autem incessū commodō.
domum servāvit. lānam fēcit. dixī. abī.

Stranger, what I say is little, stand here and read it through.
Here is the unbeautiful tomb of a beautiful woman.
Her parents gave her the name Claudia.
She loved her husband with her heart.
She bore two sons. Of these, she leaves one
Upon the earth, the other she places beneath the earth.
She was elegant in her speech, and graceful in her gait.
She looked after her home. She worked her wool. I have spoken. Go on your way.

CHAPTER 28
Impersonal Verbs

Impersonal verbs do not have a specific subject; instead, their subject is an unidentified "it." Examples in English would be "It is raining," "It upsets me to hear this," "It happens to be a sunny day," "It pleases me that you are here." Impersonal verbs generally use only the third person singular or, occasionally, the infinitive. A small number, however, of the verbs discussed here are also used as personal verbs: for example, *placeō* and *iuvō*.

As in English, impersonal verbs are used to describe the weather:

fulgurat 1	it (there) is lightning
lūcescit, lūcescere 3	it is getting light
pluit, pluere, pluit 3	it is raining
tonat, tonāre, tonuit 1	it is thundering
(ad)vesperascit, (ad)vesperascere, (ad)vesperāvit 3	it becomes evening

Some impersonal verbs refer to feelings, with the person who feels in the accusative:

miseret, miserēre, miseruit 2	it causes pity
paenitet, paenitēre, paenituit 2	it causes regret
piget, pigēre, piguit 2	it causes vexation
pudet, pudēre, puduit 2	it causes shame
taedet, taedēre, taesum est 2 semi-deponent	it causes tedium

With these verbs, the cause of the feeling can be either a noun in the genitive or a verb in the infinitive:

Genitive of the cause	**Infinitive**
hostium nostrōrum mē miseret.	*porcōs meōs abiisse mē miseret.*
I am sorry for our enemies.	I am sorry that my pigs have gone away.
avāritiae tuae tē paenitet?	*paenitet mē hōc fēcisse.*
Do you regret your greed?	I regret having done this.
stultitiae meae piget magistrum.	*mēcum in lūdō sedēre tē piget?*
The teacher is vexed by my stupidity.	Does it irritate you to sit in school with me?
gracilis porcī pudet agricolam.	*hōc facere mē tunc nōn puduit, fēcisse nunc pudet.*
The farmer is ashamed of his skinny pig.	I was not ashamed then to do this, but I'm ashamed now to have done it.
taedet nōs hōrum veterum librōrum.	*taedet nōs in lūdō sedēre.*
We are bored with these old books.	We are bored with sitting in school.

Other impersonal verbs, also expressing a feeling or moral judgment, take the accusative of the person affected, but only with an infinitive:

decet, decēre, decuit 2	it suits, it is fitting
dēdecet, dēdecēre, dēdecuit 2	it disgraces
dēlectat 1	it pleases
iuvat, iuvāre, iūvit 1	it pleases

bonum ducem **decet** *hostibus parcere.*	**It is fitting** for a good general to spare the enemy.
mē **nōn iūvit** *herī ad lūdum īre.*	**It did not please** me to go to school yesterday. I didn't like going to school yesterday.

Other impersonal verbs of feeling and judgment take the dative of the person affected and an infinitive:

displicet, displicēre, displicuit 2	it is displeasing
libet, libēre, libuit 2	it is pleasant
licet, licēre, licuit 2	it is permissible
placet, placēre, placuit 2	it is pleasing
prōdest, prōdesse, prōfuit irreg.	it is beneficial

placet mihi tē vidēre.	I am pleased to see you.
mihi displicuit audīre tē tuum librum nōn attulisse.	I was displeased to hear that you had not brought your book.
tibi prōderit librōs tuōs tēcum ferre.	It will be good for you to bring your books with you.
cūr domum abīre nōbīs nōn licēbit?	Why will we not be allowed to leave for home?

Certain verbs, some of which you have already learned in their regular uses, and some of which are compounds of familiar verbs, can be used impersonally. When they are, they introduce a result clause, and they follow the regular rules for sequence of tenses. Among these verbs are a group that all mean "it happens":

- **accidit, accidere, accidit** 3 a compound of *cadō*
- **contingit, contingere, contigit** 3 a compound of *tangō*
- **ēvenit** a compound of *veniō*
- **fit** the third person singular of *fīō*

Three other common examples are

- **efficitur** 3 *i*-stem   it is brought about
- **restat** 1   it remains
- **sequitur** 3   it follows

Here are examples of how to use these forms in impersonal sentences:

saepe fit ut lupī ē silvā veniant.	It often happens that wolves come out of the wood.
ergō sequitur ut porcī infēlīcēs sint.	Therefore it follows that the pigs are unhappy.
restābat ut pastor lupōs in silvam ageret.	It remained for the shepherd to drive the wolves into the wood.

necesse est and **opus est** mean "it is necessary." They take the dative of the person affected and either an infinitive or a clause, which may or may not be introduced by *ut*. If they introduce a clause, the verb in the clause will be in the present subjunctive in primary sequence, and in the imperfect subjunctive in secondary sequence. **oportet, oportēre, oportuit** 2 "it is proper" takes the accusative of the person affected and either an infinitive or a clause with or without *ut*.

Infinitive	**Subjunctive clause**
nōbīs opus est urbem fortiter dēfendere.	*opus est (ut) urbem fortiter dēfendāmus.*
We must defend the city bravely.	We must defend the city bravely.
nōbīs necesse erat urbem fortiter dēfendere.	*necesse erat (ut) urbem fortiter dēfenderēmus.*
We needed to defend the city bravely.	We needed to defend the city bravely.
pastōrem oportet porcōs pascere.	*pastor porcōs pascat oportet.*
A shepherd should feed his pigs.	A shepherd should feed his pigs.

Notā Bene

opus est can also take an ablative of the thing needed; for example, *opus est mihi librīs multīs* "I need many books."

The words **interest** and **rēfert** mean "it concerns," "it is in the interest of." They introduce either an infinitive or an *ut*-clause with the verb in the present subjunctive in primary sequence, and the imperfect subjunctive in secondary sequence.

For the person designated by *interest*, there are two possible options:

- the genitive
- the ablative feminine singular form of the pronominal adjective: *meā, tuā*, etc.

The genitive is not an option for *rēfert* in Classical Latin. In *meā rēfert*, *meā* modifies *rē*, the abl. sing. of *rēs*. An alternative to *interest* with the genitive, *meā interest*, developed by analogy with *meā rēfert*, even though *meā* has nothing to agree with here.

A subjunctive clause with *interest* or *rēfert* is rarely negative, but, if it is, the negative is *nē*.

With genitive of the person affected	**With abl. fem. sing. of the pronom. adj.**
Caesaris interest hodiē domī remanēre. It is in Caesar's interest to stay at home today.	*tuā interest hodiē domī remanēre.* It is in your interest to stay home today.
cīvium omnium interest ut Brūtus Caesarem interficiat. It is in the interest of all the citizens that Brutus should kill Caesar.	*vestrā rēfert ut Brūtus Caesarem interficiat.* It is in your interest that Brutus should kill Caesar.
Rōmānōrum interest nē Caesar rex fīat. It concerns the Romans that Caesar should not become king.	*nostrā interest, Rōmānī, nē Caesar rex fīat.* It concerns us, Romans, that Caesar should not become king.

As a variation on this idiom, you can use a demonstrative pronoun in the neuter nominative singular to indicate the thing that is of interest. For example:

hōc Caesaris nōn interest. This is not in Caesar's interest.	*hōc meā nōn interest/rēfert.* This is not in my interest.

Here, however, the demonstrative pronoun *hōc* is the subject, so *interest* or *rēfert* is not really impersonal.

fore (*futūrum esse*) *ut . . .*

One way to translate a sentence such as "Caesar knew that our city would be destroyed by the enemy" is to use the future passive infinitive, *dēlētum īrī*:

sciēbat Caesar urbem nostram ab hostibus dēlētum īrī.	(lit. Caesar knew our city to be about to be destroyed by the enemy.)

We saw in Chapter 21, however, that the Romans seem to have avoided using the future passive infinitive. An alternative is the impersonal use of the future infinitive of *sum*, *futūrum esse*, or its indeclinable equivalent, *fore*.

sciēbat Caesar fore/futūrum esse ut urbs nostra ab hostibus dēlērētur.	(lit. Caesar knew that it would be that our city was destroyed by the enemy.)

Here the infinitive is used impersonally to introduce the *ut*-clause, which follows the normal rules for sequence of tenses and negation as if it were a result clause.

The *fore/futūrum esse* construction is also useful in some instances of indirect questions, when the verb is one that does not have a future active infinitive: *nolle*, for example. Here is how the future active infinitive is normally used in indirect questions:

scit pastor porcum agrum relictūrum esse.	The shepherd knows that the pig will leave the field.

But with a verb that has no future active infinitive, you must use *futūrum esse* or, more commonly, *fore*.

scit pastor fore ut porcus agrum relinquere nōlit.	The shepherd knows that the pig will not wish to leave the field. (lit. The shepherd knows that it will be that the pig does not wish to leave the field.)

Impersonal Passive

You remember that intransitive verbs cannot normally be used in the passive. They are used in the passive, however, as a way of referring impersonally to an action that was in fact performed by specific individuals. This idiom, which has no real equivalent in English, is used especially to emphasize the action itself rather than those who do it. For example:

diū pugnātum est.	The fighting went on for a long time. (lit. It was fought for a long time.)
curritur ex omnibus partibus urbis.	People come running from all parts of the city. (lit. It is run from all parts of the city.)
post multōs diēs Rōmam ventum est.	Rome was reached after many days. (lit. It was come to Rome after many days.)

An impersonal use of the passive is also a way of getting around the normal rule by which intransitive verbs that take a dative or ablative can't be used passively.

You remember that when a transitive verb is put into the passive, the direct object becomes the subject, while the subject becomes an agent in the ablative:

Active	**Passive**
porcōs agricola amat.	*porcī ab agricolā amantur.*
The farmer loves the pigs.	The pigs are loved by the farmer.

However, if the verb is intransitive and takes, say, a dative of reference instead of an accusative, this simple switch is not possible. Instead, you must use the passive verb impersonally. There is no subject; the person or thing affected by the action remains in the dative, and a personal agent is expressed with *ā/ab* and the ablative.

Active	Passive
porcīs agricola parcit.	*parcitur porcīs ab agricolā.*
The farmer spares the pigs.	The pigs are spared by the farmer. (lit. It is spared to the pigs by the farmer.)
porcīs parcis.	*parcitur porcīs ā tē.*
You spare the pigs.	The pigs are spared by you. (lit. It is spared to the pigs by you.)
nautae pīrātīs resistunt.	*pīrātīs resistitur ā nautīs.*
The sailors resist the pirates.	The pirates are resisted by the sailors. (lit. It is resisted to the pirates by the sailors.)
mihi numquam persuādēbit dominus crūdēlis ut hōc faciam.	*mihi numquam ā dominō crūdēlī persuādēbitur ut hōc faciam.*
My cruel master will never persuade me to do this.	I will never be persuaded by my cruel master to do this. (lit. It will never be persuaded to me by my cruel master that I should do this.)

As this impersonal passive construction is somewhat complicated, it is not surprising that the active construction is much more common.

Prōlūsiōnēs

Parse the words in bold.

1. quae nōn puduit ferre, **tulisse** pudet. (Ovid)
2. aliter cum tyrannō, aliter cum amīcō **vīvitur**. (Cicero)
3. mē ipsum **amēs** oportet, nōn mea, sī vērī amīcī futūrī sumus. (Cicero)
4. nōn semper **mihi** licet dīcere "nōlō." (Seneca the Younger)
5. tempus erit, quō **vōs** speculum vīdisse pigēbit. (Ovid)
6. incertum est quam longa cuiusque **nostrum** vīta futūra sit. (Cicero)
7. an quisquam est alius līber, nisi dūcere vītam **cui** licet ut libuit? (Persius)
8. noscere hōc prīmum decet, quid facere victor **dēbeat**, victus patī. (Seneca the Younger)
9. pudeat illōs quī ita in studiīs sē abdidērunt, ut ad vītam commūnem nullum fructum prōferre **possint**. (Cicero)
10. praeferre patriam līberīs **rēgem** decet. (Seneca the Younger)

Translate (as a review of the various uses of the subjunctive).

tam magnī sunt hippopotamī ut crocodīlī eīs exitiō nōn possint esse, sed in flūmine opus est remaneant ut muscās vītent. saepe fit ut "crocodīlī stultī mihi nocēre cōnentur!" vōciferent. "magis mihi displiceant (mīrābile dictū!), sī minōrēs sint. sī tam parvī fuissent quam hae muscae, ē flūmine fūgissem. cum tam magnus sim, nōn timeō nē mē pungant crocodīlī. muscās tamen timeō, cum tam parvae sint. dummodo in flūmine maneam, nōn potest fierī ut mē pungant. sī nōn abierint muscae, quōmodo ē flūmine exīre poterō? num eās iuvat mē pungere quod piger pinguisque sim? nēmō mihi persuādeat ut aquam relinquam, nam nōn dubium est quīn futūrum sit ut multa vulnera parva patiar. ē flūmine alium hippopotamum mittam oportet quī muscās interficiat. utinam pennās habeam, nam tum muscās sequar. nesciō cūr abīre nōlint. ē flūmine exīre timeō, et vereor ut aquam relinquere possim. muscae, nōn crocodīlī, sunt animālia quae timeam. cum muscae abierint, herbā dulcī pascar. sequitur ergō, muscae, ut vōbīs imperem ut abeātis. capitī meō nē laeserītis! maneamne ego in flūmine dum vōbīs placeat abīre?"

Translate.

1. sī quis erit quī nesciat quid dē Aenēā scrīpserit Vergilius, ad mea verba animum breve tempus vertat oportet!

2. in prīmō librō, Iuppiter fīliae suae, Venerī, pollicētur fore ut Rōmānīs imperium sine fīne det.

3. in secundō, dum advesperascit, Troiānīs libet omnibus vīnum bibere; arbitrantur enim nōn opus esse moenia urbis dēfendant.

4. in tertiō, sociōrum tuōrum, Aenēā, nōs miseret per mare tam diū frustrā nāvigantium.

5. in quartō, rēgīnam novae urbis, Karthāginis, tantō amōre arsisse paenitet.

6. in quīntō, per celebrēs lūdōs et mūnera magna necesse est exsequiīs patris fungātur fīlius.

7. in sextō, per tenebrās tristēs perque alta silentia noctis ītur in Ēlysium.

8. in septimō, Latīnus, rex Latīnōrum, negat fīliam Turnō, rēgī Rutulōrum, nuptūram esse, et sequitur ut Rutulī cum Troiānīs pugnent.

9. in octāvō, quae dē scūtō Aenēae narrāvit poēta quem nōn iuvet audīre?

10. in nōnō, mē pudeat sī nihil dē Nīsō Euryalōque referam.

11. tum fit ut in decimō puer audax, nōmine Pallās, tristia Troiānōs moritūrus in arma sequātur.

12. in undecimō, ācriter pugnātur neque Troiānōrum rēfert Camillae, puellae cum fortī tum volucrī, resistere.

13. in duodecimō, restat ut mortem Turnī narret Vergilius.

14. multōs dēlectat dē ultimīs ultimī librī versibus verba multa perdere, sed nēminī prōsit dē morte aut Turnī aut Vergiliī ipsīus querī.

15. omnēs Vergiliī carmen decet admīrārī.

16. Many months ago, it was a pleasure for the students to give food to the teacher's pig, for they had never been in the countryside and wanted to learn the habits of pigs and of the other animals.

17. I think some students are sorry now that they promised to feed the pig every day.

18. While it rained and thundered, they had to go to the field, and soon it turned out that no one was whispering softly to the pig.

19. Surely it's a disgrace for a teacher to be reading a book under a tree while all the students are feeding the greedy pig and fighting against wolves?

20. What would happen if there were lightning while we drove the pig back home?

21. If only the wolves would carry off our teacher's pig, for it bores me to stay with it in the field all day.

22. I should open the gate, for the pig might perhaps like to run into the forest and play with the wolves.

23. I don't think it's in the pig's interest to live near the teacher's garden, for there's no doubt that within a few days it'll be taken to the Forum.

24. In the Forum, many people would admire the pig so much that they would not be ashamed to buy the huge animal for a large amount of gold.

25. Soon, pig, you will regret coming to the city!

Lectiōnēs Latīnae

Lege, Intellege

War with the Germans

aciē triplicī īnstitūtā et celeriter VIII mīlium itinere cōnfectō, prius ad hostium castra pervēnit Caesar quam quid agerētur sentīre possent Germānī, quī perterritī sunt et celeritāte adventūs nostrī et discessū suōrum. mīlitēs nostrī in castra irrūpērunt. quō locō quī celeriter arma capere potuērunt paulisper nostrīs restitērunt atque inter carrōs impedīmentaque proelium commīsērunt; at reliqua multitūdō puerōrum mulierumque (nam cum omnibus suīs domō excesserant et Rhēnum trānsierant) passim fugere coepit, contrā quōs Caesar equitātum mīsit. Germānī post tergum clāmōre audītō, cum suōs interficī vidērent, armīs abiectīs et signīs mīlitāribus relictīs sē ex castrīs ēiēcērunt, et cum ad cōnfluentem Mosae et Rhēnī pervēnissent, reliquā fugā dēspērātā, magnō numerō interfectō, reliquī sē in flūmen praecipitāvērunt atque ibi timōre, lassitūdine, vī flūminis oppressī periērunt. nostrī ad ūnum omnēs incolumēs, perpaucīs vulnerātīs, ex tantī bellī timōre sē in castra recēpērunt. Caesar eōs quōs in castrīs retinuerat dīmīsit. at illī, supplicia cruciātūsque Gallōrum veritī, quōrum agrōs vexāverant, remanēre sē apud eum velle dīxērunt. hīs Caesar lībertātem concessit.

—Caesar, *Dē Bellō Gallicō* 4.14–15

carrus, -ī masc. 2 waggon

tergum, -ī neut. 2 back

ad ūnum "to a man"

supplicium, -iī neut. 2 punishment

1. What frightened the Germans when Caesar arrived at their camp?
2. Had the Germans left their wives and children on the other side of the Rhine?
3. How far did Caesar's army march to attack the German camp?
4. How many of Caesar's men were killed in this attack?
5. Why did the German survivors wish to stay with Caesar?

Ars Poētica

Ovid's *Metamorphōsēs* IV
Explain the function of the words in bold.

1. *quid **mihi** fingere prōdest?*
   What good does it do me to pretend?

2. *mors mihi mūnus erit; decet haec dare dōna **novercam**.*
   Death will be a gift to me; it befits a mother-in-law to give me these gifts. [Hercules complaining about Juno's cruelty.]

3. *mē miseram, quod nōn nascī **mihi** contigit illīc!*
   Poor me, that I did not have the luck to be born there!

4. *pudet haec opprōbria nōbīs*
   *et dīcī **potuisse** et nōn potuisse refellī.*
   It's a shame that these insults could be said to us and could not be refuted.

5. *nec prōfuit **hydrae***
   crescere per damnum gemināsque resūmere vīrēs.
   It did the hydra no good that it increased and gathered double strength through the harm it suffered.

6. *"terrās licet" inquit "et undās*
   ***obstruat**: et caelum certē patet; ībimus illāc:*
   *omnia **possideat**, nōn possidet āera Mīnōs."*
   "He can block the land and the waves," he said: "the sky also certainly lies open; we'll go that way: Even if he possesses everything, Minos [the king of Crete] does not possess the air."

7.
       iuvat esse sub undīs
et modo tōta cavā summergere membra palūde,
*nunc **prōferre** caput, summō modo gurgite nāre.*
It pleases them [people changed into frogs] to be under the waves and sometimes to submerge their limbs entirely in the hollow marsh, now to raise their heads out, sometimes to swim on top of the whirling water.

8. *paenituit iūrasse **patrem**: quī terque quaterque*
concutiens illustre caput "temerāria" dixit
*"vox mea facta tuā est; utinam prōmissa **licēret***
nōn dare! confiteor, sōlum hōc tibi, nāte, negārem.
dissuādēre licet: nōn est tua tūta voluntās!
magna petis, Phaethōn, et quae nec vīribus istīs
mūnera conveniant nec tam puerīlibus annīs:
sors tua mortālis, nōn est mortāle, quod optās.
plūs etiam, quam quod superīs contingere possit,
*nescius affectās; **placeat** sibi quisque licēbit,*
nōn tamen igniferō quisquam consistere in axe
mē valet exceptō; vastī quoque rector Olympī,
quī fera terribilī iaculātur fulmina dextrā,
*nōn **agat** hōs currūs: et quid **Iove** maius habēmus?"*
His father [Phaethon's father, the sun god] was sorry he had sworn: shaking his distinguished head three or four times, he said, "My voice has been made rash by yours; if only I could not give my promises! I admit, this would be the only thing that I'd deny you, my son. I can dissuade you: your wish is not a safe one! You seek great things, Phaethon, and gifts such as do not suit that strength of yours nor your years that are so boyish: your fate is mortal, what you wish for is not mortal. In your ignorance, you aim for even more than could be given to the gods above; even if everyone pleases himself, nevertheless no one except me is strong enough to stand in the fire-bearing chariot. Even the ruler of vast Olympus, who hurls his fierce lightning bolts with his terrible right hand, could not drive this chariot: and what do we have that is greater than Jupiter?

Aurea Dicta

1. *ā rectā conscientiā nōn oportet discēdere.* (Cicero)
2. *alterī vīvās oportet, sī tibi vīs vīvere.* (Seneca the Younger)
3. *cui peccāre licet, peccat minus.* (Ovid)
4. *dixisse mē aliquandō paenituit, tacuisse numquam.* (Valerius Maximus)
5. *lēgem brevem esse oportet quō facilius ab imperītīs teneātur.* (Seneca the Younger)
6. *mē nōn sōlum piget stultitiae meae, sed etiam pudet.* (Cicero)
7. *miseret tē aliōrum, tuī nec miseret nec pudet.* (Plautus)
8. *necesse est facere sumptum, quī quaerit lucrum.* (Plautus)

imperītus, -a, -um inexperienced

sumptus, -ūs masc. 4 expenditure

Lūsūs

Thēsaurus Verbōrum

Body Parts II

artus, -ūs masc. 4	limb	manus, -ūs fem. 4	hand
auris, -is fem. 3	ear	nārēs, nārium fem. 3	nose
calx, calcis fem. 3	heel	ōs, ōris neut. 3	mouth
caput, capitis neut. 3	head	os, ossis neut. 3	bone
cervix, cervīcis fem. 3	(nape of the) neck	pectus, pectoris neut. 3	chest
cor, cordis neut. 3	heart	pellis, -is fem. 3	skin
crūs, crūris neut. 3	leg	pēs, pedis masc. 3	foot
dens, dentis masc. 3	tooth	pollex, -icis masc. 3	thumb
faciēs, -iēī fem. 5	face	pulmō, pulmōnis masc. 3	lung
femur, feminis neut. 3	thigh	rēnēs, rēnium masc. 3	kidneys
frons, frontis fem. 3	forehead	sanguis, sanguinis masc. 3	blood
genū, -ūs neut. 4	knee	unguis, -is masc. 3	finger-nail
iecur (= *jecur*), iecoris neut. 3	liver	venter, ventris masc. 3	belly
inguen, -inis neut. 3	groin	viscera, viscerum neut. 3	entrails
latus, lateris neut. 3	side	vultus, -ūs masc. 4	face

Etymologiae Antīquae

Parallel Etymologizing

Some Latin etymologies are matched in Greek, the only other language of consequence to the Romans, even when the words in the two languages are themselves quite different. In some cases, this will be coincidental, but often the existence of the Greek etymology may be supposed to have inspired the Latin one.

caelebs, caelibis masc. 3 "bachelor." Unmarried men live a life like that of the celestial gods (*caeles, -itis* masc. 3). Similarly, the Greeks linked the term for a young unmarried man, ἠΐθεος (*eïtheos*), to the word for god, θεός (*theos*).

Dīs, Dītis masc. 3. The god of the Underworld is rich (*dīves, dīvitis*) because all things arise from the earth and return to it. Similarly, the Greek god of the Underworld, Πλούτων (*Ploutōn*), was also linked with wealth, πλοῦτος (*ploutos*).

Līber, Līberī masc. 2. The god of wine frees (*līberō* 1) us from our cares. Similarly, the Greek god of wine, Bacchus, was also known as Lyaios (from λύειν [*luein*] "release").

lūdus, -ī masc. 2 "school." By the standard etymological technique of explaining a word in terms of its opposite (*ē contrāriō*; see the etymology section in Chapter 27), the Romans defined a school as a place where one is *not* allowed to play (*lūdo, -ere, lūsī, lūsum* 3). The Greeks similarly used the same word, σχολή (*schole*), for both "leisure" and "school."

Mars, Martis masc. 3. Wars are fought by men (*mās, maris* masc. 3). Similarly, the Greek god of war, Ares, was associated especially with men, ἄρσενες (*arsenes*).

mundus, -ī masc. 2 "universe." The universe is arranged in an elegant (*mundus, -a, -um*) manner. Similarly, the Greeks used the same term, κόσμος (*kosmos*), for the universe and for elegance (hence our word "cosmetics").

Thunderbolts in three languages: The general Scipio the Elder, called "Africanus," defeated Hannibal decisively at Zama in 202 BC, and his adopted son Scipio Aemilianus destroyed Carthage in 146. At *Aeneid* 6.842, Virgil describes the two Scipios as *duo fulmina bellī*, which means "two thunderbolts of war," implying a favorable contrast with Hannibal, whose family name, Barca, means "thunderbolt" in Punic. Another layer in this etymological play comes from the fact that σκηπτός (*skeptos*), which sounds like *Scīpiō*, means "thunderbolt" in Greek.

virtūs, virtūtis fem. 3 and the Greek term ἀρετή (*arete*) are used predominantly of correct moral behavior (as our word "virtue" suggests). The original meaning of both words, however, is "bravery," that is, behaving like a *vir* or an ἄρσην (*arsen* "man"), both words for the male gender, not for human beings.

Vīta Rōmānōrum

Pompeian Graffiti

More than two thousand inscriptions have been discovered in the ruins of Pompeii. They allow us a glimpse into the inhabitants' ordinary life, which was suddenly terminated by the eruption of Vesuvius on August 24 and 25, AD 79: lovers' scribblings, election slogans, advertisements for games, and so on. Since abbreviation and unorthodox spelling are especially common in graffiti, some of the following have been expanded and standardized:

Vibius Restitutus hīc sōlus dormīvit et Urbānam suam dēsīderābat.
Vibius Restitutus slept alone here, and pined for his darling Urbana.

Restitutus multās dēcēpit saepe puellās.
Restitutus has often deceived many girls.

Cestilia, rēgīna Pompeiānōrum, anima dulcis, valē.
Farewell, Cestilia, queen of the Pompeians, sweet soul.

Marcus Spendūsam amat.
Marcus loves Spendusa.

Cornēlia Helena amātur ab Rūfō.
Cornelia Helena is loved by Rufus.

Marcellus Praenestīnam amat et nōn cūrātur.
Marcellus loves a girl from Praeneste and is ignored.

Staphylus hīc cum Quiētā.
Staphylus (was) here with Quieta.

Samius Cornēliō: suspendere.
Samius to Cornelius: go hang yourself!

Virgula Tertiō suō: indecens es.
Virgula to her darling Tertius: you're disgusting.

suspīrium puellārum Celadus Thrax.
Celadus the Thracian [gladiator] for whom all the girls sigh.

Eutychis Graeca assibus II mōribus bellīs.
Eutychis, a Greek girl, two cents, nice character.

C. Iūlium Polybium IIvirum mūliōnēs rogant.
The mule-drivers ask [you to elect] Gaius Julius Polybius as *duovir* [one of the chief magistrates].

miximus in lectō; fateor, peccāvimus, hospes.
　　sī dīcēs "quārē?," nulla matella fuit.
I [lit. we] have wet the bed; I confess, I [lit. we] have done wrong, innkeeper.
　　If you ask "Why?" there was no chamber pot.

Decimī Lucrētī Satrī Valentis flāminis gladiātōrum paria decem pugnābunt.
Ten pairs of gladiators owned by the priest Decimus Lucretius Satrius Valens will fight.

N[umerius] *POPIDIVS N*[umeriī] *F*[īlius] *CELSĪNVS | AEDEM ĪSIDIS TERRAE MŌTŪ CONLAPSAM | Ā FVNDĀMENTŌ P*[ecūniā] *S*[uā] *RESTITVIT. HVNC DĒCVRIŌNĒS OB LĪBERĀLITĀTEM | CVM ESSET ANNŌRVM SEX ORDINĪ SVŌ GRĀTĪS ADLĒGĒRVNT.*

Numerius Popidius Celsinus, son of Numerius, restored the temple of Isis from the ground up at his own expense, after it had been destroyed by an earthquake. In consideration of his generosity, the Town Council inducted him into their order without charge when he was six years old. [He presumably had parental encouragement.]

APPENDIX 1
Latin Readings

It is important to gain confidence in Latin pronunciation as soon as possible, for correct pronunciation will make learning the language much easier. The recordings online (www.hackettpublishing.com/classicallatin) are designed to help you achieve this.

Latin is an unusually simple language to pronounce correctly (largely because we do not know how the Romans actually spoke their language, and correctness of pronunciation is therefore inevitably determined to some extent by familiar modern conventions). Before listening to the recordings, you may wish to read through the section on pronunciation in the Introduction. It will, however, be sufficient to bear a few basic principles in mind as you listen:

- long vowels are indicated in the transcript by a superscript macron (-)
- *c* and *g* are always hard
- *h* at the beginning of a word is always pronounced
- *i* is sometimes a consonant, pronounced as a *y*
- *v* is pronounced as a *w*
- Latin is easy to pronounce

As you listen, concentrate on the sound of Latin, and, at least to begin with, do not pay any attention to the meaning. You will see some of these sentences again, as you work through the course, when they will be used to illustrate specific points of grammar.

Verba Rōmānōrum 1 (Words of the Romans 1)

1. **carpe diem, quam minimē crēdula posterō.** (Horace)
   Enjoy the day, trusting as little as possible in the next.

2. **vēnī, vīdī, vīcī.** (Caesar)
   I came, I saw, I conquered.

3. **omnia vincit amor.** (Virgil)
   Love conquers all things.

4. **labor omnia vincit improbus.** (Virgil)
   Unremitting labor conquers all things.

5. **aliud agendī tempus, aliud quiescendī.** (Cicero)
   There is one time for action, another for resting.

6. **alterī vīvās oportet, sī tibi vīs vīvere.** (Seneca the Younger)
   You should live for another person, if you wish to live for yourself.

7. **bonum ex malō nōn fit.** (Seneca the Younger)
   Good does not arise out of evil.

8. **confessiō conscientiae vox est.** (Seneca the Elder)
   Confession is the voice of conscience.

9. **corpora nostra lentē augescunt, cito exstinguuntur.** (Tacitus)
   Our bodies grow slowly, but they are quickly extinguished.

10. **disce legendō.** (Ps.-Cato)
    Learn by reading.

11. **dīves quī fierī vult, et cito vult fierī.** (Juvenal)
    A person who wishes to become rich also wishes to become rich quickly.

12. **doctrīna est fructus dulcis rādīcis amārae.** (Ps.-Cato)
    Learning is a sweet fruit with a bitter root.

13. **effugere nēmō id potest quod futūrum est.** (Cicero)
    No one can escape what is going to happen.

14. **ēmit morte immortālitātem.** (Quintilian)
    He bought immortality through his death.

15. **facile vincere nōn repugnantēs.** (Cicero)
    It is easy to defeat those who do not fight back.

16. **fāta regunt hominēs.** (Juvenal)
    The fates rule mankind.

17. **fortūna opēs auferre potest, nōn animum.** (Seneca the Younger)
    Fortune can take away our wealth, but not our spirit.

18. **frequens imitātiō transit in mōrēs.** (Quintilian)
    Frequent imitation passes into habit.

19. **hōc ūnum certum est, nihil esse certī.** (Seneca the Younger)
    This one thing is certain, nothing is certain.

20. **hominēs vitia sua et amant simul et ōdērunt.** (Seneca the Younger)
    People both love and hate their own flaws at the same time.

21. **in rēbus dubiīs plūrimī est audācia.** (Publilius Syrus)
    In uncertain matters, boldness is worth the most.

22. **inhūmānum verbum est ultiō.** (Seneca the Younger)
    Vengeance is an inhuman word.

23. **iniūriam (= *injūriam*) quī factūrus est iam fēcit.** (Seneca the Younger)
    A person who is going to commit an injury has already done so.

24. **intemperantia omnium perturbātiōnum māter est.** (Cicero)
    Intemperance is the mother of all derangements.

25. **īra odium generat, concordia nūtrit amōrem.** (Ps.-Cato)
    Anger generates hatred, but harmony fosters love.

26. **longa est vīta, sī plēna est.** (Seneca the Younger)
    Life is long, if it is full.

27. **maximum remedium īrae mora est.** (Seneca the Younger)
    Delay is the greatest remedy for anger.

28. **meliōra sunt ea quae nātūrā quam illa quae arte perfecta sunt.** (Cicero)
    What has been accomplished by nature is better than what has been accomplished by artifice.

29. **multa sunt quae ego nescīre mālō.** (Cicero)
    There are many things which I prefer not to know.

30. **multī mentiuntur ut dēcipiant, multī quia dēceptī sunt.** (Seneca the Younger)
    Many people lie in order to deceive, many because they have been deceived.

31. **mūtārī fāta nōn possunt.** (Cicero)
    The fates cannot be altered.

32. **nātūrā homō mundum et ēlegans animal est.** (Seneca the Younger)
    By nature, man is a neat and elegant animal.

33. **nātūrae iūra (= *jūra*) sacra sunt etiam apud pīrātās.** (Seneca the Elder)
    The laws of nature are sacred even among pirates.

34. **nātūrāle est magis nova quam magna mīrārī.** (Seneca the Younger)
    It is natural to admire new things more than great things.

35. **nāvis quae in flūmine magna est in marī parvula est.** (Seneca the Younger)
    A ship which is big in a river is tiny in the sea.

36. **nē damnent quae nōn intellegunt.** (Quintilian)
    People should not criticize what they do not understand.

37. **nēminem pecūnia dīvitem fēcit.** (Seneca the Younger)
    Money has made no one rich.

38. **nēmō adeō ferus est ut nōn mītescere possit.** (Horace)
    No one is so savage that he cannot become mild.

39. **nihil agendō hominēs male agere discunt.** (Columella)
    By doing nothing, people learn to act badly.

40. **nihil sibi quisquam dē futūrō dēbet prōmittere.** (Seneca the Younger)
    No one should promise himself anything about the future.

41. **nōlīte velle quod fierī nōn potest.** (Cicero)
    Do not wish for what cannot happen.

42. **nōn ut diū vīvāmus cūrandum est, sed ut satis.** (Seneca the Younger)
    We should not worry about living for a long time, but about living sufficiently.

43. **num, tibi cum faucēs ūrit sitis, aurea quaeris pōcula?** (Horace)
    When thirst is burning your throat, you don't demand golden cups, do you?

44. **numquam temeritās cum sapientiā commiscētur.** (Cicero)
    Rashness is never combined with wisdom.

45. **nusquam est quī ubīque est.** (Seneca the Younger)
A person who is everywhere is nowhere.

46. **ōdērunt peccāre bonī virtūtis amōre.** (Horace)
Good people shun wrongdoing because of their love of virtue.

47. **omnēs hominēs aut līberī sunt aut servī.** (Justinian's *Dīgestā*)
Everyone is either free or a slave.

48. **omnēs sē ipsōs nātūrā dīligunt.** (Cicero)
Everyone naturally loves himself.

49. **omnia etiam fēlīcibus dubia sunt.** (Seneca the Younger)
Everything is in doubt, even for those who are fortunate.

50. **omnia quae tū vīs ea cupiō.** (Plautus)
I wish for everything that you want.

51. **plūs potest quī plūs valet.** (Plautus)
The person with more strength has more power.

52. **post glōriam invidia sequitur.** (Sallust)
Envy follows after glory.

53. **quod dare nōn possīs verbīs prōmittere nōlī.** (Ps.-Cato)
Do not promise with words what you cannot give.

54. **quod sequitur fugiō; quod fugit ipse sequor.** (Ovid)
Whatever pursues, I flee; whatever flees, I myself pursue.

55. **quot hominēs, tot sententiae.** (Terence)
There are as many opinions as there are people.

56. **saepius pauper et fidēlius rīdet.** (Seneca the Younger)
A poor person laughs more often and more honestly.

57. **sagittā Cupīdō cor meum transfixit.** (Plautus)
Cupid has shot my heart through with an arrow.

58. **sērum auxilium post proelium.** (Livy)
Help (comes) late after the battle.

59. **spēs spem excitat, ambitiōnem ambitiō.** (Seneca the Younger)
Hope stirs hope, ambition ambition.

60. **tot mala sum passus quot in aethere sīdera lūcent.** (Ovid)
I have suffered as many bad things as there are stars shining in the sky.

Verba Rōmānōrum II

1. **ab honestō vir bonus nullā rē dēterrēbitur.** (Seneca the Younger)
A good man will be deterred from decency by nothing.

2. **ācerrima proximōrum odia sunt.** (Tacitus)
The hatreds of those closest are sharpest.

3. **adversus hostēs necessāria est īra.** (Seneca the Younger)
Anger is necessary against one's enemies.

4. **aliīs quod triste et amārum est, hōc tamen esse aliīs possit praedulce vidērī.** (Lucretius)
What to some people is depressing and bitter may nevertheless seem to others to be very sweet.

5. **aliīs tempora dēsunt, aliīs tempora supersunt.** (Seneca the Younger)
Some people lack time, others have too much time.

6. **aliquid crastinus diēs ad cōgitandum nōbīs dabit.** (Cicero)
Tomorrow will give us something to think about.

7. **amantium caeca iūdicia** (= *jūdicia*) **sunt.** (Cicero)
The judgments of lovers are blind.

8. **aspiciunt oculīs superī mortālia iustīs** (= *justīs*). (Ovid)
The gods above look with just eyes on mortal affairs.

9. **aut rīdenda omnia aut flenda sunt.** (Seneca the Younger)
Everything should be either laughed at or wept over.

10. **avāritia bēlua fera, immānis, intoleranda est.** (Sallust)
Greed is a wild beast, huge, intolerable.

11. **bellum nec timendum nec prōvocandum.** (Pliny the Younger)
War is neither to be feared nor to be provoked.

12. **bonitās nōn est pessimīs esse meliōrem.** (Seneca the Younger)
Being better than the worst is not goodness.

13. **brevissima ad dīvitiās per contemptum dīvitiārum via est.** (Seneca the Younger)
The shortest way to riches is through the spurning of riches.

14. **cito fit quod deī volunt.** (Petronius)
What the gods want happens quickly.

15. **crēdēbās dormientī haec tibi confectūrōs deōs?** (Terence)
Did you suppose that the gods would make these things happen for you while you slept?

16. **cum mentior et mentīrī mē dīcō, mentior an vērum dīcō?** (Aulus Gellius)
When I tell a lie and say that I am telling a lie, am I telling a lie or speaking the truth?

17. **deōs nēmō sānus timet.** (Seneca the Younger)
No sane person fears the gods.

18. **dignus es porcōs pascere.** (Martial)
You are fit to feed pigs.

19. **dīvīna nātūra dedit agrōs, ars hūmāna aedificāvit urbēs.** (Varro)
Divine nature gave fields, human skill built cities.

20. **dolōris medicīnam ā philosophiā petō.** (Cicero)
From philosophy I seek medicine for pain.

21. **dūcunt volentem fāta, nōlentem trahunt.** (Seneca the Younger)
    The fates lead the willing, but drag the unwilling.

22. **ego adulescentulōs existimō in scholīs stultissimōs fierī, quia nihil ex eīs quae in ūsū habēmus aut audiunt aut vident.** (Petronius)
    I believe that young people become very stupid in the schools, since they neither hear nor see any of those things which we consider useful.

23. **ēnumerat mīles vulnera, pastor ovēs.** (Propertius)
    The soldier counts his wounds, the shepherd his sheep.

24. **errāre mālō cum Platōne quam cum istīs vēra sentīre.** (Cicero)
    I prefer to be wrong with Plato than to hold true opinions with those fellows.

25. **etiam sine magistrō vitia discuntur.** (Seneca the Younger)
    Vices are learned even without a teacher.

26. **factum fierī infectum nōn potest.** (Terence)
    What has been done cannot be made undone.

27. **fateor saepe peccasse; homō sum.** (Petronius)
    I confess I have often made mistakes; I am human.

28. **fertilior seges est aliēnīs semper in agrīs.** (Ovid)
    Crops are always more fertile in other people's fields.

29. **firmissima est inter parēs amīcitia.** (Quintus Curtius)
    Friendship is always firmest among equals.

30. **fortūna in omnī rē dominātur.** (Sallust)
    Fortune controls everything.

31. **genus est mortis male vīvere.** (Ovid)
    Living badly is a sort of death.

32. **ignāviā nēmō immortālis factus est.** (Sallust)
    No one has been made immortal through laziness.

33. **in fugā foeda mors est, in victōriā glōriōsa.** (Cicero)
    Death in flight is shameful, in victory glorious.

34. **incrēdibile est quam facile etiam magnōs virōs dulcēdō ōrātiōnis abdūcat ā vērō.** (Seneca the Younger)
    It is incredible how easily the sweetness of a speech leads even great men away from the truth.

35. **lītore quot conchae, tot sunt in amōre dolōrēs.** (Ovid)
    There are as many sorrows in love as there are shells on the shore.

36. **longius aut propius mors sua quemque manet.** (Propertius)
    Farther away or nearer at hand, each person's death awaits them.

37. **lūdit in hūmānīs dīvīna potentia rēbus.** (Ovid)
    The power of the gods plays amidst human affairs.

38. **maior (= *major*) frāter dīvidat patrimōnium, minor ēligat.** (Seneca the Elder)
    Let the elder brother divide the inheritance, the younger one choose.

39. **maior (= *major*) ignōtārum rērum est terror.** (Livy)
Fear of unknown things is greater.

40. **mālō prospicere quam acceptā iniūriā (= *injūriā*) ulciscī.** (Terence)
I prefer to be on the lookout than to take vengeance after suffering a wrong.

41. **malus bonum malum esse vult ut sit suī similis.** (Plautus)
The bad person wants the good person to be bad, so that he should be like him himself.

42. **manet incolumis mundus, īdem semper erit, quoniam semper fuit īdem.** (Manilius)
The world remains safe, it will always be the same, since it has always been the same.

43. **medicus nihil aliud est quam animī consōlātiō.** (Petronius)
A doctor is nothing but a source of consolation for the mind.

44. **moritur omne quod nascitur.** (Minucius Felix)
Everything which is born dies.

45. **mors dolōrum omnium exsolūtiō est et fīnis, ultrā quem mala nostra nōn exeunt.** (Seneca the Younger)
Death is a release and end of all pains, beyond which our ills do not extend.

46. **mors nec bonum nec malum est.** (Seneca the Younger)
Death is neither a good thing nor a bad thing.

47. **mors somnō similis est.** (Cicero)
Death is like sleep.

48. **mortālia facta perībunt.** (Horace)
Mortal deeds will perish.

49. **nātūra mūtārī nōn potest.** (Cicero)
Nature cannot be changed.

50. **nātūram sī sequēmur ducem, numquam aberrābimus.** (Cicero)
If we follow nature as our guide, we will never go astray.

51. **nēmō patriam, quia magna est, amat, sed quia sua.** (Seneca the Younger)
No one loves his country because it is great, but because it is his own.

52. **nescīs quid vesper sērus vehat.** (Varro)
You do not know what the late evening brings.

53. **nihil difficile amantī.** (Cicero)
Nothing is difficult for a lover.

54. **nihil est bellō fūnestius.** (Seneca the Younger)
Nothing is more deadly than war.

55. **nihil est mortī tam simile quam somnus.** (Cicero)
Nothing is so like death as sleep.

56. **nihil est quod deus efficere nōn possit.** (Cicero)
There is nothing which god cannot bring about.

57. **nihil est quod longinquitās temporis nōn efficere possit.** (Cicero)
There is nothing which length of time cannot bring about.

58. **nihil perpetuum, pauca diūturna sunt.** (Seneca the Younger)
Nothing is permanent, few things last for a long time.

59. **nīl admīrārī prope rēs est ūna sōlaque quae possit facere et servāre beātum.**
(Horace)
To be surprised at nothing is almost the one and only thing which can make and
keep a person happy.

60. **nōn bonus est hominī somnus post prandium.** (Plautus)
Sleep after lunch is not good for a person.

61. **nōn census nec clārum nōmen avōrum sed probitās magnōs ingeniumque facit.**
(Ovid)
Not wealth nor the famous name of one's ancestors but rather honesty and genius
make people great.

62. **nōn miscentur contrāria.** (Seneca the Younger)
Opposites do not mix.

63. **nōn omnēs eadem mīrantur amantque.** (Horace)
Not everyone admires and likes the same things.

64. **nōn omnēs quī habent citharam sunt citharoedī.** (Varro)
Not everyone who has a lyre is a lyre-player.

65. **nōn quaerit aeger medicum ēloquentem, sed sānantem.** (Seneca the Younger)
A sick person does not look for an eloquent doctor, but one who cures him.

66. **nōn quia difficilia sunt nōn audēmus, sed quia nōn audēmus difficilia sunt.**
(Seneca the Younger)
It is not because they are difficult that we do not dare (to do) things; rather they are
difficult because we do not dare (to do) them.

67. **nōs nōn plūris sumus quam bullae.** (Petronius)
We are worth no more than bubbles are.

68. **nulla flendī est maior** (= *major*) **causa, quam flēre nōn posse.** (Seneca the Elder)
There is no greater reason for weeping than not to be able to weep.

69. **numquam aliud nātūra, aliud sapientia dīcit.** (Juvenal)
Nature never says one thing, wisdom another.

70. **occultae inimīcitiae magis timendae sunt quam apertae.** (Cicero)
Hidden enmities are more to be feared than open ones.

71. **omnem crēde diem tibi dīluxisse suprēmum.** (Horace)
Believe that every day has dawned for you for the last time.

72. **omnēs immemorem beneficiī ōdērunt.** (Cicero)
Everyone detests a person who forgets a favor.

73. **omnia praeclāra rāra.** (Cicero)
All excellent things are rare.

74. **omnis vīta servitium est.** (Seneca the Younger)
All of life is slavery.

75. **onerātus magis sum quam honōrātus.** (Livy)
I am more burdened than honored.

76. **opprime, dum nova sunt, mala sēmina morbī.** (Ovid)
Check the evil seeds of disease while they are fresh.

77. **optimōs vītae diēs effluere prohibē.** (Seneca the Younger)
Stop the best days of your life from flowing away.

78. **palleat omnis amans; hīc est color aptus amantī.** (Ovid)
Every lover should be pale; that color suits a lover.

79. **parēs cum paribus facillimē congregantur.** (Cicero)
Like gather together with like very easily.

80. **parva levēs capiunt animōs.** (Ovid)
Small things captivate light minds.

81. **perīculōsius est timērī quam dēspicī.** (Seneca the Younger)
It is more dangerous to be feared than to be despised.

82. **piger ipse sibi obstat.** (Seneca the Younger)
A lazy person is an obstacle to himself.

83. **plūs alimentī est in pāne quam in ullō aliō.** (Celsus)
There is more nourishment in bread than in anything else.

84. **post mortem nihil est, ipsaque mors nihil.** (Seneca the Younger)
There is nothing after death, and death itself is nothing.

85. **potior dignitās sine vītā quam vīta sine dignitāte.** (Valerius Maximus)
Honor without life is better than life without honor.

86. **potior perīculōsa lībertās quiētō servitiō.** (Sallust)
Freedom with danger is better than tranquil slavery.

87. **praeferre patriam līberīs rēgem decet.** (Seneca the Younger)
A ruler should value his country more than his children.

88. **prīma virtūs est vitiō carēre.** (Quintilian)
Being without vice is the first virtue.

89. **quam caeca avāritia est!** (Cicero)
How blind greed is!

90. **quās dederis, sōlās semper habēbis opēs.** (Martial)
The only wealth you will always have is what you have given away.

91. **quid lībertāte pretiōsius?** (Pliny the Younger)
What is more valuable than freedom?

92. **quidquid bene dictum est ab ullō meum est.** (Seneca the Younger)
Whatever has been well said by anyone is mine.

93. **quidquid servātur cupimus magis.** (Ovid)
Whatever is guarded we desire more.

94. **quod bonum est, bonōs facit.** (Seneca the Younger)
What is good makes people good.

95. **quod parum nōvit, nēmo docēre potest.** (Ovid)
No one can teach what he scarcely knows.

96. **quod tuum est, meum est, omne meum est autem tuum.** (Plautus)
What is yours is mine, and all that is mine is yours.

97. **quot caelum stellās, tot habet tua Rōma puellās.** (Ovid)
Your Rome has as many girls as the sky has stars.

98. **regitur fātīs mortāle genus.** (Seneca the Younger)
The human race is controlled by the fates.

99. **rēs est forma fugax.** (Seneca the Younger)
Beauty is a fleeting thing.

100. **semper est honestum virum bonum esse, semper est ūtile.** (Cicero)
It is always decent to be a good man, it is always useful.

101. **senectūs est nātūrā loquācior.** (Cicero)
Old age is by nature rather garrulous.

102. **sī ūnam rem sērō fēceris, omnia opera sērō faciēs.** (Cato)
If you do one thing late, you will do all your tasks late.

103. **sōlem ē mundō tollere videntur, quī amīcitiam ē vītā tollunt.** (Cicero)
Those who remove friendship from life seem to remove the sun from the world.

104. **suāve marī magnō turbantibus aequora ventīs, ē terrā magnum alterius spectāre labōrem.** (Lucretius)
When the winds are tossing the waters in a great sea, it is pleasant to watch another person's great difficulty from the land.

105. **sunt aliquid mānēs: lētum nōn omnia fīnit.** (Propertius)
The shades of the dead are something; death does not end everything.

106. **sunt apud infernōs tot mīlia formōsārum.** (Propertius)
There are among those below so many thousands of beautiful women.

107. **tanta vīs probitātis est, ut eam etiam in hoste dīligāmus.** (Cicero)
Honesty has such power that we appreciate it even in an enemy.

108. **tantī est, quantī fungus putridus.** (Plautus)
He is worth as much as a rotten mushroom.

109. **temerāriīs remediīs gravēs morbī cūrantur.** (Seneca the Elder)
Serious diseases are treated with risky remedies.

110. **tempus in agrōrum cultū consūmere dulce est.** (Ovid)
It is pleasant to spend time in cultivating one's fields.

111. **timidum dēmentia somnia terrent.** (Propertius)
Mad dreams terrify a timid person.

112. **tot sine amōre virī, tot sunt sine amōre puellae!** (Ovid)
There are so many men without love, so many girls without love!

113. **tranquillās etiam naufragus horret aquās.** (Ovid)
A person who has been shipwrecked shudders even at calm waters.

114. **tū mihi sōla placēs: placeam tibi sōlus!** (Propertius)
You alone please me: may I alone please you!

115. **ūsus efficācissimus rērum omnium magister.** (Pliny the Elder)
Practice is the most effective teacher in all affairs.

116. **ūtilius regnō est, meritīs acquīrere amīcōs.** (Ps.-Cato)
It is worth more than a kingdom to acquire friends by one's merits.

117. **vērus amīcus est is quī est tamquam alter īdem.** (Cicero)
A true friend is one who is as it were a second self.

118. **vīlius argentum est aurō, virtūtibus aurum.** (Horace)
Silver is cheaper than gold, gold than virtues.

119. **vīta et mors iūra** (= *jūra*) **nātūrae sunt.** (Sallust)
Life and death are laws of nature.

120. **vītae sequere nātūram ducem.** (Seneca the Younger)
Follow nature as your guide in life.

The Forms of Nouns, Pronouns, Adjectives, and Verbs

Noun Declensions[1]

	First	**Second**		
Singular				
Nom.	puella	dominus[2]	puer[3]	saxum
Gen.	puellae	dominī	puerī	saxī
Dat.	puellae	dominō	puerō	saxō
Acc.	puellam	dominum	puerum	saxum
Abl.	puellā	dominō	puerō	saxō
Plural				
Nom.	puellae	dominī	puerī	saxa
Gen.	puellārum	dominōrum	puerōrum	saxōrum
Dat.	puellīs	dominīs	puerīs	saxīs
Acc.	puellās	dominōs	puerōs	saxa
Abl.	puellīs	dominīs	puerīs	saxīs

	Third[4]		**Fourth**		**Fifth**[5]
Singular					
Nom.	flōs	carmen	portus	cornū	diēs
Gen.	flōris	carminis	portūs	cornūs	diēī
Dat.	flōrī	carminī	portuī	cornū	diēī
Acc.	flōrem	carmen	portum	cornū	diem
Abl.	flōre	carmine	portū	cornū	diē

---

1. First declension nouns are introduced in Chapter 2, second in Chapter 5, third in Chapter 8, fourth and fifth in Chapter 11.

2. Note also the exceptional vocative singular of nouns of the *dominus*-type, *domine. vir, virī*, masc. 2 "man" has the nominative and vocative singular *vir*, and the word otherwise declines like *dominus*.

3. For the distinction between nouns such as *puer, puerī* and *magister, magistrī*, see Chapter 5.

4. For the small number of third declension nouns that do not conform to these paradigms, such as *ars, artis*, and *mare, maris*, see Chapter 8.

5. Fifth declension nouns that are monosyllabic in the nom. sing., such as *rēs*, have a short *e* as the penultimate syllable in the gen. and dat. sing.; see Chapter 11.

	Third		Fourth		Fifth
Plural					
Nom.	flōrēs	carmina	portūs	cornua	diēs
Gen.	flōrum	carminum	portuum	cornuum	diērum
Dat.	flōribus	carminibus	portibus	cornibus	diēbus
Acc.	flōrēs	carmina	portūs	cornua	diēs
Abl.	flōribus	carminibus	portibus	cornibus	diēbus

Pronoun Declensions[6]

Demonstrative Pronouns

	Masc.	Fem.	Neut.	Masc.	Fem.	Neut.
Singular						
Nom.	hīc	haec	hōc	ille[7]	illa	illud
Gen.	huius	huius	huius	illīus	illīus	illīus
Dat.	huic	huic	huic	illī	illī	illī
Acc.	hunc	hanc	hōc	illum	illam	illud
Abl.	hōc	hāc	hōc	illō	illā	illō
Plural						
Nom.	hī	hae	haec	illī	illae	illa
Gen.	hōrum	hārum	hōrum	illōrum	illārum	illōrum
Dat.	hīs	hīs	hīs	illīs	illīs	illīs
Acc.	hōs	hās	haec	illōs	illās	illa
Abl.	hīs	hīs	hīs	illīs	illīs	illīs

	Masc.	Fem.	Neut.	Masc.	Fem.	Neut.
Singular						
Nom.	is	ea	id	īdem	eadem	idem
Gen.	eius	eius	eius	eiusdem	eiusdem	eiusdem
Dat.	eī	eī	eī	eīdem	eīdem	eīdem
Acc.	eum	eam	id	eundem	eandem	idem
Abl.	eō	eā	eō	eōdem	eādem	eōdem
Plural						
Nom.	eī	eae	ea	eīdem	eaedem	eadem
Gen.	eōrum	eārum	eōrum	eōrundem	eārundem	eōrundem
Dat.	eīs	eīs	eīs	eīsdem	eīsdem	eīsdem
Acc.	eōs	eās	ea	eōsdem	eāsdem	eadem
Abl.	eīs	eīs	eīs	eīsdem	eīsdem	eīsdem

---

6. For pronouns, see Chapters 17 and 18.

7. *iste, ista, istud* declines like *ille, illa, illud*.

Personal Pronouns[8]

	First	Second	Third
Singular			
Nom.	ego	tū	—
Gen.	meī	tuī	suī
Dat.	mihi	tibi	sibi
Acc.	mē	tē	sē
Abl.	mē	tē	sē
Plural			
Nom.	nōs	vōs	—
Gen.	nostrum (-ī)	vestrum (-ī)	suī
Dat.	nōbīs	vōbīs	sibi
Acc.	nōs	vōs	sē
Abl.	nōbīs	vōbīs	sē

Intensive Pronoun

	Masc.	Fem.	Neut.
Singular			
Nom.	ipse	ipsa	ipsum
Gen.	ipsīus	ipsīus	ipsīus
Dat.	ipsī	ipsī	ipsī
Acc.	ipsum	ipsam	ipsum
Abl.	ipsō	ipsā	ipsō
Plural			
Nom.	ipsī	ipsae	ipsa
Gen.	ipsōrum	ipsārum	ipsōrum
Dat.	ipsīs	ipsīs	ipsīs
Acc.	ipsōs	ipsās	ipsa
Abl.	ipsīs	ipsīs	ipsīs

Relative Pronoun

	Masc.	Fem.	Neut.
Singular			
Nom.	quī	quae	quod
Gen.	cuius	cuius	cuius
Dat.	cui	cui	cui
Acc.	quem	quam	quod
Abl.	quō	quā	quō
Plural			
Nom.	quī	quae	quae
Gen.	quōrum	quārum	quōrum
Dat.	quibus	quibus	quibus
Acc.	quōs	quās	quae
Abl.	quibus	quibus	quibus

Interrogative Pronoun[9]

	Masc.	Fem.	Neut.
Singular			
Nom.	quis	quis	quid
Gen.	cuius	cuius	cuius
Dat.	cui	cui	cui
Acc.	quem	quem	quid
Abl.	quō	quō	quō
Plural			
Nom.	quī	quae	quae
Gen.	quōrum	quārum	quōrum
Dat.	quibus	quibus	quibus
Acc.	quōs	quās	quae
Abl.	quibus	quibus	quibus

8. For the distinction between reflexive and non-reflexive pronouns, see Chapter 17.

9. The interrogative pronominal adjective is the same as the relative pronoun in all its forms.

Indefinite Pronouns

	Masc.	Fem.	Neut.	Masc.	Fem.	Neut.
Singular						
Nom.	aliquis[10]	aliqua	aliquid[11]	quīdam	quaedam	quiddam[12]
Gen.	alicuius	alicuius	alicuius	cuiusdam	cuiusdam	cuiusdam
Dat.	alicui	alicui	alicui	cuidam	cuidam	cuidam
Acc.	aliquem	aliquam	aliquid	quendam	quandam	quiddam
Abl.	aliquō	aliquā	aliquō	quōdam	quādam	quōdam
Plural						
Nom.	aliquī	aliquae	aliqua	quīdam	quaedam	quaedam
Gen.	aliquōrum	aliquārum	aliquōrum	quōrundam	quārundam	quōrundam
Dat.	aliquibus	aliquibus	aliquibus	quibusdam	quibusdam	quibusdam
Acc.	aliquōs	aliquās	aliqua	quōsdam	quāsdam	quaedam
Abl.	aliquibus	aliquibus	aliquibus	quibusdam	quibusdam	quibusdam

Adjective Declensions[13]

First/Second Declension Adjectives

	Masc.	Fem.	Neut.	Masc.	Fem.	Neut.
Singular						
Nom.	cārus[14]	cāra	cārum	miser[15]	misera	miserum
Gen.	cārī	cārae	cārī	miserī	miserae	miserī
Dat.	cārō	cārae	cārō	miserō	miserae	miserō
Acc.	cārum	cāram	cārum	miserum	miseram	miserum
Abl.	cārō	cārā	cārō	miserō	miserā	miserō
Plural						
Nom.	cārī	cārae	cāra	miserī	miserae	misera
Gen.	cārōrum	cārārum	cārōrum	miserōrum	miserārum	miserōrum
Dat.	cārīs	cārīs	cārīs	miserīs	miserīs	miserīs
Acc.	cārōs	cārās	cāra	miserōs	miserās	misera
Abl.	cārīs	cārīs	cārīs	miserīs	miserīs	miserīs

10. The nom. masc. sing. of the pronominal adj. is *aliquī*.

11. The nom. and acc. neut. sing. of the pronominal adj. is *aliquod*.

12. The nom. and acc. neut. sing. of the pronominal adj. is *quoddam*.

13. For first and second declension adjectives, see Chapter 6, for third (including the irregular *dīves, pauper, vetus,* and those of the type *ācer, ācris, ācre*), see Chapter 9. For the comparative and superlative forms of adjectives, see Chapter 12.

14. Note also the exceptional vocative singular masculine of adjectives of the *cārus*-type, *cāre*.

15. For the distinction between adjectives such as *miser, misera, miserum* and *pulcher, pulchra, pulchrum*, see Chapter 6.

Third Declension Adjectives

	Masc./Fem.	Neut.	Masc./Fem.	Neut.
Singular				
Nom.	dulcis	dulce	audax	audax
Gen.	dulcis	dulcis	audācis	audācis
Dat.	dulcī	dulcī	audācī	audācī
Acc.	dulcem	dulce	audācem	audax
Abl.	dulcī	dulcī	audācī	audācī
Plural				
Nom.	dulcēs	dulcia	audācēs	audācia
Gen.	dulcium	dulcium	audācium	audācium
Dat.	dulcibus	dulcibus	audācibus	audācibus
Acc.	dulcēs	dulcia	audācēs	audācia
Abl.	dulcibus	dulcibus	audācibus	audācibus

Comparative and Superlative Forms of Adjectives[16]

	Masc./Fem.	Neut.	Masc.	Fem.	Neut.
Singular					
Nom.	cārior	cārius	cārissimus[17]	cārissima	cārissimum
Gen.	cāriōris	cāriōris	cārissimī	cārissimae	cārissimī
Dat.	cāriōrī	cāriōrī	cārissimō	cārissimae	cārissimō
Acc.	cāriōrem	cārius	cārissimum	cārissimam	cārissimum
Abl.	cāriōre	cāriōre	cārissimō	cārissima	cārissimō
Plural					
Nom.	cāriōrēs	cāriōra	cārissimī	cārissimae	cārissima
Gen.	cāriōrum	cāriōrum	cārissimōrum	cārissimārum	cārissimōrum
Dat.	cāriōribus	cāriōribus	cārissimīs	cārissimīs	cārissimīs
Acc.	cāriōrēs	cāriōra	cārissimōs	cārissimās	cārissima
Abl.	cāriōribus	cāriōribus	cārissimīs	cārissimīs	cārissimīs

---

16. For superlative forms of the type *līberrimus* and *facillimus*, and for irregular comparative and superlative forms of adjectives and adverbs, see Chapter 12.

17. Note also the exceptional vocative singular masculine of adjectives of the *cārus*-type, *cārissime*.

Irregular Adjectives[18]

	Masc.	Fem.	Neut.
Nom.	ūnus	ūna	ūnum
Gen.	ūnīus	ūnīus	ūnīus
Dat.	ūnī	ūnī	ūnī
Acc.	ūnum	ūnam	ūnum
Abl.	ūnō	ūnā	ūnō

Verb Conjugations

Principal Parts of Regular Verbs

First	amō	amāre	amāvī	amātum
Second	moneō	monēre	monuī	monitum
Third	mittō	mittere	mīsī	missum
Fourth	audiō	audīre	audīvī	audītum
Third *i*-stem	capiō	capere	cēpī	captum

Active Indicative

Present

1st Sing.	amō	moneō	mittō	audiō	capiō
2nd Sing.	amās	monēs	mittis	audīs	capis
3rd Sing.	amat	monet	mittit	audit	capit
1st Pl.	amāmus	monēmus	mittimus	audīmus	capimus
2nd Pl.	amātis	monētis	mittitis	audītis	capitis
3rd Pl.	amant	monent	mittunt	audiunt	capiunt

Future

1st Sing.	amābō	monēbō	mittam	audiam	capiam
2nd Sing.	amābis	monēbis	mittēs	audiēs	capiēs
3rd Sing.	amābit	monēbit	mittet	audiet	capiet
1st Pl.	amābimus	monēbimus	mittēmus	audiēmus	capiēmus
2nd Pl.	amābitis	monēbitis	mittētis	audiētis	capiētis
3rd Pl.	amābunt	monēbunt	mittent	audient	capient

18. Here *ūnus* represents an irregular type of adjective, with a gen. sing. in *-īus* and a dat. sing. in *-ī*; see Chapter 13. Most numbers are indeclinable adjectives; see Chapter 10.

Imperfect

1st Sing.	amābam	monēbam	mittēbam	audiēbam	capiēbam
2nd Sing.	amābās	monēbās	mittēbās	audiēbās	capiēbās
3rd Sing.	amābat	monēbat	mittēbat	audiēbat	capiēbat
1st Pl.	amābāmus	monēbāmus	mittēbāmus	audiēbāmus	capiēbāmus
2nd Pl.	amābātis	monēbātis	mittēbātis	audiēbātis	capiēbātis
3rd Pl.	amābant	monēbant	mittēbant	audiēbant	capiēbant

Perfect

1st Sing.	amāvī	monuī	mīsī	audīvī	cēpī
2nd Sing.	amāvistī	monuistī	mīsistī	audīvistī	cēpistī
3rd Sing.	amāvit	monuit	mīsit	audīvit	cēpit
1st Pl.	amāvimus	monuimus	mīsimus	audīvimus	cēpimus
2nd Pl.	amāvistis	monuistis	mīsistis	audīvistis	cēpistis
3rd Pl.	amāvērunt	monuērunt	mīsērunt	audīvērunt	cēpērunt

Fut. Perf.

1st Sing.	amāverō	monuerō	mīserō	audīverō	cēperō
2nd Sing.	amāveris	monueris	mīseris	audīveris	cēperis
3rd Sing.	amāverit	monuerit	mīserit	audīverit	cēperit
1st Pl.	amāverimus	monuerimus	mīserimus	audīverimus	cēperimus
2nd Pl.	amāveritis	monueritis	mīseritis	audīveritis	cēperitis
3rd Pl.	amāverint	monuerint	mīserint	audīverint	cēperint

Pluperfect

1st Sing.	amāveram	monueram	mīseram	audīveram	cēperam
2nd Sing.	amāverās	monuerās	mīserās	audīverās	cēperās
3rd Sing.	amāverat	monuerat	mīserat	audīverat	cēperat
1st Pl.	amāverāmus	monuerāmus	mīserāmus	audīverāmus	cēperāmus
2nd Pl.	amāverātis	monuerātis	mīserātis	audīverātis	cēperātis
3rd Pl.	amāverant	monuerant	mīserant	audīverant	cēperant

Passive Indicative

Present

1st Sing.	amor	moneor	mittor	audior	capior
2nd Sing.	amāris	monēris	mitteris	audīris	caperis
3rd Sing.	amātur	monētur	mittitur	audītur	capitur
1st Pl.	amāmur	monēmur	mittimur	audīmur	capimur
2nd Pl.	amāminī	monēminī	mittiminī	audīminī	capiminī
3rd Pl.	amantur	monentur	mittuntur	audiuntur	capiuntur

Future

1st Sing.	amābor	monēbor	mittar	audiar	capiar
2nd Sing.	amāberis	monēberis	mittēris	audiēris	capiēris
3rd Sing.	amābitur	monēbitur	mittētur	audiētur	capiētur
1st Pl.	amābimur	monēbimur	mittēmur	audiēmur	capiēmur
2nd Pl.	amābiminī	monēbiminī	mittēminī	audiēminī	capiēminī
3rd Pl.	amābuntur	monēbuntur	mittentur	audientur	capientur

Imperfect

1st Sing.	amābar	monēbar	mittēbar	audiēbar	capiēbar
2nd Sing.	amābāris	monēbāris	mittēbāris	audiēbāris	capiēbāris
3rd Sing.	amābātur	monēbātur	mittēbātur	audiēbātur	capiēbātur
1st Pl.	amābāmur	monēbāmur	mittēbāmur	audiēbāmur	capiēbāmur
2nd Pl.	amābāminī	monēbāminī	mittēbāminī	audiēbāminī	capiēbāminī
3rd Pl.	amābantur	monēbantur	mittēbantur	audiēbantur	capiēbantur

Perfect

1st Sing.	amātus sum[19]	monitus sum	missus sum	audītus sum	captus sum
2nd Sing.	amātus es	monitus es	missus es	audītus es	captus es
3rd Sing.	amātus est	monitus est	missus est	audītus est	captus est
1st Pl.	amātī sumus	monitī sumus	missī sumus	audītī sumus	captī sumus
2nd Pl.	amātī estis	monitī estis	missī estis	audītī estis	captī estis
3rd Pl.	amātī sunt	monitī sunt	missī sunt	audītī sunt	captī sunt

Fut. Perf.

1st Sing.	amātus erō	monitus erō	missus erō	audītus erō	captus erō
2nd Sing.	amātus eris	monitus eris	missus eris	audītus eris	captus eris
3rd Sing.	amātus erit	monitus erit	missus erit	audītus erit	captus erit
1st Pl.	amātī erimus	monitī erimus	missī erimus	audītī erimus	captī erimus
2nd Pl.	amātī eritis	monitī eritis	missī eritis	audītī eritis	captī eritis
3rd Pl.	amātī erunt	monitī erunt	missī erunt	audītī erunt	captī erunt

---

19. Note that, for reasons of space, such forms omit the fem. and neut. endings, -a, -um, and -ae, -a.

Pluperfect

1st Sing.	amātus eram	monitus eram	missus eram	audītus eram	captus eram
2nd Sing.	amātus erās	monitus erās	missus erās	audītus erās	captus erās
3rd Sing.	amātus erat	monitus erat	missus erat	audītus erat	captus erat
1st Pl.	amātī erāmus	monitī erāmus	missī erāmus	audītī erāmus	captī erāmus
2nd Pl.	amātī erātis	monitī erātis	missī erātis	audītī erātis	captī erātis
3rd Pl.	amātī erant	monitī erant	missī erant	audītī erant	captī erant

Active Subjunctive

Present

1st Sing.	amem	moneam	mittam	audiam	capiam
2nd Sing.	amēs	moneās	mittās	audiās	capiās
3rd Sing.	amet	moneat	mittat	audiat	capiat
1st Pl.	amēmus	moneāmus	mittāmus	audiāmus	capiāmus
2nd Pl.	amētis	moneātis	mittātis	audiātis	capiātis
3rd Pl.	ament	moneant	mittant	audiant	capiant

Imperfect

1st Sing.	amārem	monērem	mitterem	audīrem	caperem
2nd Sing.	amārēs	monērēs	mitterēs	audīrēs	caperēs
3rd Sing.	amāret	monēret	mitteret	audīret	caperet
1st Pl.	amārēmus	monērēmus	mitterēmus	audīrēmus	caperēmus
2nd Pl.	amārētis	monērētis	mitterētis	audīrētis	caperētis
3rd Pl.	amārent	monērent	mitterent	audīrent	caperent

Perfect

1st Sing.	amāverim	monuerim	mīserim	audīverim	cēperim
2nd Sing.	amāverīs	monuerīs	mīserīs	audīverīs	cēperīs
3rd Sing.	amāverit	monuerit	mīserit	audīverit	cēperit
1st Pl.	amāverīmus	monuerīmus	mīserīmus	audīverīmus	cēperīmus
2nd Pl.	amāverītis	monuerītis	mīserītis	audīverītis	cēperītis
3rd Pl.	amāverint	monuerint	mīserint	audīverint	cēperint

Pluperfect

1st Sing.	amāvissem	monuissem	mīsissem	audīvissem	cēpissem
2nd Sing.	amāvissēs	monuissēs	mīsissēs	audīvissēs	cēpissēs
3rd Sing.	amāvisset	monuisset	mīsisset	audīvisset	cēpisset
1st Pl.	amāvissēmus	monuissēmus	mīsissēmus	audīvissēmus	cēpissēmus
2nd Pl.	amāvissētis	monuissētis	mīsissētis	audīvissētis	cēpissētis
3rd Pl.	amāvissent	monuissent	mīsissent	audīvissent	cēpissent

Passive Subjunctive

Present

1st Sing.	amer	monear	mittar	audiar	capiar
2nd Sing.	amēris	moneāris	mittāris	audiāris	capiāris
3rd Sing.	amētur	moneātur	mittātur	audiātur	capiātur
1st Pl.	amēmur	moneāmur	mittāmur	audiāmur	capiāmur
2nd Pl.	amēminī	moneāminī	mittāminī	audiāminī	capiāminī
3rd Pl.	amentur	moneantur	mittantur	audiantur	capiantur

Imperfect

1st Sing.	amārer	monērer	mitterer	audīrer	caperer
2nd Sing.	amārēris	monērēris	mitterēris	audīrēris	caperēris
3rd Sing.	amārētur	monērētur	mitterētur	audīrētur	caperētur
1st Pl.	amārēmur	monērēmur	mitterēmur	audīrēmur	caperēmur
2nd Pl.	amārēminī	monērēminī	mitterēminī	audīrēminī	caperēminī
3rd Pl.	amārentur	monērentur	mitterentur	audīrentur	caperentur

Perfect

1st Sing.	amātus sim	monitus sim	missus sim	audītus sim	captus sim
2nd Sing.	amātus sīs	monitus sīs	missus sīs	audītus sīs	captus sīs
3rd Sing.	amātus sit	monitus sit	missus sit	audītus sit	captus sit
1st Pl.	amātī sīmus	monitī sīmus	missī sīmus	audītī sīmus	captī sīmus
2nd Pl.	amātī sītis	monitī sītis	missī sītis	audītī sītis	captī sītis
3rd Pl.	amātī sint	monitī sint	missī sint	audītī sint	captī sint

Pluperfect

1st Sing.	amātus essem	monitus essem	missus essem	audītus essem	captus essem
2nd Sing.	amātus essēs	monitus essēs	missus essēs	audītus essēs	captus essēs
3rd Sing.	amātus esset	monitus esset	missus esset	audītus esset	captus esset
1st Pl.	amātī essēmus	monitī essēmus	missī essēmus	audītī essēmus	captī essēmus
2nd Pl.	amātī essētis	monitī essētis	missī essētis	audītī essētis	captī essētis
3rd Pl.	amātī essent	monitī essent	missī essent	audītī essent	captī essent

Present Imperatives

Active

Sing.	amā	monē	mitte	audī	cape
Pl.	amāte	monēte	mittite	audīte	capite

Passive

Sing.	amāre	monēre	mittere	audīre	capere
Pl.	amāminī	monēminī	mittiminī	audīminī	capiminī

Infinitives

Pres. Act.	Fut. Act.	Perf. Act.	Pres. Pass.	Fut. Pass.	Perf. Pass.
amāre	amātūrus esse	amāvisse	amārī	amātum īrī	amātus esse
monēre	monitūrus esse	monuisse	monērī	monitum īrī	monitus esse
mittere	missūrus esse	mīsisse	mittī	missum īrī	missus esse
audīre	audītūrus esse	audīvisse	audīrī	audītum īrī	audītus esse
capere	captūrus esse	cēpisse	capī	captum īrī	captus esse

Participles

	Masc./Fem.	Neut.
Singular		
Nom.	amans	amans
Gen.	amantis	amantis
Dat.	amantī	amantī
Acc.	amantem	amans
Abl.	amantī (amante)[20]	amantī (amante)
Plural		
Nom.	amantēs	amantia
Gen.	amantium	amantium
Dat.	amantibus	amantibus
Acc.	amantēs	amantia
Abl.	amantibus	amantibus

Gerunds

Nom.	—	—	—
Gen.	amandī	audiendī	sequendī
Dat.	amandō	audiendō	sequendō
Acc.	amandum	audiendum	sequendum
Abl.	amandō	audiendō	sequendō

---

20. For these forms of the ablative singular, see Chapter 19.

Gerundives

	Masc.	Fem.	Neut.
Singular			
Nom.	amandus[21]	amanda	amandum
Gen.	amandī	amandae	amandī
Dat.	amandō	amandae	amandō
Acc.	amandum	amandam	amandum
Abl.	amandō	amandā	amandō
Plural			
Nom.	amandī	amandae	amanda
Gen.	amandōrum	amandārum	amandōrum
Dat.	amandīs	amandīs	amandīs
Acc.	amandōs	amandās	amanda
Abl.	amandīs	amandīs	amandīs

Irregular Verbs

Active Indicative

Present

1st Sing.	sum	possum	eō	volō	nōlō	mālō
2nd Sing.	es	potes	īs	vīs	nōn vīs	māvīs
3rd Sing.	est	potest	it	vult	nōn vult	māvult
1st Pl.	sumus	possumus	īmus	volumus	nōlumus	mālumus
2nd Pl.	estis	potestis	ītis	vultis	nōn vultis	māvultis
3rd Pl.	sunt	possunt	eunt	volunt	nōlunt	mālunt

Future

1st Sing.	erō	poterō	ībō	volam	nōlam	mālam
2nd Sing.	eris	poteris	ībis	volēs	nōlēs	mālēs
3rd Sing.	erit	poterit	ībit	volet	nōlet	mālet
1st Pl.	erimus	poterimus	ībimus	volēmus	nōlēmus	mālēmus
2nd Pl.	eritis	poteritis	ībitis	volētis	nōlētis	mālētis
3rd Pl.	erunt	poterunt	ībunt	volent	nōlent	mālent

---

21. Note also the exceptional vocative singular masculine form, *amande*.

Imperfect

1st Sing.	eram	poteram	ībam	volēbam	nōlēbam	mālēbam
2nd Sing.	erās	poterās	ībās	volēbās	nōlēbās	mālēbās
3rd Sing.	erat	poterat	ībat	volēbat	nōlēbat	mālēbat
1st Pl.	erāmus	poterāmus	ībāmus	volēbāmus	nōlēbāmus	mālēbāmus
2nd Pl.	erātis	poterātis	ībātis	volēbātis	nōlēbātis	mālēbātis
3rd Pl.	erant	poterant	ībant	volēbant	nōlēbant	mālēbant

Perfect	fuī etc.	potuī etc.	iī/īvī etc.	voluī etc.	nōluī etc.	māluī etc.
Fut. Perf.	fuerō etc.	potuerō etc.	ierō/īverō etc.	voluerō etc.	nōluerō etc.	māluerō etc.
Pluperfect	fueram etc.	potueram etc.	ieram/īveram etc.	volueram etc.	nōlueram etc.	mālueram etc.

Active Subjunctive

Present

1st Sing.	sim	possim	eam	velim	nōlim	mālim
2nd Sing.	sīs	possīs	eās	velīs	nōlīs	mālīs
3rd Sing.	sit	possit	eat	velit	nōlit	mālit
1st Pl.	sīmus	possīmus	eāmus	velīmus	nōlīmus	mālīmus
2nd Pl.	sītis	possītis	eātis	velītis	nōlītis	mālītis
3rd Pl.	sint	possint	eant	velint	nōlint	mālint

Imperfect

1st Sing.	essem	possem	īrem	vellem	nōllem	māllem
2nd Sing.	essēs	possēs	īrēs	vellēs	nōllēs	māllēs
3rd Sing.	esset	posset	īret	vellet	nōllet	māllet
1st Pl.	essēmus	possēmus	īrēmus	vellēmus	nōllēmus	māllēmus
2nd Pl.	essētis	possētis	īrētis	vellētis	nōllētis	māllētis
3rd Pl.	essent	possent	īrent	vellent	nōllent	māllent

Perfect	fuerim etc.	potuerim etc.	ierim/īverim etc.	voluerim etc.	nōluerim etc.	māluerim etc.
Pluperfect	fuissem etc.	potuissem etc.	iissem/īvissem etc.	voluissem etc.	nōluissem etc.	māluissem etc.

	Infinitives			Imperative	Participles		Gerund
Pres. Act.	Fut. Act.	Perf. Act.		Pres. Act.	Pres. Act.	Fut. Act.	
esse	futūrus esse/fore	fuisse		es or estō, este or estōte		futūrus, -a, -um	
posse		potuisse					
īre	itūrus esse	īvisse/iisse		ī, īte	iens, euntis	itūrus, -a, -um	eundī
velle		voluisse			volens, volentis		
nolle		nōluisse		nōlī, nōlīte	nōlens, nōlentis		
malle		māluisse					

Active Indicative

	Present	Future	Imperfect		
1st Sing.	ferō	feram	ferēbam		
2nd Sing.	fers	ferēs	ferēbās	**Perfect**	tulī, etc.
3rd Sing.	fert	feret	ferēbat	**Fut. Perf.**	tulerō, etc.
1st Pl.	ferimus	ferēmus	ferēbāmus	**Pluperfect**	tuleram, etc.
2nd Pl.	fertis	ferētis	ferēbātis		
3rd Pl.	ferunt	ferent	ferēbant		

Passive Indicative

	Present	Future	Imperfect		
1st Sing.	feror	ferar	ferēbar		
2nd Sing.	ferris	ferēris	ferēbāris	**Perfect**	lātus sum, etc.
3rd Sing.	fertur	ferētur	ferēbātur	**Fut. Perf.**	lātus erō, etc.
1st Pl.	ferimur	ferēmur	ferēbāmur	**Pluperfect**	lātus eram, etc.
2nd Pl.	feriminī	ferēminī	ferēbāminī		
3rd Pl.	feruntur	ferentur	ferēbantur		

Active Subjunctive

	Present		Imperfect		
1st Sing.	feram		ferrem		
2nd Sing.	ferās		ferrēs	**Perfect**	tulerim, etc.
3rd Sing.	ferat		ferret	**Pluperfect**	tulissem, etc.
1st Pl.	ferāmus		ferrēmus		
2nd Pl.	ferātis		ferrētis		
3rd Pl.	ferant		ferrent		

Passive Subjunctive

	Present	Imperfect		
1st Sing.	ferar	ferrer		
2nd Sing.	ferāris	ferrēris	**Perfect**	lātus sim, etc.
3rd Sing.	ferātur	ferrētur	**Pluperfect**	lātus essem, etc.
1st Pl.	ferāmur	ferrēmur		
2nd Pl.	ferāminī	ferrēminī		
3rd Pl.	ferantur	ferrentur		

Infinitives

Pres. Act.	Fut. Act.	Perf. Act.	Pres. Pass.	Fut. Pass.	Perf. Pass.
ferre	lātūrus esse	tulisse	ferrī	lātum īrī	lātus esse

Present Active Imperative
fer, ferte

Present Active Participle
ferens, ferentis

Future Active Participle
lātūrus, -a -um

Perfect Passive Participle
lātus, -a, -um

Gerund
ferendī, etc.

Gerundive
ferendus, -a, -um

Indicative

	Present	Future	Imperfect		
1st Sing.	fīō	fīam	fīēbam		
2nd Sing.	fīs	fīēs	fīēbās	**Perfect**	factus sum, etc.
3rd Sing.	fit	fīet	fīēbat	**Fut. Perf.**	factus erō, etc.
1st Pl.	fīmus	fīēmus	fīēbāmus	**Pluperfect**	factus eram, etc.
2nd Pl.	fītis	fīētis	fīēbātis		
3rd Pl.	fīunt	fīent	fīēbant		

Subjunctive

	Present	Imperfect		
1st Sing.	fīam	fierem		
2nd Sing.	fīās	fierēs	**Perfect**	factus sim, etc.
3rd Sing.	fīat	fieret	**Pluperfect**	factus essem, etc.
1st Pl.	fīāmus	fierēmus		
2nd Pl.	fīātis	fierētis		
3rd Pl.	fīant	fierent		

Present Imperative
fī, fīte

Perfect Passive Participle
factus, -a, -um

Gerundive
faciendus, -a, -um

Infinitives

Present (Active)
fierī

Future (Passive)
factum īrī

Perfect (Passive)
factus esse

The following lists include most of the commonest Latin words that are found in only one form. All but a very few are among the two thousand words most commonly used in Latin. A large percentage of them have not appeared elsewhere in the book because they are indeclinable, and it is not therefore necessary to learn how they are adapted for use in a sentence.[1] You will, however, meet most of them frequently when you read Latin texts. Some such indeclinable words are included elsewhere in the book but not repeated here; see esp. Chapters 10 (numbers) and 12 (adverbs). Drills to help you memorize these words are online at www.hackettpublishing.com/classicallatin.

Prepositions (those marked with an asterisk are also used as adverbs)

With the Accusative:

ad	to	**ob**	against, on account of
adversus (adversum)*	against	**penes**	in the power of
ante*	before, in front of	**per**	along, through
apud	at the house of	**pōne***	behind
circā (circum)*	around	**post***	after, behind
circiter*	approximately	**praeter***	except, past
cis (citrā*)	on this side of	**prope***	near
clam*	unknown to	**propter***	near, on account of
contrā*	against	**secundum**	along, according to
ergā	toward	**sub**	to under
extrā*	outside	**subter***	under
in	into, on to	**super***	to above
infrā*	below	**suprā***	above
inter	between	**trans**	across
intrā*	within	**ultrā***	beyond
iuxtā*	beside	**versus***	toward[2]

With the Ablative:

ā/ab	from, by	**cum**	with
clam*	unknown to	**dē**	down from, about
cōram*	in the presence of	**ē/ex**	from, out of

---

1. There is a similar core of indispensable words in English. Despite the preponderant influence of Latin on modern English vocabulary (see the Introduction), there are about seventy-five words of Germanic origin used more frequently than the commonest Latinate word ("number"), and only four of those ("other," "about," "many," "into") have more than one syllable.

2. *Versus* is placed after the noun it governs.

in	in, on	**sine**	without
palam*	in sight of	**sub**	under
prae	in front of	**super***	above, concerning
prō	on behalf of, instead of		

Adverbs, Conjuctions, and Particles[3]

ac conj.	and	**dum** conj.	while, until, provided that
adeō adv.	so		
adhūc adv.	still	**ecce (en)** interjection	look!
admodum adv.	very, extremely	**enim** conj.	for
aliās adv.	at another time	**eō** adv.	to there
alibī adv.	elsewhere	**equidem** adv.	indeed
aliquandō adv.	at some time	**ergō** conj.	therefore
aliquantō adv.	to some extent	**et** conj.	and
aliter adv.	otherwise	**etenim** conj.	for
an conj.	or, whether	**etiam** adv.	also, even
ante adv.	before	**etiamsī** conj.	even if
anteā adv.	before	**etsī** conj.	even if
anteāquam adv.	before	**fer(m)ē** adv.	almost
antequam conj.	before	**fors(it)an** adv.	perhaps
at conj.	but	**fortasse** adv.	perhaps
atque conj.	and	**forte** adv.	by chance
atquī conj.	but	**haud** adv.	not
aut conj.	or	**haudquāquam** adv.	by no means
autem conj.	but, and	**herī** adv.	yesterday
clam adv.	secretly	**hīc** adv.	here
cottīdiē adv.	every day	**hinc** adv.	from here
crās adv.	tomorrow	**hodiē** adv.	today
cum conj.	since, when, although	**hūc** adv.	to here
cūr adv.	why	**iam** adv.	now, already
dēhinc adv.	then	**ibi** adv.	there
deinde adv.	then	**idcircō** adv.	therefore
dēmum adv.	at last	**ideō** adv.	therefore
dēnique adv.	at last	**igitur** conj.	therefore
diū adv.	for a long time	**illīc** adv.	there
dōnec conj.	until	**illinc** adv.	from there

---

3. The distinction between adverbs and conjunctions is not always clear. Five hundred years ago, Erasmus acknowledged the problem: "I know a certain polymath, skilled in Greek, Latin, mathematics, philosophy and medicine, who is now sixty years old, and has, to the exclusion of all else, been torturing and crucifying himself for more than twenty years in the study of grammar, supposing that he will be happy, if he is permitted to live long enough to determine for certain how the eight parts of speech are to be distinguished, a thing which no Greek and no Roman has ever yet been able fully to achieve. As if it were a matter to be decided through warfare, if someone made a conjunction of a word which actually belongs with adverbs" (*Praise of Folly* 49).

illūc adv.	to there	**nusquam** adv.	nowhere
immō particle	rather	**ōlim** adv.	one day
inde adv.	from there	**omnīnō** adv.	entirely
insuper adv.	moreover	**paene** adv.	almost
interdum adv.	now and then	**palam** adv.	openly
intereā adv.	meanwhile	**pariter** adv.	equally
interim adv.	meanwhile	**partim** adv.	partly
intrō adv.	inside	**parum** adv.	too little
intus adv.	inside	**paulātim** adv.	gradually
istīc adv.	there	**paulō** adv.	by a little
istinc adv.	from there	**paulum** adv.	slightly
istūc adv.	to there	**plērumque** adv.	generally
ita adv.	so	**posteā** adv.	afterward
itaque conj.	therefore	**postquam** adv., conj.	after
item adv.	in the same way	**postrēmō** adv.	finally
iterum adv.	again	**postrīdiē** adv.	on the next day
māne adv.	early in the morning	**potius** adv.	rather
modo adv.	only	**praesertim** adv.	especially
mox adv.	soon	**praestō** adv.	at hand
nam conj.	for	**praetereā** adv.	moreover
namque conj.	for	**prīdiē** adv.	on the day before
-ne particle	introducing a question	**priusquam** conj.	before
nē conj.	lest	**procul** adv.	far away
nē . . . quidem	not even	**profectō** adv.	certainly
nec (neque) conj.	nor	**proinde** conj.	accordingly
necne conj.	or not	**prope** adv.	near
necnōn conj.	furthermore	**proptereā** adv.	on that account
nempe particle	indeed	**prorsus** adv.	thoroughly, indeed
nēquāquam adv.	nowhere	**prout** conj.	according as
nēquīquam adv.	in vain	**publicō** adv.	in public
neu (nēve) conj.	and . . . not	**quā** adv.	by which way, how
nihilōminus adv.	nevertheless	**quam** adv.	how, than
nimis adv.	too much	**quamdiū** adv.	how long
nimium adv.	too much	**quamobrem** adv.	why
nisi (nī) conj.	unless	**quamquam** conj.	although
noctū adv.	by night	**quamvīs** conj.	although
nōn adv.	not	**quandō** adv.	when
nondum adv.	not yet	**quandōque** adv.	sometimes
nonne particle	introducing a question	**quāpropter** adv.	therefore
nonnumquam adv.	sometimes	**quārē** adv.	why
num particle	introducing a question, whether	**quasi** conj.	as if
		quātenus adv.	as far as
numquam adv.	never	**-que** conj.	and
nunc adv.	now	**quemadmodum** adv.	how
nūper adv.	recently	**quia** conj.	because

quid adv.	why	**sponte** adv.	spontaneously
quidem particle	indeed	**statim** adv.	immediately
quīn adv., conj.	why not?, indeed, that . . . not	**subitō** adv.	suddenly
		tam adv.	so
quippe conj.	seeing that	**tamen** conj.	however
quō conj.	to where	**tametsī** conj.	even though
quoad adv.	to the extent that	**tamquam** conj.	as if
quōcumque adv.	(to) wherever	**tandem** adv.	at last
quod conj.	because	**temere** adv.	rashly
quōminus conj.	whereby . . . not	**tot** adj.	so many
quōmodo adv.	how	**tum (tunc)** adv.	then
quondam adv.	once upon a time	**ubi** conj.	when, where
quoniam conj.	because	**ubi** adv.	where
quoque conj.	also	**ubicumque** adv.	wherever
quot adj.	how many	**ubīque** adv.	everywhere
quotannīs adv.	every year	**umquam** adv.	ever
repente adv.	suddenly	**ūnā** adv.	together
rursus adv.	again	**unde** adv.	from where
saepe adv.	often	**undique** adv.	everywhere
saltem adv.	at least	**usquam** adv.	anywhere
sānē adv.	indeed	**usque** adv.	continuously
satis adv.	enough	**ut** adv., conj.	as, how, in order that, etc.[4]
scīlicet particle	of course		
secus adv.	differently	**utinam** particle	if only
sed conj.	but	**utīque** adv.	certainly
semper adv.	always	**utpote** conj.	in as much as
seu (sīve) conj.	whether	**utrum** conj.	whether
sī conj.	if	**-ve** conj.	or
sīc adv.	thus	**vel** conj.	or
sīcut conj.	just as	**velut** adv.	just as
simul adv.	together, simultaneously	**vērō** adv.	but, truly
		vidēlicet adv.	plainly
sīn conj.	but if	**vix** adv.	almost
sōlum adv.	only	**vulgō** adv.	in general

---

4. The range of meanings of *ut* is too great for them all to be listed here. See the index.

APPENDIX 4
English–Latin Vocabulary

The number in the right-hand column refers to the chapter in which the word is first found.

able (be) *possum, posse, potuī* irreg.	4	**and** *ac, atque, et* conj.	2
about *dē* prep. (+ abl.)	3	-*que* enclitic particle	4
above *suprā* adv.	12	**and not**. *nec* adv., conj	4
absent (be) *absum, abesse, āfuī*	7	**anger** *īra, īrae* fem. 1	3
abundance *cōpia, cōpiae* fem. 1	6	**angry** (be) *īrascor, īrascī, īrātus sum* 3 (+ dat.)	17
accept *accipiō, -ere, accēpī, acceptum* 3 *i*-stem	7	**animal** *animal, animālis* neut. 3	8
accustomed (I am) *soleō, solēre, solitus sum* 2	15	**announce** *nuntiō* 1	21
across *trans* prep. (+ acc.)	2	**another** *alius, alia, aliud*	13
add *addō, addere, addidī, additum* 3	7	**any** *ullus, -a, -um*	13
admire *mīror* 1	15	**appearance** *speciēs, specieī* fem. 5	11
adornment *decus, decoris* neut. 3	16	**approach** *appropinquō* 1 (+ dat.)	17
after *post* prep. (+ acc.)	2	**arise** *orior, orīrī, ortus sum* 4	15
postquam conj.	7	**arms** *arma, armōrum* neut. 2	10
again *iterum, rursus* adv.	6	**army** *exercitus, exercitūs* masc. 4	11
against *contrā* prep. (+ acc.)	2	**around** *circā, circum* adv., prep. (+ acc.)	5
ago *abhinc* adv.	15	**art** *ars, artis* fem. 3	8
all *omnis, omne*	9	**as . . . as possible** *quam* adv. (+ superl.)	12
ally *socius, sociī* masc. 2	14	**ask** (for) *rogō* 1	16
almost *ferē* adv.	7	**at first** *prīmō* adv.	12
paene adv.	3	**at last** *tandem* adv.	3
alone *sōlus, -a, -um*	13	**at some time** *ōlim* adv.	12
along *per* prep. (+ acc.)	5	**Athens** *Athēnae, Athēnārum* fem. 1	10
already *iam* adv.	7	**attack** *aggredior, aggredī, aggressus sum* 3 *i*-stem	15
also *etiam* adv.	13	**attention** *opera, operae* fem. 1	20
altar *āra, ārae* fem. 1	3	**autumn** *autumnus, autumnī* masc. 2	15
although *cum* conj.	27	**avenge** *ulciscor, ulciscī, ultus sum* 3	15
quamquam adv.	7	**avoid** *vītō* 1	4
quamvīs adv.	27	**away from** see **from**	
always *semper* adv.	4	**back** *tergum, tergī* neut. 2	7
ambush *insidiae, insidiārum* fem. 1	10	**bad** *malus, -a, -um*	6
amount *cōpia, cōpiae* fem. 1	3	**badly** *male* adv.	12

barbarian *barbarus, -a, -um*	6	**bridge** *pons, pontis* masc. 3	8
battle *proelium, proeliī* neut. 2	7	**bring back** *referō, referre, retulī, relātum* irreg.	7
pugna, pugnae fem.	14	**bring down** *dēferō, deferre, dētulī, dēlātum* irreg.	7
battle line *aciēs, aciēī* fem. 5	11	**bring into** *īnferō, īnferre, intulī, illātum* irreg.	7
be a slave to *serviō, servīre, servīvī,*		**bring out of** *efferō, efferre, extulī, ēlātum* irreg.	7
servītum 4 (+ dat.)	17	**bring through** *perferō, perferre, pertulī,*	
be unwilling *nōlō, nolle, nōluī* irreg.	10	*perlātum* irreg.	7
beautiful *pulcher, pulchra, pulchrum*	6	**bring under** *sufferō, sufferre, sustulī, sublātum*	
because *quia, quod, quoniam* conj.	3	irreg.	7
become *fīō, fierī, factus sum* irreg.	15	**broad** *lātus, -a, -um*	6
before *ante* prep. (+ acc.)	3	**brother** *frāter, frātris* masc. 3	8
antequam conj.	7	**brought about** (it is) *efficitur, efficī, effectum*	
priusquam conj.	27	*est* impers. 3 *i*-stem	28
begin *incipiō, incipere, incēpī, inceptum* 3 *i*-stem	7	**build** *aedificō* 1	7
coepī, coepisse 3 (began)	19	**bull** *taurus, taurī* masc. 2	5
behind *post* prep. (+ acc.)	2	**burden** *onus, oneris* neut. 3	16
believe (a person) *crēdō, -ere, crēdidī,*		**burn** *ardeō, ardēre, arsī* intrans. 2	19
crēditum 3 (+ dat.)	17	**business** *negōtium, negōtiī* neut. 2	7
below *īnfrā* adv.	12	**but** *at, sed* conj.	2
beneficial (it is) *prōdest, prōdesse, prōfuit*		*tamen* adv.	7
irreg. (+ dat. + inf.)	28	**buy** *emō, emere, ēmī, emptum* 3	16
besiege *oppugnō* 1	3	**by chance** *forte* adv.	11
best *optimus, -a, -um* superl. adj. (*bonus*)	12	**Caesar** *Caesar, Caesaris* masc. 3	11
better *melior, melius* compar. adj. (*bonus*)	12	**call back** *revocō* 1	7
big *magnus, -a, -um*	6	**call together** *convocō* 1	7
bigger *maior, maius* compar. adj. (*magnus*)	12	**call** *vocō* 1	1
biggest *maximus, -a, -um* superl. adj. (*magnus*)	12	**camp** *castra, castrōrum* neut. 2	10
black *niger, nigra, nigrum*	6	**care** *cūra, cūrae* fem. 1	16
blood *sanguis, sanguinis* masc. 3	8	**carry** *ferō, ferre, tulī, lātum* irreg.	4
body *corpus, corporis* neut. 3	8	*portō* 1	4
bold *audax, audācis*	9	**carry from** *auferō, auferre, abstulī, ablātum* irreg.	7
boldness *audācia, audāciae* fem. 1	2	**carry to** *afferō, afferre, attulī, allātum*	7
book *liber, librī* masc. 2	5	**cause** *causa, -ae* fem. 1	16
booty *praeda, praedae* fem. 1	2	**cause to fall** *caedō, caedere, cecīdī, caesum* 3	7
born (I am) *nascor, nascī, nātus sum* 3	15	**cavalry** *equitātus, equitātūs* masc. 4	11
both *et* conj., *-que* enclitic particle	4	**cave** *spēlunca, spēluncae* fem. 1	3
boy *puer, puerī* masc. 2	5	**centurion** *centuriō, centuriōnis* masc. 3	14
brave *fortis, forte*	9	**chariot** *currus, currūs* masc. 4	11
break *frangō, frangere, frēgī, fractum* 3	3	**children** *līberī, līberōrum* masc. 2	10

citadel *arx, arcis* fem. 3	8
citizen *cīvis, cīvis* masc. 3	8
city *urbs, urbis* fem. 3	8
close *claudō, claudere, clausī, clausum* 3	7
cold *frīgidus, -a, -um*	6
column (esp. of soldiers) *agmen, agminis* neut. 3	14
come *veniō, venīre, vēnī, ventum* 4	4
comfort *sōlācium, sōlāciī* neut. 2	16
commander *imperātor, imperātōris* masc. 3	11
complain *queror, querī, questus sum* 3	15
confess *fateor, fatērī, fassus sum* 2	15
conquer *superō* 1	14
vincō, vincere, vīcī, victum 3	1
consul *consul, consulis* masc. 3	11
country house *villa, villae* fem. 1	3
countryside *rūs, rūris* neut. 3	15
courage *virtūs, virtūtis* fem. 3	8
cow *vacca, vaccae* fem. 1	4
crime *scelus, sceleris* neut. 3	11
cruel *crūdēlis, crūdēle*	9
cultivate *colō, colere, coluī, cultum* 3	19
cure *remedium, remediī* neut. 2	16
custom *mōs, mōris* masc. 3	10
danger *perīculum, perīculī* neut. 2	16
dare *audeō, audēre, ausus sum* 2	15
dark *niger, nigra, nigrum*	6
darkness *tenebrae, tenebrārum* fem. 1	10
daughter *fīlia, fīliae* fem. 1	2
day *diēs, diēī* masc./fem. 5	11
dear (to) *cārus, -a, -um* (+ dat.)	6
death *mors, mortis* fem. 3	8
deep *altus, -a, -um*	6
defend *dēfendō, dēfendere, dēfendī, dēfensum* 3	14
delay *moror, morārī, morātus sum* 1	15
deliverance *salūs, salūtis* fem. 3	16
deny *negō* 1	21
deserve *mereor, merērī, meritus sum* 2	15
despise *contemnō, -ere, contempsī, contemptum* 3	19
destroy *dēleō, dēlēre, dēlēvī, dēlētum* 2	14
perdō, perdere, perdidī, perditum 3	7
destruction *exitium, exitiī* neut. 2	16
deter *dēterreō, dēterrēre, dēterruī, dēterritum* 2	24
die *morior, morī, mortuus sum* 3 i-stem	15
difficult *difficilis, difficile*	9
disgrace *dēdecus, dēdecoris* neut. 3	16
opprobrium, opprobriī neut. 2	16
disgraces (it) *dēdecet, dēdecēre, dēdecuit* 2 (+ acc. + inf.)	28
displeasing (it is) *displicet, displicēre, displicuit* 2 (+ dat. + inf.)	28
dissuade *dissuādeō, -ēre, dissuāsī, dissuāsum* 2 (+ dat.)	17
distrust *diffīdō, diffīdere, diffīsus sum* 3 (+ dat.)	17
divine *dīvīnus, -a, -um*	6
divinity *nūmen, nūminis* neut. 3	8
do *faciō, facere, fēcī, factum* 3 i-stem	4
agō, agere, ēgī, actum 3	4
dog *canis, canis* masc./fem. 3	8
don't *nōlī, nōlīte* imperative verb	1
door *iānua, iānuae* fem. 1	2
doubt *dubitō* 1	25
doubtful *dubius, -a, -um*	25
down from *dē* prep. (+ abl.)	3
dream *somnium, somniī* neut. 2	7
drink *bibō, bibere, bibī* 3	1
drive *agō, agere, ēgī, actum* 3	4
dry *āridus, -a, -um*	6
duty *officium, officiī* neut. 2	7
earth *terra, terrae* fem. 1	4
easily *facile* adv.	9
easy *facilis, facile*	9
eight *octō*	10
eight each *octōnī, -ae, -a*	10
eight hundred *octingentī, -ae, -a*	10
eight hundredth *octingentēsimus, -a, -um*	10
eight times *octiēs*	10
eighteen *duodēvigintī*	10

eighteenth *duodēvīcēsimus, -a, -um*	10	**farther** *ulterior, -ius* compar. adj.	12
eighth *octāvus, -a, -um*	10	**farthest** *extrēmus, -a, -um* superl. adj.	12
eightieth *octōgēsimus, -a, -um*	10	*ultimus, -a, -um* superl. adj.	2
eighty *octōgintā*	10	**fat** *pinguis, pingue*	9
either *uter, utra, utrum*	13	**fate** *fātum, fātī* neut. 2	7
either . . . or . . . *vel . . . vel . . .*	3	**father** *pater, patris* masc. 3	8
aut . . . aut . . .	3	**favor** *faveō, favēre, fāvī, fautum* 2 (+ dat.)	17
eleven *undecim*	10	**fear** *metuō, metuere, metuī* 3	1
eleventh *undecimus, -a, -um*	10	*timeō, timēre, timuī* 2	1
Elysium *Ēlysium, Ēlysiī* neut. 2	10	*vereor, verērī, veritus sum* 2	15
embrace *amplector, amplectī, amplexus sum* 3	15	**fear** *metus, metūs* masc. 4	11
emperor *imperātor, imperātōris* masc. 3	11	*timor, timōris* masc. 3	16
empty *inānis, ināne*	9	**feed** (trans.) *pascō, pascere, pāvī, pastum* 3	4
end *fīnis, fīnis* masc. 3	8	**feed on** *vescor, vescī* defective 3 (+ abl.)	18
enemy *hostis, hostis* masc. 3	8	**feel** *sentiō, sentīre, sensī, sensum* 4	21
enjoy *fruor, fruī, fructus sum* 3 (+ abl.)	18	**few** *paucī, -ae, -a*	6
entrails *exta, extōrum* neut. 2	10	**field** *ager, agrī* masc. 2	5
envy *invideō, invidēre, invīdī, invīsum* 2 (+ dat.)	17	**fierce** *ferox, ferōcis*	9
epistle *litterae, litterārum* fem. 1	11	**fifteen** *quindecim*	10
especially *praesertim* adv.	3	**fifteenth** *quintus, -a, -um decimus, -a, -um*	10
estimate *aestimō* 1	16	**fifth** *quintus, -a, -um*	10
even *etiam* adv.	13	**fiftieth** *quinquāgēsimus, -a, -um*	10
evening (it becomes) *(ad)vesperascit, -ere, -āvit* 3	28	**fifty** *quinquāgintā*	10
every *omnis, omne*	9	**fight** *pugnō* 1	3
every day *cottīdiē* adv.	3	**find** *reperiō, reperīre, repperī, repertum* 4	1
everywhere *passim* adv.	12	*inveniō, invenīre, invēnī, inventum* 4	4
ewe-lamb *agna, agnae* fem. 1	5	**find out** *noscō, noscere, nōvī, nōtum* 3	21
example *exemplum, exemplī* neut. 2	16	**fire** *ignis, ignis* masc. 3	8
exclaim *exclāmō* 1	21	**first** *prīmus, -a, -um*	10
eye *oculus, oculī* masc. 2	7	**fish** *piscis, piscis* masc. 3	8
face *faciēs, faciēī* fem. 5	11	**fitting** (it is) *decet, decēre, decuit* 2 (+ acc. + inf.)	28
vultus, vultūs masc. 4	11	**five** *quinque*	10
fall *cadō, cadere, cecidī* 3	7	**five each** *quīnī, -ae, -a*	10
family *familia, familiae* fem. 1	2	**five hundred** *quingentī, -ae, -a*	10
famous *celeber, celebris, celebre*	9	**five times** *quinquiēs*	10
far away *procul* adv.	7	**flame** *flamma, flammae* fem. 1	2
farmer *agricola, agricolae* masc. 1	2	**flee** *fugiō, fugere, fūgī* 3 *i*-stem	14
		fleet *classis, classis* fem. 3	8

flock *grex, gregis* masc. 3   8
   pecus, pecudis fem. 3   8
flower *flōs, flōris* masc. 3   8
flying *volucer, volucris, volucre*   9
follow *sequor, sequī, secūtus sum* 3   15
food *cibus, cibī* masc. 2   7
foot *pēs, pedis* masc. 3   11
foot soldier *pedes, peditis* masc. 3   14
for a long time *diū* adv.   5
for *enim* particle   5
   nam particle   5
   namque conj.   5
forbid *interdīcō, interdīcere, interdixī,*
   interdictum 3 (+ dat.)   24
   vetō, vetāre, vetuī, vetitum 1   24
force *cōgō, cōgere, coēgī, coactum* 3   7
force *vīs* fem. irreg. 3   10
forces (military) *cōpiae, cōpiārum* fem. 1   10
forget *oblīviscor, oblīviscī, oblītus sum* 3 (+ gen.)   18
forgive *ignoscō, ignoscere, ignōvī, ignōtum* 3
   (+ dat.)   17
form *speciēs, speciēī* fem. 5   11
former *prior, prius* compar. adj.   12
fort *castrum, castrī* neut. 2   10
fortieth *quadrāgēsimus, -a, -um*   10
fortune *fortūna, fortūnae* fem. 1   3
forty *quadrāgintā*   10
forum *forum, forī* neut. 2   7
fountain *fons, fontis* masc. 3   8
four *quattuor*   10
four each *quaternī, -ae, -a*   10
four hundred *quadringentī, -ae, -a*   10
four times *quater*   10
fourteen *quattuordecim*   10
fourteenth *quartus, -a, -um decimus, -a, -um*   10
fourth *quartus, -a, -um*   10
free *līber, lībera, līberum*   6
free *līberō* 1   4
freedom *lībertās, lībertātis* fem. 3   11

friend (female) *amīca, amīcae* fem. 1   5
friend (male) *amīcus, amīcī* masc. 2   5
frighten *terreō, terrēre, terruī, territum* 2   1
from *ā/ab* prep. (+ abl.)   2
from here *hinc* adv.   12
from there *inde* adv.   17
   illinc adv.   12
from where *unde* adv.   15
frost *gelū, gelūs* neut. 4   11
fruit *fructus, fructūs* masc. 4   11
funeral rites *exsequiae, -ārum* fem. 1   11
game *lūdus, lūdī* masc. 2   5
games *lūdī, lūdōrum* masc. 2 (in the circus,
   amphitheater, etc.)   10
garden *hortus, hortī* masc. 2   5
gate *porta, portae* fem. 1   2
gather *cōgō, cōgere, coēgī, coactum* 3   8
gift *dōnum, dōnī* neut. 2   5
   mūnus, mūneris neut. 3   8
girl *puella, puellae* fem. 1   2
give *dō, dare, dedī, datum* 1   1
gladiator *gladiātor, gladiātōris* masc. 3   11
glory *glōria, glōriae* fem. 1   16
   laus, laudis fem. 3   16
go *eō, īre, iī* (or *īvī*), *itum* irreg.   4
go away *abeō, abīre, abiī/abīvī* irreg.   4
go back *regredior, regredī, regressus sum* 3
   i-stem   15
   redeō, redīre, rediī/redīvī irreg.   4
go forward *prōgredior, prōgredī, prōgressus*
   sum 3 *i*-stem   15
go into *ingredior, ingredī, ingressus sum* 3 *i*-stem   15
   ineō, inīre, iniī/inīvī irreg.   4
go out *ēgredior, ēgredī, ēgressus sum* 3 *i*-stem   15
   exeō, exīre, exiī/exīvī irreg.   4
go through *pereō, perīre, periī/perīvī* irreg.   4
go to *adeō, adīre, adiī/adīvī* irreg.   4
god *deus, deī* masc. 2   5
goddess *dea, deae* fem. 1   2

gold *aurum, aurī* neut. 2 — 5

good *bonus, -a, -um* — 6

gradually *paulātim* adv. — 12

grape *ūva, ūvae* fem. 1 — 4

greatly *magnopere* adv. — 12

greed *avāritia, avāritiae* fem. 1 — 2

greedy *avārus, -a, -um* — 6

ground *humus, humī* fem. 2 — 15

hand *manus, manūs* fem. 4 — 11

handsome *pulcher, pulchra, pulchrum* — 6

happens (it) *accidit, accidere, accidit* impers. 3 — 28

   ēvenit, ēvenīre, ēvēnit impers. 4 — 28

   contingit, contingere, contigit impers. 3 — 28

happy *fēlix, fēlīcis* — 9

harbor *portus, portūs* masc. 4 — 11

harm *laedō, laedere, laesī, laesum* 3 — 4

   noceō, nocēre, nocuī, nocitum 2 (+ dat.) — 17

hate *ōdī, ōdisse* defective 3 — 19

hatred *odium, odiī* neut. 2 — 16

have *habeō, habēre, habuī, habitum* 2 — 1

head *caput, capitis* neut. 3 — 8

heal *medeor, medērī* 2 (+ dat.) — 17

healthy *salūber, salūbris, salūbre* — 9

hear *audiō, audīre, audīvī, audītum* 4 — 1

heaven *caelum, caelī* neut. 2 — 5

heavenly *caelestis, caeleste* — 9

heavy *gravis, grave* — 9

he-goat *caper, caprī* masc. 2 — 5

helmet *galea, galeae* fem. 1 — 14

help *iuvō, iuvāre, iūvī, iūtum* 1 — 3

help *auxilium, auxiliī* neut. 2 — 16

herd *grex, gregis* masc. 3 — 8

   pecus, pecudis fem. 3 — 8

here *hīc* adv. — 12

high *altus, -a, -um* — 6

higher *superior, -ius* compar. adj. — 14

highest *suprēmus, -a, -um* superl. adj. — 14

hill *collis, collis* masc. 3 — 8

himself etc. *suī* reflex. pers. pron. — 17

hinder *impediō, impedīre, impedīvī, impedītum* 4 — 24

   obstō, obstāre, obstitī 1 (+ dat.) — 24

hindrance *impedīmentum, impedīmentī* neut. 2 — 16

hold *teneō, tenēre, tenuī, tentum* 2 — 3

honor *honor, honōris* masc. 3 — 16

hope *spērō* 1 — 21

hope *spēs, speī* fem. 5 — 11

horn *cornū, cornūs* neut. 4 — 11

horseman *eques, equitis* masc. 3 — 14

hour *hōra, hōrae* fem. 1 — 15

house *casa, casae* fem. 1 — 2

   aedēs, aedium fem. 3 — 10

   domus, domūs fem. 4 — 11

household gods *penātēs, penātium* masc. 3 — 10

how *quam* adv. — 12

   quōmodo adv. — 4

how many *quot* indecl. adj. — 13

how much *quantus, -a, -um* — 13

how often *quotiens* adv. — 13

however *tamen* adv. — 7

huge *ingens, ingentis* — 9

human being *homō, hominis* masc./fem. 3 — 9

humble *humilis, humile* — 9

hundred *centum* — 10

hundred each *centēnī, -ae, -a* — 10

hundredth *centēsimus, -a, -um* — 10

I *ego, meī* pers. pron. — 17

if *sī* conj. — 2

if only *utinam* particle — 22

ignorant *ignārus, -a, -um* — 16

immediately *statim* adv. — 6

immortal *immortālis, immortāle* — 9

impede *impediō, impedīre, impedīvī, impedītum* 4 — 24

   obstō, obstāre, obstitī 1 (+ dat.) — 24

implore *ōrō* 1 — 24

   precor 1 — 24

in *in* prep. (+ abl.) — 2

in front of *ante* prep. (+ acc.) — 3

in the morning *māne* adv. — 3

in vain *frustrā* adv. — 3

increase (intrans.) *crescō, crescere, crēvī, crētum* 3 — 19

increase (trans.) *augeō, augēre, auxī, auctum* 2 — 19

injury *damnum, damnī* neut. 2 — 16

innermost *intimus, -a, -um* superl. adj. — 12

inside *intrā* adv. — 12

interior *interior, -ius* compar. adj. — 12

into *in* prep. (+ acc.) — 2

invade *invādō, invādere, invāsī, invāsum* 3 — 14

iron *ferrum, ferrī* neut. 2 — 5

island *insula, insulae* fem. 1 — 2

Italy *Ītalia, Ītaliae* fem. 1 — 2

journey *iter, itineris* neut. 3 — 11

kill *interficiō, interficere, -fēcī, -fectum* 3 *i*-stem — 14

    caedō, caedere, cecīdī, caesum 3 — 7

king *rex, rēgis* masc. 3 — 8

knee *genū, genūs* neut. 4 — 11

know *sciō, scīre, scīvī* 4 — 21

know (do not) *nesciō, nescīre, nescīvī* 4 — 21

lack *careō, carēre, caruī* 2 (+ abl.) — 18

    egeō, egēre, eguī 2 (+ abl.) — 18

land *terra, terrae* fem. 1 — 4

later *posterior, -ius* compar. adj. — 12

latest *postrēmus, -a, -um* superl. adj. — 12

laugh *rīdeō, rīdēre, rīsī, rīsum* 2 — 3

law *lex, lēgis* fem. — 8

    iūs, iūris neut. 3 — 8

lazy *piger, pigra, pigrum* — 6

lead *dūcō, dūcere, duxī, ductum* 3 — 1

leader *dux, ducis* masc. 3 — 8

learn *discō, discere, didicī* 3 — 7

leave *relinquō, relinquere, relīquī, relictum* 3 — 7

legion *legiō, legiōnis* fem. 3 — 14

leisure *ōtium, ōtiī* neut. 2 — 7

lenient (I am) *indulgeō, indulgēre, indulsī, indultum* 2 (+ dat.) — 17

lest *quōminus* conj. — 24

letter *epistula, epistulae* fem. 1 — 7

letter of the alphabet *littera, litterae* fem. 1 — 10

lie down *iaceō, iacēre, iacuī* 2 — 14

life *vīta, vītae* fem. 1 — 3

light (it is getting) *lūcescit, lūcescere* 3 — 28

light *levis, leve* — 9

light *lūmen, lūminis* neut. 3 — 8

    lux, lūcis fem. 3 — 8

lightning (it is) *fulgurat* 1 — 28

like *similis, simile* (+ gen. or dat.) — 9

live *vīvō, vīvere, vixī, victum* 3 — 1

long *longus, -a, -um* — 6

look at *aspiciō, -ere, aspexī, aspectum* 3 *i*-stem — 19

lose *āmittō, āmittere, āmīsī, āmissum* 3 — 4

    perdō, perdere, perdidī, perditum 3 — 7

love *amō* 1 — 1

love *amor, amōris* masc. 3 — 8

lower class of citizens *plebs, plēbis* fem. 3 — 10

lower *inferior, -ius* compar. adj. — 12

lowest *infimus, -a, -um* superl. adj. — 12

lucky *fēlix, fēlīcis* — 9

madness *insānia, insāniae* fem. 1 — 10

magistrate *magistrātus, magistrātūs* masc. 4 — 11

make *faciō, facere, fēcī, factum* 3 *i*-stem — 4

man *vir, virī* masc. 2 — 5

many see **much**

mare *equa, equae* fem. 1 — 5

marriage *nuptiae, nuptiārum* fem. 1 — 10

marry (of a woman) *nūbō, nūbere, nupsī, nuptum* 3 (+ dat.) — 17

master *dominus, dominī* masc. 2 — 5

matters (it) *interest, interesse, interfuit* impers. — 28

    rēfert, rēferre, rētulit impers. — 28

meanwhile *interim* adv. — 12

mind *animus, animī* masc. 2 — 7

    mens, mentis fem. 3 — 8

missile *tēlum, tēlī* neut. 2 — 7

mistress *domina, dominae* fem. 1 — 5

mob *turba, turbae* fem. 1 — 3

money *pecūnia, pecūniae* fem. 1 — 2

month *mensis, mensis* masc. 3	15	
moon *lūna, lūnae* fem. 1	3	
morals *mōrēs, mōrum* masc. 3	10	
more *magis* compar. adv.	12	
more *plūs* compar. adj. (*multus*)	12	
mortal *mortālis, mortāle*	9	
most *plūrimus, -a, -um* superl. adj. (*multus*)	12	
mother *māter, mātris* fem. 3	8	
mountain *mons, montis* masc. 3	8	
move *moveō, movēre, mōvī, mōtum* 2	7	
much *multum* adv.	12	
much, pl. **many** *multus, -a, -um*	6	
must *dēbeō, dēbēre, dēbuī, dēbitum* 2	1	
my *meus, -a, -um*	6	
myself etc. *ipse, ipsa, ipsum* pron., pronom. adj.	17	
name *nōmen, nōminis* neut. 3	9	
near *prope* prep. (+ acc.)	5	
nearer *propior, propius* compar. adj.	12	
nearest *proximus, -a, -um* superl. adj.	12	
necessary (it is) *necesse est* impers.	28	
opus est impers.	28	
neck *collum, collī* neut. 2	7	
neither *neuter, neutra, neutrum*	13	
neither . . . nor . . . *nec . . . nec . . .*	4	
never *numquam* adv.	4	
new *novus, -a, -um*	6	
night *nox, noctis* fem. 3	8	
nine *novem*	10	
nine each *novēnī, -ae, -a*	10	
nine hundred *nōngentī, -ae, -a*	10	
nine times *noviēs*	10	
nineteen *undēvīgintī*	10	
ninety *nōnāgintā*	10	
ninth *nōnus, -a, -um*	10	
no one *nēmō, nullīus*	13	
nobility *nōbilitās, nōbilitātis* fem. 3	10	
none *nullus, -a, -um*	13	
nor *nec* adv., conj.	4	
not *nōn* adv.	2	

not even *nē . . . quidem*	13	
not much *parum* adv.	12	
not only . . . but also . . . *cum . . . tum . . .*	13	
nothing *nihilum, nihilī* neut. 2	16	
now *iam* adv.	7	
nunc adv.	4	
number *numerus, numerī* masc. 2	7	
obey *obsequor, obsequī, obsecūtus sum* 3 (+ dat.)	17	
obtain *adipiscor, adipiscī, adeptus sum* 3	15	
of such a sort *tālis, -e*	13	
offer *offerō, offerre, obtulī, oblātum* irreg.	7	
often *saepe* adv.	5	
old *vetus, veteris*	9	
old age *senectūs, senectūtis* fem. 3	11	
omen *ōmen, ōminis* neut. 3	11	
on *in* prep. (+ abl.)	2	
on behalf of *prō* prep. (+ abl.)	3	
onto *in* prep. (+ acc.)	2	
once *semel*	10	
one *ūnus, -a, -um*	10	
one (in pl., **some**) **. . . another** (in pl., **others**)		
alius . . . alius . . .	13	
one each *singulī, -ae, -a*	10	
one hundred times *centiēs*	10	
one thousand each *millēnī, -ae, -a*	10	
one thousand times *mīliēs*	10	
only *modo* adv.	13	
sōlum adv.	13	
tantum adv.	13	
only *sōlus, -a, -um*	15	
onset *impetus, impetūs* masc. 4	11	
open *aperiō, aperīre, aperuī, apertum* 4	7	
or (of a particular set of alternatives) *aut* conj.	3	
(of any number and type of alternatives)		
vel conj.	3	
order *imperō* 1 (+ dat.)	17	
iubeō, iubēre, iussī, iussum 2	14	
other see **another**		
other (**the**) *alter, altera, alterum*	13	

ought to *dēbeō, dēbēre, dēbuī, dēbitum* 2   1

our *noster, nostra, nostrum*   6

out of *ē/ex* prep. (+ abl.)   2

outer *exterior, -ius* compar. adj.   12

outside *extrā* adv.   12

owe *dēbeō, dēbēre, dēbuī, dēbitum* 2   1

own, his (her/its/their) *suus, -a, -um*   17

owner *domina, dominae* fem. 1   5

     dominus, dominī masc. 2   5

pain *dolor, dolōris* masc. 3   8

part *pars, partis* fem. 3   8

partly *partim* adv.   12

peace *pax, pācis* fem. 3   8

people *populus, populī* masc. 2   7

perform *fungor, fungī, functus sum* 3 (+ abl.)   18

perhaps *fortasse* adv.   3

perish *pereō, perīre, periī*   4

permissible (it is) *licet, licēre, licuit* 2 (+ dat. + inf.)   28

persuade *persuādeō, -ēre, persuāsī, persuāsum* 2 (+ dat.)   17

piety *pietās, pietātis* fem. 3   11

pig *porca, porcae* fem. 1   4

     porcus, porcī masc. 2   5

pirate *pīrāta, pīrātae* masc. 1   2

pity (it causes) *miseret, miserēre, miseruit* 2 (+ acc. + gen. or inf.)   28

place *pōnō, pōnere, posuī, positum* 3   4

plain *campus, campī* masc. 2   5

play *lūdō, lūdere, lūsī, lūsum* 3   1

pleasant (it is) *libet, libēre, libuit* 2 (+ dat. + inf.)   28

please *placeō, placēre, placuī, placitum* 2 (+ dat.)   17

pleases (it) *dēlectat* 1 (+ acc. + inf.)   28

     iuvat, iuvāre, iūvit 1 (+ acc. + inf.)   28

     placet, placēre, placuit 2 (+ dat. + inf.)   28

plow *arō* 1   4

pluck *carpō, carpere, carpsī, carptum* 3   4

plunder *praeda, praedae* fem. 1   2

     spolia, spoliōrum neut. 2   10

poem *carmen, carminis* neut. 3   8

poet *poēta, poētae* masc. 1   2

poison *venēnum, venēnī* neut. 2   7

poor *pauper, pauperis*   9

port *portus, portūs* masc. 4   11

pour *fundō, fundere, fūdī, fūsum* 3   3

power *potentia, potentiae* fem. 1   2

     vīrēs, vīrium fem. 3   10

powerful *potens, potentis*   9

praise *laudō* 1   7

pray *precor, precārī, precātus sum* 1   15

prefer *mālō, malle, māluī* irreg.   10

prevent *prohibeō, prohibēre, prohibuī, prohibitum* 2   24

priest(ess) *sacerdōs, sacerdōtis* masc./fem. 3   8

profit *lucrum, lucrī* neut. 2   16

promise *polliceor, pollicērī, pollicitus sum* 2   15

     prōmittō, prōmittere, prōmīsī, prōmissum 3   21

proper (it is) *oportet, oportēre, oportuit* 2 (+ acc. + inf.)   28

provided that *dum(modo)* conj.   27

punishment *poena, poenae* fem. 1   7

pure *pūrus, -a, -um*   6

put to flight *fugō* 1   14

queen *rēgīna, rēgīnae* fem. 1   7

raining (it is) *pluit, pluere, pluit* 3   28

ram-lamb *agnus, agnī* masc. 2   5

read *legō, legere, lēgī, lectum* 3   1

recently *nūper* adv.   6

regret (it causes) *paenitet, paenitēre, paenituit* 2 (+ acc. + gen. or inf.)   28

rejoice *gaudeō, gaudēre, gāvīsus sum* 2   15

remain *maneō, manēre, mansī* 2   7

remains (it) *restat* 1 impers.   28

remains *reliquiae, reliquiārum* fem.1   10

remember *meminī, meminisse* defective 3 (+ gen.)   18

repel *pellō, pellere, pepulī, pulsum* 3   4

reply *respondeō, respondēre, respondī,*	
responsum 2	21
resist *resistō, resistere, restitī* 3 (+ dat.)	17
rest *quiēs, quiētis* fem. 3	10
restrain *retineō, retinēre, retinuī, retentum* 2	24
rich *dīves, dīvitis*	9
riches *dīvitiae, dīvitiārum* fem. 1	10
rise *surgō, surgere, surrexī, surrectum* 3	3
river *flūmen, flūminis* neut. 3	8
road *via, viae* fem. 1	3
rock *saxum, saxī* neut. 2	5
Roman *Rōmānus, -a, -um*	6
Rome *Rōma, Rōmae* fem. 1	2
rose *rosa, rosae* fem. 1	2
rough *asper, aspera, asperum*	6
run *currō, currere, cucurrī, cursum* 3	19
rush *impetus, impetūs* masc. 4	11
sacred (to) *sacer, sacra, sacrum* (+ dat.)	6
sad *tristis, triste*	9
safe *incolumis, incolume*	9
sail *nāvigō* 1	7
sailor *nauta, nautae* masc. 1	2
same *īdem, eadem, idem* pron., pronom. adj.	17
savage *saevus, -a, -um*	6
say *dīcō, dīcere, dixī, dictum* 3	1
says/said (he [she, it]) *ait* defective	7
inquit defective	7
school *lūdus, lūdī* masc. 2	5
sea *mare, maris* neut. 3	8
second *secundus, -a, -um*	10
alter, -a, -um	10
see *videō, vidēre, vīdī, vīsum* 2	1
seek *petō, -ere, petiī* (or *-īvī*)*, petītum* 3	
(+ *ā*/*ab* + abl.)	1
quaerō, -ere, quaesīvī, quaesītum 3	
(+ *ā*/*ab* + abl.)	24
seem *videor, vidērī, vīsus sum* 2	15
seize *rapiō, rapere, rapuī, raptum* 3 *i*-stem	1
sell *vendō, vendere, vendidī, venditum* 3	16

Senate *senātus, senātūs* masc. 4	11
Senate(-house) *cūria, cūriae* fem. 1	3
send *mittō, mittere, mīsī, missum* 3	1
serious *gravis, grave*	9
set on fire *accendō, -ere, accendī, accensum* 3	19
set out *proficiscor, proficiscī, profectus sum* 3	15
seven *septem*	10
seven each *septēnī, -ae, -a*	10
seven hundred *septingentī, -ae, -a*	10
seven times *septiēs*	10
seventeen *septemdecim*	10
seventeenth *septimus, -a, -um decimus, -a, -um*	10
seventh *septimus, -a, -um*	10
seventieth *septuāgēsimus, -a, -um*	10
seventy *septuāgintā*	10
shame (it causes) *pudet, pudēre, puduit* 2	
(+ acc. + gen. or inf.)	28
shame *pudor, pudōris* masc. 3	16
shameful *turpis, turpe*	9
sharp *ācer, ācris, ācre*	9
she-goat *capella, capellae* fem. 1	4
shepherd *pastor, pastōris* masc. 3	8
shield *scūtum, scūtī* neut. 2	14
ship *nāvis, nāvis* fem. 3	8
shore *lītus, lītoris* neut. 3	11
ōra, ōrae fem. 1	2
short *brevis, breve*	9
should *dēbeō, dēbēre, dēbuī, dēbitum* 2	1
shout *clāmō* 1	7
show *monstrō* 1	7
ostendō, ostendere, ostendī, ostentum 3	4
sick *aeger, aegra, aegrum*	6
silence *silentium, silentiī* neut. 2	7
silver *argentum, argentī* neut. 2	5
similar to *similis, simile* (+ gen. or dat.)	9
since *cum* conj.	27
sing *cano, canere, cecinī* 3	19
cantō 1	21
sister *soror, sorōris* fem. 3	8

sit *sedeō, sedēre, sēdī, sessum* 2	1	**spare** *parcō, parcere, pepercī, parsum* 3 (+ dat.)	17
six *sex*	10	**speak** *loquor, loquī, locūtus sum* 3	15
six each *sēnī, -ae, -a*	10	**spear** *hasta, hastae* fem. 1	14
six hundred *sescentī, -ae, -a*	10	**speech** *ōrātiō, ōrātiōnis* fem. 3	11
six times *sexiēs*	10	**spoils** *spolia, spoliōrum* neut. 2	10
sixteen *sēdecim*	10	**spontaneously** *sponte* adv.	11
sixth *sextus, -a, -um*	10	**spring** *vēr, vēris* neut. 3	15
sixty *sexāgintā*	10	**stallion** *equus, equī* masc. 2	5
sky *caelum, caelī* neut. 2	5	**stand** *stō, stāre, stetī, statum* 1	3
slave (female) *serva, servae* fem. 1	5	**star** *astrum, astrī* neut. 2	5
slave (male) *servus, servī* masc. 2	5	*stella, stellae* fem. 1	3
sleep *dormiō, dormīre, dormīvī, dormītum* 4	3	**statue** *statua, statuae* fem. 1	2
sleep *somnus, somnī* masc. 2	3	**stealthily** *furtim* adv.	12
slip *lābor, lābī, lapsus sum* 3	15	**still** *adhūc* adv.	3
slow *lentus, -a, -um*	6	**stride** *gradior, gradī, gressus sum* 3 *i*-stem	15
small *parvus, -a, -um*	6	**strong** *fortis, forte*	9
smaller *minor, minus* compar. adj. (*parvus*)	12	**student** (female) *discipula, discipulae* fem. 1	5
smallest *minimus, -a, -um* superl. adj.		**student** (male) *discipulus, discipulī* masc. 2	5
(*parvus*)	12	**study** *studeō, studēre, studuī* 2 (+ dat.)	17
so *tam* adv.	13	**stupid** *stultus, -a, -um*	6
so (in such a way) *ita* adv.	23	**stupidity** *stultitia, stultitiae* fem. 1	10
sīc adv.	23	**suddenly** *subitō* adv.	7
so (to such an extent) *adeō* adv.	23	**suffer** *patior, patī, passus sum* 3 *i*-stem	15
so many *tot* indecl. adj.	13	**suits** (it) *decet, decēre, decuit* 2 (+ acc. + inf.)	28
so much *tantus, -a, -um*	13	**summer** *aestās, aestātis* fem. 3	15
so often *totiens* adv.	13	**surely** *nonne*, interrogative particle (invites	
soft *mollis, molle*	9	affirmative answer)	4
soldier *mīles, mīlitis* masc. 3	8	**surely not** *num*, interrogative particle	
some *nonnullus, -a, -um*	13	(invites negative answer)	4
some(one) *quīdam, quaedam, quid(quod)dam*		**sweet** *dulcis, dulce*	9
pron., pronom. adj.	18	**swift** *celer, celeris, celere*	9
aliqui(s), aliquid(-quod) pron.,		**sword** *gladius, gladiī* masc. 2	14
pronom. adj.	18	**take** *capiō, capere, cēpī, captum* 3 *i*-stem	1
son *fīlius, fīliī* masc. 2	5	**take possession of** *potior, potīrī, potītus sum* 4	
song *carmen, carminis* neut. 3	8	(+ gen. or abl.)	18
soon *mox* adv.	6	**take vengeance upon** *ulciscor, ulciscī,*	
soul *anima, animae* fem. 1	7	*ultus sum* 3	15
souls of the dead *mānēs, mānium* masc. 3	10	**tavern** *taberna, tabernae* fem. 1	2
sow *porca, porcae* fem. 1	4	**teach** *doceō, docēre, docuī, doctum* 2	7

teacher *magister, magistrī* masc. 2	5	**three** *trēs, tria*	10
tear(-drop) *lacrima, lacrimae* fem. 1	2	**three each** *ternī, -ae, -a*	10
tedium (it causes) *taedet, taedēre, taesum est* 2		**three hundred** *trecentī, -ae, -a*	10
(+ acc. + gen. or inf.)	28	**three times** *ter*	10
tell *narrō* 1	21	**throng** *turba, turbae* fem. 1	3
tell a lie *mentior, mentīrī, mentītus sum* 4	15	**through** *per* prep. (+ acc.)	5
temple *aedēs, aedis* fem. 3	10	**throw** *iaciō, iacere, iēcī, iactum* 3 *i*-stem	14
templum, templī neut. 2	5	**thundering** (it is) *tonat, tonāre, tonuit* 1	28
ten *decem*	10	**time** *tempus, temporis* neut. 3	8
ten each *dēnī, -ae, -a*	10	**tired** *fessus, -a, -um*	6
ten times *deciēs*	10	**to** *ad* prep. (+ acc.)	2
tenth *decimus, -a, -um*	10	**to here** *hūc* adv.	12
territory *fīnēs, fīnium* masc. 3	8	**to there** *illūc* adv	12
than *quam* adv. (+ compar.)	12	**to where** *quō* adv.	15
thanks *grātiae, grātiārum* fem. 1	10	**today** *hodiē* adv.	5
that *ille, illa, illud* pron., pronom. adj.	17	**tolerate** *tolerō* 1	3
is, ea, id pron., pronom. adj.	17	**tomorrow** *crās* adv.	5
iste, ista, istud pron., pronom. adj.	17	**tooth** *dens, dentis* masc. 3	8
the one . . . the other . . . *alter . . . alter . . .*	13	**touch** *tangō, tangere, tetigī, tactum* 3	3
then *tum/tunc* adv.	4	**tower** *turris, turris* fem. 3	8
there *illīc* adv.	12	**town** *oppidum, oppidī* neut. 2	7
therefore *ergō* conj.	3	**trap** *insidiae, insidiārum* fem. 1	10
igitur conj.	3	**tree** *arbor, arboris* fem. 3	8
itaque conj.	3	**truly** *vērō* adv.	11
thin *gracilis, gracile*	12	**trust** *crēdō, -ere, crēdidī, crēditum* 3 (+ dat.)	17
thing *rēs, reī* fem. 5	11	*fīdō, fīdere, fīsus sum* 3 (+ abl.)	18
think *arbitror* 1	15	**trust** *fidēs, fideī* fem. 5	11
existimō 1	21	**truth** *vēritās, vēritātis* fem. 3	11
putō 1	21	**try** *cōnor* 1	15
reor, rērī, ratus sum 2	15	**tuft of wool** *floccus, floccī* masc. 2	16
third *tertius, -a, -um*	10	**turn** *vertō, vertere, vertī, versum* 3	19
thirteen *tredecim*	10	**twelfth** *duodecimus, -a, -um*	10
thirteenth *tertius, -a, -um decimus, -a, -um*	10	**twelve** *duodecim*	10
thirtieth *trīcēsimus, -a, -um*	10	**twentieth** *vīcēsimus, -a, -um*	10
thirty *trīgintā*	10	**twenty each** *vīcēnī, -ae, -a*	10
this *hīc, haec, hōc* pron., pronom. adj.	17	**twenty one** *vīgintī et ūnus, -a, -um*	10
thousand *mille*	10	**twenty times** *vīciēs*	10
thousandth *millēsimus, -a, -um*	10	**twenty** *vīgintī*	10
threats *minae, minārum* fem. 1	10	**twice** *bis*	10

two *duo, duae, duo* 10

two each *bīnī, -ae, -a* 10

two hundred *ducentī, -ae, -a* 10

two hundredth *duocentēsimus, -a, -um* 10

ugly *dēformis, dēforme* 9

unaware (be) *ignōrō* 1 21

under (to) *sub* prep. (+ acc.) 2

under *sub* prep. (+ abl.) 2

understand *intellegō, intellegere, intellexī,*
 intellectum 3 21

unhappy *infēlix, infēlīcis* 9

unless *nisi* conj. 26

unlike *dissimilis, dissimile* (+ gen. or dat.) 9

unlucky *infēlix, infēlīcis* 9

unwilling (I am) *nōlō, nolle, nōluī* irreg. 11

urge *hortor* 1 15

 suādeō, suādēre, suāsī, suāsum 2 (+ dat.) 17

use *ūsus, ūsūs* masc. 4 16

use *ūtor, ūtī, ūsus sum* 3 (+ abl.) 18

verse *versus, versūs* masc. 4 11

vexation (it causes) *piget, pigēre, piguit* 2
 (+ acc. + gen. or inf.) 28

victor *victor, victōris* masc. 3 14

victory *victōria, victōriae* fem. 1 3

virtue *virtūs, virtūtis* fem. 3 8

voice *vox, vōcis* fem. 3 8

walk *ambulō* 1 7

wall *mūrus, mūrī* masc. 2 5

walls (of a city) *moenia, moenium* neut. 3 10

war *bellum, bellī* neut. 2 7

warm *calidus, -a, -um* 6

warn *moneō, monēre, monuī, monitum* 2 1

watch *spectō* 1 1

water *aqua, aquae* fem. 1 3

wave *fluctus, fluctūs* masc. 4 11

 unda, undae fem. 1 2

weapons *arma, armōrum* neut. 2 10

weep *fleō, flēre, flēvī, flētum* 2 7

well *bene* adv. 12

what *quis, quid* interrog. pron. 18

what sort of *quālis, -e* 13

when *cum* conj. 3

 quandō adv. 4

where *ubi* adv. 4

where *ubi* interrogative particle 4

whether *an, utrum* particle 4

 introducing indirect question *num* 25

which *quī, quae, quod* interrog. pronom. adj. 18

 quī, quae, quod rel. pron. 18

which (of two) *uter, utra, utrum* 13

while *dum* conj. 3

whisper *susurrō* 1 21

who *quī, quae, quod* rel. pron. 18

 quis, quid interrog. pron. 18

whole *tōtus, -a, -um* 13

why *cūr* adv. 4

wife *uxor, uxōris* fem. 3 8

wild animal *fera, ferae* fem. 1 4

wild boar *aper, aprī* masc. 2 5

wind *ventus, ventī* masc. 2 7

wine *vīnum, vīnī* neut. 2 5

wing (of a battle line) *cornū, cornūs* neut. 4 11

winter *hiems, hiemis* fem. 3 15

wisdom *sapientia, sapientiae* fem. 1 10

wish *cupiō, cupere, cupīvī, cupitum* 3 *i*-stem 7

 volō, velle, voluī irreg. 10

with *cum* prep. (+ abl.) 2

without *sine* prep. (+ abl.) 2

woman *fēmina, fēminae* fem. 1 5

 mulier, mulieris fem. 3 8

wood *silva, silvae* fem. 1 4

word *verbum, verbī* neut. 2 7

word for word *verbātim* adv. 12

work *labōrō* 1 4

work *labor, labōris* masc. 3 8

 opus, operis neut. 3 8

worse *dēterior, -ius* compar. adj. 12

 peior, peius compar. adj. (*malus*) 12

worship *colō, colere, coluī, cultum* 3 — 19

worst *dēterrimus, -a, -um* superl. adj. — 12
      pessimus, -a, -um superl. adj. (*malus*) — 12

wound *vulnerō* 1 — 14

wound *vulnus, vulneris* neut. 3 — 14

wretched *miser, misera, miserum* — 6

write *scrībō, scrībere, scrīpsī, scrīptum* 3 — 7

year *annus, annī* masc. 2 — 15

yesterday *herī* adv. — 5

yield *cēdō, cēdere, cessī, cessum* 3 — 19

yoke *iugum, iugī* neut. 2 — 7

you *tū, tuī* pers. pron. — 17

young man *iuvenis, iuvenis* masc. 3 — 11

your (sing.) *tuus, -a, -um* — 6

your (pl.) *vester, vestra, vestrum* — 6

APPENDIX 5
Latin–English Vocabulary

The number in the right-hand column refers to the chapter in which the word is first found.

(ad)vesperascit, -ere, -āvit 3 *it becomes evening* 28

ā/ab prep. (+ abl.) *from* 2

abdūcō, -ere, abduxī, abductum 3 *lead away* 7

abeō, abīre, abiī/abīvī irreg. *go away* 4

abhinc adv. *ago* 15

absum, abesse, āfuī irreg. *be absent* 7

ac conj. *and* 2

accendō, -ere, accendī, accensum 3 *set on fire* 19

accidit, accidere, accidit impers. 3 *it happens* 28

accipiō, -ere, accēpī, acceptum 3 *i*-stem *accept* 7

ācer, ācris, ācre *sharp, fierce* 9

aciēs, aciēī fem. 5 *battle line* 11

actum see **agō**

ad prep. (+ acc.) *to* 2

addō, addere, addidī, additum 3 *add* 7

adeō adv. *so, to such an extent* 23

adeō, adīre, adiī/adīvī irreg. *go to* 4

adeptus see **adipiscor**

adhūc adv. *still* 3

adipiscor, adipiscī, adeptus sum 3 *obtain* 15

adsum, adesse, adfuī irreg. *be present* 7

aedēs, aedis fem. 3 *temple*, pl. *house* 10

aedificō 1 *build* 7

aeger, aegra, aegrum *sick* 6

aestās, aestātis fem. 3 *summer* 15

aestimō 1 *estimate* 16

afferō, afferre, attulī, allātum irreg. *carry to* 7

ager, agrī masc. 2 *field* 5

aggredior, aggredī, aggressus sum 3 *i*-stem *attack* 15

agmen, agminis neut. 3 *column* (esp. of soldiers) 14

agna, agnae fem. 1 *ewe-lamb* 5

agnus, agnī masc. 2 *ram-lamb* 5

agō, agere, ēgī, actum 3 *drive, do, spend (of time)* 4

agricola, agricolae masc. 1 *farmer* 2

ait defective *he (she, it) says or said* 7

aliquī, aliqua, aliquod indef. pronom. adj. *some* 18

aliquis, aliqua, aliquid indef. pron. *someone/something* 18

alius, alia, aliud *another* 13

alius . . . alius . . . *one (in pl., some) . . . another (in pl., others)* 13

alter . . . alter . . . *the one . . . the other . . .* 13

alter, altera, alterum *the other, the second* 13

altus, -a, -um *high, deep* 6

ambulō 1 *walk* 7

amīca, amīcae fem. 1 *female friend* 5

amīcus, amīcī masc. 2 *male friend* 5

āmittō, āmittere, āmīsī, āmissum 3 *lose* 4

amō 1 *love* 1

amor, amōris masc. 3 *love* 8

amplector, amplectī, amplexus sum 3 *embrace* 15

an particle *or, whether* 4

anima, animae fem. 1 *soul* 7

animal, animālis neut. 3 *animal* 8

animus, animī masc. 2 *mind* 7

annōn particle *or not* 4

annus, annī masc. 2 *year* 15

ante prep. (+ acc.) *before, in front of* 3

antequam conj. *before* 7

aper, aprī masc. 2 *wild boar* 5

aperiō, aperīre, aperuī, apertum 4 *open*	7	**bīnī, -ae, -a** *two each*	10
appropinquō 1 (+ dat.) *approach*	17	**bis** *twice*	10
aqua, aquae fem. 1 *water*	3	**bonus, -a, -um** *good*	6
āra, ārae fem. 1 *altar*	3	**brevis, breve** *short*	9
arbitror 1 *think*	15	**cadō, cadere, cecidī** 3 *fall*	7
arbor, arboris fem. 3 *tree*	8	**caedō, caedere, cecīdī, caesum** 3 *cause to fall,*	
ardeō, ardēre, arsī 2 intrans. *burn*	19	*kill*	7
argentum, argentī neut. 2 *silver*	5	**caelestis, caeleste** *heavenly*	9
āridus, -a, -um *dry*	6	**caelum, caelī** neut. 2 *sky, heaven*	5
arma, armōrum neut. 2 *arms, weapons*	10	**Caesar, Caesaris** masc. 3 *Caesar*	11
arō 1 *plow*	4	**calidus, -a, -um** *warm*	6
ars, artis fem. 3 *art*	8	**campus, campī** masc. 2 *plain*	5
arx, arcis fem. 3 *citadel*	8	**canis, canis** masc./fem. 3 *dog*	8
as, assis neut. 3 *the smallest Roman coin*	16	**cano, canere, cecinī** 3 *sing*	19
asper, aspera, asperum *rough*	6	**cantō** 1 *sing*	21
aspiciō, -ere, aspexī, aspectum 3 *i*-stem *look at*	19	**capella, capellae** fem. 1 *she-goat*	4
astrum, astrī neut. 2 *star*	5	**caper, caprī** masc. 2 *he-goat*	5
at conj. *but*	2	**capiō, capere, cēpī, captum** 3 *i*-stem *take*	1
Athēnae, Athēnārum fem. 1 *Athens*	10	**caput, capitis** neut. 3 *head*	8
atque conj. *and*	2	**careō, carēre, caruī** 2 (+ abl.) *lack*	18
audācia, audāciae fem. 1 *boldness*	2	**carmen, carminis** neut. 3 *song, poem*	8
audax, audācis *bold*	9	**carpō, carpere, carpsī, carptum** 3 *pluck*	4
audeō, audēre, ausus sum 2 *dare*	15	**cārus, -a, -um** (+ dat.) *dear (to)*	6
audiō, audīre, audīvī, audītum 4 *hear*	1	**casa, casae** fem. 1 *house*	2
auferō, auferre, abstulī, ablātum irreg.		**castrum, castrī** neut. 2 *fort,* pl. *camp*	10
carry from	7	**causa, -ae** fem. 1 *cause*	16
augeō, augēre, auxī, auctum 2 trans. *increase*	19	**causā** (+ gen.) *for the sake of*	16
aurum, aurī neut. 2 *gold*	5	**cecidī** see **cadō**	
ausus see **audeō**		**cecīdī** see **caedō**	
aut conj. *or* (of a particular set of alternatives)	3	**cecinī** see **canō**	
aut . . . aut *either . . . or*	3	**cēdō, cēdere, cessī, cessum** 3 *yield*	19
autumnus, autumnī masc. 2 *autumn*	15	**celeber, celebris, celebre** *famous*	9
auxilium, auxiliī neut. 2 *help*	16	**celer, celeris, celere** *swift*	9
avāritia, avāritiae fem. 1 *greed*	2	**centiēs** *one hundred times*	10
avārus, -a, -um *greedy*	6	**centum** *one hundred*	10
barbarus, -a, -um *barbarian*	6	**centuriō, centuriōnis** masc. 3 *centurion*	14
bellum, bellī neut. 2 *war*	7	**cēpī** see **capiō**	
bene adv. *well*	12	**certō** 1 *struggle*	4
bibō, bibere, bibī 3 *drink*	1	**cessī** see **cēdō**	

ceteri, -a, -um *the other*	13
cibus, cibī masc. 2 *food*	7
circā and **circum** adv., prep. (+ acc.) *around*	5
cīvis, cīvis masc. 3 *citizen*	8
clāmō 1 *shout*	7
classis, classis fem. 3 *fleet*	8
claudō, claudere, clausī, clausum 3 *close*	7
coēgī see **cōgō**	
coepī, coepisse defective 3 *began*	19
cōgō, cōgere, coēgī, coactum 3 *gather, force*	7
collis, collis masc. 3 *hill*	8
collum, collī neut. 2 *neck*	7
colō, colere, coluī, cultum 3 *cultivate, worship*	19
conferō, conferre, contulī, collātum irreg. *bring together*	16
cōnor 1 *try*	15
consul, consulis masc. 3 *consul*	11
contemnō, -ere, contempsī, contemptum 3 *despise*	19
contingit, contingere, contigit impers. 3 *it happens*	28
contrā prep. (+ acc.) *against*	2
convocō 1 *call together*	7
cōpia, cōpiae fem. 1 *amount, supply*, pl. *military forces*	3
cornū, cornūs neut. 4 *horn, wing (of a battle line)*	11
corpus, corporis neut. 3 *body*	8
cottīdiē adv. *every day*	3
crās adv. *tomorrow*	5
crēdō, -ere, crēdidī, crēditum 3 (+ dat.) *trust, believe* (a person)	17
crescō, crescere, crēvī, crētum 3 intrans. *increase*	19
crēvī see **cresco**	
crūdēlis, crūdēle *cruel*	9
cum conj. *when, since, although*	3
cum prep. (+ abl.) *with*	2
cum . . . tum . . . *not only . . . but also*	13

cupiō, cupere, cupīvī, cupitum 3 *i*-stem *wish, desire*	7
cūr adv. *why*	4
cūra, cūrae fem. 1 *care*	16
cūria, cūriae fem. 1 *Senate(-house)*	3
currō, currere, cucurrī, cursum 3 *run*	19
currus, currūs masc. 4 *chariot*	11
damnum, damnī neut. 2 *injury*	16
dē prep. (+ abl.) *down from, about*	3
dea, deae fem. 1 *goddess*	2
dēbeō, dēbēre, dēbuī, dēbitum 2 *owe, ought to, must, should*	1
decem *ten*	10
decet, decēre, decuit 2 (+ acc. + inf.) *it suits, it is fitting*	28
deciēs *ten times*	10
decimus, -a, -um *tenth*	10
decus, decoris neut. 3 *honor, adornment*	16
dēdecet, dēdecēre, dēdecuit 2 (+ acc. + inf.) *it disgraces*	28
dēdecus, dēdecoris neut. 3 *disgrace*	16
dedī see **dō**	
dēfendō, dēfendere, dēfendī, dēfensum 3 *defend*	14
dēferō, deferre, dētulī, dēlātum irreg. *bring down*	7
dēformis, dēforme *ugly*	9
dēlectat 1 (+ acc. + inf.) *it pleases*	28
dēleō, dēlēre, dēlēvī, dēlētum 2 *destroy*	14
dēnī, -ae, -a *ten each*	10
dens, dentis masc. 3 *tooth*	8
dēterior, -ius compar. adj. *worse*	12
dēterreō, dēterrēre, dēterruī, dēterritum 2 *deter*	24
dēterrimus, -a, -um superl. adj. *worst*	12
deus, deī masc. 2 *god*	5
dīcō, dīcere, dixī, dictum 3 *say*	1
didicī see **discō**	
diēs, diēī masc./fem. 5 *day*	11

differō, differre, distulī, dīlātum irreg.
    disperse, postpone — 7

difficilis, difficile *difficult* — 9

diffīdō, diffīdere, diffīsus sum 3 (+ dat.)
    distrust — 17

discipula, discipulae fem. 1 *female student* — 5

discipulus, discipulī masc. 2 *male student* — 5

discō, discere, didicī 3 *learn* — 7

displicet, displicēre, displicuit 2 (+ dat. + inf.)
    it is displeasing — 17

dissimilis, dissimile (+ gen. or dat.) *unlike* — 9

dissuādeō, -ēre, dissuāsī, dissuāsum 2 (+ dat.)
    dissuade — 17

diū adv. *for a long time* — 5

dīves, dīvitis *rich* — 9

dīvīnus, -a, -um *divine* — 6

dīvitiae, dīvitiārum fem. 1 *riches* — 10

dō, dare, dedī, datum 1 *give* — 1

doceō, docēre, docuī, doctum 2 *teach* — 7

dolor, dolōris masc. 3 *pain* — 8

domina, dominae fem. 1 *mistress, owner* — 5

dominus, dominī masc. 2 *master, owner* — 5

domus, domūs fem. 4 *house* — 11

dōnum, dōnī neut. 2 *gift* — 5

dormiō, dormīre, dormīvī, dormītum 4 *sleep* — 3

dubitō (1) *doubt* — 25

dubius, -a, -um *doubtful* — 25

ducentī, -ae, -a *two hundred* — 10

dūcō, dūcere, dūxī, ductum 3 *lead* — 1

dulcis, dulce *sweet* — 9

dum conj. *while, provided that* — 3

dummodo conj. *provided that* — 27

duo, duae, duo *two* — 10

duodecim *twelve* — 10

duodecimus, -a, -um *twelfth* — 10

duodēvīcēsimus, -a, -um *eighteenth* — 10

duodēvīgintī *eighteen* — 10

dux, ducis masc. 3 *leader* — 8

ē/ex prep. (+ abl.) *out of* — 2

ēdūcō, -ere, ēdūxī, ēductum 3 *lead out* — 7

efferō, efferre, extulī, ēlātum irreg. *bring
    out of* — 7

efficitur, efficī, effectum est impers. 3 *i*-stem
    it is brought about — 28

egeō, egēre, eguī 2 (+ abl.) *lack* — 18

ēgī see **agō**

ego, meī pers. pron. *I* — 17

ēgredior, ēgredī, ēgressus sum 3 *i*-stem *go out* — 15

Ēlysium, Ēlysiī neut. 2 *Elysium* — 10

emō, emere, ēmī, emptum 3 *buy* — 16

enim particle *for* — 5

eō, īre, iī (*or* **īvī**), **itum** irreg. *go* — 4

epistula, epistulae fem. 1 *letter* — 7

equa, equae fem. 1 *mare* — 5

eques, equitis masc. 3 *horseman* — 14

equitātus, equitātūs masc. 4 *cavalry* — 11

equus, equī masc. 2 *stallion* — 5

ergō conj. *therefore* — 3

et conj. *and* — 2

etiam adv. *also, even* — 13

ēvenit, ēvenīre, ēvēnit impers. 4 *it happens* — 28

exclāmō 1 *exclaim* — 21

exemplum, exemplī neut. 2 *example* — 16

exeō, exīre, exiī (*or* **exīvī**) irreg. *go out* — 4

exercitus, exercitūs masc. 4 *army* — 11

existimō 1 *think* — 21

exitium, exitiī neut. 2 *destruction* — 16

exsequiae, -ārum fem. 1 *funeral rites* — 10

exta, extōrum neut. 2 *entrails* — 10

exterior, -ius compar. adj. *outer* — 12

extrā adv., prep. (+ acc.) *outside* — 12

extrēmus, -a, -um superl. adj. *farthest* — 12

faciēs, faciēī fem. 5 *face* — 11

facile adv. *easily* — 12

facilis, facile *easy* — 9

faciō, facere, fēcī, factum 3 *i*-stem *do, make* — 4

familia, familiae fem. 1 *family, household* — 2

fassus see **fateor**

fateor, fatērī, fassus sum 2 *confess*	15
fātum, fātī neut. 2 *fate*	7
faveō, favēre, fāvī, fautum 2 (+ dat.) *favor*	17
fēcī see **faciō**	
fēlix, fēlīcis *happy, lucky*	9
fēmina, fēminae fem. 1 *woman*	5
fera, ferae fem. 1 *wild animal*	4
ferē adv. *almost*	7
ferō, ferre, tulī, lātum irreg. *carry*	4
ferox, ferōcis *fierce*	9
ferrum, ferrī neut. 2 *iron*	5
fessus, -a, -um *tired*	6
fidēs, fideī fem. 5 *trust*	11
fīdō, fīdere, fīsus sum 3 (+ abl.) *trust*	17
fīlia, fīliae fem. 1 *daughter*	2
fīlius, fīliī masc. 2 *son*	5
fīnis, fīnis masc. 3 *end*, pl. *territory*	8
fīō, fīerī, factus sum irreg. *become*	15
flamma, flammae fem. 1 *flame*	2
fleō, flēre, flēvī, flētum 2 *weep*	7
floccus, floccī masc. 2 *tuft of wool*	16
flōs, flōris masc. 3 *flower*	8
fluctus, fluctūs masc. 4 *wave*	11
flūmen, flūminis neut. 3 *river*	8
fons, fontis masc. 3 *fountain, spring*	8
fore fut. act. inf. of **sum, esse, fuī** irreg.	28
fortasse adv. *perhaps*	3
forte adv. *by chance*	11
fortis, forte *strong, brave*	9
fortūna, fortūnae fem. 1 *fortune*	3
forum, forī neut. 2 *forum*	7
fractum see **frangō**	
frangō, frangere, frēgī, fractum 3 *break*	3
frāter, frātris masc. 3 *brother*	8
frēgī see **frangō**	
frīgidus, -a, -um *cold*	6
fructus see **fruor**	
fructus, fructūs masc. 4 *fruit*	11
fruor, fruī, fructus sum 3 (+ abl.) *enjoy*	18
frustrā adv. *in vain*	3
fūdī see **fundō**	
fugiō, fugere, fūgī 3 *i*-stem *flee*	14
fugō 1 *put to flight*	14
fuī see **sum**	
fulgurat 1 *it is lightning*	28
functus see **fungor**	
fundō, fundere, fūdī, fūsum 3 *pour*	3
fungor, fungī, functus sum 3 (+ abl.) *perform*	18
furtim adv. *stealthily*	12
galea, galeae fem. 1 *helmet*	14
gaudeō, gaudēre, gāvīsus sum 2 *rejoice*	15
gāvīsus see **gaudeō**	
gelū, gelūs neut. 4 *frost*	11
genū, genūs neut. 4 *knee*	11
gladiātor, gladiātōris masc. 3 *gladiator*	11
gladius, gladiī masc. 2 *sword*	14
glōria, glōriae fem. 1 *glory*	16
gracilis, gracile *thin*	12
gradior, gradī, gressus sum 3 *i*-stem *stride*	15
grātia, grātiae fem. 1 *favor*, pl. *thanks*	10
grātiā (+ gen.) *for the sake of*	16
gravis, grave *heavy, serious*	9
grex, gregis masc. 3 *flock*	8
habeō, habēre, habuī, habitum 2 *have*	1
hasta, hastae fem. 1 *spear*	14
herī adv. *yesterday*	5
hīc adv. *here*	12
hīc, haec, hōc pron., pronom. adj. *this*	17
hiems, hiemis fem. 3 *winter*	15
hinc adv. *from here*	12
hodiē adv. *today*	5
homō, hominis masc./fem. 3 *human being*	8
honor, honōris masc. 3 *honor*	16
hōra, hōrae fem. 1 *hour*	15
hortor 1 *urge*	15
hortus, hortī masc. 2 *garden*	5
hostis, hostis masc. 3 *enemy*	8
hūc adv. *to here*	12

humilis, humile *humble* 9

humus, humī fem. 2 *ground* 15

iaceō, iacēre, iacuī 2 *lie down* 14

iaciō, iacere, iēcī, iactum 3 *i*-stem *throw* 14

iam adv. *now, already* 7

iānua, iānuae fem. 1 *door* 2

ibi adv. *there* 12

īdem, eadem, idem pron., pronom. adj.
   the same 17

iēcī see **iaciō**

igitur conj. *therefore* 3

ignārus, -a, -um *ignorant* 16

ignis, ignis masc. 3 *fire* 8

ignōrō 1 *be unaware* 21

ignōscō, ignoscere, ignōvī, ignōtum 3
   (+ dat.) *forgive* 17

ille, illa, illud pron., pronom. adj. *that* 17

illīc adv. *there* 12

illinc adv. *from there* 12

illūc adv. *to there* 12

immortālis, immortāle *immortal* 9

impedīmentum, impedīmentī neut. 2
   hindrance 16

impediō, impedīre, impedīvī, impedītum 4
   hinder, impede 24

imperātor, imperātōris masc. 3 *commander,*
   emperor 11

imperō 1 (+ dat.) *order* 17

impetus, impetūs masc. 4 *rush, onset* 11

in prep. (+ abl.) *in, on* 2

in prep. (+ acc.) *into, on to* 2

inānis, ināne *empty* 9

incipiō, incipere, incēpī, inceptum 3 *i*-stem
   begin 7

incolumis, incolume *safe* 9

inde adv. *from there* 12

indulgeō, indulgēre, indulsī, indultum 2
   (+ dat.) *be lenient to* 17

infēlix, infēlīcis *unhappy, unlucky* 9

inferior, -ius compar. adj. *lower* 12

inferō, inferre, intulī, illātum irreg. *bring into* 7

infimus, -a, -um superl. adj. *lowest* 12

infrā adv. *below* 12

ingens, ingentis *huge* 9

ingredior, ingredī, ingressus sum 3 *i*-stem
   go into 17

inquit defective *he (she, it) says* or *said* 7

insānia, insāniae fem. 1 *madness* 10

insidiae, insidiārum fem. 1 *ambush* 10

insula, insulae fem. 1 *island* 2

intellegō, intellegere, intellexī, intellectum 3
   understand 21

interdīcō, interdīcere, interdixī, interdictum
   3 (+ dat.) *forbid* 24

interest, interesse, interfuit impers. irreg.
   it matters 28

interficiō, interficere, -fēcī, -fectum 3 *i*-stem
   kill 14

interim adv. *meanwhile* 12

interior, -ius compar. adj. *interior* 12

intimus, -a, -um superl. adj. *innermost* 12

intrā adv. *inside* 12

invādō, invādere, invāsī, invāsum 3 *invade* 14

inveniō, invenīre, invēnī, inventum 4 *come*
   upon, find 4

invideō, invidēre, invīdī, invīsum 2 (+ dat.)
   envy 17

ipse, ipsa, ipsum intensive pron., pronom. adj.
   myself etc. 17

īra, īrae fem. 1 *anger* 3

īrascor, īrascī, īrātus sum 3 (+ dat.) *be angry*
   with 17

is, ea, id pron., pronom. adj. *that* 17

iste, ista, istud pron., pronom. adj. *that* 17

ita adv. *so (in such a way)* 23

Ītalia, Ītaliae fem. 1 *Italy* 2

itaque conj. *therefore* 3

iter, itineris neut. 3 *journey* 11

iterum adv. *again*	6
iubeō, iubēre, iussī, iussum 2 *order*	14
iugum, iugī neut. 2 *yoke*	7
iūs, iūris neut. 3 *law*	8
iussī see **iubeō**	
iuvat, iuvāre, iūvit 1 (+ acc. + inf.) *it pleases*	28
iuvenis, iuvenis masc. 3 *young man*	11
iuvō, iuvāre, iūvī, iūtum 1 *help*	3
lābor, lābī, lapsus sum 3 *slip*	15
labor, labōris masc. 3 *work, toil*	8
labōrō 1 *work*	4
lacrima, lacrimae fem. 1 *tear(-drop)*	2
laedō, laedere, laesī, laesum 3 *harm*	4
lapsus see **lābor**	
lātum see **ferō**	
lātus, -a, -um *broad*	6
laudō 1 *praise*	7
laus, laudis fem. 3 *glory*	16
legiō, legiōnis fem. 3 *legion*	14
legō, legere, lēgī, lectum 3 *read*	1
lentus, -a, -um *slow*	6
levis, leve *light*	9
lex, lēgis fem. 3 *law*	8
līber, lībera, līberum *free*	6
liber, librī masc. 2 *book*	5
līberī, līberōrum masc. 2 *children*	10
līberō 1 *free*	4
lībertās, lībertātis fem. 3 *freedom*	11
libet, libēre, libuit 2 (+ dat. + inf.) *it is pleasant*	28
licet, licēre, licuit 2 (+ dat. + inf.) *it is permissible*	28
littera, litterae fem. 1 *letter of the alphabet*, pl. *letters of the alphabet, epistle, literature*	10
lītus, lītoris neut. 3 *shore*	11
longus, -a, -um *long*	6
loquor, loquī, locūtus sum 3 *speak*	15
lūcescit, lūcescere 3 *it is getting light*	28
lucrum, lucrī neut. 2 *profit*	16
lūdō, lūdere, lūsī, lūsum 3 *play*	1
lūdus, lūdī masc. 2 *game, school*, pl. *games (in the circus, amphitheater, etc.)*	5
lūmen, lūminis neut. 3 *light*	8
lūna, lūnae fem. 1 *moon*	3
lupa, lupae fem. 1 *she-wolf*	5
lupus, lupī masc. 2 *male wolf*	5
lux, lūcis fem. 3 *light*	8
magis compar. adv. *more*	12
magister, magistrī masc. 2 *teacher*	5
magistrātus, magistrātūs masc. 4 *magistrate*	11
magnopere adv. *greatly*	12
magnus, -a, -um *big*	6
maior, maius compar. adj. (**magnus**) *bigger*	12
male adv. *badly*	12
mālō, malle, māluī irreg. *prefer*	10
malus, -a, -um *bad*	6
māne adv. *in the morning*	3
maneō, manēre, mansī 2 *remain*	7
mānēs, mānium masc. 3 *the souls of the dead*	10
manus, manūs fem. 4 *hand*	11
mare, maris neut. 3 *sea*	8
māter, mātris fem. 3 *mother*	8
maximus, -a, -um superl. adj. (**magnus**) *biggest*	12
medeor, medērī 2 (+ dat.) *heal*	17
melior, melius compar. adj. (**bonus**) *better*	12
meminī, meminisse defective 3 (+ gen.) *remember*	18
memor, memoris *mindful*	16
mens, mentis fem. 3 *mind*	8
mensis, mensis masc. 3 *month*	15
mentior, mentīrī, mentītus sum 4 *tell a lie*	15
mereor, merērī, meritus sum 2 *deserve*	15
metuō, metuere, metuī 3 *fear*	1
metus, metūs masc. 4 *fear*	11
meus, -a, -um *my*	6
mīles, mīlitis masc. 3 *soldier*	8
mīliēs *one thousand times*	10
mille *a thousand*	10

millēnī, -ae, -a *one thousand each* — 10

millēsimus, -a, -um *thousandth* — 10

minae, minārum fem. 1 *threats* — 10

minimus, -a, -um superl. adj. (**parvus**) *smallest* — 12

minor, minus compar. adj. (**parvus**) *smaller* — 12

mīror 1 *admire* — 15

miser, misera, miserum *wretched* — 6

miseret, miserēre, miseruit 2 (+ acc. + gen. or inf.) *it causes pity* — 28

mīsī see **mittō**

mittō, mittere, mīsī, missum 3 *send* — 1

modo adv. *only* — 13

moenia, moenium neut. 3 *city walls* — 10

mollis, molle *soft* — 9

moneō, monēre, monuī, monitum 2 *warn* — 1

mons, montis masc. 3 *mountain* — 8

monstrō 1 *show* — 7

morior, morī, mortuus sum 3 *i*-stem *die* — 15

moror, morārī, morātus sum 1 *delay* — 15

mors, mortis fem. 3 *death* — 8

mortālis, mortāle *mortal* — 9

mortuus see **morior**

mōs, mōris masc. 3 *custom* pl. *morals, character* — 9

moveō, movēre, mōvī, mōtum 2 *move* — 7

mox adv. *soon* — 6

mulier, mulieris fem. 3 *woman* — 8

multum adv. *much* — 12

multus, -a, -um *much*, pl. *many* — 6

mūnus, mūneris neut. 3 *gift* — 8

mūrus, mūrī masc. 2 *wall* (in general) — 5

nam particle *for* — 5

namque conj. *for* — 5

narrō 1 *tell* — 21

nascor, nascī, nātus sum 3 *be born* — 13

nātus see **nascor**

nauta, nautae masc. 1 *sailor* — 2

nāvigō 1 *sail* — 7

nāvis, nāvis fem. 3 *ship* — 8

-ne enclitic particle *introduces a question* — 4

nē adv., conj. *introduces various types of clause* — 23

nē . . . quidem *not even* — 13

nec adv., conj. *and not, nor* — 4

nec . . . nec . . . *neither . . . nor . . .* — 4

necesse est impers. *it is necessary* — 28

necne conj. *or not* — 25

negō 1 *deny* — 21

negōtium, negōtiī neut. 2 *business* — 7

nēmō, nullīus *no one* — 13

nesciō, nescīre, nescīvī 4 *do not know* — 21

neuter, neutra, neutrum *neither* — 13

niger, nigra, nigrum *black, dark* — 6

nihilum, nihilī neut. 2 *nothing* — 16

nimis adv. *too much* — 16

nisi conj. *unless, if . . . not* — 28

nōbilitās, nōbilitātis fem. 3 *nobility, the upper class* — 10

noceō, nocēre, nocuī, nocitum 2 (+ dat.) *harm* — 17

nōlī, nōlīte imperative verb (+ inf.) *don't* — 1

nōlō, nolle, nōluī irreg. *be unwilling* — 10

nōmen, nōminis neut. 3 *name* — 8

nōn adv. *not* — 2

nōn modo (sōlum, tantum) . . . *not only* — 13

nōnāgintā *ninety* — 10

nōngentī, -ae, -a *nine hundred* — 10

nonne interrogative particle *surely* (invites affirmative answer) — 4

nonnullus, -a, -um *some* — 13

nōnus, -a, -um *ninth* — 10

noscō, noscere, nōvī, nōtum 3 *find out*, perf. *know* — 21

noster, nostra, nostrum *our* — 6

novem *nine* — 10

novēnī, -ae, -a *nine each* — 10

nōvī see **noscō**

noviēs *nine times* — 10

novus, -a, -um *new* — 6

nox, noctis fem. 3 *night* — 8

nūbō, nūbere, nupsī, nuptum 3 (+ dat.) *marry* (of a woman) — 17

nullus, -a, -um *no, none* — 13

num interrogative particle *surely not* (invites negative answer) — 4
  introducing indirect question *whether* — 25

nūmen, nūminis neut. 3 *divinity* — 8

numerus, numerī masc. 2 *number* — 7

numquam adv. *never* — 4

nunc adv. *now* — 4

nuntiō 1 *announce* — 21

nūper adv. *recently* — 6

nupsī see **nūbō**

nuptiae, nuptiārum fem. 1 *marriage* — 10

oblīviscor, oblīviscī, oblītus sum 3 (+ gen.) *forget* — 18

obsequor, obsequī, obsecūtus sum 3 (+ dat.) *obey* — 17

obstō, obstāre, obstitī 1 (+ dat.) *hinder, impede* — 24

octāvus, -a, -um *eighth* — 10

octiēs *eight times* — 10

octō *eight* — 10

octōnī, -ae, -a *eight each* — 10

oculus, oculī masc. 2 *eye* — 7

ōdī, ōdisse defective 3 *hate* — 19

odium, odiī neut. 2 *hatred* — 16

offerō, offerre, obtulī, oblātum irreg. *offer* — 7

officium, officiī neut. 2 *duty* — 7

ōlim adv. *at some time* — 12

ōmen, ōminis neut. 3 *omen* — 11

omnis, omne *all, every* — 9

onus, oneris neut. 3 *burden* — 16

opera, operae fem. 1 *attention* — 20

oportet, oportēre, oportuit 2 (+ acc. + inf.) *it is proper* — 28

oppidum, oppidī neut. 2 *town* — 7

opprobrium, opprobriī neut. 2 *disgrace* — 16

oppugnō 1 *besiege* — 3

optimus, -a, -um superl. adj. (**bonus**) *best* — 12

opus, operis neut. 3 *work* — 8

opus est impers. (+ abl.) *it is necessary* — 28

ōra, ōrae fem. 1 *shore* — 2

ōrātiō, ōrātiōnis fem. 3 *speech* — 11

orior, orīrī, ortus sum 4 *arise* — 15

ōrō 1 *implore* — 24

ortus see **orior**

ostendō, ostendere, ostendī, ostentum 3 *show* — 4

ōtium, ōtiī neut. 2 *leisure* — 7

paene adv. *almost* — 3

paenitet, paenitēre, paenituit 2 (+ acc. + gen. or inf.) *it causes regret* — 28

parcō, parcere, pepercī, parsum 3 (+ dat.) *spare* — 17

pars, partis fem. 3 *part* — 8

partim adv. *partly* — 12

parum adv. *too little* — 12

parvus, -a, -um *small* — 6

pascō, pascere, pāvī, pastum 3 *feed* — 4

passim adv. *everywhere* — 12

passus see **patior**

pastor, pastōris masc. 3 *shepherd* — 8

pater, patris masc. 3 *father* — 8

patior, patī, passus sum 3 *i*-stem *suffer, allow* — 15

paucī, -ae, -a *few* — 6

paulātim adv. *gradually* — 12

pauper, pauperis *poor* — 9

pāvī see **pascō**

pax, pācis fem. 3 *peace* — 8

pecūnia, pecūniae fem. 1 *money* — 2

pecus, pecudis fem. 3 *flock, herd* — 8

pedes, peditis masc. 3 *foot soldier* — 14

peior, peius compar. adj. (**malus**) *worse* — 12

pellō, pellere, pepulī, pulsum 3 *drive, repel* — 4

penātēs, penātium masc. 3 *household gods* — 10

pepercī see **parcō**

pepulī see **pellō**

per prep. (+ acc.) *through, along* — 5

perdō, perdere, perdidī, perditum 3 *lose, destroy* — 7

pereō, perīre, periī (or **perīvī**) irreg. *go through, perish* — 4

perferō, perferre, pertulī, perlātum irreg. *bring through, endure* — 7

perīculum, perīculī neut. 2 *danger* — 16

persuādeō, -ēre, persuāsī, persuāsum 2 (+ dat.) *persuade* — 17

pēs, pedis masc. 3 *foot* — 11

pessimus, -a, -um superl. adj. (**malus**) *worst* — 12

petō, -ere, petiī (or **-īvī**), **petītum** 3 (+ *ā/ab* + abl.) *seek* — 1

pietās, pietātis fem. 3 *piety* — 11

piger, pigra, pigrum *lazy* — 6

piget, pigēre, piguit 2 (+ acc. + gen. or inf.) *it causes vexation* — 28

pinguis, pingue *fat* — 9

pīrāta, pīrātae masc. 1 *pirate* — 2

piscis, piscis masc. 3 *fish* — 8

placeō, placēre, placuī, placitum 2 (+ dat.) *please* — 17

placet, placēre, placuit 2 (+ dat. + inf.) *it is pleasing* — 28

plebs, plēbis fem. 3 *the lower class of citizens* — 10

plēnus, -a, -um (+ gen. or abl.) *full* — 16

pluit, pluere, pluit 3 *it is raining* — 28

plūrimus, -a, -um superl. adj. (**multus**) *most* — 12

plūs, plūris compar. adj. (**multus**) *more* — 12

poena, poenae fem. 1 *punishment* — 7

poēta, poētae masc. 1 *poet* — 2

polliceor, pollicērī, pollicitus sum 2 *promise* — 15

pōnō, pōnere, posuī, positum 3 *place* — 4

pons, pontis masc. 3 *bridge* — 8

populus, populī masc. 2 *people* — 7

porca, porcae fem. 1 *pig* — 4

porcus, porcī masc. 2 *pig* — 5

porta, portae fem. 1 *gate* — 2

portō 1 *carry* — 4

portus, portūs masc. 4 *port, harbor* — 11

possum, posse, potuī irreg. *be able* — 4

post prep. (+ acc.) *behind, after* — 2

posterior, -ius compar. adj. *later* — 12

postquam conj. *after* — 7

postrēmus, -a, -um superl. adj. *latest* — 12

posuī see **pōnō**

potens, potentis *powerful* — 9

potentia, potentiae fem. 1 *power* — 2

potior, potīrī, potītus sum 4 (+ gen. or abl.) *take possession of* — 18

praeda, praedae fem. 1 *booty, plunder* — 2

praesertim adv. *especially* — 3

precor 1 *implore* — 15

prīmō adv. *at first* — 12

prīmus, -a, -um *first* — 10

prior, prius compar. adj. *former* — 12

priusquam conj. *before* — 27

prō prep. (+ abl.) *on behalf of* — 3

procul adv. *far away* — 7

prōdest, prōdesse, prōfuit (+ dat. + inf.) *it is beneficial* — 28

proelium, proeliī neut. 2 *battle* — 7

proficiscor, proficiscī, profectus sum 3 *depart* — 15

prōgredior, prōgredī, prōgressus sum 3 i-stem *go forward* — 15

prohibeō, prohibēre, prohibuī, prohibitum 2 *prevent* — 24

prōmittō, prōmittere, prōmīsī, prōmissum 3 *promise* — 21

prope prep. (+ acc.) *near* — 5

propior, propius compar. adj. *nearer* — 12

proximus, -a, -um superl. adj. *nearest* — 12

pudet, pudēre, puduit 2 (+ acc. + gen. or inf.) *it causes shame* — 28

pudor, pudōris masc. 3 *shame* — 16

puella, puellae fem. 1 *girl* — 2

puer, puerī masc. 2 *boy* — 5

pugna, pugnae fem. 1 *battle* — 14

pugnō 1 *fight* — 3
pulcher, pulchra, pulchrum *beautiful, handsome* — 6
pūrus, -a, -um *pure* — 6
putō 1 *think* — 21
quadrāgintā *forty* — 10
quadringentī, -ae, -a *four hundred* — 10
quaerō, -ere, quaesīvī, quaesītum 3 (+ ā/ab + abl.) *seek* — 24
quālis, -e *what sort of, as* — 13
quam adv. (+ compar.) *than*, (+ superl.) *as . . . as possible, how, as* — 12
quamquam adv. *although* — 7
quamvīs adv. *although* — 27
quandō adv. *when* — 4
quantus, -a, -um *how much/great, as* — 13
quartus, -a, -um *fourth* — 10
quater *four times* — 10
quaternī, -ae, -a *four each* — 10
quattuor *four* — 10
-que enclitic particle *and, both* — 4
queror, querī, questus sum 3 *complain* — 15
quī, quae, quod interrog. pronom. adj. *which* — 18
quī, quae, quod rel. pron. *who, which* — 18
quia conj. *because* — 3
quīdam, quaedam, quid(quod)dam indef. pron., pronom. adj. *some(one)* — 18
quiēs, quiētis fem. 3 *rest* — 10
quīn adv., conj. introduces various types of clause — 24
quīndecim *fifteen* — 10
quīngentī, -ae, -a *five hundred* — 10
quīnī, -ae, -a *five each* — 10
quīnquāgintā *fifty* — 10
quīnque *five* — 10
quīnquiēs *five times* — 10
quīntus, -a, -um *fifth* — 10
quis, quid interrog. pron. *who, what* — 18
quō adv. *to where* — 15

quod conj. *because* — 3
quōminus conj. *lest* — 24
quōmodo adv. *how* — 4
quoniam *because* — 3
quot indecl. adj. *how many, as* — 13
quotiens adv. *how often, as* — 13
rapiō, rapere, rapuī, raptum 3 *i*-stem *seize* — 1
ratus see **reor**
redeō, redīre, rediī irreg. *go back* — 4
redūcō, -ere, -duxī, -ductum 3 *lead back* — 7
referō, referre, retulī, relātum irreg. *bring back* — 7
rēfert, rēferre, rētulit impers. *it matters* — 28
rēgīna, rēgīnae fem. 1 *queen* — 7
regredior, regredī, regressus sum 3 *i*-stem *go back* — 15
relinquō, relinquere, relīquī, relictum 3 *leave, abandon* — 7
reliquiae, reliquiārum fem. 1 *remains* — 10
remedium, remediī neut. 2 *cure* — 16
reor, rērī, ratus sum 2 *think* — 15
reperiō, reperīre, repperī, repertum 4 *find* — 1
repperī see **reperiō**
rēs, reī fem. 5 *thing* — 11
resistō, resistere, restitī 3 (+ dat.) *resist* — 17
respondeō, respondēre, respondī, responsum 2 *reply* — 21
restat 1 impers. *it remains* — 28
retineō, retinēre, retinuī, retentum 2 *restrain* — 24
revocō 1 *call back* — 7
rex, rēgis masc. 3 *king* — 8
rīdeō, rīdēre, rīsī, rīsum 2 *laugh, mock* — 3
rogō 1 *ask (for)* — 16
Rōma, Rōmae fem. 1 *Rome* — 2
Rōmānus, -a, -um *Roman* — 6
rosa, rosae fem. 1 *rose* — 2
rursus, adv. *again* — 6
rūs, rūris neut. 3 *countryside* — 15
sacer, sacra, sacrum (+ dat.) *sacred (to)* — 6
sacerdōs, sacerdōtis masc./fem. 3 *priest(ess)* — 8

Appendix 5

saepe adv. *often*	5	**sexiēs** *six times*	10
saevus, -a, -um *savage*	6	**sextus, -a, -um** *sixth*	10
salūber, salūbris, salūbre *healthy*	9	**sī** conj. *if*	2
salūs, salūtis fem. 3 *deliverance*	16	**sīc** adv. *so (in such a way)*	23
sanguis, sanguinis masc. 3 *blood*	11	**silentium, silentiī** neut. 2 *silence*	7
sapientia, sapientiae fem. 1 *wisdom*	10	**silva, silvae** fem. 1 *wood, forest*	4
satis *enough*	16	**similis, simile** (+ gen. or dat.) *like, similar to*	9
saxum, saxī neut. 2 *rock*	5	**sine** prep. (+ abl.) *without*	2
scelus, sceleris neut. 3 *crime*	11	**singulī, -ae, -a** *one each*	10
sciō, scīre, scīvī 4 *know*	21	**socius, sociī** masc. 2 *ally*	14
scrībō, scrībere, scripsī, scriptum 3 *write*	7	**sōlācium, sōlāciī** neut. 2 *comfort*	16
scūtum, scūtī neut. 2 *shield*	16	**soleō, solēre, solitus sum** 2 *be accustomed*	15
secundus, -a, -um *second*	10	**sōlum** adv. *only*	13
sed conj. *but*	2	**sōlus, -a, -um** *only, alone*	13
sed etiam *but also*	13	**somnium, somniī** neut. 2 *dream*	7
sēdecim *sixteen*	10	**somnus, somnī** masc. 2 *sleep*	7
sedeō, sedēre, sēdī, sessum 2 *sit*	1	**soror, sorōris** fem. 3 *sister*	8
semel *once*	10	**speciēs, speciēī** fem. 5 *form, appearance*	11
semper adv. *always*	4	**spectō** 1 *watch*	1
senātus, senātūs masc. 4 *Senate*	11	**spēlunca, spēluncae** fem. 1 *cave*	3
senectūs, senectūtis fem. 3 *old age*	11	**spērō** 1 *hope*	21
sēnī, -ae, -a *six each*	10	**spēs, speī** fem. 5 *hope, expectation*	11
sensī see **sentiō**		**spolia, spoliōrum** neut. 2 *plunder, spoils*	10
sentiō, sentīre, sensī, sensum 4 *feel, perceive*	21	**sponte** adv. *spontaneously*	11
septem *seven*	10	**statim** adv. *immediately*	6
septemdecim *seventeen*	10	**statua, statuae** fem. 1 *statue*	2
septēnī, -ae, -a *seven each*	10	**stella, stellae** fem. 1 *star*	3
septiēs *seven times*	10	**stetī** see **stō**	
septimus, -a, -um *seventh*	10	**stō, stāre, stetī, statum** 1 *stand*	3
septingentī, -ae, -a *seven hundred*	10	**studeō, studēre, studuī** 2 (+ dat.) *study,*	
septuāgintā *seventy*	10	*be eager*	17
sequor, sequī, secūtus sum 3 *follow*	15	**stultitia, stultitiae** fem. 1 *stupidity*	10
serva, servae fem. 1 *female slave*	5	**stultus, -a, -um** *stupid*	6
serviō, servīre, servīvī, servītum 4 (+ dat.)		**suādeō, suādēre, suāsī, suāsum** 2 (+ dat.) *urge*	17
be a slave to	17	**sub** prep. (+ abl.) *under*	2
servus, servī masc. 2 *male slave*	5	**sub** prep. (+ acc.) *(to) under*	2
sescentī, -ae, -a *six hundred*	10	**subitō** adv. *suddenly*	7
sex *six*	10	**sufferō, sufferre, sustulī, sublātum** irreg.	
sexāgintā *sixty*	10	*bring under, endure*	7

suī reflex. pers. pron. *himself* etc. 17

sum, esse, fuī irreg. *be* 4

superior, -ius compar. adj. *higher* 12

superō 1 *conquer* 14

suprā adv. *above* 12

suprēmus, -a, -um superl. adj. *highest* 12

surgō, surgere, surrexī, surrectum 3 *rise* 3

surrexī see **surgō**

susurrō 1 *whisper* 21

suus, -a, -um *his (her/its/their) own* 17

taberna, tabernae fem. 1 *tavern* 2

taedet, taedēre, taesum est 2 (+ acc. + gen. or inf.) *it wearies* 28

tālis, -e *of such a sort* 13

tam adv. *so, as* 13

tamen, adv. *but, however* 7

tandem adv. *at last* 3

tangō, tangere, tetigī, tactum 3 *touch* 3

tantum adv. *only* 13

tantus, -a, -um adj. *so much/great* 13

taurus, taurī masc. 2 *bull* 5

tēlum, tēlī neut. 2 *missile* 7

templum, templī neut. 2 *temple* 5

tempus, temporis neut. 3 *time* 8

tenebrae, tenebrārum fem. 1 *darkness* 10

teneō, tenēre, tenuī, tentum 2 *hold* 3

ter *three times* 10

tergum, tergī neut. 2 *back* 7

ternī, -ae, -a *three each* 10

terra, terrae fem. 1 *earth, land* 4

terreō, terrēre, terruī, territum 2 *frighten* 1

tertius, -a, -um *third* 10

tetigī see **tangō**

timeō, timēre, timuī 2 *fear* 1

timor, timōris masc. 3 *fear* 16

tolerō 1 *tolerate* 3

tonat, tonāre, tonuit 1 *it is thundering* 28

tot indecl. adj. *so many* 13

totiens adv. *so often* 13

tōtus, -a, -um *whole* 13

trans prep. (+ acc.) *across* 2

trecentī, -ae, -a *three hundred* 10

tredecim *thirteen* 10

trēs, tria *three* 10

trīgintā *thirty* 10

tristis, triste *sad* 9

tū, tuī pers. pron. *you* 17

tulī see **ferō**

tum/tunc adv. *then* 4

turba, turbae fem. 1 *crowd, mob* 3

turpis, turpe *shameful* 9

turris, turris fem. 3 *tower* 8

tuus, -a, -um *your* (sing.) 6

ubi adv. *where, when* 4

ulciscor, ulciscī, ultus sum 3 *avenge, take vengeance upon* 15

ullus, -a, -um *any* 13

ulterior, -ius compar. adj. *farther* 12

ultimus, -a, -um superl. adj. *farthest* 12

ultus see **ulciscor**

unda, undae fem. 1 *wave* 2

unde adv. *from where* 12

undecim *eleven* 10

undecimus, -a, -um *eleventh* 10

undēvīgintī *nineteen* 10

ūnus, -a, -um *one* 10

urbs, urbis fem. 3 *city* 8

ūsus, ūsūs masc. 4 *use, experience* 16

ut conj. introduces various types of clause 23

uter, utra, utrum *which* (of two), *either* 13

utinam particle *if only* 22

ūtor, ūtī, ūsus sum 3 (+ abl.) *use* 18

utrum particle introduces a question, *whether* 4

ūva, ūvae fem. 1 *grape* 4

uxor, uxōris fem. 3 *wife* 8

vacca, vaccae fem. 1 *cow* 4

vel conj. *or* (of any number and type of alternatives) 3

vel . . . vel . . . *either . . . or . . .*	3	**videō, vidēre, vīdī, vīsum** 2 *see*	1
vendō, vendere, vendidī, venditum 3 *sell*	16	**videor, vidērī, vīsus sum** 2 *seem*	15
venēnum, venēnī neut. 2 *poison*	7	**vīgintī** *twenty*	10
veniō, venīre, vēnī, ventum 4 *come*	4	**villa, villae** fem. 1 *country house*	3
ventus, ventī masc. 2 *wind*	7	**vincō, vincere, vīcī, victum** 3 *conquer*	1
vēr, vēris neut. 3 *spring*	15	**vīnum, vīnī** neut. 2 *wine*	5
verbātim adv. *word for word*	12	**vir, virī** masc. 2 *man, husband*	5
verbum, verbī neut. 2 *word*	7	**vīrēs** see **vīs**	
vereor, verērī, veritus sum 2 *fear*	15	**virtūs, virtūtis** fem. 3 *courage, virtue*	8
vēritās, vēritātis fem. 3 *truth*	11	**vīs** fem. irreg. 3 *force*; pl. *strength*	10
vērō adv. *truly*	11	**vīta, vītae** fem. 1 *life*	3
versus, versūs masc. 4 *verse*	11	**vītō** 1 *avoid*	4
vertō, vertere, vertī, versum 3 *turn*	19	**vīvō, vīvere, vixī, victum** 3 *live*	1
vescor, vescī defective 3 (+ abl.) *feed on*	18	**vixī** see **vīvō**	
vester, vestra, vestrum *your* (pl.)	6	**vocō** 1 *call*	1
vetō, vetāre, vetuī, vetitum 1 *forbid*	24	**volō, velle, voluī** irreg. *wish*	10
vetus, veteris *old*	9	**volucer, volucris, volucre** *flying, swift*	9
via, viae fem. 1 *road, way*	3	**vox, vōcis** fem. 3 *voice*	8
vīcī see **vincō**		**vulnerō** 1 *wound*	14
vīciēs *twenty times*	10	**vulnus, vulneris** neut. 3 *wound*	14
victor, victōris masc. 3 *victor*	14	**vultus, vultūs** masc. 4 *face*	11
victōria, victōriae fem. 1 *victory*	3		

Index by Subject

Index by Subject

comparative (*continued*)
meaning and uses, 125, 130
with the ablative of comparison, 131
with *quam*, 130
concessive clauses
with *cum*, 324f.
expressed by participles and the ablative absolute, 221ff.
with *quamquam/quamvīs*, 328
conditional sentences
defined, 313
protasis expressed by a participle or the ablative absolute, 221ff.
sī with the indefinite pronoun/pronominal adjective, 315f.
types, 314f.
conjugation
defective, s.v.
deponent, s.v.
irregular forms, s.v.
perfect system
active voice of all indicative tenses, 71f.
passive voice of all indicative tenses, 151f.
subjunctive, Chapter 22
present system
present active indicative and imperative, 1ff.
present passive indicative and imperative, 149
future and imperfect active indicative, 29f.
future and imperfect passive indicative, 150
subjunctive, Chapter 22
principal parts, 5
semi-deponent verbs, 166f.
consecutive clauses, *see* result
correlatives, Chapter 13
cum
conjunction, 323ff.
preposition, 16, 20, 22, 196

dative
defined, 16
agent with the gerund of obligation, 238
double dative, 180f.
indirect object, 16
possession, 179
predicate, 180f.
reference, 179f.
with certain adjectives, 65
with impersonal verbs, 338ff.
with intransitive verbs, 197f.
declension
adjectives
first/second declension, 60
third declension, 93ff.
comparative, s.v.
indeclinable, 103
superlative, s.v.

nouns *see* gerund, participles, pronouns, etc.
first declension, 17
second declension, 51f.
third declension, 84, 86
fourth declension, 115
fifth declension, 115f.
defective verbs
ait, 77
coepī, 226
fīō, 166
inquit, 77
meminī, 210
ōdī, 226
vescor, 210
deliberative questions, 267f.
demonstrative pronouns/pronominal adjectives, 191ff.
deponent verbs
defined, 164
conjugation
imperative and indicative, Chapter 14
infinitive, Chapter 14, 247
participles, 220f., 246, subjunctive, 260
semi-deponent verbs, s.v.
description
ablative of, 182
genitive of, 178
direct statement (contrasted with indirect), 245
double accusative, 182
double dative, 180f.
doubting, clauses of, 304
dum/dummodo, 325f.
duration, *see* extent, accusative of

enclitics
defined, 44
enim, 54
nam(que), 54
-ne, 44
-que, 44
tamen, 77
exclamation
with the accusative, 181
with correlative adjectives and adverbs, 138f.
exhortations
defined, 267
introducing primary sequence only, 280
as the origin of clauses of fearing, 305
extent, accusative of, 182

fearing, clauses of, 305
fifth declension, *see* declension
final clauses, *see* purpose
first conjugation, *see* conjugation
first declension, *see* declension
fourth conjugation, *see* conjugation
fourth declension, *see* declension

410

used in an ablative absolute construction, 223ff.
used as adjectives, 218
used as nouns, 223
partitive genitive, 127f., 177
parts of speech, *see* adjectives, adverbs, nouns,
prepositions, pronouns, verbs
passive periphrastic (gerundive of obligation), 237f.
passive voice, *see* voice
perfect system, *see* conjugation
perfect tense
compared to the imperfect tense, 74
in conditional sentences, 314f.
forms, *see* conjugation
meaning and translation, 74
referring to present time, 74, 277
with the subjunctive used as a main verb
exhortations, 267
potential, 269
with the subjunctive used in a subordinate clause,
see sequence of tenses
person
defined, 1
contrasted with impersonal verbs, 337
with the subjunctive used as a main verb
deliberative questions, 267f.
exhortations, 267
personal pronouns/pronominal adjectives, 62, 194ff., 249f.
place expressions
locative, 168
with cities, towns, and small islands, 168
with prepositions, 20f.
pluperfect tense
in conditional sentences, 314f.
with *cum* meaning "whenever," 323
forms, *see* conjugation
meaning and translation, 74
with the subjunctive used as a main verb
potential, 269
wishes, 268
with the subjunctive used in a subordinate clause,
see sequence of tenses
possession
dative of, 179
genitive of, 16
personal pronominal adjectives, 62
reflexive vs. non-reflexive, 195, 249f.
postpositive, *see* enclitics
potential main clauses, 269
predicate
in an ablative absolute construction, 225
adjectives, 62
dative, 180f.
genitive of characteristic, 178
nominative, 41, 167
prepositions, 20f.
present system, *see* conjugation

present tense
in conditional sentences, 314f.
forms, *see* conjugation
meaning and translation, 4f.
with the subjunctive used as a main verb
deliberative questions, 267f.
exhortations, 267
potential, 269
wishes, 268
with the subjunctive used in a subordinate clause,
see sequence of tenses
preventing, *see* hindering/preventing, clauses of
price, ablative of, 183
principal parts
defined, 5
absence of the fourth principal part of intransitive
verbs, 152
priusquam, 327
prohibition, *see* exhortations
pronouns/pronominal adjectives, Chapters 17 and 18.
See also demonstrative, indefinite, intensive, interrogative, personal, reflexive, relative
pronunciation, Appendix 1, xvi
of certain pronouns, 191
protasis, *see* conditional sentences
punctuation, xviii
purpose
accusative form of the supine, 238
contrasted with result, 282
gerund(ive) with *ad*, *grātiā*, and *causā*, 235ff.
not expressed with the infinitive, 278
predicate dative, 180
relative clause of, 293
ut or *nē* with the subjunctive, 278ff.

quam
with *ante* and *post*, 328
with the comparative and superlative, 130
as a correlative, 138
distinguished from *quōmodo*, 139
in questions and exclamations, 138f.
quamquam/quamvīs, 76, 328
questions
alternative ("double"), 40, 303f.
deliberative, 267f.
direct, 40f.
indirect, 302ff.
quīn, 292, 304
quod, 20, 32, 327

reference, dative of, 179f.
reflexive
defined, 194f.
forms, 195f.
contrasted with the intensive, 197
in indirect statement, 249f.

Index Auctōrum

Chapter 1

Lege, Intellege	Ampelius
Ars Poētica	Publilius Syrus
Vīta Rōmānōrum	Pliny the Elder

Chapter 2

Lege, Intellege	Florus
Ars Poētica	Publilius Syrus
Vīta Rōmānōrum	Petronius

Chapter 3

Lege, Intellege	Solinus
Ars Poētica	Ovid
Mors Rōmānōrum	Lucretius

Chapter 4

Lege, Intellege	[Apicius]
Ars Poētica	Publilius Syrus
Vīta Rōmānōrum	Pliny the Younger

Chapter 5

Lege, Intellege	Ampelius
Ars Poētica	Publilius Syrus
Vīta Rōmānōrum	Donatus

Chapter 6

Lege, Intellege	Ampelius
Ars Poētica	Publilius Syrus
Vīta Rōmānōrum	Cicero

Chapter 7

Lege, Intellege	Ampelius
Ars Poētica	Ovid
Mors Rōmānōrum	Valerius Maximus

Chapter 8

Lege, Intellege	Caesar
Ars Poētica	Publilius Syrus
Vīta Rōmānōrum	Aulus Gellius

Chapter 9

Lege, Intellege	Eutropius
Ars Poētica	Ovid
Vīta Rōmānōrum	Justinian

Chapter 10

Lege, Intellege	Eutropius
Ars Poētica	Ovid
Vīta Rōmānōrum	Aulus Gellius

Chapter 11

Lege, Intellege	Pliny the Elder
Ars Poētica	Ovid
Vīta Rōmānōrum	Seneca the Younger

Chapter 12

Lege, Intellege	Vegetius
Ars Poētica	Ovid
Vīta Rōmānōrum	Cicero

Chapter 13

Lege, Intellege	Vegetius
Ars Poētica	Ovid
Vīta Rōmānōrum	Cicero, Columella

Chapter 14

Lege, Intellege	Eutropius
Ars Poētica	Virgil
Vīta Rōmānōrum	Pliny the Elder

Chapter 15

Lege, Intellege	Eutropius
Ars Poētica	Virgil
Vīta Rōmānōrum	Augustus

Chapter 16

Lege, Intellege	Seneca the Elder
Ars Poētica	Virgil
Vīta Rōmānōrum	Cicero

Chapter 17

Lege, Intellege	Justinian
Ars Poētica	Catullus
Vīta Rōmānōrum	Suetonius

Chapter 18

Lege, Intellege	Tacitus
Ars Poētica	Catullus
Vīta Rōmānōrum	Ovid, Seneca the Elder

Chapter 19

Lege, Intellege	[Aurelius Victor]
Ars Poētica	Martial
Vīta Rōmānōrum	Cicero, Pliny the Elder

Chapter 20

Lege, Intellege	Caesar
Ars Poētica	Horace
Vīta Rōmānōrum	Plautus

Chapter 21

Lege, Intellege	Livy
Ars Poētica	Martial
Vīta Rōmānōrum	Suetonius

Chapter 22

Lege, Intellege	Caesar
Ars Poētica	Juvenal
Vīta Rōmānōrum	Suetonius

Chapter 23

Lege, Intellege	Cato
Ars Poētica	Phaedrus
Vīta Rōmānōrum	Suetonius

Chapter 24

Lege, Intellege	Cicero
Ars Poētica	Juvenal
Mors Rōmānōrum	Dying Words of the Emperors

Chapter 25

Lege, Intellege	Livy
Ars Poētica	Ovid
Vīta Rōmānōrum	Valerius Maximus

Chapter 26

Lege, Intellege	Cicero, Macrobius
Ars Poētica	Ovid
Vīta Rōmānōrum	Vegetius

Chapter 27

Lege, Intellege	Cicero
Ars Poētica	Ovid
Mors Rōmānōrum	Epitaphs

Chapter 28

Lege, Intellege	Caesar
Ars Poētica	Ovid
Vīta Rōmānōrum	Pompeian Graffiti

List of Illustrations and Credits

Cover. Nero (r. AD 54–68) and his mother, Julia Agrippina (the Younger), who was the emperor Claudius' fourth wife. She probably murdered him, to make way for Nero, who resented her power and had her killed. The inscription on the coin, AGRIPP(īna) AUG(usta) DĪVĪ CLAUD(iī) NERŌNIS MĀTER (Agrippina Augusta, wife of the god Claudius, mother of Nero), is indicative of the hold which she exerted over him.

P. 7   Aeneas fleeing from Troy with the Palladium (a sacred image of Athena) and his father Anchises. The coin was minted for his descendant, Julius Caesar.

P. 13   Venus, the goddess of love, daughter of Jupiter and ancestor of the Julian family.

P. 23   Jupiter, the king of the Roman gods.

P. 27   Mars, the god of war, coming to Rhea Silvia, who is destined to be the mother of Romulus and Remus.

P. 33   Romulus and Remus suckled by the she-wolf.

P. 37   Janus, the two-faced god of gates and beginnings. The month January is named after him.

P. 45   Nero (r. AD 54–68). His youthful good looks were long gone before his assassination.

P. 49   Vitellius. Nero committed suicide in early June AD 68, fleeing from Galba's soldiers; Otho's troops murdered Galba on January 15 AD 69; Otho committed suicide on April 16, ousted by Vitellius, who reigned until December 22, to be replaced by Vespasian.

P. 55   Rome, helmeted and ready for war.

P. 58   Victory driving a four-horsed chariot.

P. 65   The Medusa, a snake-haired monster, often used as a totem to avert evil. Greek mythological figures are not commonly found on Roman coinage.

P. 69   A Roman military camp.

P. 77   S(enātus) P(opulus)Q(ue) R(ōmānus) MEMORIAE AGRIPPĪNAE. The elder Agrippina, widow of Germanicus, was a much admired figure. Her status within the Julio-Claudian family reflects the complexities of dynastic politics, for she was sister-in-law, stepdaughter and daughter-in-law to Tiberius (who may have poisoned her).

P. 82   Pan, god of herding and the countryside, one of the many deities adopted from Greece. Here the moneyer, Gaius Vibius Pansa, is punning on his own name.

P. 87   The goddess Peace.

P. 92   LĪBERTĀS (Freedom), on a coin minted by Brutus in 54 BC, a decade before the assassination of Julius Caesar.

P. 97   Mars, the god of war.

P. 101   A trophy commemorating Caesar's conquest of Gaul in the 50s BC.

P. 108   Augustus, the first and greatest of the emperors (r. 27 BC–AD 14).

P. 112   The emperor Geta (r. AD 211, jointly with his brother Caracalla, who is said to have killed him in their mother's arms). He liked to puzzle grammarians by asking them for the names of the sounds that particular animals make.

P. 118   FIDĒS EXERCITUUM (The Loyalty of the Armies). This coin, issued by Vitellius, emphasizes the role of the army in appointing emperors and in maintaining their authority. In intervals during the battle in which Vespasian ousted him from power, Vitellius' troops are said to have shared their provisions with Vespasian's army.

P. 122   AEGYPTŌ CAPTĀ (After the Capture of Egypt). A coin issued by Augustus in 28 BC, celebrating the defeat of Antony and Cleopatra.

P. 131   A trophy, on a coin minted by Brutus in late 42 BC, just before he and the other assassins of Julius Caesar were defeated at Philippi by Antony and Octavian.

P. 135   OPTIMŌ PRINCIPĪ (To the best Emperor). A coin issued in honor of Trajan (r. AD 98–117).

P. 142   The temple of Vesta, the goddess of the hearth, is one of the most distinctive features of the Forum Romanum.

P. 146   Magistrates were escorted by officials known as *lictōrēs*, who carried the *fascēs*, bundles of rods with an axe, symbols of their authority to scourge or execute criminals. This coin was issued by Brutus, the assassin of Julius Caesar.

P. 157 Vespasian (r. AD 69–79). It is partly fortuitous, but partly also an indication of the precarious nature of the imperial system, that, in the first 200 years of the Empire, Vespasian was the only emperor to be succeeded by his own son (in his case, by both of his sons, Titus and Domitian).

P. 161 An elephant fighting a snake. Scientists in antiquity debated whether elephants had knee joints. Representations of animals on Roman coins are sometimes not of a very high standard.

P. 169 Valerian, co-emperor with his son Gallienus from AD 253 to 260, when he was captured by Shapur I of Persia, who is said to have used him as a mounting-block when he got on his horse.

P. 173 Diocletian. The half-century before Diocletian seized power in AD 284 was a period of unusual instability, with dozens of emperors and usurpers. He ruled until 305, when he felt strong enough to abdicate, compelling his co-ruler Maximian to do the same. He lived on as a private citizen for about seven years in his magnificent palace near Split in Dalmatia (now Croatia), where he prided himself on growing large cabbages.

P. 183 Standards of Antony's twelfth legion.

P. 188 From a military issue of coinage by Antony, just before he and Cleopatra were defeated by Octavian at Actium in 31 BC.

P. 199 Cleopatra VII, queen of Egypt. Ancient sources praise her intelligence rather than her beauty.

P. 203 Mark Antony. Defeat at Actium ended Antony's hopes of power in Rome, but, through his marriage to Octavian's sister Octavia, he was the grandfather of Claudius, great-grandfather of Caligula, and great-great-grandfather of Nero.

P. 211 HERCULĒS MŪSĀRUM (Hercules as Leader of the Muses).

P. 215 Neptune, the god of the sea, acknowledging his support for Octavian at Actium. The letters *SC* are a standard abbreviation, denoting that the coin was minted *senātūs consultō* "by decree of the Senate"

P. 227 A rather robust peacock, on a coin minted in honor of the deified Paulina, wife of Maximinus Thrax (r. AD 235–238).

P. 231 SPQR SIGNĪS RECEPTĪS (SPQR after the Recovery of the Standards), celebrating the restoration to Augustus in 20 BC of the standards that Crassus had lost to the Parthians in the disastrous Battle of Carrhae 33 years earlier.

P. 239 Commodus (r. AD 180–192) frequently fought as a gladiator, armed with iron weapons whereas his opponents had lead ones.

P. 243 OB CĪVĒS SERVĀTŌS (On account of the Saving of Citizens). The inscription and the civic crown of oak leaves commemorate Galba's rescue of Rome from the tyranny of Nero. Galba was murdered in January AD 69, after a reign of seven months.

P. 251 Hadrian (r. AD 117–138). He is said to have introduced the fashion for wearing a beard either in deference to Greek philosophers or to hide facial scars.

P. 256 Julius Caesar, on a coin issued perhaps only days before his assassination. The garland, which he wore by special dispensation of the Senate, hid his baldness.

P. 269 Tiberius (r. AD 14–27). This coin is sometimes known as the "Tribute Penny," on the assumption that Jesus pointed to this image in arguing that Jews should pay taxes to Rome, "rendering unto Caesar the things that are Caesar's" (St. Matthew 22.21).

P. 274 Caligula (r. AD 37–41), the first of the really worthless emperors. Suetonius says that he enjoyed wallowing in piles of coins.

P. 282 A splendid Celtic portrayal of a horse. The coin was issued in Britain about the time of the Claudius' invasion in AD 43.

P. 287 DĪVUS CLAUDIUS AUGUSTUS, i.e., Claudius the God. In Seneca's *Apocolocyntōsis*, Augustus uses his maiden speech in the Olympian Council to protest that, if the gods allow Claudius to be a god, no one will believe that *they* are gods.

P. 294 SER(vius) GALBA IMP(erātor) CAESAR AUG(ustus) TR(ibūnus) P(lēbis). Tacitus said of Galba that "everyone agreed that he would have made a fine emperor, if only he had not been emperor."

P. 299 Otho (r. January 15–April 16 AD 69). According to ancient sources, the most commendable aspect of his life was the brave way in which he committed suicide.

P. 306 Victory setting up a trophy.

P. 310 Depositing a vote in an election urn. Since the term for a voting enclosure was *ovīle* (lit. "sheep pen"), the procedure may not always have been quite as dignified as this portrayal suggests.

P. 316 DĪVUS IŪLIUS. The fiery-tailed comet that symbolized the deification of Julius Caesar.

P. 321 Poppaea, the second wife of Nero. She liked to bathe in donkey's milk to keep her skin youthful. Nero is said to have burned more than a whole year's output of Arabian incense at her funeral (having killed her by kicking her in the stomach when she was pregnant).

P. 328 Septimius Severus (r. AD 193–211) was the first emperor of Carthaginian ancestry. About a century earlier, Domitian had put a senator to death because he had named two of his slaves after Hannibal and his brother, Mago.

P. 334 Maximinus Thrax (r. AD 235–238) was the first ruling emperor known to have taken part in a battle. According to the frequently rather implausible *Historia Augusta*, he often drank 7 gallons of wine in a day, along with 40 or 60 pounds of meat, but never ate vegetables, and was 8 feet 6 inches tall.

P. 342 Pegasus, the winged horse.

P. 347 A rather jolly, but not very accurate, representation of a hippopotamus, one of the animals that appeared in the games put on by Philip the Arab in AD 247/248 to celebrate the thousandth anniversary of Rome.